SHADES OF BLACK

SHADES OF BLACK

CONRAD BLACK – HIS RISE AND FALL

RICHARD SIKLOS

M&S

Library and Archives Canada Cataloguing in Publication

Siklos, Richard, 1965-
Shades of Black : Conrad Black – his rise and fall / Richard Siklos. – Rev. ed.

Includes index.
ISBN 0-7710-8071-9

1. Black, Conrad. 2. Publishers and publishing–Canada–Biography.
3. Newspaper publishing–History–20th century.
I. Title.

PN4913.B56S53 2004   070.5'092   C2004-904572-5

We acknowledge the financial support of the Government of Canada through the Book Publishing Industry Development Program and that of the Government of Ontario through the Ontario Media Development Corporation's Ontario Book Initiative. We further acknowledge the support of the Canada Council for the Arts and the Ontario Arts Council for our publishing program.

The excerpt from *Best Seat in the House* by Robert Fulford, on page 167, is reprinted by kind permission of the author.

Typeset in Bembo by M&S, Toronto
Printed and bound in Canada

This book is printed on acid-free paper that is
100% ancient forest friendly (100% post-consumer recycled).

McClelland & Stewart Ltd.
The Canadian Publishers
481 University Avenue
Toronto, Ontario
M5G 2E9
www.mcclelland.com

1 2 3 4 5   08 07 06 05 04

For my mother, Suzanne Siklos,
and in memory of my father, Sandor Alex Siklos.

"I sometimes think of what future historians will say of us. A single sentence will suffice for modern man: He fornicated and read the papers."

Albert Camus, The Fall

"It's no trick to make a lot of money if all you want is to make a lot of money."

Mr. Bernstein, from Citizen Kane

CONTENTS

Introduction

"ET TU, BRUTE"

For a man with Conrad Black's sense of place and history, an AT&T teleconference may not have been his choice of venue for his own corporate beheading. Black was at his Park Avenue apartment at 10 a.m. on Tuesday, January 20, 2004, when he phoned into a board meeting of Hollinger International, the Chicago-based newspaper company he had founded, which owned the Telegraph newspaper group in London, the *Chicago Sun-Times*, and the *Jerusalem Post*.

As the ultimate owner of a 72 per cent voting interest in Hollinger International, Black conducted his affairs with a swagger that was based on certain immutable beliefs: he called the shots and he controlled his board. If shareholders didn't like his act they could sell their stock and take a hike. On and off for a quarter century, he had operated in the grey areas of business where little is straightforward, rules are meant to be prodded and bent, and personal advantage is the single objective. It's a risky path, but in all those years he had usually come out on top. Even when he hadn't, there was often someone else to blame.

Black was very good at this game. It had brought him fame, fortune, a peerage, a brainy wife who looked like a movie star, and a Gulfstream IV jet that ferried the couple among their splendid homes in London, New York, Palm Beach, and Toronto. In their lifestyles, Lord Black of Crossharbour and Lady Black dwelled among the mega-rich in the social mesosphere, the place above the stratosphere where the air is thin and meteors burn up.

Black's hand-selected Hollinger board was stocked with – in addition to his wife, the columnist Barbara Amiel – a high ratio of dignitaries of the right, including former U.S. secretary of state Henry Kissinger, former Defense Policy Board chairman Richard Perle, four-term Illinois governor James Thompson, and retired U.S. ambassadors Richard Burt and Raymond Seitz. Their elevated stature reflected Black's carefully cultivated persona as a Renaissance magnate, equally adept at delivering euphuistic speeches in Britain's House of Lords, penning weighty biographies, and overseeing a cash-spinning media empire. He and Kissinger, whom he'd known for two decades, were especially close. Indeed, Conrad and Barbara had spent the last American Thanksgiving at Henry and Nancy Kissinger's home in Connecticut. "I realize the allegation is about that I am somewhat of a seeker of celebrities, and in one sense I suppose that's true," Black once said. "But my purpose is that celebrities who are justly celebrated can be very useful to you."

For two months before the teleconference, Black's life had been turned upside down by an internal revolt unlike any other big corporate blow-up of recent years. The nightmare had started in November 2003, when Black and several top associates were accused by a special committee of the Hollinger board of taking US$32 million from the company without authorization; Black agreed to step down as chief executive of his company, and the others resigned or were fired. The situation had grown uglier in the weeks since. Over the weekend of January 16–18, the feud between Black and his beloved board escalated into all-out corporate war or, as he would growl into his telephone, a "series of Pearl Harbor attacks." On Friday, January 16, Hollinger fired Black as chairman and sued him and several associates for the more than US$300 million they were alleged to have plundered from the company. At the same time, without consulting Black, Hollinger signed a Securities and Exchange Commission court order that would stymie any attempt by Black to replace the insurgents.

Combative at the best of times, Black held fast. He denied any wrongdoing and on Sunday the 18th shot back with a surprise counter-move: he announced a deal to sell Hollinger's Canadian holding company to Sir David and Sir Frederick Barclay, self-made identical-twin billionaires. Selling out at this moment would be the ultimate kiss-off to his accusers and give Black the war chest to regroup and fight on.

Now, three days later, the board was meeting to ratify Black's ouster as chairman and the lawsuit against him, and it was becoming painfully clear that celebrity friendships have their limits. The meeting began at 10:10 a.m. with the directors announcing their presence on the line one by one.

Gordon Paris – a chief Black nemesis who had led the investigation into Hollinger's finances and had been appointed interim chief executive in November – called for the ratification of Black's removal as chairman. Black's wife objected, demanding an explanation, because the November agreement had stipulated that her husband would retain the title. Raymond Seitz replied that at least one reason to remove Black was that he had invoked the Fifth Amendment when summoned before the Securities and Exchange Commission a few weeks earlier. The other directors felt Black's stance had motivated the SEC to take action against the company. Beyond that, Seitz said he preferred not to provide a detailed explanation of his own reasons for supporting the move. He was "sure all the other members each have valid reasons and there would be no benefit to recording them all here." Amiel shot back that his reasons were "extraneous."

Nonetheless, when the motion was put to a vote it passed easily, with only the Blacks opposed out of nine directors present and Dan Colson, Black's long-time friend and Hollinger's chief operating officer, abstaining. With that, Black was out as chairman and Paris was appointed to the post.

Next, Paris proposed the creation of a corporate review committee to evaluate Black's deal with the Barclays and, if necessary, try to thwart it; the committee would consist of all the directors except the Blacks and Colson, ostensibly because Colson was a shareholder in Black's private holding company, Ravelston Corp., which stood to benefit from the Barclay deal. Once again Barbara protested, noting that she wasn't a Ravelston shareholder. One of Hollinger's lawyers came on the line and explained that she had economic and other interests in the Barclay deal through her husband, to which Amiel huffed: "That's an interesting legal theory – that by virtue of marriage one could be deemed to have a conflicting interest." In smoother times, it was the sort of thing she might have taken up in one of her feisty columns in the *Daily Telegraph* or *Maclean's*.

Once more, the Blacks voted against and Colson abstained. Kissinger said he supported the motion but abstained on the question of Amiel's exclusion from the new committee. Paris counted Kissinger's vote as an abstention, and again the motion passed.

Paris then raised the subject of the massive lawsuit that had just been filed against Black, former Hollinger president David Radler, their associates, and their Canadian holding companies, accusing them of ripping off Hollinger on annual management fees paid to Ravelston, dividends paid to the parent company, Hollinger Inc., and other matters. Black said that while the board was not the place to argue the merits of this lawsuit, he wanted it put on the record that the action was "frivolous and fictitious," and any suggestion that he and Radler "should be working pro bono" or that dividends should be returned was absolutely ludicrous. He was shocked that the board could be party to such a spurious complaint. Moreover, he added ominously, "Anyone supporting this defamation and action will feel part of the response to this."

Paris called for the meeting's secretary to note Black's objections and Thompson called for a vote. Graham Savage, another member of the board's special committee, seconded the motion, and Paris called for a roll call around the virtual table. Once again, everyone present voted in favour except Black and Amiel, who voted against, and Colson, who abstained. This time, Black listened, thunderstruck, as Kissinger's disembodied, gravelly baritone voted "yesss" to approve a lawsuit that could crush his friend.

"Henry, did you just vote against me?"

"Yesss," Kissinger repeated into the phone.

"*Et tu, Brute*," replied Black.

Later in the meeting, Kissinger asked to make a statement to board. He had been a friend of Lord Black's for decades, he said, and had made serious efforts to "find a reconciliation" between Black and the directors who opposed him. Kissinger wanted to make clear that while he was not supporting every allegation in the complaint, he was supporting the right of the board's independent directors to defend the shareholders in court when every other avenue to reconciliation was closed, notwithstanding all his personal efforts to defuse the situation. "The shareholders do not need protection from me," Black retorted.

Kissinger then asked that his earlier abstention on the vote regarding the corporate review committee be changed to a vote in favour. He had simply wanted a chance to state his views on the complaint, and was now satisfied. The meeting was adjourned at 11:20, and the members of the newly formed committee began their meeting immediately via a new conference call number that was not shared with the Blacks. A few hours later, Black scrawled out a fax and sent it to the Barclay brothers to report the day's events and plot his next countermove. "It was an unpleasant meeting this morning," Black wrote. "They have high-jacked the company."

Black had always been a military buff, but as a teenager in Toronto, he found his calling when he read W.A. Swanberg's *Citizen Hearst*, a biography of William Randolph Hearst. He was enamoured of the power and influence of the legendary press baron. "All his life, Hearst had a conviction, often outrageous but sometimes magnificent, that the rules that applied to others didn't apply to him," Black once wrote about his hero. He applied a similar conviction to his early career as a Canadian conglomerateur and then to the way he ran Hollinger International, the Chicago-based company that since 1996 had been traded on the New York Stock Exchange. Beginning with the takeover of London's prestigious *Daily Telegraph* in 1986, Black and his partner, David Radler, built Hollinger over the following decade into the world's third-largest newspaper company by circulation, ranking behind only Rupert Murdoch's News Corporation and

America's Gannett. It was a stage from which Black made grand statements about politics, policy, and the industry he aimed to dominate.
"There's a terrible amount of self-righteous claptrap about a sacred
trust," went a typical barb. "If the small guy's guardian is the media,
then the small guy·is in bigger trouble than I thought."

Black revelled in the role. The moneyed and the mighty congregated at his and Barbara's table, whether it was for summer cocktails
in London each June, for the Blacks' Christmas buffet in Toronto, or
at the annual Hollinger Dinner. The dinners were a feature event for
the company, which spent as much as US$1 million for them. Guest
speakers included Ronald Reagan and Margaret Thatcher, Tom Wolfe
and Condoleezza Rice. "The one thing I remember about the
Hollinger Dinner is there seemed to be quite a – how should I say –
upscale crowd," said Wolfe. "Black struck me as very thoughtful. He
certainly seemed well informed on public affairs, and serious."

Now, like the protagonist in Wolfe's novel *A Man in Full*, Black
had been humiliatingly stripped of his Gulfstream. Somewhere amid
the euphoria of the late 1990s, his majestic vision for Hollinger ran
out of gas, at least from the perspective of those who owned stock in
it. Despite all the excitement about media fuelled by the technology
and Internet bubble, Hollinger's share performance as a publicly traded
company during the greatest bull market of all time was uninspired.
Even after the company sold most of its North American newspapers
between 1998 and 2000 in an effort to reduce its heavy debts, its stock
languished. News of a series of lucrative payments made by Hollinger
to Black, Radler, other executives, and their private Canadian holding
company, Ravelston, began to raise investors' hackles at a time when
corporate scandals had begun to sweep America. This backlash was
inconvenient to Black, and he initially dismissed it. "This is a guy
who at his annual meeting said that the corporate governance movement was a fad," said the Hollinger director Richard Burt. "It is like
saying computers are a fad, you know?"

Although Black worshipped American-style success and postured
as a great defender of capitalism, he seemed to have become heedless
of the idea of pay for performance. For example, Hollinger's top five
executives were paid a total of US$33.5 million in compensation in

2003, according to the company's lawsuit against Black. For that same amount, Hollinger could have hired the top five officers at the newspaper companies Washington Post, Dow Jones, and Knight Ridder combined and still have had US$5 million left over. (Plus, those three companies combined had revenues roughly seven times larger than Hollinger's.) "The only way one can possibly understand what's happened here is to use Lord Black's paradigm," said Herbert Denton, a banker who had advised shareholders on their legal actions against Black. "If you're the proprietor it's like droit de seigneur – he's not working for the papers, they're working for him."

Black maintained that everything had been done in broad daylight. If shareholders had a beef with his remuneration, then that beef was really with Hollinger's distinguished board, which, he contended, had approved all of it – including the controversial US$32 million in payments. For all his study of history and the frailties of great leaders, as he approached sixty Black did not seem to comprehend either that the shareholder revolt would turn his exalted directors against him, or, more seriously, that the allegations against him would evolve well beyond greed and high-handed behaviour into possible fraud and even potentially criminal acts. "Pursuing a grand vision and building a successful company are perfectly fine objectives, but the law sets standards on how you go about it," said Richard Breeden, the former Securities and Exchange Commission chairman who advised the Hollinger board on the investigations that led to Black's ouster. "You don't get a licence to violate fiduciary duties to shareholders because you have grandiose ambitions, and your past success doesn't mean you can just take whatever you want."

Black never wanted to be seen as a garden-variety businessman, and the corporate scandal that would bring him down would be uniquely his own. Unlike Worldcom or Enron, his was a successful, healthy company worth as much as US$2 billion and producing some of the world's best-read newspapers. As far as he was concerned the allegations against him and his firing were the result of a "smear job" by "truly wicked people" – Breeden, Paris, and the star-studded Hollinger board – who had turned against him to protect their own gilded derrières. "There's a serious war going on here that's far beyond corporate governance versus Conrad Black," said Edward Greenspan, Black's Toronto lawyer and a long-time friend. "Not that Conrad Black will ever be the poster child for corporate governance."

If anything was predictable about Black's demise as a press baron, it was the degree to which he brought it on himself. When news of the scandal first broke in November, Black could have accepted that he had made some mistakes, set the stage for a graceful departure from the scene, and announced plans to move on to a new, quieter stage of life. And that is precisely what Black initially agreed to do. But, true to form, he soon changed course, hired an armada of lawyers, and set out to reclaim control of his company in a vicious fight against his own beloved board that he almost certainly could not win and that could cost him everything. This had always been his way.

PART ONE

MAN OF DESTINY

Chapter One

HIS FATHER'S SON

The caricature of Lord Black of Crossharbour – roguish, pompous, unsentimental, avaricious, a man of letters and history, charmer of political celebrities, champion of the right – is self-invented, but only up to a point. He is his father's son, and his father was a wealthy, erudite man who cultivated an air of superiority in himself and his family, who conducted his affairs with the utter conviction that he was always in the right, even when it led to conflict and cut short his own career. To look for clues to what propelled Conrad Black on his spectacular and ultimately disastrous path to the loftiest echelons of media moguldom, a good place to start is 10 Toronto Street, the former Toronto post office built in 1853 that has served as the centre of Black's business operations since 1978. Walk through the two sets of double doors; pad across the elegant green and gold carpet, ignoring the nineteenth-century French paintings of the Barbizon school that hang on soothing pale yellow walls; pass the reception desk and turn right into the anteroom that leads to the boardroom. There hangs a painting of a handsome, bespectacled, grey-haired man in suit and tie sitting patiently in his study, a chess set in the foreground, as if he were waiting for a game to begin. The man in the portrait is George Montegu Black Jr. Conrad called him Father.

An accomplished executive and investor, George Black stood nearly six and a half feet tall and could seem variously charming, imperious, or otherworldly. A voracious reader with a passion for history and great men, he was a droll raconteur with an unusually grandiloquent style. "As Coleridge once observed of the ancient mariner, I have strange power of speech," he once said. Betty Black frequently advised her husband to "shorten things up," to which George would mutter, "Well, for God's sake, if you're going to express something, express it."

Betty doted on Conrad and his older brother, Montegu. To friends of the Black children she was a gracious hostess who took pride in running a proper household, complete with cook, nanny, butler, and chauffeur. Toronto, the city where the Blacks lived, was safe, clean, predictable, and controlled by people very much like themselves.

The picture of George Black as a paragon of the brewing industry is summed up by a 1955 profile in *Saturday Night* magazine: "He has tried his hand at most sports and games of skill. In his view none can compare in challenge or excitement with big business; none requires more skill or better timing. His work, which is his way of life, has only one major rival – his family: his wife, his young sons, Montegu and Conrad, and his comfortable home."

George Black grew up in the prairie city of Winnipeg, where he was born on June 3, 1911, to George Montegu Black Sr. and Gertrude Maxwell Black. The Blacks hailed from New England and lived in Halifax for a time, where George Montegu Sr.'s father, George Anderson Black, worked for the Hudson's Bay Company.

Born in 1875 and having moved to Winnipeg as a boy, the first George Montegu Black worked throughout western Canada, primarily in real estate and insurance, and was a junior partner of the original Viscount Rothermere, Harold Harmsworth. Black was not in the top echelon of Winnipeg "society," but he was an extremely well-connected man, garnering lengthy entries in *Who's Who*. As the 1920s progressed, many of his ventures did not, but his main enterprise became a controlling stake in Western Breweries, a holding company he created in 1927 to amalgamate four breweries in Saskatchewan and Manitoba and a ginger-ale plant. The business suffered during the Depression; Western Breweries stock nose-dived from a high of $10.50 in 1930 to $2.50 in 1931, resulting in the suspension of its dividends, a main source of family income. But the family funds remained sufficiently liquid that George Jr. wanted for little and was sent to Appleby College, a preparatory boarding school in Oakville, near Toronto. This was followed by a short stint at Montreal's McGill University – the brevity due to a bout of double pneumonia that sent him home during his first year. Back in Winnipeg in 1930, he enrolled at the University of Manitoba and fell for Elizabeth Jean Riley, a figure-skating champion universally known as Betty, beginning a courtship he later described as lasting "seven financially lean years."

Black received a general arts degree from the University of Manitoba in 1933, and his first job was with the accounting firm of Millar, Macdonald and Co., where he worked by day while attending lectures and studying for his chartered accountancy certificate by night. In 1937, his labours began to pay off: he earned his accountant's degree, joined the family brewery as controller, and married his sweetheart in an Anglican ceremony.

The Riley family was among Winnipeg's most prominent, possessing the stalwart, rock-solid airs of its main business, life insurance. Betty Riley's father, Conrad Stephenson Riley, traced his roots to Beverly, Yorkshire. Her great-grandfather, Thomas Riley, moved in the early 1850s to London where, with his father-in-law, he is said to have purchased a "fractional interest" in a newly launched newspaper, the *Daily Telegraph and Courier*.

At the turn of the twentieth century, Winnipeg, where George Black and Conrad Riley eventually settled, was going through boom times. After the completion of the Canadian Pacific Railway in 1886 and until the opening of the Panama Canal in 1914, Winnipeg was the leading gateway for commerce to the unexploited Canadian west. It became the biggest grain centre on the continent, and from a population of about 14,000 in 1883, when Conrad Riley arrived in Winnipeg, the city swelled to more than 165,000 by 1912.

The Rileys found their fortune in the burgeoning field of insurance. In 1895, Conrad's father, Robert Riley, set up the Canadian Fire

Insurance Company, which he followed with Canadian Indemnity Company and Northern Trusts Company. As a young man, Conrad Riley possessed considerable athletic prowess, and his feats as a rowing champion later earned him induction to the Canadian Sports Hall of Fame. At the apex of his career, his blue-chip directorships included Royal Bank of Canada, Winnipeg Electric Company, Beaver Lumber Company, Great-West Life, and Montreal Trust. In the 1940s, a magazine profile described Riley as one of the fifty men in control of Canada's finances, which he dismissed as "a big untrue."

George Black Jr. was grateful that during his long courtship of Betty, his future father-in-law "bore my callow unsophistication with benign indulgence." A future in the family brewery and a stable life with Betty in one of the fine homes of Armstrong Point seemed preordained for George until 1940, when he decided to join the war effort. His first thought was to enlist in the army, but he was rejected because of failing eyesight. "After all," he said later, "there's no point in having a great big tall blind man standing in a trench looking like an idiot." Black signed up with the Royal Canadian Air Force, which was in need of accountants as well as aces. On Dominion Day, July 1, 1940, George kissed Betty goodbye and climbed aboard a Trans-Canada Airlines flight from Winnipeg to Ottawa, with orders to report to air force headquarters. There, he was seconded to the office of the deputy minister of national defence for air, James Duncan, who wanted him to assist in setting up the British Commonwealth Air Training Plan. To avoid the discomfort of having a low-ranking officer advising senior commanders, Black was removed from duty and placed in a civilian role. With typical imperiousness, he later described the men he served as "a hopeless bunch of ghouls. They were totally incapable of handling anything without some assistance."

One person whom Black found to his liking was the renowned industrialist Edward Plunket (E.P.) Taylor. In December 1940, Black was invited by James Duncan to an informal dinner at Ottawa's Château Laurier hotel where Taylor was the guest of honour. Taylor was serving as the civilian right hand of the minister of munitions, C.D. Howe, and the pair had recently been plucked from cold

Atlantic seas after the ship on which they were steaming toward England was torpedoed by the Germans.

Taylor, born in Ottawa, the son of a small-town banker, had built up and acquired a large swath of businesses, largely in the food and beverage industries. He was the quintessential top-hatted Canadian capitalist of the day, a cigar-chomping beer baron and racehorse owner of larger-than-life proportions. Over dinner, Black was impressed by this man ten years his senior who seemed the fount of an endless stream of ideas. Likewise, Taylor, who had started his empire with a small brewery owned by his grandfather, made a mental note to keep an eye on Black.

Several months later, once the training program was off the ground, Black was recruited to help set up an aircraft propeller manufacturing operation, Canadian Propellers, in Montreal. Not long after the birth of the Blacks' first child, George Montegu III, on August 6, 1940, Betty and the baby joined him in Montreal. By the war's end, Canadian Propellers had built and shipped 12,500 propellers; rising to executive vice-president, Black had directed the operations of 800 workers. When the company was wound up in the summer of 1945, it had accumulated a surplus of $5,000, which was donated to the mechanical engineering department at nearby McGill University. "So if anybody says that I was a war profiteer," Black later commented, "they're goddamned liars."

One day in July 1944, Black was surprised to receive a call from E.P. Taylor, saying he was in Montreal and inviting George to lunch. As Black's office was far from the centre of town, he arranged for Taylor to dine at the Black home on Cedar Avenue. Black's instructions to Betty, who was pregnant with their second child, were, "Hold onto your hat, buy some steaks!"

During after-dinner drinks on the patio, Taylor eased into the purpose of his call. "George, this war isn't going to last forever . . ." What were his plans? Black hadn't really thought it through but answered that he expected to return to the family brewing business. Taylor agreed that he should go into the business, but not back in Winnipeg, saying, "I think you should come to Toronto and work with me."

Conrad Moffat Black* was born a few weeks later, on August 25, 1944, the day Paris was liberated from the Nazis. His stay in Montreal would be brief, as a weekend visit to Toronto that George and Betty made in November had culminated in a job offer from Taylor. Nearly a year later Black reported to work at Taylor's Canadian Breweries Ltd. (CBL) in Toronto, as executive assistant to the president, Clive Betts, at a salary of $15,000 a year. Yet from early on it was clear that George Black's ambitions extended beyond being a mere salary man.

In autumn 1945 Taylor was the driving force of a group of industrialists who decided to pool resources and create a closed-end investment holding company. Modelling their venture after a U.S. company called Atlas (which itself took a substantial initial stake), Taylor and his cronies called it Argus, taking the name from the all-seeing giant of Greek mythology, reputed to have a hundred eyes. The philosophy behind the corporate Argus worked well in the business climate of the mid-century, long before the advent of corporate raiders and buyout funds: then, a small but dominant shareholding in a company, represented by a forceful presence on the board of directors, could actually have a controlling influence – particularly if that director was Taylor or, in later years, his crafty partner, Bud McDougald. While many businessmen were hunkering down for another bust after the lean years of the Second World War and the Great Depression before it, Taylor and company correctly reckoned it was the dawn of an era of prosperity and growth.

The Argus plan was to acquire significant shareholdings in a small number of operating companies without controlling shareholders. Initially, five corporations, including CBL, Massey-Harris, and Dominion Stores, accounted for nearly 80 per cent of its approximately $13.5 million of assets.

Though the extent of his holdings would not come to light until three decades later, George Black was one of Argus's original shareholders, and he continued to buy in over the years. He joined the board in 1951, and never sold his Argus shares. Later, he explained that he was impressed by the "quadrumvirate" who ruled Argus: Taylor,

---

* The middle name, Moffat, was his paternal grandmother's maiden name.

Lt. Col. Eric Phillips, Wallace McCutcheon, and Bud McDougald – all business greats of their day.

From the moment he set foot in Canadian Breweries' executive offices at O'Keefe House in Toronto on October 1, 1945, Black was caught up in Taylor's expansionist plans. Black quickly displayed an aptitude for administration and a disdain for unions. As far as the product went, he preferred spirits to beer. "He thought of himself as an organization man, and he felt if a company had a good organization chart, then it should work," said one of his contemporaries. "'There should be a policy of delegation down the lines of the organization chart' – and that was it. Well, delegation was fine, but you've got to have competent people to delegate to."

Black's star rose quickly when he was assigned to head a turn-around of CBL's flagging Cleveland subsidiary, Brewing Corporation of America, later to be renamed Carling Brewing. The company had recently moved from washing and reusing its bottles to non-returnable ones, which, along with the new cartons that carried them, were defective. "God, there was beer and blood and broken glass all over thousands of stores," Black recalled. "So, naturally, it was a first-rate disaster. It was an imperial military fuck-up, like the Charge of the Light Brigade."

By the time Black became president of Carling in 1950, new bottle-washing machines had been bought, but sales had faltered badly; the company was losing some $300,000 a month. Black fired staff to get costs in line and started building up the business again. "I've fired so many people in my life that it's sort of an art," Black later boasted. "I can do it without bitterness." Carling returned to profitability, and in January 1950, six months shy of his thirty-ninth birthday, Black was named president of Canadian Breweries.

Just prior to Black's appointment as CBL's president, another of Taylor's brewing subsidiaries, Brewers and Distillers of Vancouver, bought out the shareholders of Western Breweries, the company George Black Sr. controlled, for a total of $8.5 million.

Western Breweries was one of numerous breweries Taylor would collect in Canada, the U.S., and Britain in his quest to command the world's largest brewery (and to pick up a peerage – an unrealized ambition). Each year between 1946 and 1950, the company met its target of 25 per cent growth. The rapid expansion naturally took its toll on the CBL organization, and in 1951 Taylor felt the company ought to be decentralized because "too many policies and decisions were being made at head office." Black, as CBL's new president, was never one to rush decisions; he would sometimes sit for long periods at his limed-oak desk, balancing a model propeller from his Montreal days between his fingers while mulling over a situation from every angle. He took several months to formulate a decentralizing plan before announcing it to CBL's fifty top managers. "I am opposed philosophically and every other way to doing complicated things in a large company in a hurry without proper consideration," he later explained.

Not only did decentralization work, but it suited Black's personal style. A night person, he would often arrive in the office at mid-morning or later and rarely spent more than a dozen hours a week there. "George *was* lazy," claimed a former CBL executive. "When he was president of Canadian Breweries he wasn't getting out of the house as fast as he should." Black took delegation to the extreme and rarely attended meetings of subsidiaries under his command. His view was that most business could be conducted over the phone and, he said, "I find the phone works just as well at home as at the office."

In the years that Black was president of Canadian Breweries, 1950 to 1959, it briefly became the world's largest and most profitable brewery; it dwarfed the U.S. giants Anheuser-Busch and Joseph Schlitz Brewing. CBL's sales during the period more than tripled, growing from $100.4 million to $333.8 million, and net profit soared from $4.9 million to $12.4 million. But his moment at the pinnacle of his profession would be brief.

Despite the unbridled growth, there were strains in the executive suite. The tensions that led to George Black falling out with E.P. Taylor can be traced in part to Black's long-held ambition to force an industry-wide strike against a united coalition of brewers. Black realized his wish in the summer of 1959, when the brewers' union called a strike at all the breweries for seven weeks. Taylor's style was to settle right away, but Black resisted – at a cost to CBL of $100,000 a day. Taylor, in Europe at the time, conveyed his annoyance to Black. On Taylor's return to Toronto, Black argued that the strike cost their competitors Molson and Labatt plenty too, and his holding the coalition together eventually led to the unions settling for less than they had originally been offered. "If you can't turn around and snarl at these guys occasionally, they'll kick you to pieces," Black explained.

Taylor did not share his protegé's view, and this was an increasing occurrence. By early 1958, Taylor had come to feel that Black had been elevated beyond his abilities. In the spring of 1959, several weeks before the strike, Taylor had suggested to Black that he recentralize the company he had decentralized eight years earlier. Black told Taylor that he was "out of his skull," which did not go over well. On October 30, 1959, Taylor met Black and reiterated his dissatisfaction with the strike and desire to recentralize. "Well, I did the best I could, Eddie," Black told him.

"I think it is time we had a new president of Canadian Breweries Ltd.," Taylor said.

"Well, that's fine with me, Eddie," Black replied. "I think your policy is nuts and I'm not going to have anything to do with it." He shook Taylor's hand, cleaned out his desk, and never returned to the Canadian Breweries office.

Relations with Taylor remained outwardly friendly, but Black became bitter as the years went by because Taylor never acknowledged that Black had been right about the direction of CBL. (The company's finances roller-coastered over the next few years, but the long-term trend was negative, and it was sold in 1968 to the cigarette giant Rothmans.) Black later said that before his final exchange with Taylor as CBL's president turned ugly, Taylor had offered him a five-year contract at $150,000 a year – double his salary – if he would stick around and do as Taylor bid. He also noted he could have swung a better pension if he'd been fired instead of quitting. But it was a matter of some pride to Black that he "retired" at age forty-eight on his own terms.

Besides, market investments during an era of unfettered post-war economic expansion had made him a rich man, and he would never return to executive life again. "I have all the money I'll ever need, and so have my sons, and so has my wife and so has my sister and so have her children," he said. "And I've made it all." In theory, George would now have more time to spend with his teenage sons.

Chapter Two

AIMLESS YOUTH

"Certainly there was a good chance for Conrad to become a total dilettante," recalled George Hayhurst, a close friend of George Black's younger son at grade school. "There were plenty of guys who had equal privilege and equal access to money who went on to do absolutely nothing." There was, however, little chance of this happening to skinny, red-haired Conrad.

For their first five years in Toronto, the Blacks lived in a home in the affluent Forest Hill district. In 1951, when Conrad was six, they moved to Park Lane Circle, in an area then at the outskirts of the city; in time it would become one of Toronto's most exclusive neighbourhoods, the Bridle Path. On part of a large parcel of the new suburb of Don Mills, which George Black had invested in with E.P. Taylor, the Blacks lived well in a picturesque estate. Set on seven and a quarter manicured acres dotted with willow trees, the house was equipped with large rooms for entertaining and a swimming pool.

With few other young people on Park Lane Circle, Conrad was often left to his own designs. His frequent companions were his books and his father. Like his older brother, Monte, before him, Conrad was sent to Toronto's Upper Canada College from the age of six. He would invite friends, sometimes two or three at a time, over to his house for weekend visits.

A favourite activity was playing the nickel slot machine George Black had provided for the playroom. Gambling and losing was no character-building exercise since Conrad possessed the key and could always open up the back for more change. Hayhurst, who sat beside Black in most classes between the ages of ten and fourteen, spent many weekends at the Black estate. "Mostly we played with the slot machine, which was a rather fantastic thing to have in those days," he recalled. "Or we'd play this game called Ships and Battleships on his pool table. The red balls would be ships and the coloured balls would be battleships. Conrad was pretty good at that."

Another preferred pastime was discussing cars, with debates over which of the latest Cadillac or Chrysler models packed the most horsepower. Sometimes they would sneak down to the garage to look at the engines or play with the newfangled automatic windows on the family cars. The centrepiece of the weekend would be Saturday lunch with Conrad and his parents in the cavernous dining hall. Meals were prepared by the cook, Thomas Dair. George Black would sit at the end of the table holding forth on a range of subjects. "His father was a bit distant and sort of looked like the great philosopher," said Hayhurst. "He sort of pontificated."

Summers for the Black children were spent at the Riley summer camp in Kenora, Ontario. There were also winter trips to Nassau, in the Bahamas, where George Black was a member of the exclusive Porcupine Club. There, the Blacks could rub shoulders with American dynasties such as the Mellons and the du Ponts. George Black believed in proper manners and "putting his sons in the picture at an early age" – it was something his own father had done for him. "I don't think it does any harm," he once explained. "And, furthermore, when you grow up, in later years, you can sometimes astound people by saying, 'Well, of course, I once shook hands with His Royal Highness, the Prince of Wales, in 1919.' I did too. I was only eight years old, but I remember."

George Black's fascination with the rich and powerful was appreciated by Conrad, but the son had bigger ambitions. According to a close friend, he vowed early on that, unlike his father, "he wasn't just going to talk about people – he was going to know them."

Conrad's parents were often still in bed when he rose for school. Occasionally Betty Black drove her son to Upper Canada College, a few miles away, but more frequently he was chauffeured by Tommy, the family's driver. The Blacks were formal at home, and dinner was served at precisely the same time every day. "To Conrad this was torment," said another friend from school days, "because he's notorious for being one of the most unpunctual figures imaginable."

The Black brothers got along well but could not have been more different. Monte Black was a joiner, Conrad was not. Affable and athletic like many of his Riley cousins, Monte physically resembled his father and adored his mother.* Bookish and cerebral, Conrad shared his namesake grandfather Riley's build for rowing but was awkward and enjoyed sports only as a spectator. The Black boys did share an interest in boats, although Monte's taste ran to the pleasure craft that glided through the cottage-country lakes north of Toronto, Conrad's to the mighty steamships and naval juggernauts that ruled the high seas. The isolation of Park Lane Circle was enhanced by Monte's departure, when Conrad was ten, for boarding school.

Invariably, people look to Black's early life for signs of what was to come. Precocious and left to create his own amusements, Conrad Black felt his capitalist urges stir early. At age eight, he recounted in a speech, he sank his "accumulated life savings of $60" into a single share of General Motors. "The Korean War was on, Stalin was still in power, it was the height of the Cold War," Black said. "To buy a share of General Motors was a wise means of participating in the growth of capitalism, supporting a great institution, and casting one's vote with the side of freedom and enterprise in the worldwide struggle with the red menace which was then generally assumed to be lurking behind every bush and under every bed."

One popular fragment of Black lore that captures the picture of the tycoon as a young man has him washing dollar bills and hanging

---

* While Conrad Black seemed to be more influenced by his father, in later life Monte seemed closer to his mother. "He had an extraordinary affection for his mother," said Sarah Band, who dated Monte in the early 1980s. "The house was full of pictures of his mother, pictures of a kind-looking woman."

them on a line to dry outside the Park Lane home. This tale, according to Black's first wife, Joanna, was embellished and recounted by one of George Black's former colleagues, Jack Campbell, to the author Peter Newman and has since become a kind of urban myth. Black had fallen in some mud and was in fact mainly engaged in the less mythical act of washing change. Campbell, recalled Joanna Black MacDonald, "had come to the house and Conrad was washing these coins. And he told Peter Newman many, many years later that he was washing dollar bills. Conrad told me that he was doing 'nothing of the sort.'"

Black himself chuckled at the recollection years later. "I was very young," he said. "I think I did actually wash mud off *one* dollar bill. But she's right – it was mainly quarters."

A similar piece of Black lore – that he spent much of his boyhood playing with toy soldiers – grew out of a 1980 CBC program that featured footage of Black as an adult engaged in a toy soldier battle with his friend Hal Jackman. The perpetuation of this image was for years a bit of a running joke between them. ("That's the only time we've ever played toy soldiers – for that TV show," recalled Jackman, who unlike Black did collect soldiers. "But I like military science, as does he; we do know the various positions of Napoleonic battles particularly. Conrad will often draw analogies to something Napoleon did in one of his battles. And that's good copy, but it's absolutely nothing to do with reality.")

Much of young Conrad's time was spent in what was intended to be a vast playroom but, as he grew older, became more of a library. Black's long-time friend Brian Stewart said, "At seventeen or eighteen, he had his own library of military encyclopedias and military books, probably not much less than a thousand books in all. Then he had his father's library on top of that."

Norman Elder, who lived next door to the Blacks for eleven years, would occasionally come over and thumb through *Who's Who* with Conrad, the boys measuring the achievements of people their parents knew. Even for Toronto in the 1950s, this was not most adolescents' idea of a good time. Black's own youthful reminiscences include David Brinkley announcing the kills in the aerial dogfights over Korea every night, and rushing "home early from school to watch the McCarthy hearings on television." Though rock 'n' roll was the rage, Black's taste ran to recordings of famous political speeches. The only contemporary music he purchased was Elvis Presley's "When My Blue Moon Turns to Gold Again." A prized recording was a copy of Franklin Delano Roosevelt's speech at Madison Square Garden, which he would play at great volume over and over. "It was an unbelievably great speech by FDR, attacking the rich, and the great rich of the Republican Party," recalled Stewart. "His father detested FDR, and this recording would play through the house with the crowd cheering. Finally his father said, 'I don't want that damn record ever played in this house again!'" Conrad continued to play it, but behind closed doors, at low volume, in the wing that served as his apartment. George Black would not live to read his son's massive biography of the president he detested, published some forty years later.

Two passions George Black did share with his younger son were chess and Napoleon, with the elder Black lending the younger numerous volumes on the latter. Also held in common was a remarkable capacity for retaining facts and figures. "His father had an outstanding memory and, I think, trained Conrad from early childhood to work on it, kind of like a muscle in the brain," said Stewart. "His father would read encyclopedias and remember 85, 90 per cent of them. Pretty astonishing. I used to pepper him with the most obscure trivia questions, like 'Who is the world's greatest bullfighter?' And he would agonize and think, and strain his brain, and sure enough he'd give the right answer."

One day, when Conrad was quite young, Taylor came over to the Blacks' house after a trip to North Carolina. Little Conrad turned up and Taylor asked him, "Where do you think North Carolina comes into the lineup of the states as to population?" Without blinking an eye, Conrad replied, "Fourteenth." "Conrad," Taylor said, "if you're right on that, I'll give you a quarter." Conrad marched upstairs and shortly returned with a gazetteer (which he had recently been studying), verifying the figure. Taylor later told George Black, "You know, that young man, judging by the shape of his skull, is going to have a tremendous brain."

By the age of twelve, Conrad's feats of memory reputedly included the length, breadth, and armament of every fighting ship on the seas, the length and tonnage of the greatest steamships, leaders of obscure countries, whole cabinets of former Canadian governments, and endless statistics from professional hockey and baseball. "You always have to be careful what you say to Conrad," a long-time friend recalled. "If you have a discussion with him, he's apt to quote back verbatim some foolish remark you made fifteen years ago."

Black's long memory was always razor-sharp when it came to recalling the eight years he spent at Upper Canada College, culminating in his expulsion at age fourteen. Black unenthusiastically pursued his studies, nurtured a distaste for authority, and claimed to have learned much about corporal punishment techniques of the 1950s.

His friends attribute his self-described feelings of rebellion to a sense of imprisonment Conrad felt in his childhood. "I know he rarely, if ever, did any work," said George Hayhurst. "In grade nine, he would have certainly been in the bottom 10 per cent of the class. He would occasionally do some work in the limousine on the way to class, but I think he felt he didn't have to do any work – and he probably didn't.

"He was a little distant. He didn't come out and scrimmage with us at recess when we played hockey or football, but he was certainly not ostracized, not by any stretch – nor did he ostracize people."

Even at a tender age, Black had inherited his father's penchant for blustery language. At UCC, he derided his prep masters (from afar) as "gauleiters." One day in 1954, Black told his chum John Fraser, "This place is a concentration camp, but most of the inmates are oblivious to the fact." The schoolboy had a way of warming to his subject. "Our pig-stupid colleagues think of this place as the universe. E.P. Taylor could buy up this land and forty more parcels like it without blinking. These jerks that control our lives are pure flotsam."

In his book *Telling Tales*, Fraser wrote that spending time with Black served as a valuable English tutorial – Fraser hadn't known what flotsam meant – for even at age ten Black talked with "big words and strong statements." Conrad, Fraser maintained, "set himself against the imposed establishment right from the beginning and always resented the power others, like masters or prefects, had over him. In addition, he had a terribly sharp tongue, which is not appreciated in the young."

Another student recalled Black as the most "ostentatiously rich" student in his class, once showing off a wallet bulging with $80 – a large sum for the late 1950s. He is remembered as someone who would inquire of his classmates how many servants they had, and one classmate recalled the brusque manner in which Black treated his nanny. Although Black didn't have many friends and was not among the school's leaders, he was likeable and had a certain panache, and his frequent tirades were rarely taken at face value. "I was impressed by him because he was an aggressive, brassy kind of guy," said one friend from Upper Canada who had not seen Black since. "He'd act tough and belligerent but he wasn't. It was his adopted mode. He was very much a Machiavellian kind of guy. His favourite book was *Napoleon and His Marshals*, and he used to love to read about how they all schemed." Sometimes Black would defy the school edict that no one was to leave the grounds at lunch by having the limousine wait just beyond the drive, where select classmates would be invited to sit with him and read comic books.

Well into middle age, Black's venom toward UCC was undiminished – although he has admitted some of the canings he received there were deserved. Nonetheless, in his memoir, *A Life in Progress*, he wrote, "All those who, by their docility or obsequiousness, legitimized the excesses of the school's penal system, the several sadists and few aggressively fondling homosexuals on the faculty, and the more numerous swaggering boobies who had obviously failed in the real world and retreated to Lilliput where they could maintain their exalted status by constant threat of battery: all gradually produced in me a profound revulsion."

The result, at age fourteen, was his decision to mount "a systematic campaign of harassment and clerical sabotage against the regime." Black's campaign began with his breaking into an office to remove himself from the school's battalion and alter the files of schoolmates he disliked. He also poached his records from the athletics director as a way of avoiding sports activities.

As the grade nine year-end approached, amid the disarray of major building renovations, Black and three accomplices, John Hornbeck, Gerry Hazelton, and Bill Koerner, stole the cache of final exams from the school office. Black then proceeded to offer them for sale on a sliding scale – based on the fact that he already knew how well most of the students in the Upper School were doing in their studies, having previously pinched and reviewed their academic records. The sale netted $1,400. "A lot of money for a fourteen-year-old in 1959," Black admitted.

To some of his contemporaries, the episode seemed more the schemings of someone craving attention and the approval of his peers than the daring act of sabotage Black has portrayed it as being. One of his co-conspirators in the exam heist dismissed the idea that Black was rebelling. "I can't imagine anything more ridiculous as a justification," he said. "I don't say I know what his motive was." This person (who even years later was still scarred by the experience and declined to have his name used on the record) claimed his own motive was to get the exams for his own use, and that he was not aware Black was selling them until it was too late. "Conrad takes the goddamn papers, and the only reason it ever came to light is because he's selling the damn things to upperclassmen," he said. Black's version differs. "I was not seeking attention," he claimed. "What happened was one of my colleagues was a little indiscreet and indicated to one of his classmates that he could help him. And then people started coming to me. I didn't set out to sell these things."

On June 9, 1959, one of Black's customers was apprehended and ratted out Black. Conrad and his cohorts were expelled, but not before George Black tried to make the case to principal Cedric Sowby that his son was merely showing strong entrepreneurial instincts. The principal announced two days later that all the boys would write new exams. "Those who had been among the most eager to purchase were suddenly transformed into the Knights of New Jerusalem," recalled John Fraser. "Overnight [Conrad] became a pariah and a number of boys even burned him in effigy on his father's front lawn."

In his memoir, Black gave a sort of apology to his accomplices in the caper. "I am neither proud nor ashamed of what happened," Black wrote. "It was an awful system whose odiousness was compounded by banality and pretension, but I was becoming somewhat fiendish and in the end inconvenienced hundreds of unoffending people, students and faculty."

Black's next academic foray was as a boarder at Trinity College School in Port Hope, Ontario, where his brother had studied. His disciplinary problems persisted, and his stay lasted less than a year. By this time he was a heavy-smoking teenager with few friends and plenty of notoriety. His last chance was at Thornton Hall in Toronto – "a bit of a cram school," said Brian Stewart, whom he met there – from which Black managed to graduate.

Armed with mediocre grades and a checkered record, Black was accepted at Carleton University in Ottawa, where he enrolled in journalism, switching to history after a semester. "I concluded the courses were more interesting if I took general arts because I was more interested in history and political science than I was in the techniques of journalism."

Being "not much of a joiner," he moved into a basement flat in the Savoy Hotel, some distance from campus. Black quickly established a regimen that included playing cards with various senators and backbenchers who also lived at the hotel, familiarizing himself with the taverns across the Ottawa River in Hull, Quebec, and attending sessions of the House of Commons. Studies took a back seat.

"[Prime Minister John] Diefenbaker's government was in a minority position at this point and its status became more tenuous throughout the fall and into the new year, 1963," Black recalled. "My progress as a freshman followed a roughly parallel course."

As he headed toward another educational disaster, his first-year history professor, Naomi Griffiths, sent Black a note telling him to get his act together. Until this point in his life, few people had challenged Black, and he responded. He and Griffiths struck up a friendship, exemplified by Black's tendency to submit voluminous essays running a considerable length over what was assigned. "He's extraordinarily hard-working and an extremely shy person," Griffiths reminisced in 1979. "He's one of those people who looks warily at others and says: 'Well I wonder what category you fit into?'"

From the Savoy, Black moved into a two-bedroom apartment in the Juliana, one of the finer buildings in Ottawa at the time. One night in his second year, Conrad met a cousin from Montreal, Jeremy Riley, at a Chinese restaurant. There he was introduced to a keen and worldly young parliamentary assistant named Peter White.

Though White was six years older than Black, they struck up a fast friendship based on a shared fascination with politics. Born in São Paolo, Brazil, where his Canadian father was Latin American sales manager for Sperry Gyroscope, White grew up in Montreal but had lived briefly in the south of France and Majorca and studied for two years in Switzerland. He had graduated from Laval University with a law degree in 1963 (one of his classmates and closer friends was Brian Mulroney, the future prime minister) but had no interest in practising law. Instead, he took a job as special assistant to Maurice Sauvé, minister of forestry and rural development in the government of Lester Pearson.

Though he worked for Sauvé, a Liberal, White was an active young Progressive Conservative. Black was a Liberal who would entertain friends with hilarious imitations of prominent parliamentarians they met, particularly Jack Pickersgill and Paul Martin Sr. "Paul Martin was very, very ponderous and extremely circumlocutory and loquacious and would take five minutes to answer a question and was very careful during those five minutes to say absolutely nothing," said White. "So Conrad got very good at giving a Paul Martin–type answer to a question in the House of Commons."

Several months after they met, out of his lease and in need of a place to stay for six months, White readily accepted when Black offered his spare bedroom in the Juliana. As a young professional with a job, White couldn't always partake in his roommate's after-hours carousing. Late one night White was rudely awakened when Black and some giggling accomplices entered his room and dumped a door from Conrad's large convertible on his bed. (One of the passengers had opened the door while Black was backing the car into his underground spot, striking a pillar and breaking the door.)

One nocturnal ritual of Black's that caught White's attention in less dramatic fashion was his late-night phone conversations with George Black. By this time the elder Black had been retired for some five years, and he rarely ventured out of Park Lane Circle. He was occasionally melancholy, but whatever demons afflicted him were amplified by severe cataracts in both his eyes and painful, debilitating arthritis in his legs.

White said, "Conrad was the apple of his father's eye. I think he saw the genius in Conrad. George was a recluse at that point in his life, living in that lovely mansion, and he would stay up till three or four in the morning. What he loved to do most of all was watch the Marx Brothers, or W.C. Fields movies, things like that, on late, late TV with some very stiff drink beside him the whole evening.

"When finally the television channels all shut down and he'd had his last drink and he couldn't think of anything else to do, he would telephone Conrad. This would happen religiously every night. Conrad had the dilemma: 'Do I go to sleep or stay up?' More often than not, he chose the latter.

"The phone would ring at three or four in the morning. They'd talk mainly about the day's events, but a great deal about history also. George would always ask Conrad what he was reading, and what were his professors saying. Roosevelt, de Gaulle, Churchill, Napoleon – they both had very serious interests in a lot of things, sort of a salon type of conversation. And it would go on for an hour and sometimes two hours."

Another favourite topic was investment, and White recalled Conrad animatedly explaining to him the share structure and internecine intrigues of Argus Corporation, where his father remained a significant investor.

The aimlessness of Black's youth continued through his undergraduate years. From his military, historical, and political interests sprang a fascination with world affairs, which was heightened by trips to Europe in the summers of 1963 and 1965. Travelling with his older brother, Monte, in 1963, Black met up with his friend Brian Stewart, who was then starting a career as a cub newspaper reporter in England and Spain. Stewart and Black spent night after night in sidewalk cafés, sipping cognac and drinking coffee, "discussing the world, where Rommel went wrong in the desert, MacArthur's greatest battles, forever listing the ten greatest this and the ten greatest that."

Black had never displayed more than a passing interest in the media, save for his flirtation with the journalism faculty. Stewart was surprised one day in Madrid to hear that his companion had added William Randolph Hearst to his roster of mostly military and political heroes. "He had just read the book *Citizen Hearst*, and it struck me as a very unusual person for Conrad to be fascinated by," recalled Stewart. "He'd go on about Hearst and quote him endlessly. I could never understand what is the interest in this guy; I mean, *a mere publisher?*"

Stewart noticed similar references to the press barons Lord Beaverbrook and Lord Northcliffe creeping into his friend's ready supply of analogies and anecdotes. During their travels, Black began to do a curious thing. Like most people on the road, they would buy a newspaper most days. But where Stewart's inclination was to peruse the front page or the sports pages, Black would turn immediately to the masthead or comment on the amount of advertising.

Through Peter White, Black and Stewart – at this point a scribe at the Oshawa *Times* – obtained tickets to the 1964 Democratic convention in Atlantic City, to see the coronation of their hero Lyndon Johnson. "Conrad clearly had a mystical love of America which is very strong to this day," said Stewart, going so far as to portray young Black driving to Atlantic City in a tableau straight out of Kerouac. "Very hard to picture now, but he loved driving, he loved the road, the highway, the movement, the bigness of America."

On the drive down, they detoured to where the Rivers Ohio, Allegheny, and Monongahela converge in Pittsburgh, and Black held forth about the might of America. The convention did not diminish his adulation. Thirty-five thousand Democrats crammed into the Atlantic City hall. One night there was a birthday party for LBJ, and Black stood among the sea of people while fireworks went off and placards waved. He was in his element. Said Stewart, "Conrad has always been impressed by the impressive – in the sense that he likes political figures to look impressive, be regal, authoritative in appearance. That's why he likes de Gaulle. He likes the grandeur of these figures, and LBJ had it then. People won't believe it now, but he sure had it in 1964."

Johnson won a decisive victory over Barry Goldwater that autumn, but it was the beginning of the end for the great Democratic machine. Perhaps it was on the drive back to Canada that Black's ideological leanings began to shift toward the right. He and Stewart had observed the first scattering of anti-Vietnam protestors at the convention, and driving back through Philadelphia they came face to face with the first major race riots of that long hot summer. In the coming liberal years of flower children, free love, and radical student protest, Black's beliefs went against the grain. He was a supporter of the Vietnam War and contemptuous of the anti-war movement.

"Social unrest had become severe in most Western countries by the late 1960s," Black later explained. "By that time, our society, as the ultimate product of tensions between left and right, had subjected itself to the crowning indignity of the so-called counterculture. There were frenzied attacks on supposed bourgeois slavishness, insipid middle-class sex practices, and the routinization of life. I was amazed at the time – and I spent some years enrolled in universities that saw a good deal of agitation of this sort – at the counterculture's ludicrous combination of nihilism and sentimentality.

"In the fifteen years from 1953, when I bought my share in General Motors, to 1968, with the riot-torn fiasco of the Democratic Party in Chicago, much of society had forgotten the unprecedented achievements of capitalism and of its bourgeois practitioners."

Black's grandiose and decidedly square ideas did not immediately translate into personal success or popularity. In the fall of 1964, with his bachelor's degree from Carleton in hand, Black enrolled at Osgoode Hall Law School in Toronto; he flunked out after one year. Another trip to Europe in the summer of 1965 was a good opportunity to weigh his diminishing options. Stewart suggested a carefree interlude of living in London for a year, working as a bus conductor, maybe selling ties at Harrods. Black sniffed that he felt he could do better. "He was really wondering what he would do with his life at that stage," said Stewart. "There was a sense of his parents being fed up. In the early sixties, right through to the seventies, there was a sliver of Conrad that was slightly Bohemian. Had he not ended up a rich businessman, he would have ended up a polemicist, or a writer on the Left Bank or something."

With few immediate options, Black thought he might move to Quebec, where Peter White was now working. White suggested Black might like to come to rural Quebec to edit a tiny weekly newspaper he owned. It was several hours away by car, but a million miles from the weight of his parents' disappointment. Black gathered some belongings and headed off for self-imposed exile in a place called Brome County.

Chapter Three

"WHERE HAS THIS BUSINESS
BEEN ALL OUR LIVES?"

There were two prominent features on the front page of the November 24, 1966, edition of the *Eastern Townships Advertiser*. One was the article about the tenth anniversary of the Stage House Restaurant, "an event of great social as well as commercial significance." The other was the letter to readers about the "new and promising era" for the *Advertiser* under the direction of Mr. C.M. Black.

Among the enthusiastic plans outlined in his letter, Peter White, as president of the Eastern Townships Publishing Co. Ltd., announced an impending revamp of the paper's format and a new distribution scheme that would quintuple circulation, taking it to some 2,100 copies. Black had already been penning editorials at the paper for about a month, and White promised, "Readers of this and succeeding issues will notice an improvement in the *Advertiser*'s news coverage and literary merit."

Sixty miles from Montreal, Black's new home, Knowlton, cradled the shore of Brome Lake, a holiday watering hole popular with English-speaking Montrealers. During the summer, the population of Knowlton swelled to about 3,000, double its winter level. White's grandfather had bought a house there in 1920, and Peter spent summers there with his parents. In the late 1950s he purchased the paper and its assets from its founder – a journalism student whose parents had a place in nearby Bondville – for $1.

Black's arrangement with White included another paper White owned in nearby Farnham, the French-language *L'Avenir de Brome-Missisquoi*. With a free circulation of about 15,000, *L'Avenir* was a much larger and more profitable paper than the *Advertiser*. White sold Black his interests in both papers for a percentage of profits, amounting to something under $500.

At the time Black took over the *Advertiser*, White's mother was living in the house in Knowlton. Black moved into her boathouse, the former residence of a Catholic priest. It was a long way from the comfort of Park Lane Circle, and Black would glare enviously across the lake at the grand home of John Bassett, owner of the *Sherbrooke Record*. The Whites' boathouse had minimal heating and insulation, and the fierce Quebec winter sometimes induced Black to pry open a window and climb inside the main house in the middle of the night in order to sleep.

At the *Advertiser*, Black handled virtually every aspect of the paper: editorial, layout, circulation, and marketing. He also wrote a rather academic column, called "Commerce," in which he enlightened the rural Quebec readership with *Wall Street Journal* detail about investing, industry, and financial markets. Friends would occasionally help him out. Once, Black ran a page from the telephone book instead of an editorial (with little complaint from readers). Filling in as editor one week, Brian Stewart scribbled a barely legible cartoon to fill a last-minute hole.

The only other employee at the *Advertiser*, two days a week, was managing editor Maureen Johnston-Main. She recalled Conrad Black as a lone and somewhat incongruous figure in what he later described as a "bucolic redoubt."

"He was a young kid who drove too quickly," she said. "He could be quite friendly, but most of the time he was quite serious. He seemed to look down his nose at folks around here."

Black made the job interesting by waging war on the local town council through heavily worded editorials and by enmeshing himself in the political machinery of the region. Stewart noticed that, in his new capacity as publisher, Black frequently polled strangers for their opinions. He'd ask the barber whether MacArthur should have stopped at the thirty-eighth parallel. The gas-pump attendant was queried about the Diefenbaker legacy. White recalled that Black was equally eager to know people's impressions of himself. "He was always very curious and anxious to know what people thought of him. Whenever he met anybody that he looked up to or that he was impressed by, he always wanted to know what they thought of him. He doesn't do that much any more, but he used to do that all the time."

Generally, said White, Black made a positive impression. "[Brian] Mulroney always had the same anxiety," he said. "I'm not a psychologist, but it's a sort of need for appreciation and recognition that I think Conrad and Mulroney and a lot of other people share."

In 1967, Canada's centenary, great political change was afoot. The Maple Leaf, Canada's new flag, had just been introduced, but nationalist sentiments were countered by growing uneasiness fuelled by a flourishing sovereignty movement in Quebec. The Vietnam War raged. Black took another stab at academic study and immersed himself in Quebec culture by enrolling at Laval, the French-language university in Quebec City. Black was one of only about a dozen Anglo students in the 600-member law faculty. His boathouse days behind him, he rented a spacious apartment overlooking the St. Lawrence River, ignoring the student ghetto where most of the Anglo clique lived.

Despite the burden of learning to speak French, Black, aged twenty-three, now excelled at his studies at Laval. His chum White was working at the nearby Quebec legislature as an aide to Premier Daniel Johnson, and through him Black became acquainted with the premier and his entourage. Black's closest friends at university were Jonathan Birks, scion of the Montreal jewellery retailing family, and Daniel Colson, the son of an Irish police detective. "We used to regularly have long boozy dinners," said Colson, "and invariably we'd end up screaming and arguing about something or other, but it was always good-natured. Conrad usually won the argument because he knew more about the historical background of virtually anything than any of us, plus he was that much more articulate than we were. So the odds were stacked.

"What I do remember vividly," he continued, "is that Conrad has always had this great fascination with power."

Through Peter White, Black also met David Radler, who later joined their newspaper-buying partnership. The son of a New York–born restaurateur, short, scrappy Radler was born and raised in Jewish Montreal, where he would watch Chuck Connors – who played the Rifleman in the television series of the same name – play first base for the Montreal Royals; Radler also hustled subscriptions to *Liberty* magazine in order to further his baseball card collection. Radler attended McGill and took his MBA at Queen's in Kingston, Ontario. He was by no means short of confidence and ambition, and in his early twenties he worked as a business consultant on native reserves in Ontario and northern Quebec, helping residents start businesses that ranged from handicraft production to grocery stores. Radler's father ran a French restaurant in Montreal called Au Lutin Qui Bouffe ("the elf who gorges himself"), which featured a concession where customers could have their photos snapped with live piglets. Au Lutin was a hangout for the provincial Union Nationale party, and it was at a party function there in 1968 that Radler was introduced to Black by their mutual acquaintance, White. Radler was as blunt and streetwise as Black was erudite and aristocratic. Both were unsentimental and intensely ambitious. It was the beginning of a relationship that would continue for thirty-five years.

Black and White's early successes at *L'Avenir* led them to set their sights on bigger game: the nearby *Sherbrooke Record*. Initial approaches by White to the *Record*'s owner, John Bassett, were brusquely rebuffed, but by spring 1969 the paper was in a precarious financial state, no longer owned by Bassett, and very much available.

The *Record* had undergone a painful strike, and Bassett had become an absentee owner. He sold the *Record* to Ivan Saunders, the newspaper's long-time general manager, essentially allowing him to give the paper a go in return for the assumption of its debts. Saunders had arranged to buy a new press, but the paper was rapidly heading toward insolvency. With losses mounting – $180,000 in less than two years – Saunders was more than willing to sell to Black and White, again for nothing more than assumption of debts and the payroll.

White suggested to Black that they bring in Radler as a partner in the venture, and over lunch one day they worked out the details. The three young men put up $20,000, most of it borrowed from banks. The paper had no assets, except the goodwill of its name and a circulation of about 8,000.

Radler and Black shared a room at Sherbrooke's Hermitage hotel the night before they assumed ownership on July 1, 1969. White opted for a cheaper room in the Royal, across the street from the *Record* offices at CPR Terrace. The fact that Black had recently inherited at least $200,000 from his grandparents might have dulled the risk of taking over the paper. But the confidence of being a rich young man was not in evidence as he nervously awaited the dawn of their new venture. "Conrad," Radler said years later, "was crapping in his pants. So was I. Don't get me wrong – I may have been worse."

White was president and Black was publisher, while Radler ran day-to-day operations at the paper. White and Black were more or less responsible for editorial matters (although an editor was nominally in charge), and Radler handled advertising, administration, and circulation. Black was somewhat of a roving owner, always involving himself in key decisions. All three would, at one time or another, sell ads, help design pages, and even deliver papers. Because they did not buy the new press as part of their deal, one of the first tasks was finding a new printing arrangement. For a while, the contract went to a competitor, the big Montreal-based media player Power Corporation, which had a plant thirty miles away in Granby. But Black may have contributed to its cancellation by arguing a position that sounds ludicrous in light of his future as a Canadian press owner. His participation in the 1969–70 Senate Special Committee on Mass Media also included a brief decrying the consolidation of media juggernauts.

"Diversity of opinion and aggressive newsgathering tend to disappear with the disappearance of competition, and public opinion could thereby become more of a hostage to private interests than a master to public policy," Black wrote in his brief. And when his submission was released publicly, he claimed, Power, against whom the tirade was partly directed, cancelled the printing contract. In an appendix to his submission Black wrote: "So serious was the deterioration of our relationship with our printers subsequent to the writing of this brief, that we were obliged to transfer our business to the only other printer in our geographic area, whose place of business is in the state of Vermont. We hold the unreasonableness of our former printers to be the total cause of the regrettable development."

In later years, rather than assail the evils of media consolidation, Black and Radler embraced its merits and preferred to say that finding this deal with another printer meant that, for a time, the *Record* laid claim to being the only daily newspaper in the world to be printed in a foreign country.

The *Record*'s biggest operational problem was that its payroll could not be justified by its revenues, especially with the debt that needed to be paid down. In the new owners' view, Saunders had been too close to his long-time employees to put them out of work, but without considerable cuts the paper would cease operation altogether. The new owners' trial-and-error approach was to start firing people and keep going until they reached the point where it became apparent that the paper would cease to function in decent form. It was a ruthless exercise, and the staff of forty-eight was soon pared to twenty-four.

Crosbie Cotton, in later life an editor at the *Calgary Herald*, began his career at the *Record* in the early 1970s by winning his job in a chess game with Peter White. He described White and the three owners as "great mentors for somebody who was starting out in the business at that time. The training that they gave to young reporters was exceptional." His job included everything from reporting to delivering papers, and being subject to a rather arbitrary remuneration system. At each week's end Black and Radler would decide how much money each reporter deserved. On the rare occasions when raises were granted, Black assured the recipient with mock seriousness that pay cuts could just as easily be imposed – "downward payroll adjustment," he called it – if performance tapered.

Cotton never saw a pay increase. "One day, I delivered papers in the morning, covered something in the afternoon, then I covered the school board that night, taking my own pictures. I got back to the office around eleven o'clock, wrote my stories, developed my pictures, and left there at three a.m." The next morning, Cotton was fined $25 – out of a weekly paycheque of $82 – "because I missed the North Hatley Ladies Auxiliary Garden Tour at eight a.m. I'll never forget that."

Lew Harris, another young reporter who worked at the *Record* for two years from 1971, recalled Black as a formal though good-humoured person who seemed far older than his twenty-seven years, but who had "a certain playfulness" and was always keen to discuss baseball. "[The owners] weren't the original blunt instrument," he insisted, noting that Black preferred to employ terms like "phase in" and "phase out" when talking about firing employees. "At one point, Black said to one of the reporters, 'We're phasing you out, Bernie.' I thought that was a funny choice of words, and sure enough, six months later he wasn't working there."

Black's legendary vocabulary was already well honed. "I used to go get a dictionary," said Cotton. "I'd get three words a day – I would find the most startling words, words that I could not fathom – and I would ask him to define what they meant. He never lost." Indeed, there were few twenty-seven-year-olds in rural Quebec who could bandy about, as Black did, such words as *scutcheon*, *tenebrous*, *dolorous*, and *calumniate*.

Radler, meanwhile, seemed to exist solely on hot dogs while gleefully paring costs wherever he could. Whenever an invoice arrived, Radler would write a cheque, date it, then put both the cheque and the bill in his desk drawer. Then he would wait until the supplier's demand for payment reached near-violent levels, and calmly produce the cheque. By 1971, the paper was producing annual profits of more than $150,000.

The owners didn't normally interfere in editorial matters, but one former reporter recalled an intervention by Radler over the *Record*'s coverage of protests by students from the two local universities against the U.S. military's testing of atomic bombs underground in Alaska. "Why aren't these same people complaining when China does nuclear testing?" Radler demanded. The *Record* was one of the few papers to come out in favour of the testing.

A more notorious episode was White's ill-fated candidacy in the 1970 Quebec provincial election. Even though White ran for the Union Nationale in Brome, which lay mostly outside the *Record's* readership area, Radler insisted on prominent coverage of White's bid. The partisanship may not have had the desired effect, but it could hardly be blamed for White's loss – the Union Nationale was soundly defeated by the Liberals throughout the province. Still, a quarter century later, the *Record's* editor, Charles Bury, claimed that on account of the White episode there were residents of Sherbrooke who still refused to read the paper.

Black played the part of publisher well, decked out in a three-piece suit, his Cadillac Eldorado – with rare front-wheel drive – parked prominently in front of the *Record* office. He also found time to submit the occasional article, most notably the opus that ran on his twenty-fifth birthday, August 25, 1969. "A Year after Chicago: Homage to LBJ" was a page-and-a-half canonization of Lyndon Baines Johnson, printed seven months after he left office, ostensibly in honour of the former president's forthcoming sixty-fifth birthday. A caption under a stern photo declared him "A great man much reviled." Beyond its sheer length, the invective-laden tirade is notable for the contrarian view Black took. Rather than the tyrant that LBJ's critics portrayed in his waning days in power, Black portrayed LBJ as a misunderstood man of compassion and vision. "A less patient and dedicated man," Black noted, "when taunted incessantly with the chant 'Hey, hey, LBJ, how many kids have you killed today?' might have been tempted to reply: 'None, unfortunately.'"

The story was sent to Johnson by the American consul in Montreal and read into the congressional record by Congressman Jake J. Pickle, a crony of Johnson's from Texas, who held his old seat in the House of Representatives. Betty Black proudly framed the personal note sent to her son from the former president thanking him for his editorial.

It was a small but instructive lesson in the power of the press and the access it can gain you. The contacts Black made through the article came in handy the following year when he decided to travel to Southeast Asia and asked Pickle if he could help him get through official channels in Saigon. On arrival in Vietnam, Black recounted,

"I announced myself to the Marine guard in the lobby of the U.S. embassy, and his jaw dropped. He picked up the phone and said, 'Mr. Black is here.' It was like the arrival of Stanley and Livingstone. They had a telegram from Secretary of State William Rogers claiming that I was a friend of LBJ – which was taking considerable liberty with the facts. So they gave me quite a tour. I met everybody who was over there."

The high point of the trip was a hard-to-come-by interview with Vietnamese president Nguyen Van Thieu, arranged by the U.S. embassy in Saigon. The resulting story, which Black wrote that day, was picked up around the world, including by the *New York Times*. Black described it as "the highlight of my sporadic career as a journalist," and it was no doubt a major coup for the obscure *Sherbrooke Record*. But there were a few townsfolk, Bury said, who looked askance at a gallivanting publisher running exclusives from Vietnam while local coverage suffered. Black, White, and Radler may have saved the paper and made themselves a small fortune in the process, but Bury – who at the time was editing a local monthly – said it was at the expense of "less coverage, more wires, and when one of them didn't feel like writing an editorial they ran an editorial from the *Winnipeg Free Press*, of all places."

Whatever criticisms may have been levelled at Black by rivals, only a few months into his ownership of the *Record* his own views of the trade were already well honed. He penned a precocious submission in 1969 to the Senate Special Committee on Mass Media headed by Keith Davey, stating, "My experience with journalists authorizes me to record that a very large number of them are ignorant, lazy, opinionated, intellectually dishonest, and inadequately supervised. The so-called 'profession' is heavily cluttered with abrasive youngsters who substitute what they call 'commitment' for insight, and, to a lesser extent, with aged hacks toiling through a miasma of mounting decrepitude. Alcoholism is endemic in both groups."

The attack, Black later claimed, was based largely on his observation that English-language journalists disposed toward the separatist cause in Quebec were engaging in "supercilious partisanship" within such institutions as the CBC, the *Montreal Star*, and the Montreal

Gazette. For the next two decades, the passage would be widely regurgitated as an indictment of Black's suitability as a press owner. In latter years, as his relationship with the media as a press owner and public figure grew ever more complex, Black played down what he'd written, pointing out the limited context for which he says it was intended. "Of course, the personal lives of journalists were never any of my business," he said at a press gathering, "and when I wrote those words it was not entirely without admiration."

Black's next move in his ascent through the ranks of the Quebec intelligentsia was to author a voluminous biography of Maurice Duplessis, the imperious former premier of Quebec, who ruled the province from 1936 until just prior to his death in 1959. It took him five years to write the exhaustive volume, entitled *Duplessis.* In it, Black was willing to forgive the premier's less appealing characteristics while building an argument for his greatness. It too might have been called *A Great Man Much Reviled.*

The tome weighed in at 743 pages and has come to be regarded as the definitive work on the Quebecer's life and career. "Like an all-seeing father, severe but benign, Maurice Duplessis rewarded the deserving, punished the unworthy, and ruled vigilantly over his brood," Black wrote.

Author and subject had much in common. The consummate right-wing Quebec statesman was a reasonable subject for Black, a blossoming Conservative. But there was more. Both enjoyed and excelled at debate, both possessed a stupendous memory, both had an aversion to playing sports beyond the occasional round of croquet. Like Black, Duplessis was, as Black wrote, "an avid devourer of bulky legal and theological tomes and political biographies." And there was a familiar ring to Duplessis's belief that "a gentleman could allow himself almost no informality, that all manner of bygone proprieties had always to be maintained." A conclusion that perhaps no one but Black could have drawn was that much of what Duplessis's critics "decried as dictatorship and corruption was really a puckish love of farce."

Despite his regard for Duplessis, Black did not gloss over the former premier's imperfections in his book. "It would be unjust to omit all reference to Duplessis' personal manner of government. He drank very heavily, was frequently intoxicated, abusive and belligerent at public ceremonies of secondary importance."

Once he had embarked on the project, Black decided to use his research for a master's degree thesis, and he enrolled part-time at McGill University. By now he had moved to a sparsely furnished apartment on Sherbrooke Street in Montreal, where he wrote into the night after tending to business during the day. Dan Colson said, "I can remember vividly going to visit Conrad many times and his apartment would be filled to the ceiling with cardboard boxes of documents and letters and research." The broadcaster Laurier LaPierre, who as a McGill history professor advised Black on his thesis, said Black was "pleasant" but "socially inept" – he rarely mixed with the other students and never seemed to have a girlfriend (a characterization Black disputed). He was guarded, though a skilled raconteur, and almost always dressed in suit and tie. When he visited LaPierre and his wife's country home, "we would say, 'Remove your tie, Conrad, for God's sake.'"

Duplessis was published in late 1976, receiving for the most part respectful reviews for the contribution it made to the historiography of Quebec. "Unevenly written and overwritten; idiosyncratic and at times bombastic, the book itself is nevertheless one of the most revealing, indiscreet, and fascinating accounts ever written of a Canadian public figure and his times," wrote a reviewer at the Montreal *Gazette*.

There were exceptions, most notably Professor Ramsay Cook of York University, whose review ran in the *Globe and Mail* just before the book's publication. The verdict was not kind, to say the least: "Verbally inflated ... badly organized ... unjustifiably long ... a ramshackle volume," were among Cook's findings.

Cook had been an outside examiner on Black's MA thesis and had written a highly critical opinion of it, which Black considered "gratuitously insulting and provoking." There is even an endnote in *Duplessis* referring to the "churlish flippancies of Ramsay Cook." On reading the review, Black, who was in Toronto, stormed over to the home of the publisher of the *Globe* in order to present his letter of response in person. It called Cook "a slanted, supercilious little twit," and he later added during a television interview that Cook had "the professional ethics of a cockroach."

Cook was taken aback by Black's ire, maintaining that (despite what Black believed) he had never requested to review the book. "I have no idea why he's so upset about my review," Cook said. "He seems to be obsessed with it."

It would be two decades before Black would write another book – this time about himself – but during those years he presented hundreds of copies of *Duplessis* to friends and those he wished to befriend, using it as a calling card that said its bearer was more than just a businessman.

During the same five years that Black toiled on *Duplessis*, he and his partners pursued the newspaper business with zeal. They made inquiries about buying the *Toronto Telegram* when it folded in 1971, but the paper's subscription lists and presses had been sold. Before long Black and his cohorts were calling their venture the Sterling Newspapers chain, after adding several other small papers, including the *Granby Leader Mail* and, in Sept-Îles, *L'Avenir de Sept-Îles Journal*. By 1976 Sterling owned nine dailies and nine weeklies. "We didn't suddenly sit down one day and decide we would become media tycoons," Black later said. "But after we bought the *Record*, we just asked ourselves: 'Where has this business been all our lives?'"

Black and Radler rang small-town publishers from coast to coast to see if they were open to bids. Ontario was the most desirable market, but they found that someone else already owned most of the choice properties – Thomson Newspapers, the juggernaut that had grown out of the small-town chain founded by Roy Thomson, the first Lord Thomson. Western Canada, however, was a relatively unexploited frontier of family operations, some of whose owners were ready to retire. Black admired Thomson's legendary profit margins and sought to emulate its success wherever he could. Black and Radler toured the west and began buying papers.

At the same time, the dwindling English population of rural Quebec – and the political mood – convinced them to begin selling their earlier acquisitions. *L'Avenir de Sept-Îles* and other Quebec papers were sold in short order; the last to go, in 1977, was the *Sherbrooke Record*. The Montreal lawyer George MacLaren bought it for $865,000, a tidy fortune for Black, Radler, and White considering that the Sterling partners had initially paid only $20,000 and that its profits had been used for other purchases.

With the focus now on the west, Radler and his new wife, Rona, moved in 1972 to Prince Rupert, British Columbia, to oversee operations. Within a few months, the Sterling stable consisted of several B.C. papers including the *Alaska Highway News* in Fort St. John, the *Terrace Daily Herald*, the *Trail Daily Times*, and the *Alberni Valley Times*. If Radler's "division" was western Canada, Black's was the east, and here he negotiated the purchase of the *Summerside Journal-Pioneer* in Prince Edward Island after St. Clair Balfour, the president of the newspaper giant Southam, suggested to him that the owners wanted to sell out and preferred a non-Thomson buyer.

According to Radler, the financial approach to each acquisition was virtually identical. For example, Sterling bought the *Alaska Highway News* for $240,000, half up front and half "on the come" – in other words, over time. Said Radler, "We used to tell the bank that we were doing a deal for $240,000 and we needed $120,000 from them. And they'd say, 'How do you propose to handle the balance?' And we'd say, 'We'll take care of it' – which we did. They didn't necessarily know how we were doing it." In other words, in those days Black and his colleagues rarely put their own money into their ventures – but by squeezing cash out of the operations they bought, they could pay down their debts.

Once they were in charge, hammering at the paper's cost structure was the priority, but profits were also generated by buying weekly papers in monopoly markets and turning them into dailies. Before long, Sterling's operating profit margins rose to between 15 and 18 per cent, levels usually surpassed only by Thomson. In 1979, a particularly rich year, its profits were 25 per cent: $4.6 million on revenue of $18.5 million.

The editorial quality of Sterling newspapers was frequently criticized for being less than sterling, an accusation that grated on Radler but had some merit. The author Peter Newman noted that when a

Pacific Western Airlines jet crashed at Cranbrook, B.C., in early 1978, coverage at the local *Daily Townsman*, a Sterling paper, relied heavily on wire stories from the Canadian Press news agency. Even this would not have been possible when, several years later, Sterling withdrew from CP in favour of its own in-house news agency.

Radler, who once (partly in jest) suggested that his contribution to journalism was the "three-man newsroom," with two of the occupants selling advertising, might well agree. He made no pretense of being in journalism for social or intellectual reasons, and believed that if newspapers focused on making serious money first, good journalism would follow. The 1981 Canadian Royal Commission on Newspapers noted in its report that it was difficult to infer what weight Sterling "gives to the objective of service" in its newspapers. "Radler told us he wrote some editorials for the Sterling papers," the report's puzzled author noted. "When asked if he was a newspaperman, he responded: 'I am a businessman.'"

In July 1974, Black returned to Toronto, having been away for eight years, at last able to hold his head high. He had gained a law degree and built a chain of newspapers, and his book was nearing completion. He knew important people and sometimes referred to himself as a historian.*

His return from Quebec to Toronto marked the first time Black displayed what would become a recurring tendency to, in effect, angrily resign from a place the way most people would from a job. On the day he departed for Toronto, July 26, 1974, Black, who had been a regular guest commentator on CBC Radio's English channel in Montreal, delivered a soliloquy slamming the Quebec government as "the most financially and intellectually corrupt in the history of the province." Even before he turned thirty, Black's linguistic skills were already weapons grade. "The English community here, still deluding itself with the illusion of Montreal as an incomparably fine

---

* Black's fascination with power had led him to Quebec's Cardinal Paul-Émile Leger, whom he got to know and nominated for the 1973 Nobel Peace Prize, obtaining the signatures of many luminaries, including former prime ministers Lester Pearson and John Diefenbaker. (The prize went to Henry Kissinger and Le Duc Tho.)

place to live, is leaderless and irrelevant, except as the hostage of a dishonest government.

"Last month one of the most moderate ministers, Guy Saint-Pierre, told an English businessman's group, 'If you don't like Quebec, you can leave it.' With sadness but with certitude, I accept that choice."

Chapter Four

COMING OF AGE

I n Toronto, Black rented an office for Sterling Newspapers in the Bank of Commerce building in the business district and set about reingratiating himself into the local scene. He became a habitué of the Toronto Club, the stuffy WASP enclave for which Argus chairman Bud McDougald had presented Black a membership on his twenty-first birthday. And he was no stranger at 10 Toronto Street, Argus's headquarters. For several years, Black's elder brother, Montegu, had been working in the securities industry, the Blacks and their father having purchased 25 per cent of a mid-sized brokerage firm, Draper, Dobie & Co., for $250,000.

The private dining room at Draper's Adelaide Street office provided a venue for weekly roast-beef lunches, at which the brothers entertained the local financial and political heavyweights in the finest Old Toronto never-too-early-for-a-stiff-cocktail tradition. Monte, a very large man with thick glasses and a linebacker's neck, provided a friendly and humorous foil for his more formal younger brother. Whereas Conrad was now in possession of three university degrees, easygoing, jocular Monte boasted "no degrees, but several attempts."

Conrad Black became more involved in the affairs of Ravelston, the private company that controlled powerful Argus and of which the Black family company, Western Dominion Investments, owned 22.4 per cent. George Black intended his sons to take over his interests in

Ravelston and had been quietly transferring his Western Dominion shares to them throughout the 1970s in order to avoid estate taxes. Conrad's emergence as a presence in Argus came in 1975, when Paul Desmarais made an unwelcome bid for control of the conglomerate. Desmarais, who rose from stewardship of his family's obscure Sudbury school-bus company to build one of Canada's most potent empires, Power Corporation, had been encouraged to bid for Argus by its co-founder E.P. Taylor. Now living in the Bahamas and with little interest in Argus affairs, Taylor believed the aging partners who ruled Argus would happily sell for the right price. What Desmarais did not take into account was that Ravelston, which beneficially owned 61 per cent of Argus, had been set up six years earlier specifically to wrest power away from Taylor on behalf of his successor as chairman, McDougald.

The son of a well-to-do Toronto financier, John A. (Bud) McDougald, like Black, did not take to Upper Canada College – he flunked out at age sixteen. His father helped him get a job at Dominion Securities, where Bud was syndicate manager by the age of twenty. The family lost its fortune during the Depression, but McDougald more than reversed that through his Argus investment and his presidency of Crown Trust. His pride was his collection of vintage cars, which he kept in the chandeliered garage at his estate, Oriole Farm, in the Toronto suburb of North York.

In rallying the defence against Desmarais, whom he portrayed publicly as an undesirable francophone interloper, McDougald sought and found in George Black's younger son an articulate and spirited ally. (This, despite the fact that George Black, like Taylor, actually endorsed the idea of liquidating Argus.) Conrad Black was unambiguously behind McDougald. "The fact is," he told one interviewer, "the key to Argus's success – and it is now surely recognized by everyone as a great and successful company – is that it has had three chairmen only, and they're all three, I can authenticate this fact, they're all three great men. Lt. Col. Eric Phillips, Mr. Taylor, and Mr. McDougald. This quality – that's consistent, continuous quality. It's a quality operation." And Desmarais? "This kamikaze raid that just came out of the blue from Montreal was an absurd development."

Though of retirement age, McDougald was not the sort to slow down. He had no children, and under the threat of Argus falling into Desmarais's grasp the murmuring began around Toronto that the heir apparent to Argus was Conrad Black, a rumour that Black made little effort to quell.

By 1976 George and Betty Black were rarely seen outside their Park Lane Circle home. Conrad attributed this largely to their failing health, particularly the condition of his sixty-five-year-old father. In the evenings, his mother would go to sleep early, but his father would stay up, sometimes all night. "He was happy enough to have people visit him in his home," recalled Black. "He wasn't a recluse in the sense of not wanting to see anybody, and he wasn't a recluse in the sense of not staying in touch. He read the paper and he watched television, so he knew what was going on. If you visited him, he was well dressed, clean-shaven, alert, and well aware of what was going on in the world. But his problem was that his eyes failed and his legs failed, so he just wasn't very mobile."

A stiff drink was never far from George Black's side, and one person close to the family wasn't sure if health was the only factor in his reclusiveness. Black spoke often of wanting to write a book but never did. "He retired at the age of forty-eight," the friend noted. "Now most people who would be able to retire at forty-eight would either have gone on to a second career or just spent their life travelling, on the golf course, writing books, whatever their interests were. But he sat there in his house and didn't go anywhere."

George and Betty Black died ten days apart in June 1976. Betty succumbed to cancer on June 19, which left George despondent and Conrad charged with trying to console him. Black recounted in his memoir, *A Life in Progress*, how they spent their last evening together. At one point, George began to climb the circular stairs in the front hall, and moments later "came the unnerving crack of straining and breaking wood, followed by the descent of my father backwards through and over the banister to the floor about ten feet below." An ambulance was called and when his father came to, he "spoke of having lost his balance on the stairs and having no desire to live." He was taken to

Scarborough General Hospital, where he told Conrad he was "a good son." Conrad did not know it would be their final exchange. "He was getting a bit incoherent and I didn't particularly want to stay around for that," he recalled. "So I came home on the understanding that they would call me if there were any developments."

Peter Newman's account of George Black's death in his 1982 biography of Conrad, *The Establishment Man*, presents a picture of an embittered man. Newman quoted George Black telling his son, "Life is hell, most people are bastards, and everything is bullshit" before his fateful walk upstairs. Conrad Black contends those words were never said. "I never heard him say that," Black said one afternoon almost two decades after George Black's death. "Certainly in his latter days he would have said things sort of approaching that, but not as bad as that." Black said his father's death was nothing more than a tragic accident, noting, "He was melancholy, but he wasn't depressive." Several hours later, the hospital called and told Black his father had died. Going through his father's things later, Black found several books on depression in his study, with passages that had been underlined.

One person who knew George Black saw his death at the age of sixty-five as the end of a slow suicide. This observer said the prospect frightened Conrad, who had himself, most acutely in the early 1970s, suffered from anxiety attacks during which he would gasp and sweat or feel nauseated. At one point, he always carried a sick bag. Black underwent psychoanalysis and even took courses toward becoming a psychoanalyst. "The physical symptoms were reminiscent of descriptions of historic death throes like those of Henry VIII or Alexander VI (Borgia)," Black wrote in his autobiography about his most serious attack, adding that it was "far more terrifying than anything else I have known." According to one person who was close to Black after his father's death, Conrad feared that depression might overtake him, that at some point he might lose control and give up on life as his father had. "It's a wonderful fear, because if you're frightened of [suicide], you're probably never going to do it," said the person. "But it leaves a big hole. It asks big questions." Black's anxiety episodes lasted sporadically into the mid-1980s, but he wrote that psychoanalysis had unearthed the root cause of the attacks – which he declined to reveal – and he had not suffered from them since.*

Although Conrad Black worked mainly out of his Sterling Newspapers office in the Bank of Commerce building in 1976, his telephone rang through to the offices of Draper, Dobie, the brokerage house run by his older brother, Monte, on nearby Adelaide Street. The instructions for the Draper, Dobie secretaries were simple: if the Sterling phone rang between nine and eleven a.m., they were to explain that Mr. Black was in a "meeting"; between eleven and two he was at "lunch"; and from two to five he was "unavailable."

En route to lunch or a chat with his brother, Conrad would cruise through the Draper, Dobie office in a vice-regal manner, often leaving the secretaries in a fluster. One of them, Shirley Walters, recalls taking down a message for him and, not knowing Black, asking a co-worker to deliver it to him. When Black was given the message, from around a corner Walters heard him declare, "Doesn't she *know* who I am?" How arrogant! she thought, but then Black came around and introduced himself and, she says, was actually quite pleasant.

The next time Walters encountered the younger Black brother, she was asked to type up a letter from Conrad to Newell Lusby, the president of Diner's Club. Black was incensed over a scandalous incident during which he was denied credit. The letter was written in the acid tone of "Don't you know who I am?" Black showed up at her desk soon after. "How did you like my letter to Newell Lusby?" he inquired with a mischievous smile. "Didn't you think it was funny?" Suddenly Walters saw Conrad Black in a different light – sure, there was arrogance, but his tongue was planted firmly in his cheek, and a self-deprecating wit lurked beneath the bluster.

Soon after, Black's permanent office moved into Draper, Dobie. He and Walters struck up a fast friendship, with Black saying to her things like, "Now that my mother's dead, you'll have to tell me when I need a haircut." Walters was bright, cheerful, down-to-earth, and as

---

* Calvin Trillin of the *New Yorker* later pointed out that Black's symptoms sounded similar to those that afflicted the fictional Mafia boss Tony Soprano.

straightforward as Black was guarded. She hailed from well outside the society circles in which Black travelled. At night, as she prepared to go home, she would often find herself, coat on, leaning against the wall in Conrad's office, fascinated by the tales of history and personalities he would recount. When *Duplessis* was published in late 1976, she was flattered to find her name among the acknowledgements (one of three people singled out as "conspicuously kind and efficient"), which she later realized was "just his way of telling me he likes me." Black did indeed take a growing interest in Walters, six years his junior. At one point she mentioned to him that her marriage was breaking up and she needed to find a lawyer. The next thing she knew an attorney was on the line, saying he had been referred by her boss.

At this point, Black was squiring a voluptuous Brazilian-born socialite, Anna Maria Marston, about Toronto. Shirley Walters felt protective toward Black, because people were making snide comments about the relationship behind his back. In the 1960s and 1970s not every young women's dream date was a fleshy man in a three-piece pinstripe suit whose small talk was about Napoleon or Disraeli. Certainly, throughout his teens and twenties, Black was awkward around women. But the era of free love had worked in his favour, and Black had what he later called "ample experience."

Even in his twenties, Laurier LaPierre said, he walked "as if he is encased in cement." It was as if his burly shoulders were held in an invisible vise. Philip Marchand wrote in *Toronto Life* on meeting thirty-three-year-old Black in 1977, "The curious sense he projects [is] of someone alone, of someone who has, almost in an unconscious way, renounced certain desirable aspects of human existence – it is impossible to imagine him passionately in love, for example, or even fully giving himself over to the joys of camaraderie, of having fun with the boys."

One day, Black phoned Walters at the office from home. "Would you work late tonight?" Black asked, explaining he had some pressing work that needed attending to. He added, "I'll take you out to dinner." This gentle approach resulted in their first date. On the way to the restaurant they circled the block as they listened on the radio in Black's car to Quebec premier René Lévesque delivering a speech in New York.

Before long, the friendship became something more. Walters could see beyond Black's stiff exterior and found an appealing vulnerability. In early 1977, she became pregnant with Black's child. This was complicated by two factors: first, although she was legally separated, Walters was not yet divorced; second, she was not sure she wanted to continue a relationship with Black, let alone marry him. Black, she recalled, impressed upon her that if they didn't get married they would never know if they were meant to be together. Shirley (who changed her name to Joanna in 1990) agreed to continue the relationship, and soon they decided to marry.

The pregnancy presented serious complications for Black – it didn't fit in with his public relations strategy. He wanted to keep news of the child being born out of wedlock out of the papers. And when their son, Jonathan Black, was born in November 1977, his father's name was purposely left off the birth registration. Until the child was roughly a year old, Jonathan's existence remained a well-guarded secret – even some close friends and relatives did not know about him until two weeks before the wedding. Neither parent felt he or she had done anything to be ashamed of, but Shirley said later that her husband was concerned that the less liberally minded likes of Bud McDougald would take a dim view of him if they knew. If only, Shirley hoped during this strange interlude, the media would stop characterizing the father of her child as "Canada's most eligible bachelor."

Chapter Five

BOY WONDER

On George Black's death, McDougald had invited the Black brothers to Oriole Farm, where he kept his collection of cars and where he bred fine horses and miniature poodles. Conrad and Monte had inherited their father's 22.4 per cent interest in Ravelston and were worried that the holding company's other shareholders, led by McDougald, might force them out. Those fears proved unfounded, as McDougald made good on a pledge to their father and invited the Black brothers to share the positions, except for that of vice-president of Argus, that their father had held. Monte filled slots on the boards of Dominion Stores and Standard Broadcasting, while Conrad took the more critical seats on the boards of Argus and Ravelston. McDougald also helped Conrad realize his ambition of becoming a director of a major Canadian bank by arranging for him to join the board of the Canadian Imperial Bank of Commerce, where George Black had also served as a director. Monte joined the board of the Toronto-Dominion Bank.

On the ides of March, March 15, 1978, McDougald died in Palm Beach. It was his seventieth birthday. At home that day, in Toronto, Conrad Black was clearly distracted by news of his mentor's death: he sliced his hand while carving a turkey. Until then, he had been primarily an up-and-coming author and self-described historian who also owned part of a small-town newspaper chain. The death of

Argus's chairman presented an opportunity for Black to leap onto the national and, potentially, international stage.

McDougald's talent, which permeated Argus, was to exercise control from a minority position through sheer force of personality and, when called upon, intimidation. His personal interest in Ravelston* was 23.6 per cent, but a similar interest was owned by the estate of his late brother-in-law, Eric Phillips, whose widow, Doris, was the sister of McDougald's wife, Maude. Typical of the opaque ways he exercised control, McDougald reinforced his control over the Phillips estate through his roles at Crown Trust, the corporate trustee of the estate.

Without McDougald, the mystique surrounding Argus soon dispersed. One of the corporations it had invested in, the farm-equipment maker Massey-Ferguson, though Canada's largest multinational, was in increasingly dismal financial health. Conrad Black later said that the all-powerful corporate octopus had, by the time of McDougald's death, become "a tired group of entries: indifferently managed companies in mature industries."** The whole point of Argus, Black concluded, was that "for fifteen years after the war, E.P. Taylor and his partners bustled around Canada buying things for their own account and then peddling them into the Argus group at handsome profits, in an era before capital gains taxes and self-dealing rules." It was not much more, concluded Black, than "a rather elegant confidence trick."

Hal Jackman, whose family interests owned 9 per cent of Argus and who joined its board in 1975, said "Argus didn't do anything in the years I was around." At a typical executive committee meeting, "McDougald would tell stories about 1929, 1916, when they used to get drunk before putting in their bids for the latest Canadian National Railway franchise, usually some off-colour story. And everybody would just sit around and listen."

---

* Ravelston was named after McDougald's grandfather's house in Scotland.

** Argus's main assets were 29 per cent of Hollinger Mines, 16 per cent of Massey-Ferguson, 17 per cent of Domtar, 26 per cent of Dominion Stores, and 48 per cent of Standard Broadcasting. Through Hollinger, the company also owned 61 per cent of Labrador Mining, 12 per cent of Iron Ore Co. of Canada, and 10 per cent of Noranda.

Still, there were some $4 billion in assets under Argus control, and through its ownership of 61 per cent of the company's voting common shares – which represented only 10 per cent of Argus's overall equity – Ravelston maintained firm control. Five groups owned Ravelston: the Blacks held 22.4 per cent through Western Dominion Investments; McDougald and Phillips held 23.6 per cent each; Canadian General Investments and an associated trust company, both headed by Col. Maxwell Meighen, the elderly son of former prime minister Arthur Meighen, held 26.5 per cent; and 3.9 per cent was owned by Gen. A. Bruce Matthews, then the executive vice-president of Argus.

The day after McDougald's death, Conrad and Montegu met Alex Barron, president of Canadian General Investments, nominally Ravelston's biggest shareholder, for dinner at Park Lane Circle, where Conrad was now living. Conrad told Barron he aspired to become a vice-president of Argus and to have Monte elected to the board. Black's recollection was that Barron left him with the impression he would support their aspirations, while Barron later said he sympathized with the Blacks but could not commit to anything.

The following week, on March 22, 1978, the Argus executive committee met to appoint the post-McDougald executive officers. Black, caught in a traffic jam on the Don Valley Parkway, arrived four minutes late and found the nominations closed – and himself and Monte shut out. It would probably have made no difference if Black had spent the previous night in the boardroom. Clearly, the elderly triumvirate of Meighen, Barron, and Matthews had no intention of inviting Conrad into the Argus inner sanctum just yet. Meighen took the chairman's office, Matthews became president, and Barron was named executive vice-president. Meighen later said that McDougald's instructions regarding Black were to "bring him along exceedingly slowly. He's too precipitous. We have to educate him." Black, of course, had a different view. He expected to be an Argus executive, which would have sent a clear signal that he was a potential successor to head the group. "We were happy to co-operate with this new triumvirate and we were prepared to live with almost any arrangement provided we got a little recognition, just a crumb of recognition."

Jackman, who was at the board table that day, didn't understand the significance of Black becoming an Argus vice-president or whatever – after all, it didn't pay much, if anything. "Look, there's been a lot of speculation in the press about me," Jackman recalled Black telling the stony-faced Argus elders. "I'm one of the heirs apparent. If I'm not an officer it will look bad, the press will read something into it." Meighen quickly replied, "We are running this company, not the press."

Beyond the older Argus partners' lack of interest in publicity in general and Black's public image in particular, they didn't take him terribly seriously – an attitude that McDougald had cultivated behind Black's back. Accepting McDougald's portrayal of Black would prove to be their critical mistake. "McDougald was a real divide-and-conquer kind of guy," said Jackman. "He would encourage Conrad while he was talking to him, then he would belittle Conrad to the others."

Had Black been given a nominal vice-presidency at Argus – like his father before him – the company's future might have turned out very differently. Instead, Meighen patronized this man less than half his age, telling Black sternly, in equestrian terms, "You're rushing your fences." He later claimed that he added, motioning to his aging accomplices, "Just take a look around, you won't have to wait long." (Black contended this was never said.)

"Well, in the interest of this company and its affiliates," Black replied, "I am not going to rock the boat at this time. But I want to tell you that we're not satisfied."

Black's pledge not to "rock the boat" was short-lived. The Black brothers weighed their options in their offices at Dominion Securities, where Monte now ran the brokerage's equity operations.* As it happened, they were not the only ones unhappy with the manner in which Meighen, Barron, and Matthews had carved up Argus's executive authority – so were Bud McDougald's widow, Maude, seventy-five, and her sister, Doris Phillips, seventy-eight. When the widows approached the Blacks about joining forces against the others, Monte said later, "Well, I need hardly tell you that was music to our ears."

---

* Draper, Dobie had been sold to Dominion Securities in 1977 and Monte became a Dominion vice-president.

The executors of the Phillips estate were also on the Blacks' side, in particular Dixon Chant. A chartered accountant who had been a close associate of Eric Phillips for many years, Chant also felt swindled out of a promised executive post at Argus. He had suffered a heart attack the previous year, and Black had visited him in hospital. Black later told Peter White that visiting Chant and joining the board of the Bank of Commerce were two "absolutely crucial" elements of his successful Argus takeover.

The first phase of Black's strategy was to acquire control of Crown Trust, the corporate trustee of the Phillips and McDougald estates. "Knowing something of the propensity of elderly ladies to change their minds," Black later explained carefully, they bought Crown "to ensure as much stability as possible for whatever course we embarked upon together."

Black also secured the willing support of the multimillionaire Nelson Davis, Bud McDougald's best friend and an old friend of the Black family. Anticipating difficulties, Conrad and Montegu had sought Davis's counsel shortly after McDougald's death. "Bide your time, bite your lips and these guys will dig their own graves," Davis advised.

In a strange sideshow that took place in this period, Black was the coy but willing target of a CBC Television crew charged with filming seven one-hour documentaries based on Peter Newman's book *The Canadian Establishment*, a who's who of the country's rich and powerful. The effect of that show and the subsequent Newman biography of Black, which focused on the Argus takeover, was the coronation of this peculiar young hybrid of businessman and intellectual as the fresh face of Canadian capitalism. In short order, images of the thirty-three-year-old Black were all over Canada's television screens, as well as its business pages.

"To meet Black in those halcyon days before his ascendancy was to be kept waiting only forty-five minutes on a mid-winter's evening," recalled Ron Graham, then a CBC Television producer. "He glided down the corridor of Dominion Securities in Toronto, tendered an apology, extended his hand low enough that an involuntary bow was required to grasp it, and said hello with an *ennui* that contradicted his quizzical gaze. The petitioner was ushered graciously into an unkempt cubicle where, surrounded by unpacked boxes, a photograph of [then prime minister] Joe Clark, a sheaf of pink phone messages, and a stack of his biography of Maurice Duplessis, Black entertained for several hours with droll verbiage, slanderous insights, and a hilarious piece of French vitriol he had just dispatched to the editor of *Le Devoir*. One laughed at his jokes, admired his intelligence, deferred to his position, and came away with the promise of an interview."

With the necessary supports in place – not least of which was an avid press following – Black pressed forward with his plan to get Argus. On May 15, 1978, Maude McDougald and Doris Phillips agreed to vote their Ravelston interests with the Blacks, creating a shareholder bloc just shy of 70 per cent. But the beauty of the deal was in the fine print of their arrangement with the two widows: the Blacks became sole owners of the right to invoke an obscure "compulsory transfer" provision in the original 1969 Ravelston shareholders' agreement. This curious provision had been included to ensure that a majority of the partners could get rid of any other partner who had grown senile or just undesirable.

The Blacks wasted little time. Two days after signing the agreement with the widows, Conrad Black and Dixon Chant served Colonel Meighen with a notice of compulsory sale of his 26.5 per cent of Ravelston. The move was made, Black later said, at the "enthusiastic urging of the ladies." The old guard was ambushed from within. "There have been no policy differences," Alex Barron told *Maclean's* magazine in bewilderment. "Relations were excellent." In fact, he added, Black had voted in favour of Meighen's appointment and had voiced no opposition.

Black shot back in the same article that Barron's assertion was "not in accord with demonstrable facts. There were substantial policy differences. Unless Alex has succumbed to a massive attack of amnesia, he should be able to recall some of them." Indeed, Barron should have recognized the most obvious policy difference of all: the effrontery to suggest that the Establishment Man was not yet ready for the exalted offices of Argus.

All ran smoothly until June 13, when Ian Anderson, a reporter at the Montreal *Gazette*, phoned Maude McDougald and Doris Phillips for comment on the story. When asked if she had empowered the Blacks to acquire Meighen's Ravelston interests for themselves, McDougald replied, "I don't think I did, but I suppose I must have." She added, "I have a bird brain about business and I don't know anything about it." Phillips, who had just returned to Toronto from a long vacation in Palm Springs, was equally flaky. "I've signed hundreds of documents since my husband died," she told Anderson. "You know more about it than I do."

As Black later said acidly, "When the inevitable publicity ensued, the ladies confected an entertaining fiction on an arsenic and old lace theme and painted me as a rapacious young man." The widows did this, he contends, because they did not want to admit publicly what they felt privately – that Meighen was a threat to their joint position as the dominant shareholders in Ravelston, and the firebrand Black would be their agent to ensure that Meighen didn't trouble them again. Now they were suggesting that Black was the proverbial wolf among the hens, using their shareholdings, the late great Bud's affections, and his legal savvy to sew up control of Argus for himself and his brother. Black's view was soon supported publicly by Nelson Davis – "I agree with everything that the Black boys have done" – and the widows' lawyer, Louis Guolla: "There is no doubt that these ladies were aware of the consequences when they signed the document, but they have been quite upset by all the publicity."

Whatever their original motive had been, the widows' reaction to the attention resulted in their attempting an end run around the Blacks. Repudiating their May 15 agreement with the Blacks, they set out to purchase Gen. Bruce Matthews's 4 per cent interest in Argus, which would have given them 51 per cent and left the Blacks out in the cold. Only a week earlier, the widows, knowing Conrad Black to be an admirer of Napoleon, had given him a wooden statue of Bonaparte that had belonged to Eric Phillips. But now they were egged on in their about-face by a third sister, Cecil Hedstrom, and by John Prusac, a wealthy real estate developer. Prusac hailed from outside Toronto's establishment circles but had been courting the sisters, harbouring barely suppressed designs of his own on Argus.

Black's key ally in the imbroglio turned out to be Dixon Chant. The Phillips estate trustee met with Prusac, the widows, and Matthews one afternoon in late June and immediately distrusted the developer. Chant was even less impressed when Prusac produced documents to purchase 51 per cent of the Ravelston shares from those present (the widows' 47 per cent and Matthews's 4). Chant wanted to read the papers through, but Prusac kept insisting he sign, that it was what "the girls" wanted. Chant refused and grew irritated. "If Bud McDougald were here," he growled, "he would have you thrown out the front door."

"You can't talk to me like that," snapped Prusac.

On hearing from Chant that the Argus prize might be snatched out of his grasp, Black consulted his lawyer, Igor Kaplan of Aird & Berlis. "On the day that Conrad heard about the ladies' ploy," Kaplan recalled, "he phoned me at home to tell me, eleven o'clock at night. I stayed awake thinking the thing through and went into the office at four in the morning. More lawyers gathered, five of us maybe, and we began to talk through the options." With Black, they decided on a course of action. First they threatened to invoke the compulsory transfer and buy the ladies' shares. It was a tactic of questionable legality, but it was a good show of force. Step two: Peter Atkinson, Aird & Berlis's bright young head of litigation, drafted a strongly worded writ suing the ladies for violating the May 15 agreement and the original Ravelston agreement. Kaplan phoned the widows' lawyers and warned them that, if necessary, the Black group would issue it.

The next day, Tuesday, June 27, during a break at a Massey-Ferguson board meeting, Black served a compulsory transfer notice on Matthews. Unlike the one served on Meighen, this notice did not contain the widows' signatures; Kaplan's legal opinion was that they were not required. The widows were overwhelmed by the Blacks' aggressive stance. On July 4, their lawyers arrived at the Black estate on Park Lane Circle to capitulate; they proposed that the Blacks buy out the McDougald-Phillips stock – a striking change of heart from their initial goal of using the Blacks to preserve Argus in Bud's spirit. The widows asked for $10 million each for their two 23.6 per cent stakes. The Blacks offered $8 million, and a price of $9.2 million each was agreed on. The brothers borrowed the entire amount; half from the Bank of Commerce, half from the Toronto-Dominion Bank, the banks on whose boards of directors the brothers sat.

Questions about the Blacks' conduct lingered, but most people wanted to know what they would do with Argus and its $4 billion in slumbering assets. Now perched atop a many-tentacled giant with interests in natural resources, chemicals, farm-equipment manufacturing, grocery retailing, and broadcasting, Conrad Black, not yet thirty-four, was already the most celebrated Canadian tycoon of his generation. The keys to 10 Toronto Street were his. "We're talking about business," commented Hal Jackman. "It's not a moral issue. There's no right and wrong in this. The prizes go to the stronger, and Conrad was the stronger."

Alongside Conrad Black's signature on the crucial compulsory-transfer document presented to Max Meighen in June was that of Shirley Gail Walters, who had become the corporate secretary at Western Dominion, the Black family company. And in the midst of the Argus imbroglio, on July 14, she and Conrad Black were married.

The Anglican ceremony was conducted by the Reverend John Erb at Grace Church on-the-Hill, where the funeral service for George Black had been held two years earlier. Monte Black and Leigh Beauchamp, Brian Stewart's girlfriend, were witnesses. After the wedding, Shirley left her bouquet of white roses with pink edges on George's and Betty Black's graves in Mount Pleasant Cemetery. The newlyweds returned to the Blacks' Park Lane Circle home, where about twenty guests drank Dom Pérignon and dined on crown roast of lamb catered by Winston's, the stuffy Toronto restaurant where Black and other power-brokers dined.

The event was part nuptial celebration and part business banquet, with much Argus strategy discussed by the pool. Throughout the evening, Black conferred with his brother, White, Radler, and

Kaplan. The groom, sporting a white carnation in the lapel of his blue suit, kept apologizing for talking business. "I'm sorry I have to keep bringing this up but I have to keep everything straight in my mind." While the wedding guests and Shirley partied into the night, the exhausted groom turned in early, alone.

Despite his professed desire to keep things quiet, a gaggle of reporters had gathered by the gate at Black's estate earlier that day, and four days later a large colour photo of the newlyweds graced the *Toronto Star*. ("Wall of Privacy Surrounds Tycoon and Four-Day Bride.") Reporters were frustrated by their inability to unearth much about the new Mrs. Black, except that she had been married for about two years previously with no children, hailed from Montreal, was the daughter of an accountant for the Canadian Imperial Bank of Commerce, and was the grand-niece of Robert Stanley Weir, the judge who wrote the English words to the national anthem, "O Canada."

Attempts to elicit interviews at the Black doorstep generated only Shirley's brief comment that she didn't want to be seen as a spouse in the Margaret Trudeau vein, and that she didn't want people to think "Conrad married his secretary." The *Star* did get hold of Margaret Barker, a friend of Shirley's, who shockingly revealed that "the new Mrs. Black has never entertained on a large scale but is 'very competent in the kitchen,' tending towards pork chops, mixed grills and chicken dishes."

More seriously, Black's effort to keep the existence of their infant son under wraps was briefly threatened when a writer for the *Globe and Mail* phoned his new mother-in-law to inquire about the rumours of a child. She didn't speak to him but quickly called Shirley. Black later explained that his only reason for keeping Jonathan's existence quiet was to protect his son. "When they phoned my mother-in-law, she phoned my wife and my wife raised it with me," recalled Black, "and I spoke to [*Globe* editor-in-chief] Dic Doyle. And he said, 'That's fine, quite right, what do we want to get into that for?'"

The press filled its pages with plenty of other Black-mania. There was no shortage of super-confident, chin-forward photos of Black, many of them featuring him thumbing through an ever-present copy of *Duplessis*. He was the *Globe and Mail*'s Report on Business "Man of the Year" for 1978, the *Toronto Star*'s "Prince of Tycoons" and *Fortune* magazine's "Boy Wonder of Canadian Business." Rod McQueen, writing for *Maclean's* magazine, tried to get a handle on Black during an interview in his office. "I'm a man of the people," Black offered drolly. "I'm a retired pensioner living on my investments." In a more serious vein, he said, "Avocationally, I'm a historian and a publisher. Fundamentally, I'm an ideologist." A slight smile never quite departed Black's lips as he searched for the right words: "I'm motivated by . . ." There was a long pause, but then Black dug deep and salvaged the thought. "It's difficult. One doesn't want to sound pretentious or superficial. I am perplexed at the erosion of conviction and the gradual descent of our society into a moral torpor. There is a great deal of hand-wringing going on; I'm reduced to reading Spengler. His theme is that the decline of civilization is as likely as the turning of autumn leaves. I have this semi-romantic notion about ideological questions. I guess there's a bit of the missionary in all of us."

Monte Black was happy to let his younger brother bask in the spotlight and make profound statements. With Conrad on a honeymoon, both literal and metaphorical, Monte, by now married more than a dozen years and with children of his own, found the Argus grab a cause of some marital discord. "We had a very difficult time," said Mariellen Black, who separated from Monte in 1981 and whose divorce was finalized in 1988. "There were some very serious security concerns about the children. We had guards on the children. There had been vandalism at the house. Our life had been severely affected by all of the fame and notoriety."

During one drive back to Toronto from their cottage in Muskoka, Mariellen said to Monte in exasperation, "I really don't understand what all of this is about. What is it worth? We live in the same house. The kids have always gone to private school. What's the benefit?"

"Well," Monte replied, "it's a Monopoly game. It's a lot of fun."

Up to this point, Monte had always had difficulty living within his means. In the 1970s he had borrowed more than $300,000 from his parents, and at a particularly low point in 1973 was given a monthly allowance by his father to get by.

Monte would not soon forget his wife's reaction on July 5, 1978, when he informed her that he and his brother had just borrowed $18.4 million to buy out Maude McDougald's and Doris Phillips's interests in Ravelston. Mariellen, he later said, "was startled that this amount of money had been borrowed and wondered how I was going to pay it back – a question I had a hard time answering at the time."

Chapter Six

FINANCIAL ENGINEERING

On the face of it, the $30 million that the Blacks ended up paying for all of Ravelston seems a small price for control of assets worth $4 billion. But any knowledgeable investor knows that there is often little relationship between the value of the assets of a company on its balance sheet and the value that investments in that company will fetch if sold, after paying off debts. (Hal Jackman, for one, believed Black paid dearly for Argus, relative to the underlying share values, although this is a tough point to prove since Argus's common shares rarely traded.) But this was all part of the illusion of Argus's influence, which Black knew – although perhaps not to the degree that he was soon to discover – was in decline.

Mariellen Black's question was a rational one: what had motivated them to gamble on Argus? Conrad Black had helped create Sterling Newspapers, on the basis of which he could boast to his Toronto contemporaries that he had made it on his own, without family money. Monte had a comfortable career in the investment industry as a vice-president of Dominion Securities. They also owned a malting business and were to inherit a further $4.2 million from their father's estate. They could also have simply sold their Ravelston stock and, based on what they paid the widows, walked away with some $9 million more.

One explanation is that Ravelston was their largest asset, and since they were "seriously disquieted about its deteriorating condition" (as Black put it) they had to do whatever they could to protect it. Second, the Blacks believed that among the factions within Ravelston only they could reverse Argus's decline by pursuing a strategy of unsentimentally disposing of assets, which Conrad Black would come to call an "asset upgrade." Perhaps the most revealing insight into Black's motivation was his statement that "my brother and I had known Argus all our lives, and while we always liked and admired Mr. Taylor and Mr. McDougald, both of whom our father had loyally served as a junior partner, we thought, in some indefinable way, that it was justly our turn." Indeed, George Black went to his grave convinced, with some justification, that Taylor had made a mistake by replacing him as Canadian Breweries' president in 1958. "I was slightly miffed at the way I thought the old Argus quadrumvirate used him, and then set him aside for a while," Conrad Black said later of his father. "In any case, to the extent I was miffed I more than compensated for that when we took over Argus."

With Conrad as president of Argus and Monte as president of Ravelston, the Blacks spent much of the summer of 1978 putting in place a new group of investors for 49 per cent of Ravelston, people from the ranks of Toronto's ruling class. Nelson Davis, Argus's new chairman, and Hal Jackman each took 16 per cent of Ravelston, and the department-store family scion Fredrik Eaton bought 4 per cent. John Finlay, Douglas Bassett, and Dixon Chant bought 1 per cent apiece, and 10 per cent went to the Blacks' cousin Ron Riley.

The Blacks were also concerned that the Argus structure was susceptible to an uninvited acquirer, most likely Paul Desmarais, who owned more of its equity but fewer of its votes after his unsuccessful takeover attempt in 1975. If Desmarais were suddenly to decide to acquire a major interest in one of the underlying Argus companies, most of which were ostensibly controlled through shareholdings ranging from 10 to 12 per cent, Argus lacked the financial muscle to counter him. One of Black's first moves once he was in charge was to cozy up to Desmarais and buy his Argus shares for about $80 million – $65 million in cash borrowed from the

Commerce and Toronto-Dominion banks and the balance in a promissory note.

This move brought Ravelston's voting interest in Argus up to 87 per cent, and a further purchase of a 9 per cent interest from Jackman brought it to 96 per cent. In December 1978, the Blacks sold Argus's 11 per cent stake in the forest products company Domtar to Macmillan Bloedel for about $70 million. As Monte explained, Domtar did not want them on the board, and the Blacks began a series of reorganizations aimed at shoring up their positions in cash-rich Hollinger Mines* and Dominion Stores. "We had to . . . eliminate those companies where we didn't have any influence and beef up and strengthen those companies where we did have an influence so we could get to a controlling position and not have to worry about being raided or being outvoted by a majority of the shareholders." As it turned out, the upshot of this exercise would be the Blacks' selling off the whole lot.

In 1979, Massey-Ferguson was the company in the Argus group with the most pressing problems. With a 140-year history and annual sales of $3 billion, venerable Massey was the largest farm-machinery company in the world. It was Argus's highest-profile holding and would be the first proving ground for Conrad Black's as yet unseen operational abilities.

Growing up, Black had observed that Bud McDougald and his Argus cronies had enjoyed much of their status as captains of industry through their Massey ownership. The Duke of Wellington and other luminaries sat on the board of directors, and important trips abroad were a regular part of the agenda. For Black, one of the perks of Massey control was the opportunity it gave him to indulge his ambition to meet and know international bigwigs. In 1980, Massey sponsored a conference at the Four Seasons Hotel in Toronto which featured Henry Kissinger and the *Economist* editor Andrew Knight as speakers. Another attendee, former British ambassador to the U.S. Peter Jay, recalled that as he and Kissinger were walking together, Black muscled him out of the way to get alongside the former U.S. secretary of state. Jay commented, "It was a revealing encounter to

---

* Hollinger Mines was renamed Hollinger Argus.

me of the technique of Conrad." (Black dismissed the account as "a wild bowdlerization.")

Operationally, Massey had been neglected in the latter McDougald years, because Argus was focused on achieving a steady flow of dividends – its only income – at the expense of Massey using its cash flow to invest internally or expand. Between 1978, when the Blacks acquired control of Argus, and 1980, external events accelerated Massey's decline: farm markets did not recover as had been predicted in the wake of the energy crisis, and rising interest rates pushed the company into default on its interest payments and debt covenants. In the year ended October 31, 1978, Massey had logged the largest loss in Canadian corporate history, $257 million.

With 40,000 shareholders, 45,000 employees, and 250 bankers in the balance, turning the company around was an epic challenge. Against this backdrop, Conrad Black moved into the boardroom-sized chairman's office at Massey-Ferguson, vacant since Eric Phillips's death fifteen years earlier. By Black's own account, by late 1978 he was spending about two thirds of his time on Massey-Ferguson business (although his newly appointed president at Massey, Victor Rice, later pegged the workload ratio at 85 per cent to 15 in favour of Argus, and it was pointed out elsewhere that the Argus offices were being redecorated at the time Black relocated). Before long, Massey's public relations department inquired whether Black would like any assistance. No, thank you, he assured them, he was more than capable of handling the press personally.

His operational skills may have been a question mark, but Black quickly showed that he could spin with the best of them. "There is mounting evidence the company is turning around," Black assured the *Globe and Mail* at the end of 1978. "The bedrock business of Massey-Ferguson is fundamentally sound. When the flood of bad news rolls, that fact encourages me. I remember the thought that institutions, like people, are strengthened through adversity."

Even as Massey's financial situation went from bad to worse, Black hoped he could restore the company – elevating its new chairman in the process – to greatness. Privately, though, he made a point of distancing himself from the company's deteriorating results and noting he was not responsible for its decline before he took over. As he wrote in a letter to Robert Anderson, president and chief executive officer of Hanna Mining, on April 28, 1980: "The fact that ill-considered management decisions and bad luck led it to the brink of insolvency must not obscure the enormous opportunity presented by this company, whose acute state of under-capitalization has made it possible for us to buy real and absolute control of it so comparatively inexpensively, while being hailed as saviours as we do so."

Under Black's eye and president Victor Rice's stewardship, the company did make fast progress. Rice slashed its international work-force by almost one third, sold off unprofitable assets (resulting in writedowns of $600 million), and eked out a small operating profit in 1979. But the turnaround was short-lived. Burdened by a debt load of $1.7 billion, soaring interest rates, and a precipitous downturn in the North American farm-machinery market, Massey failed to meet the conditions imposed by its lenders, for the second year in a row. Unless terms were renegotiated by November 1, 1980 – and this meant a new equity issue – Massey would be bankrupt.

Black said he was willing to put more Argus money, perhaps $100 million, into Massey. But the company needed much more, and without guarantees from the Ontario and federal governments, lenders were leery of becoming more deeply involved. "I am amazed by the number of so-called financial experts who are luxuriating in the view that I am some sort of a punch-drunk prize-fighter on the ropes," Black said to a journalist from *Maclean's* magazine. "Well, screw them."*

---

* Black's bluster could sometimes be too much even for himself. In the same article, Black declared: "I am a historian by vocation, and by that bar I will be judged." More than a decade later, he said, "I thought to myself as soon as I said it: 'That is a terribly pompous thing to say. What does history care about this?'" Black was reminded of the statement while observing a parliamentary debate in the British House of Commons. "One of the members of the government said, 'History will judge something or other,' and another MP, Peter Tapsell, said, 'I think history will have other things to do.' And that's exactly how I felt at the time but I didn't put it to myself as well as that."

As feisty as he was publicly, Black slowly distanced himself from the Massey fray throughout 1980. In May, he relinquished the posts of chairman and chief executive to Rice but retained the post of chairman of the board's executive committee. Argus's investment in Massey was written down to nothing on its books. But he continued to push for government assistance, meeting and corresponding with Industry Minister Herb Gray, a move that did not sit well with his critics. Dixon Chant, then Argus's executive vice-president and a director of Massey, said, "Herb Gray's remark to us was that as long as those fat cats at 10 Toronto Street weren't going to put any money in, the federal government wasn't going to put any money in. So we knew we had to do something and stir them up. So then they didn't have any fat cat to criticize and they eventually had to put up money. Strange how those things happen sometimes."

What Black did next took just about everyone by surprise. Chant recalled that Black lumbered down the hall on the second floor of 10 Toronto Street on the afternoon of October 1, 1980, and declared that he had decided to give Argus's 16 per cent interest in Massey – worth nearly $30 million – to Massey's pension funds. This would eliminate the barrier to government assistance, and Black would (publicly, at least) continue to profess his desire for Argus to participate in Massey's resurrection. As he later explained, "I was not prepared to tolerate for one more day the allegation that I was attempting to be bailed out." The move also allowed Black to claim for Argus a capital tax loss of $39 million. "The truth of the matter is he was taking a big tax write-off and abandoning the company," said Victor Rice. "His perception of what he was doing and reality were two different things."

Rice's perception was that Black and especially David Radler, who had emerged as Argus's operations kingpin, were young men in over their heads, unequipped to deal with a business of Massey's size and complexity. "Radler's the interferer and there's no way you could run anything with Radler around," he said. For a $3 billion company, Rice joked, Radler seemed preoccupied with questions like "How many pencils and notepads can we save on today?"

In his 1981 book, *Massey at the Brink*, the journalist Peter Cook called Black's decision to walk away from Massey "as surprising and controversial as any business decision ever made in Canada." Black's position was that by withdrawing his effective controlling share-holding from Massey, he cleared the way for the government to move forward with its plans for aid. Yet federal officials later said they were working all along on the premise that Argus would be involved in some way. And with Argus's withdrawal, Massey's already jittery banks became even more agitated.

Wrote Cook: "For a self-appointed spokesman for free enterprise like Black to withdraw from Massey was to admit that something very fundamental had gone wrong. He was, after all, declaring that a great Canadian company – with 133 years of history behind it – would be better served by putting itself in the hands of governments and banks than by enjoying the continued participation of its largest private shareholder. Tactically, he may have acted in the best interests of himself and his friends who ran Hollinger Argus. But the precedent of admitting defeat, and leaving the problems to be solved by others, was hardly a helpful one."

Black's withdrawal was harshly criticized in editorials in the *Toronto Star* and *Toronto Sun*. The boy wonder became an *enfant terrible* overnight. The Liberal *Star*, under the headline "Black Left Massey in Lurch," called the stock giveaway "the sort of irresponsible, self-serving action that has no place in the top echelons of the Canadian marketplace." Black replied swiftly in a letter to the editor. "I worked at Massey-Ferguson for nearly two years for no pay and played a modest role in the greatest year-to-year improvement of results in Canadian history. Argus's presence as holder of a modest but traditionally strategic share position was being used as a pretext for governments to do nothing for Massey-Ferguson, while Argus was being accused of seeking a bail-out to which we were, in fact, opposed . . .

"What then possessed the editors of the *Star* to produce this gratuitous drivel about my 'morality and social responsibility'? My associates and I acted as we did because it was the right thing to do. The *Star*'s editorial performance, on the same subject, consisted of misinformed comment from a familiar source, uttered with the conviction that self-righteous ignorance can alone impart."

The *Toronto Sun* erroneously suggested – and soon corrected – that by giving away Argus's Massey shares, Black had got rid of some $2 billion in debts. Black wrote to the *Sun*: "For the record (not that the *Sun* is a newspaper of record for anyone who doesn't suffer from lip-strain after ten seconds of silent reading), the *Sun*'s theory that we should mortgage all the assets of our other companies, which are all prospering and have hundreds of thousands of other shareholders, to bail Massey out of a mess that none of us had any hand in creating, is too asinine to merit further reply."

Despite the bombast, both Conrad and Monte Black later admitted that the Massey episode was something of which neither was particularly proud. "We were sitting there worrying about Massey – Massey, Massey, Massey, that's all we did," recalled one Argus insider. "The actual investment, in the final analysis, was peanuts, but I guess it was the prestige company." And, once Massey was free of its Argus ties, Victor Rice did arrange a refinancing of the company and led it back to health, reinvented as an auto-parts company and renamed Varity ("Var" being Rice's own initials). Indeed, perhaps the most stinging indictment of Black's brief stewardship of Massey is that $1 invested in Massey stock when Argus walked away from it would have been worth $75 by 1999. Under his direction, Rice estimated, a total of nearly US$8 billion in new value was created, magnitudes more than any company run by Black would ever achieve. Around the time the company that had become LucasVarity was acquired by TRW in 1999, Rice and his wife ran into Black and his second wife, Barbara Amiel, at Royal Ascot Ladies' Day. The four ended up having dinner together, with Black acting as though he were the magnanimous mentor who had given his protegé Rice his chance. "I was being a success so he was trying to vicariously live off my success, which was rather strange," recalled Rice.

Shortly after buying into Argus, and before unloading the Massey stake, Black almost quit the newspaper business. In fall 1978, he and his partners agreed to sell Sterling Newspapers to the media group Maclean Hunter. Sterling, which by this time had nine regional dailies and nine weeklies (all in British Columbia, except for the paper in Summerside, Prince Edward Island), was put up for sale as a means of raising much-needed cash to finance the Ravelston buyout of Argus.* Maclean Hunter agreed to pay $14 million, subject to due diligence, and Black later asserted that its chairman, Donald Campbell, tried to "chisel $1.5 million off the purchase price" at the eleventh hour. Campbell claimed the price was based on a multiple-of-earnings formula, but Sterling's audited results for the year ended June 30, 1978, "did not produce" the expected multiple. David Radler, who was handling the sale, said merely that the idea of selling was a "mistake" and that he was relieved it fell apart.

In 1980, Sterling was folded into Western Dominion Investments after a committee of the independent (that is, non–Black) directors at Ravelston, in a rare show of dissent, rejected a proposal to buy it. Monte himself later noted, "The major item on the balance sheet of Sterling Newspapers was goodwill, and goodwill is air and wind." Nonetheless, in addition to providing cash flow to help finance Black's holdings in Ravelston, the amalgamation of Sterling into WDI brought his newspaper partners, Peter White and David Radler, into the Argus adventure as full partners.**

Black might have been prepared to sell Sterling, but he had not lost interest in newspapers. He had his sights on bigger prey: FP Publications, a federation of eight old family newspapers, including Toronto's *Globe and Mail*, Canada's establishment journal. The chain also included the *Times* and *Colonist* papers in Victoria, the *Winnipeg Free Press* (from which the FP name was derived), the *Ottawa Journal*, and a well-regarded news service. Its *Montreal Star* had recently been closed after failing to recover from a lengthy strike, and a few of the five family blocs controlling the company were ready to sell out. John

---

* Other steps included the sale by the Blacks of Crown Trust to the Winnipeg-based financier Izzy Asper, who would figure again as a buyer of Black's assets more than two decades later.

** The Blacks' 51 per cent interest in Ravelston at this time was held through Western Dominion Investments. About 65 per cent of WDI was owned by Warspite, the Black brothers' joint investment company. As a result of the Sterling deal, Radler owned about 13.5 per cent of WDI, White about 12.5 per cent, and Conrad Black 9 per cent.

Bassett and George Gardiner, president of the investment firm Gardiner Watson, invited Black to join them in a bid for the chain. He accepted. "You've got to take these opportunities when they come and sort it out later," Black explained afterwards, "as long as you're not overextending yourself financially."

In late November 1979, Black found himself sitting beside *Globe* publisher Roy Megarry at a luncheon for Alberta premier Peter Lougheed given by the lawyer (and future prime minister) John Turner. Rumours of his bid were already about, and Megarry greeted him by saying, "I understand you're negotiating with FP. I think that's great." After lunch, Megarry offered Cardinal Emmett Carter, head of Toronto's archdiocese, the use of his car, and Black gave Megarry a lift to the *Globe*. As Black recalled it, they parked in front of the *Globe* on Front Street and "chatted" for about ten minutes.

The publisher came away convinced that Black was dead set against his plan to transform the *Globe* into a national newspaper. Black claimed he only said that while he didn't object to the idea, he thought the *Globe* should ensure it maintained its position in Toronto. According to Black, Megarry's parting words were, "Well, I'm not against this. It is not a negative thing and it could be really a good thing for us. I'm not against it." Black replied, "We'll be in touch."

Black later said he felt Megarry was "extremely disingenuous" when he proceeded to confer with the *Globe*'s editor, Dic Doyle, telling him: "We will have to do something about this." Whatever impression Megarry might have given Black, the idea of his group assuming ownership of the *Globe* was received with something less than warmth, although most of the opposition was directed toward Bassett, who, as publisher of the *Toronto Telegram*, had demonstrated a hands-on and in-your-face style. Some at the *Globe* had either left the *Telegram* under Bassett or lost their jobs when the paper folded in 1971, and had no desire to work for him again.

The uneasy *Globe* staff were gathered in the newsroom by Megarry. He announced that he couldn't substantiate the rumours of a bid by Black and his group, and rallied support for an employee buyout. Despite the spirited financial pledges of the journalists, by January FP was sold to the billionaire Kenneth Thomson for $165 million. The Black-Gardiner-Bassett group had dropped out of the running some $40 million earlier, but not before Black had delivered a scathing letter for publication – an occurrence that was becoming routine – to the *Globe*, accusing Megarry of being "indiscreet and amateurish," adding that "we are not the ravaging dragon trying to defile the virgin *Globe and Mail*."

Black had plenty to keep himself occupied with besides trying to buy newspapers. His hallmark quickly became the incessant shuffling of companies within the Argus group. Between 1978, when he and his brother took over Argus, and 1984, its holdings were reorganized no fewer than eight times. To fans, Black was a grandmaster moving his pieces around the board or a general orchestrating a battle on a number of fronts. To critics, it looked like nothing so much as an elaborate shell game. "He's just getting rich," the Montreal investment counsellor Stephen Jarislowsky told the *Financial Post*. "If you look at it, he buys in cheap, at a discount, then he liquidates the assets at a higher value. It's very simple. But he's not doing anything for shareholders in the meantime."

A 1984 report by the analyst David Ramsay at Wood Gundy in Toronto cited a "Black Factor" that depressed the value of some of the companies' stocks by an estimated 10 per cent. Black responded with his own theory that this so-called "factor" worked to his advantage, because he could buy back shares and do more reorganizations at attractive prices, generating more value out of Argus's moribund companies. How or when the rest of the shareholders would benefit, though, was far from clear.

Never one for a simple explanation when a complex military analogy will do, Black later talked about the Argus years in terms of "Napoleon's famous maxim that force equals mass times velocity. As the Argus group was a collection of passive minority shareholdings in rather tired companies and the only cash flow was dividends, there was no mass, in Napoleonic terms. So our only strength came from velocity, as in Napoleon's first famous campaign, in Italy in 1796 and 1797. On that occasion he marched and counter-marched 30,000 untrained ragged conscripts around with such skill that he bundled the much superior Austrians right out of Italy, while rarely actually giving battle. I hope it is not too self-indulgent to consider our activities at Argus in our first six or seven years a pallid adaptation of those tactics. We had to conduct a war of manoeuvre because we had no financial divisions with which to fight a pitched battle."

So complex did Black's dealings become during this period that Jack Boultbee, his private accountant, plotted organization charts of the Black empire on wallet-sized cards so that he could see which company owned what at any particular moment. The destination of Black's manoeuvres may have been unclear, but the more the organization charts shifted, the more Black's ambitions grew, and so did his notoriety.

Chapter Seven

THE HANNA BRAWL

During the late morning of June 27, 1980, Conrad Black appeared in the doorway of George Humphrey Jr.'s office on the twenty-sixth floor of the Hanna Mining Company's Cleveland, Ohio, headquarters. In addition to being a descendant of Hanna's founder and a member of its largest group of shareholders, Humphrey was also Hanna's vice-president of sales. Among the myriad corporate interests Black and his brother controlled through their Argus group was a 10.5 per cent interest in the Iron Ore Company of Canada, and Conrad Black served as a director.[*]

Hanna owned 26.5 per cent of Iron Ore and managed it under agreement. Black was in the building to attend the Iron Ore board meeting that day. The association between Hanna and Argus was of long standing, and Black had taken an active interest in the American company's affairs since getting to know former Hanna chairman George M. (Bud) Humphrey Sr. through board meetings at Massey-Ferguson and at Labrador Mining – in which Hanna had a 20 per cent interest.

---

[*] The interest in Iron Ore was held 7.5 per cent by Hollinger Argus, formerly Hollinger Mines, and 3 per cent by Labrador Mining and Exploration. Hollinger Argus owned 67 per cent of Labrador Mining.

The Black Companies in 1981

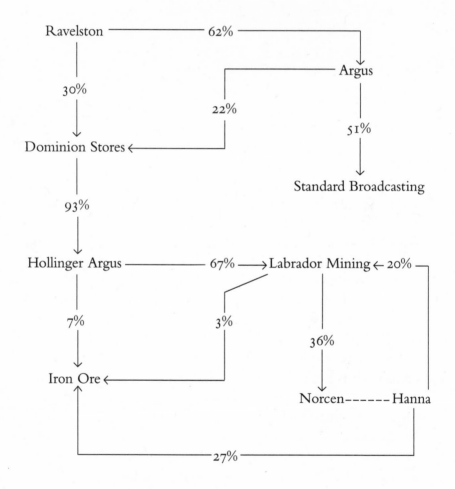

Bud's son George did not know the visitor in his doorway well, but Black seemed to know much about him. The Hanna board had appointed its first non-family chief executive, Bob Anderson, after Bud's death the previous year, and Black asked Humphrey how he felt about his family being "shunted out of the mainstream" of Hanna's management. The scenario was familiar to Black, and his instincts were correct; Humphrey was not happy about it. "He was extremely embittered at what he felt to be the unfair treatment by the incumbent Hanna management of his family and himself," Black said later, "and he was severe in his criticism of the management and very troubled because he was part of the management and his family was still heavily invested in the company stock and he was in a very serious quandary about what to do."

Black offered some cautious advice. He said that from his vantage point, as an Iron Ore shareholder, Hanna seemed to be in very capable hands under Anderson. At the same time, he could relate to George's dissatisfaction, having made his own name in the wake of the death of another Bud. He told Humphrey that his situation "was to me a little reminiscent of some of the treatment my brother and I received for a time after the death of the former chairman of our company, who was not personally related but a man we knew very well, and that I could sympathize with him but I thought patience would be rewarded."

Black said he had some ideas about collaborating with the Humphrey family on the ownership of Hanna, and when, several weeks later, Black joined Humphrey and his wife for dinner at their home in Gates Hills, Ohio, the conversation continued, but at considerably greater length. Humphrey reiterated his disgruntlement, and Black noted that Hanna looked like an "interesting vehicle" for expansion into the United States because of the long corporate association with Argus. Humphrey mentioned that he would like to run Hanna someday. Black emphasized that he was not trying to "exploit any factionalism" within Hanna and that his potential involvement was "one of conciliation." Black continued to praise Hanna and its management, and said that if George or any member of his family objected to Black's becoming involved with Hanna on a friendly basis, he would not proceed. Both men agreed to mull the idea over.

Black was enamoured not just of Hanna but of the notion of expanding into the U.S. and into the resource sector in particular. In late 1979, Black had begun to absorb Norcen Energy Resources, a Calgary-based oil and gas producer with no dominant shareholder, into the ever-shifting Argus stable. Through Labrador Mining, where he was vice-chairman, Black began to buy 10 per cent of Norcen on December 12 of that year. The next day he phoned Norcen chief executive Edward Bovey, with whom he was on friendly terms. Bovey asked Black his intentions, and he said Labrador might wish to buy more shares at some point but did not aspire to more than 50 per cent and "did not wish to relegate Norcen to the role of subsidiary."

Subsidiary or not, around mid-January 1980, Black decided to bring his interest in Norcen up to 36 per cent and effective control. Bovey soon retired, and Black became vice-chairman and later chairman. Edward Battle, a Texas-born petroleum engineer who had been with Norcen since 1957 and its president since 1975, was named chief executive. Once in command at Norcen, the Black brothers planned to assemble a powerful resource group that could take maximum advantage of tax shelters, available to oil and gas exploration at the time, to protect their earnings from Hollinger Mines. As Montegu Black noted: "In the companies that we had in Argus Corporation, the one with the money and horsepower was always Hollinger." That horsepower was derived largely from its interest in Iron Ore. Hollinger earned most of its cash flow from royalties on Iron Ore's sales of up to 16 million tons of iron pellets per year to U.S. steel companies. Labrador Mining received a sales commission of 5 per cent, which could amount to as much as $50 million annually. Under its management agreement, Hanna's appointed CEO of Iron Ore was the labour lawyer Brian Mulroney, whose political aspirations were well known and who, like Black, had studied law at Laval University. Mulroney and Black were both directors of the Canadian Imperial Bank of Commerce, as was Bovey.*

Hanna seemed to fit Black's criteria for expansion, as well as his personal ambitions. Founded in 1853 by Mark Hanna, the company

---

* Mulroney also sat on the board of Black-controlled Standard Broadcasting.

had iron ore fields in Minnesota and northern Michigan that fuelled a powerful financial and political machine. Mark Hanna virtually ruled the Republican Party in the late 1800s and is credited with engineering the election of William McKinley as president in 1896.

On a personal level, Black was now a big fish in Canada, but he was already growing disenchanted with his public image there and the country's business climate. He was impressed by the course the U.S. economy was taking, especially since Ronald Reagan's election in 1980. In 1978, the year he took control of Argus, Black began to spend his winters in Palm Beach, the bastion of dynastic opulence on Florida's Atlantic coast. To winter there was not only to follow in the footsteps of Bud McDougald but to rub shoulders with the cream of America's super-rich. "Palm Beach isn't everyone's cup of tea," Black once remarked. "Some people are offended by the extreme opulence, but I find it sort of entertaining."

In Hanna, Black found a venerable company, without any controlling shareholder, that was suffering the brunt of recession and a crisis among its main customers, the U.S. steel industry. Hanna generated profits of US$44 million on sales of US$290 million in the year ended December 31, 1981. The Humphreys, Mark Hanna's heirs, held a cumulative interest in Hanna Mining estimated at 20 per cent, amplified by connections and shareholdings with such American dynasties as the Mellons, the Bechtels, and the Graces.

Black later spoke of the Hanna episode as "a fierce litigious and regulatory firefight which entertained the financial press and its devotees for almost a year." But for Black it was more: after the rise of his corporate star in Canada, his move on Hanna was chief among a string of controversies that added a darker shade to Black's reputation. The Hanna battle and its aftermath led him to attack institutions and friendships in a country where he had rapidly risen to sudden prominence, and for others to judge Black more warily and to question his integrity and business tactics. What's more, it would lead to a legal outcome that would come back to haunt Black nearly a quarter century later.

For now, Hanna had the same elements as his successful Ravelston power play, right down to unhappy heirs and a grieving widow. The next Humphrey family member to encounter Conrad Black was George Humphrey's mother, Louise (Lulu) Humphrey, Bud's bejewelled widow. The backdrop was a white-tie tribute to Canada at the Metropolitan Opera House in New York on April 4, 1981, almost ten months after Black's encounter with George. In attendance were about sixty Canadians, led by Prime Minister Pierre Trudeau, whose date for the evening was the Texas model and socialite Lacey Neuhaus. Lulu, one of the opera's patrons, knew Black was an acquaintance of her son and of her daughter who lived in Toronto, and she arranged for him to be seated beside her, at table 10. They spoke at length, and at one point the Humphrey matriarch criticized Hanna management and told Black she was concerned about her sons' careers. She asked Black to keep in touch. He recalled, "I floated very gingerly with her the idea of whether, if we bought some shares, that would be regarded as a friendly or an unfriendly thing by her family. She replied, 'No, not at all,' that in fact they would be 'delighted if we bought some shares.'"

As Hanna's representative, George Humphrey arrived in Toronto the following month for Labrador Mining's annual meeting; afterwards Conrad and Monte invited him to meet them privately at their offices at 10 Toronto Street. Conrad again raised the possibility of an investment in Hanna, on a friendly basis – then asked that Humphrey keep their conversations private. Next, he spoke to Brian Mulroney, who assured Black he would "diplomatically present that case" to his masters at Hanna when called upon.

In August 1981, a full year after his dinner at George Humphrey's home, Black and Norcen president Edward Battle laid plans to buy up to 4.9 per cent of Hanna's outstanding stock on the open market – any more would have to be disclosed to the U.S. Securities and Exchange Commission. On Saturday, August 15, at around seven p.m., Black phoned Humphrey at his holiday home in Maine and said he was now contemplating buying into Hanna on an "imminent basis." He reiterated that he wanted to proceed only on friendly terms, and that he would be willing to buy shares from the Humphreys if they had any they were prepared to sell. Humphrey did not react as Black expected. The situation had changed completely, he told Black. He had recently been elected to the Hanna board of directors, which gave him more security about his family's interests, and he was now fully committed to working with Hanna management. Their conversation was short. "This was around the dinner hour and I didn't want to spend all night on the phone with Conrad Black," he later recalled.

Undeterred by Humphrey's brush-off, the next Monday Norcen began making open-market purchases of Hanna stock through Michael Biscotti, the chief trader at Dominion Securities Ames. Three days later, Battle arranged for a $20 million line of credit from the Canadian Imperial Bank of Commerce (where Black was a director) to purchase up to 4.9 per cent of Hanna's stock. The account, not part of Norcen's normal operating lines of credit, was assigned a secret account number, and bank officers were under orders not to deliver statements to Norcen's offices.

By September 9, Norcen had accumulated 58,000 shares, about 2 per cent of the company. That day, the executive committee of Norcen's board met in Calgary and discussed the Hanna investment. The minutes for the meeting included the entry, "U.S. Acquisition: Mr. Battle stated that the Company, subsequent to telephone contact with the members of the executive committee, had initiated through stock market transactions the acquisition of a 4.9 per cent stock interest in a U.S. company listed on the New York stock exchange with the ultimate purpose of acquiring a fifty-one per cent position at a later date." This would later prove to be a very contentious statement.

By the end of October, Norcen owned 4.9 per cent of Hanna. Black planned to contact Hanna management at this point but changed his mind after he received what he described as an unsolicited phone call from James (Jimmy) Connacher, the head of Gordon Securities in Toronto.

Connacher offered Black a huge block of Hanna stock, about 575,000 shares. Although it would mean a departure from Black's previous plan of staying below the public disclosure threshold until approaching management, and the shares were several dollars above the market price at $37, Black accepted after speaking to his brother and Battle. He later claimed in court – where this escapade would soon be headed – that Connacher gave no indication he was aware

Black had already bought Hanna shares, and that he did not say how Gordon had accumulated the block. "He did not tell me," said Black, "and I did not ask." Chalk it up to clairvoyance.

At three-thirty p.m. on October 28, 1981, Carl Nickels, Hanna's executive vice-president, was on the phone with Mulroney speculating about who was buying all the shares in Hanna. Although Mulroney must have surmised it was Black, he apparently did not say so. According to Nickels's intelligence, there was an open purchase order for the shares at Gordon. Meanwhile Black had tried to contact Hanna's CEO, Bob Anderson, but he was away in Brazil. In the midst of his chat with Mulroney, Nickels's secretary brought him a note saying that Conrad Black was on the other line.

Nickels finished his conversation with Mulroney and, putting two and two together, picked up the phone and barked, "What the hell are you doing, Conrad?" Black quickly told Nickels that Norcen had acquired an 8.8 per cent stake in Hanna "for investment purposes," and that they had no ulterior motive – they were fans of Hanna's management and looking to find a way to diversify into the United States.

Black told Nickels he and Norcen were "absolutely friendly buyers, and had no sinister motives." Black gave his word not to buy any more shares until he met Anderson. He and Norcen's chief executive, Edward Battle, would fly to Cleveland as soon as possible.

That night, Black phoned Mulroney and asked him to make good on his pledge to assure his Hanna masters "that I didn't have cloven feet and wear horns." His objective, "in the best of all possible worlds," he told Mulroney, was a stake in Hanna around 20 per cent – about the size of Hanna's investment in Labrador Mining and Exploration.

The next day, Black talked with George Humphrey, who told Black his purchases had caused consternation among management. "He used a football metaphor with which I was not altogether familiar," recalled Black. "He said that he welcomed it 'as long as we are not blind-sided, and I am sure we won't be,' and I am afraid my knowledge of football is such that I was uncertain of what he meant."

Nickels, after his telephone conversation with Black, had phoned the investment banker Goldman Sachs and ordered a full report on the man. Goldman Sachs delivered a stinging document, compiled largely from Canadian press reports, portraying him as a shuffler of assets. The report was presented at a Hanna board meeting convened on November 3. After recounting his conversation with Black to the board, Nickels talked about the "problem areas" he foresaw with Black's investment. One, Nickels later explained, was "the general overall impact that Conrad Black – that a Conrad Black – would have on the type of partnership arrangements that we have, where we have really a very close fiduciary relationship, where you would never expect a man sitting next to you as a partner to turn around and start buying you without talking to you." The Hanna board voted unanimously to oppose Black as an investor.

The next day, Black and Edward Battle met Bob Anderson and Nickels in a first-floor conference room at the Sheraton Hopkins Hotel near Cleveland's Hopkins Airport. Black had been warned that Anderson possessed a volatile personality, and Anderson kicked off the meeting by telling Black in no uncertain terms that he wanted Norcen to "peel off" its shares – to sell them.

At one point during the meeting, Nickels told Black he considered him a "paper shuffler." Black took umbrage and pointed out that he and his brother had drawn value out of a group of companies which had been run in "a somewhat anachronistic manner." Pointing to his pocket, Black claimed that along the way he and Monte had increased the equity of Ravelston, the private company atop Argus, by some $200 million.

The meeting lasted ninety minutes. Before they parted, Black asked Anderson, "Could you give us any incentive to sell our shares?" But Hanna's CEO steadfastly refused to consider some ideas Black threw out, including a trade of Norcen's Hanna shares for Hanna's Labrador Mining shares or a standstill agreement. As they flew back to Toronto, Black and Battle surveyed the wreckage of their planned "amicable arrangement" with Hanna. They now had 8.8 per cent of the company but no workable plan.

The next day Black ran into Mulroney at a directors' meeting. Mulroney reported that he had tried to ease the way with Hanna, as Black had asked, but the reception was so cold he thought Norcen had no serious option but to do as Anderson said and sell its shares. Mulroney said he was beginning to feel like the "jam in the sandwich."

On November 9, 1981, Norcen filed its required Schedule 13-D with the Securities and Exchange Commission. The document declared that the purpose of Norcen's transaction was "to acquire an investment position in Hanna." It also stated that Norcen would review its position "from time to time" and might seek to acquire further shares or sell them. There was no mention of the resolution cited in the minutes of the Norcen executive committee two months earlier: that the ultimate purpose was to acquire 51 per cent of Hanna. On the advice of Norcen's U.S. counsel, Black had instructed that the SEC filing be "as short and antiseptic as possible."

Later that month, William Kilbourne, Norcen's chief legal officer and the man responsible for keeping minutes of board and executive committee meetings, asked the high-powered New York law firm Cravath, Swaine & Moore to prepare research about state and federal laws that applied to buying control of Hanna. Kilbourne later said he was merely "preparing for all possible contingencies."

Around the same time, Black decided to approach the Humphrey family once again. On the Thanksgiving weekend, he called Lulu Humphrey at her home in Tallahassee, Florida, and explained that he had bought shares but was now immobilized and wondering what to do with them. The matriarch deferred the matter to her son and principal financial adviser, Gilbert Watts Humphrey, known as Watts. Black told Watts he was "somewhat flabbergasted at the militancy of Mr. Anderson's request" not to buy any more shares and added that "we didn't want to rock the boat and we just sincerely didn't know what to do." Watts agreed that a meeting might be useful.

On December 21, Conrad Black, Monte Black, and Edward Battle visited Watts at his home in Sewickley, Pennsylvania. Black again said he was interested in getting involved with those who had significant interests in Hanna, specifically the Mellons, the Bechtels, and the Graces, using terms such as "those are very good people to be associated with" and "they are substantial and their interests are broad-ranging." He asked if Watts could foresee "any useful collaboration" between him and the family, with the proviso that it could not be perceived to be hostile toward management. Watts appeared interested and said he would consult other family members and Paul Mellon, a significant Hanna shareholder and his neighbour.

Several weeks later, on Friday, February 5, 1982, Watts Humphrey, Monte Black, and Edward Battle held a follow-up meeting over lunch at Sewickley's Edgewood Club. Shortly into the lunch, Battle said Norcen was "ready to go" with a tender offer. This surprised Watts. Over the past few weeks he had decided he didn't want to pursue an alliance with the Norcen people, but he did not say so. Battle said Norcen was willing to give the Humphreys an option to purchase a percentage of the stock acquired under the offer. The meeting ended with no commitments, and that night Watts called his brother George and learned of the talks his brother had held with the Blacks earlier. Watts thought over the situation all weekend, then called Monte Black and explained that he had problems with Norcen's approach and had decided not to go along with them. He sensed disappointment on the other end of the line during the ten-minute phone call.

Norcen's attempts at a partnership with the Humphrey clan were a flop but did have a positive effect: word of the meetings with Watts reached Hanna chief executive Bob Anderson. Accompanied by Nickels and George Humphrey, Anderson travelled to 10 Toronto Street to meet the Blacks and Battle. This was much more to Conrad's liking. Anderson said he now might consider the Blacks' earlier idea of swapping Hanna's Labrador shares for Norcen's Hanna shares. Black was interested, while Battle, seeing no obvious benefit in that for Norcen, pressed the idea of Norcen achieving a 25 to 30 per cent stake in Hanna and entering into a standstill agreement under which it would agree to buy no more shares for a period of time.*

Anderson and Nickels flew to Palm Beach for a follow-up meeting with Black and Battle at Conrad's winter home. There they presented a one-page swap agreement, which included a commitment from Black not to buy further Hanna shares for ten years. Black

---

* Norcen wanted to own at least 20 per cent of Hanna because, under Canadian accounting rules, it could then incorporate Hanna's earnings into its own profit and loss statements, rather than merely account for its shareholding as an investment.

now agreed with Battle that there was nothing in such a deal for Norcen and continued to press the idea of a 20 per cent investment, which included buying Hanna shares out of its treasury. Anderson replied that he was not authorized by his board to discuss anything but the swap proposal. Nothing would be resolved that night. Black took his guests outside for a drink, then back to the airport.

The Blacks decided it was time to play hardball. A dozen days later the brothers assembled their legal and banking advisers at Conrad's Florida *pied-à-terre* and developed a strategy for a possible tender offer. A climactic meeting with Anderson was set for 4:30 p.m. on Friday, April 2, 1982, again in the first-floor conference room of Cleveland's Sheraton Hopkins Hotel. Anderson and Nickels were surprised when Battle and Monte Black arrived without Conrad. In Palm Beach, Shirley Black was seven months pregnant with their second child and feeling ill, and Conrad did not want to leave her. The Hanna executives were even more surprised when Battle kicked off the proceedings by saying, "I am here today to tell you, number one, that on Monday morning the board of directors of Norcen has authorized me to go for a tender offer for 51 per cent of the Hanna Mining stock."

Battle added that Norcen had retained as counsel Lehman Brothers Kuhn Loeb and the renowned New York takeover lawyer Joe Flom of the firm Skadden Arps.* The hostile bid could be avoided, Battle continued, only if Hanna accepted a standstill agreement that gave Norcen the ability to buy 30 per cent of its shares, but no more, for the next five years. Most of the shares would be bought from Hanna's treasury, which would give it needed capital. In return, Norcen wanted board representation and a say in how Hanna could spend the $70 million or so Norcen proposed to invest in the company. Norcen considered the condition a reasonable means of protecting its investment; to Anderson and his team, it was nothing but a clever tactic for locking up control. (Given that Black controlled Norcen with 36 per cent of its stock,

---

* Norcen had already arranged another special line of credit with the Bank of Commerce for $400 million – approved at a board meeting when Mulroney happened to be absent.

this was not an unreasonable view.) Battle added that he and Black had a private plane departing from Hopkins Airport at seven-fifteen p.m. If they did not hear from Hanna by then, they would launch the takeover offer. If, however, Hanna was willing to negotiate a standstill, Battle would stay through the weekend to finalize the details. One way or another, the Blacks' two-year-long ambition to become a major shareholder in Hanna and break into the American big leagues would be achieved.

Norcen had, Anderson told the Hanna executives, put them "in an awful box and put a gun to our head." He said he would consider the proposal and another meeting was arranged for Sunday morning at the offices of Hanna's Cleveland law firm, Jones, Day, Reavis & Pogue. Anderson telephoned Conrad and asked him to attend, but Black did not make the trip to Cleveland. Privately, Black thought that it would appear to his brother and to Battle that he lacked faith in their abilities if he were to re-enter the negotiations now. At the Sunday meeting, Anderson presented a counter-offer that would allow Norcen a 20 per cent interest, a ten-year (rather than five-year) standstill clause, and no control over board decisions. After a half-hour break, Battle came back to the meeting and threw copies of Hanna's proposal on the conference room table, declaring, "I'm not even going to bother with these agreements because they are completely unacceptable. They are not what we want." Monte Black added, "You have moved so far from our position that there is nothing here to negotiate." This incensed the Hanna executives, who felt they had in fact come a very long way – from wanting Norcen to own no Hanna shares to allowing the Blacks and their associates the 20 per cent they had earlier claimed was their ambition all along. (Conrad had called it "the best of all possible worlds." Apparently also long forgotten were Conrad's early assurances, similar to those made to the former Ravelston partners, that he did not wish to rock the boat.) The meeting ended and the Canadian executives boarded their jet.

Anderson again telephoned Conrad Black and asked him to intervene. But Black said later he did not want to overrule Battle and particularly Monte by getting directly involved in trying to salvage the negotiations. "Our thought was that we had a real good shot to negotiate something," Black recalled. "So I thought that they might not negotiate all the way through it on Sunday and I could come in later. But then the whole thing collapsed. That was not what we were expecting."

Nevertheless, on Monday morning, Norcen followed through on its threat and launched its tender offer at US$45 a share. Hanna stock, which had been trading in the US$26–$27 range, had risen to almost US$32 on rumours of a bid. Hanna was ready to respond. Barely an hour after the bid was announced, Hanna filed a fraud and racketeering suit in the United States District Court for the Northern District of Ohio, Eastern Division, against Norcen, Conrad Black, Montegu Black, Edward Battle, and Lehman Brothers Kuhn Loeb. Hanna claimed that Norcen had made false disclosures to the Securities and Exchange Commission about their intentions in order to depress Hanna stock, and a temporary restraining order against the bid was issued that day by the court. Now Black had a major battle on his hands. No fewer than thirty-seven lawyers from Jones, Day, Reavis & Pogue, Hanna's firm, were soon dispatched across the continent to put together the case against Norcen. Meanwhile, Black and his lawyers prepared an aggressive defence for the case, set to be heard in Cleveland ten days later.

On April 10, two lawyers from Jones, Day descended on Black in Palm Beach to take his deposition. The Hanna counsel, led by lawyer John Straugh, questioned Black for nearly twelve combative hours. "He had some cardinal in tow," recalled Straugh.* "He was without doubt the brightest man I have cross-examined. He was also arrogant and cocksure." Black knew the entire affair had gone badly and would later talk about the court challenge with more than his usual metaphoric vigour. "It was the adventures of King Pyrrhus, rather than MacArthur and Napoleon," he said. "That was a real fifteen-round main event we had going for a while there."

---

* Indeed, Black was joined by Norcen vice-president William Kilbourne, three Cravath Swaine lawyers representing him, and, elsewhere in his house, his friend Cardinal Emmett Carter, archbishop of Toronto.

In gathering evidence, the Hanna lawyers believed they had unearthed indisputable proof of Norcen's illegal behaviour – and the document bore Conrad Black's signature. The key piece of evidence was the September 9 minutes of the Norcen executive committee, prepared by William Kilbourne and signed by Black, which authorized the initial purchase of 4.9 per cent of Hanna, "with the ultimate purpose of acquiring a fifty-one per cent position at a later date."

Although it was standard procedure for him to review the minutes and sign them, Black said he did not sign the minutes in question until some two months after the September 9 meeting. The minutes were disclosed in an amended 13-D filing by Norcen to the SEC on April 9, with the explanation that the notion of 51 per cent was intended by Battle as a "corporate goal consistent with Norcen's long-range planning to be achieved by Norcen over a period in excess of five years." Although he had signed the document, as far as Black was concerned the error was in Kilbourne's preparation of it. For his part, Kilbourne was miffed at Black for not shouldering any of the responsibility. "He elected to find fault elsewhere and I was convenient," Kilbourne said years later. "He's determined that he's right, and when you're determined that you're right, you have to put it on someone else's back."

Norcen's defence would also reveal in embarrassing detail the extent of George Humphrey's disgruntlement with Bob Anderson before Humphrey was made a director, and it would attempt to show that Black had been encouraged all along by members of the Humphrey family.

In Palm Beach, Hanna's lawyer John Straugh pressed Black about the details of the September 9 meeting, and Black explained that the 51 per cent idea came up only when Battle "tossed it off as an ultimate possibility." Black proved to be a smug and rambunctious deponent.

"Now you are leading the witness," he told Straugh during one exchange.

"I'm what?"

"You are leading the witness a little tendentiously."

"Let me explain to you," Straugh countered, "that is permitted under cross-examination in our country."

"I'm not suggesting it isn't permitted, I'm suggesting I would rephrase in my own words what I'm saying, if I may."

Black argued that it wasn't a big deal what the minutes said; that they represented an intent to take over Hanna was a "misleading conclusion."

The minutes, Straugh said, suggested "that the initiation of the stock market transactions referred to were undertaken with the ultimate purpose of acquiring a fifty-one per cent position at a later date, doesn't it?"

"It would be entirely possible to derive that erroneous impression, yes," Black replied.

Straugh asked if Battle had ever used the term "investment purpose" – which eventually appeared on the SEC filing – during the executive committee meeting.

"No," said Black, "it is not a phrase that leaps to the tongue very readily."

"I wasn't asking you about the extent to which the phrase leaps or doesn't leap to the tongue or anywhere else," Straugh snapped. "Did anyone else, including yourself, describe this stock acquisition program as one for 'investment purposes'?"

"I don't recall anyone doing so. It was just . . . that could be taken as tautology in the use of the word investment, however."

"Could be taken as what?"

"Tautology: self-evidently true."

"I understand the meaning of that word and others in the English language."

The case came to trial before Judge John Manos on April 15 in Cleveland's U.S. District Courthouse. "The defendants' repeated misrepresentations concerning their plan to gain control of Hanna were not the result of inadvertence or indecision," Patrick McCartan of Jones, Day told Manos in his opening statement, "but, instead, were part of a carefully constructed plan to accomplish their objective in a market they intended to deceive and to manipulate in order to acquire control of Hanna at the lowest possible price."

For two of the hearing's several days, Black took the stand. He was furious that he was being sued under the federal anti-racketeering law. Originally passed in 1970 as part of the government's anti-Mob campaign, RICO (the Racketeer Influenced and Corrupt Organizations Act) had become popular in corporate battles because, under it, plaintiffs could ask for triple fines. Even though this was a civil RICO action, Black bristled at its suggestion of crookedness. Judge Manos called Black into his chambers, possibly because he thought that Black had done poorly under cross-examination and ought to consider settling the case while he could. In his memoirs, Black reminisced that Manos told him, "In twenty years, you are the finest witness I ever had in my court." (Judge Manos had no such recollection.)

Black didn't settle, and on June 11, Manos granted Hanna's request for a preliminary injunction against Norcen, calling Norcen's construction of the record "strained and unpersuasive." Contrary to the defendants' contention that Norcen's intent to make a tender offer for Hanna was formulated on the eve of the bid, Manos found the evidence "established conclusively" that Norcen contemplated the action as early as November 9, 1981, if not earlier; yet Norcen had described its intent as "investment" in the 13-D filing it made that day and on three other occasions. Black and Norcen immediately appealed the decision to the U.S. Court of Appeals in Cincinnati, receiving approval for an expedited appeal.

In late June, the SEC withdrew charges that Black and Norcen had made false and misleading statements related to Hanna when Black and Norcen signed a consent decree. They admitted no previous wrongdoing but promised to refrain from future securities law infractions. A consent decree can be a fairly standard wrist slap in securities cases under which neither guilt nor innocence is established. However, violation of a consent decree by an individual, even decades after its signing, can lead to criminal charges.

The episode came to a sudden end in early July when Black negotiated a $90 million truce with Hanna that saw Norcen accept a deal much like proposals that it had previously rejected: Norcen purchased 1.25 million treasury shares at US$45 – the tender offer price – which, added to its 8.8 per cent, brought its holdings up to 20 per cent. Norcen agreed to an eight-year standstill; the two Black brothers and Battle were added to the Hanna board, with Conrad

Black joining the executive committee. Norcen also purchased Hanna's 20 per cent interest in Labrador Mining and Exploration and its 40 per cent stake in another subsidiary, Hollinger North Shore Exploration, doubling its share of the royalties from the Iron Ore Company in the process.

"I never had any fears how it was going to end up," Black declared at the time. "It's all atmospherics in the United States. They never believed a goddamn word of all that bunk about racketeering. But some of our more credulous and Boy-Scoutish locals sure believed it."

In private, Black was considerably less self-assured, said Peter White. As far as White could tell, his long-time friend and business partner was "paranoid" about the legal challenges mounted against him. "Conrad was astounded, I think, at the strength and the force and the viciousness of the response" from Hanna, said White. "He certainly didn't expect to be accused of racketeering for what he did." White recalled walking down the second-floor hall at 10 Toronto Street one day in the midst of the episode and finding Black pacing around his office.

"Peter, they are out to get me," Black announced. "But they won't."

The truce with Hanna and the SEC, it turned out, was far from the end of the matter. It was just Act One in what Black came to call an "Orwellian drama" – with himself in the lead role. At some point after Black's corporate ascent some four years earlier, the Metropolitan Toronto Police Department's fraud squad had opened an active file on his activities, spurred by the private complaints made by stockbrokers who knew members of the squad. Those who followed Black's moves drew an analogy to Robert Vesco, an American financier who looted millions from investors through a pyramid of mutual fund companies and then fled to a life of grandeur in Central America. The more the police watched Black's Byzantine transactions, which all resulted in Black's private holding company, Ravelston, getting richer, the more suspicious they grew. No complaints were made by minority shareholders in companies Black controlled to the police or the Ontario Securities Commission, despite whispers that Black's moves were oppressive to them.

"He had the argument in every instance that there was a valid corporate purpose for what he was doing," said one person who had access to the police file. "But the consequence was undeniable, that his private holding company [Ravelston] – which had nothing to begin with – kept getting richer and richer. And it was that money that he eventually used when he essentially left Canada and went over and bought into the newspaper business in England."

Black himself would happily agree that he increased his wealth through his corporate manoeuvres. But the suggestion that his asset stripping was in some way illegal was a far more serious matter. The piece of the puzzle that the Toronto police zeroed in on during the Hanna proceedings was a decision taken by the Norcen board of directors in Calgary on October 16, 1981 – at the same directors' meeting where the board ratified the executive committee's decision to buy up to 4.9 per cent of Hanna – to buy up to 4.99 per cent of its own shares, a fairly common practice by companies that believe their stock to be undervalued by the market. In order to buy back the Norcen stock, the directors approved a draft of a notice that was to be sent to all shareholders. This notice, or "issuer bid circular," invited shareholders to sell their shares and, as prescribed by Ontario securities law, disclosed any material changes the company had planned. "Norcen has no present plans or proposals for material changes in its affairs," stated the material sent to shareholders on October 28 and 29, 1981.

The purpose of material-change disclosure is to ensure that the market is fully informed when making a decision. Had Norcen disclosed that it was planning a major acquisition, the value of its shares might have increased or decreased.

The police also believed that the stock buyback was a step toward firming up Black's control over Norcen. Before the buyback, Black held 36 per cent of Norcen indirectly through Labrador Mining and Exploration. As a result of cancelling 4.99 per cent of Norcen's shares, Black's interest would increase slightly – not a great difference, but one that would cost Norcen $33.7 million and Labrador nothing.

The police believed that Black was taking steps to prevent Hanna from responding to his advances with a takeover bid for the smaller company, Norcen.

As tenuous as the police's hypothesis might have sounded to Black, to them it was as plausible as the official explanation: that buy-backs increase the value of the remaining shares.*

The Toronto police suspected that the issuer bid may have been a forgery as defined in the Criminal Code: a false document on which other people might rely. They were confident enough of their suspicions to act. Robert Barbour and Robert Greig, both sergeants with the fraud squad, drew up three search warrants with the help of Crown attorney Brian Johnston. The warrants listed forgery and the related charge of uttering as the suspected offences.

On May 13, 1982 – while Judge Manos's judgment on the Norcen bid for Hanna was being awaited in Cleveland – the search warrants for documents related to the takeover were executed against three Toronto law firms. Black later said he felt the police had every right to investigate him or anybody else, but he also claimed his phones were being illegally tapped by the police. He was particularly incensed that warrants were served on Hanna's Canadian lawyers, Outerbridge Barristers & Solicitors and Davies, Ward and Beck. Serving Hanna's lawyers meant the Toronto police investigation was drawn to the attention of Judge Manos, then in the midst of his deliberations.

The same day that the warrants were served, Black angrily phoned Roy McMurtry, Ontario's attorney general. So did Fred Huycke, a long-time acquaintance of McMurtry's and a lawyer at Osler Hoskin, which was representing Norcen. An urgent meeting was requested by both men, on the grounds that someone within McMurtry's ministry was interfering with a U.S. legal action.

Late that Thursday afternoon, Black, Huycke, and Paul Saunders, the Cravath, Swaine lawyer who was in town counselling Black on the Hanna case, strode into McMurtry's eighteenth-floor office just around the corner from 10 Toronto Street. There, McMurtry was joined

---

* Moreover, the interest paid on money borrowed to buy back shares is a tax-deductible expense.

by the head of his department's civil section, Blenus Wright, and Deputy Minister Rendall Dick. The attorney general was surprised by Black's allegations that the U.S. case was being improperly influenced by the police investigation in Canada; he was unaware of any Canadian criminal investigation into Black. He later claimed that had he known, he would never have granted the meeting. Nonetheless, McMurtry sat and listened as Black protested his innocence and railed against the smear campaign he felt was being mounted against him. McMurtry's surprise grew when Black also claimed that Brian Johnston, the Crown attorney, had phoned Judge Manos in Cleveland, and that Manos had been forwarded a copy of one of the Canadian search warrants. Indeed, the heart of Black's charge was that Hanna had been feeding the Toronto police information in the hope that news of the investigation would reach the Cleveland court. It was all done, Black growled, "in such a way as to make it look like we're routinely regarded as criminals in our home jurisdiction, and this is terribly damaging to us."

McMurtry later said he had rarely heard anything as conspiratorial in his seven and a half years as attorney general. Johnston later denied that he had called Manos and said instead that a member of Manos's staff had contacted him. As for Black's assertion that serving Hanna's lawyers with search warrants was unnecessary and designed to influence the Cleveland proceedings, the Crown attorney and police claimed that they believed that swift access to Hanna's case files was critical. If Hanna and Norcen reached a friendly settlement out of court – which indeed happened several weeks later – key documents could be harder to obtain. Johnston said he considered that serving Hanna with a warrant would give Anderson and his colleagues more public relations ammunition to use against Black but he was certain they would not be influenced by "partisan" considerations.

Black was convinced that Brian Mulroney, in trying to serve his most powerful masters – Hanna – had played a role in this. Black learned that Sam Wakim, an old undergraduate roommate of Mulroney's, who was now a lawyer representing Hanna and Iron Ore, was an acquaintance of Johnston's. While Black and Mulroney were always friendly, and Mulroney continued to phone Black to offer his assistance, Black was suspicious of the Iron Ore CEO's true motives.

"I have always got along well with him, and, in general, we like each other," Black wrote in his autobiography. "But his protestations of helpfulness and innocence on this and a few other occasions were hard to endure, not so much for their smarminess as by their implicit presumption of cavernous naïveté on my part."

Mulroney dismissed Black's assertions. "I can guarantee you," he said later, "that any suggestion that my conduct was anything other than friendly, constructive, and fully ethical at all times, is improper and unacceptable. That's for sure."*

In their discussions on May 13, McMurtry told Black he doubted that the stock buyback at issue was a criminal act. He ordered his officials to review whether it was an offence and, if so, whether it fell under the purview of the Criminal Code or securities legislation. (If it was the criminal offence of forgery, as the police were suggesting, the accused could face prison terms; a securities conviction frequently resulted in a small fine, and rarely in a jail sentence.)

After Black's meeting with McMurtry, Crown attorney Johnston was pulled from the case. Although Black later said he made it clear that he was in no way attempting to get the attorney general to curb the investigation – and McMurtry later confirmed this – the meeting and Johnston's subsequent removal gave rise to this speculation. And Black did not stop with McMurtry: he also complained in person to Metropolitan Toronto chairman and police commissioner Paul Godfrey, and to Metropolitan Toronto Police chief Jack Ackroyd. To the media, it appeared that Black was a bigwig using his personal power and contacts to influence the judicial system. Remarkably, Black maintained that his only motive in petitioning high-ranking officials was altruism: he was standing up for the little guy who found himself similarly persecuted but lacked his means. "I'm willing to take up the cudgels for those less able to defend themselves than I."

Someone other than Black might have opted to lie low. But after Norcen and Hanna had reached a settlement and the SEC consent

---

* Whatever animosity Black felt didn't prevent him from supporting Mulroney's campaign to become prime minister, and during Mulroney's years in power Black was awarded the Order of Canada and later made a member of the Privy Council.

decree had been signed, the Toronto police investigation plodded on for some eighteen intense months – and Black's rancour only grew. In the months after Black's initial meeting with McMurtry, Norcen cooperated fully, with Black and Norcen's directors sitting through hours of police questioning; there was no need for search warrants to be served on them. But when the investigators tried to widen their probe to look at the affairs of other companies in the Black orbit during the previous three years, Black felt like the object of a witch hunt.

Normally, the Christmas Day editions of Toronto newspapers are light on hard news and local controversy. But the December 25, 1982, edition of the *Globe and Mail* included an unusual piece by the reporter Jock Ferguson. "Early yesterday a reporter was jolted awake by a call from Mr. Black, best known for his acquisitive habits of buying and reshuffling corporations," Ferguson wrote, "who complained for an hour about the way his corporate and personal reputation were being harmed by what he called 'a spectacle of public cowardice.'" Black was incensed by an earlier article Ferguson had written about a provincial committee hearing, at which McMurtry had testified that Johnston had been pulled from the Norcen file because he was not a specialist in securities law, rather than (as Black said McMurtry had told him) because he had committed improprieties. McMurtry also disparaged Black's continuing public commentary on the case.

Since their May 13 meeting, Black told Ferguson, he had run into McMurtry at an Ontario government luncheon for former U.S. secretary of state Alexander Haig and had challenged him to lay charges or wind up the investigation. But according to Black, although McMurtry had said the investigation "stank," he had also said that he could do nothing as "a lot of police were going round saying I'm in your pocket."

"It's a capricious investigation that's damaging innocent people's reputations," Black complained. Black subsequently heard from another journalist that McMurtry had been disquieted by Black's comments, and his wife, Maria, said publication of the story had "certainly spoiled Christmas morning."

"Isn't that *tragic*," Black aped. "Poor Maria!"

The attorney general denied that he had said that the case stank and denied the comment about being in the pocket of the police. He responded publicly by wondering what fuelled Black's imagination. "Maybe we should all try it," McMurtry mused in *Maclean's*, "because obviously his imagination has produced some degree of financial success." Less facetiously, he added: "I find this not only highly unusual, bizarre, peculiar – I find it absolutely inexplicable that a man in his position would not deal with any concerns he had through normal channels as opposed to debating the issue through the media."

Some of Black's friends also wondered if Black's comments were goading the attorney general and police. "If you're the attorney general of the province, you say to yourself, 'That guy's going to get it with both barrels,'" was Hal Jackman's assessment. "And that's exactly what happened. And so [Conrad] brought the whole bloody thing on himself."

John Fraser, Black's friend from his Upper Canada College days, wrote that Black invited him to lunch at Winston's restaurant during this tense period. Fraser was aware of the police investigation – indeed, there had been "some gleeful speculative analysis" in the press that very morning – but the matter was hardly discussed during the lunch. In the middle of the meal, Black was talking when Fraser noticed a large cockroach emerging from the wood panelling behind his companion's head. "Nice place you brought me to," Fraser said, pointing out the insect.

He recalled, "Conrad turned his head and then, in quick succession, without any pause, he started snapping his fingers and bellowed out a summons like General de Gaulle at a staff meeting: 'Mr. Arena!' he shouted at the hapless owner, Johnny Arena. Everyone stopped talking. Arena lumbered across his dining room with two liveried *garçons* in tow.

" 'Yes, Mr. Black. What is the problem?'

" 'Mr. Arena,' barked Black, pointing to the cockroach and making sure everybody was hanging on each word, 'I told you if you ever let *Roy* into this restaurant, I would never come back. Eliminate him.' "

Although he was determined to convey a defiant manner to the Winston's crowd, these were not easy times for Black. For eighteen months, he had endured visions of the police descending on his office or, worse yet, his home, with television crews in tow to chronicle the spectacle of corporate Canada's *enfant terrible* being handcuffed and led away.

"He was as wounded over that whole affair as anyone could possibly be," recalled his friend and lawyer Peter Atkinson. "I know because I lived with it virtually every day. He would constantly call, usually in the evening, from his home, when the anxiety of it all would get to him. Just the concern, 'Could these police officers really be so stupid as to lay charges? Am I going to face a search warrant? Are they suddenly going to show up at my door and cuff me and walk me off to the station?'" At home, when Black was feeling particularly anxious about the investigation, his wife would assure him that his reaction was normal, that if he were *not* upset about being under investigation, she would be worried about him.

Eleven months after the warrants were served, on April 14, the Ontario Securities Commission announced that it had concluded its investigation into Black and Norcen and would not lay charges. But two weeks later, the cover of *Maclean's* featured a story by Linda McQuaig and Ian Austen on the Black investigation, centring on a leaked 138-page internal Ontario Securities Commission report into the Norcen affair.

The report called for twenty-six charges of misrepresentation and other violations of the Ontario Securities Act to be laid in connection with the Hanna bid. Nine of the proposed charges were against Black himself, nine against Battle, and eight against Norcen. The recommendations not only were made by the OSC's investigators, Gary Curran and David Knight, but were backed by Roy McMurtry. Yet the commission unanimously, and on more than one occasion, decided not to proceed with the charges. Its media release said, in part, that there were "not sufficient grounds to support a recommendation to prosecute or to institute any other proceedings against Norcen or any of its officers or directors under the Securities Act." OSC chairman Peter Dey was dismayed that the report had been made public and said it was "not unusual at all" for the commission to reject the recommendations of its staff. Nonetheless, the article pointed out that charges under the

Securities Act were strongly recommended by McMurtry himself, via two of his Crown attorneys most experienced in securities matters. When the *Maclean's* journalists phoned McMurtry's office for an interview, he declined, through a spokesman, to comment, citing again "the ongoing criminal investigation." Black was outraged: "We have been completely exonerated by the most authoritative body on the matter," Black told the magazine, "and the fact is that the attorney general and the police have a great deal of explaining to do about what they've been doing for the past eleven months."

In the end, no explanation was forthcoming, no charges were laid, and McMurtry, after an internal investigation, said that there was "no evidence" to support Black's original claim that Hanna's lawyers had been manipulating the Canadian justice system for their own gain in a Cleveland court. Black fumed over the *Maclean's* article's insinuation that he or members of Norcen's eminent board of businessmen and lawyers had somehow conspired to pay off the entire Ontario Securities Commission.

One outcome of the episode was that Black, claiming his faith in Canada's legal system had been shaken, acquired a large security company through his private company, Ravelston. Now he had a veritable army of blue-blazered security guards (described by his wife as "rent-a-meatballs") and more seasoned experts who could sweep 10 Toronto Street for bugs and wiretaps. "I suppose I overreacted a bit, but it's very tiresome, you know, picking up the phone and having it tapped," Black said a decade later. "I mean, once they get their whole bungling bureaucratic intimidation monitoring apparatus fixed on somebody, it is a terrible nuisance. As if I am some common criminal or something! And if I'd actually done anything wrong I would have taken it in better spirit than I did."

Chapter Eight

A DARKER SHADE

Evident less and less in Argus's various corporate reorganizations, divestitures, and controversies was Monte Black. Under the fraternal division of labour, Monte was chairman of Dominion Stores and Standard Broadcasting. His forte, developed during his career in the stockbroking business, was his grasp of numbers and investment strategies. Conrad's big brother was jovial and known for his appreciation of things big – big cars, a big Muskoka cottage with big mahogany boats filling its seventeen-slip boathouse, big cigars, big three-piece pinstripe suits. It was Monte who arranged for a local sculptor to create the Black logo of an eagle eating a snake, which he had replicated as hood ornaments for their cars and emblazoned on the tail of their Canadair Challenger jet. "He's not keen on the spotlight, but he loves the big life," Sarah Band, a Toronto businesswoman who was involved with Monte for three years after he separated from his wife, said in the early 1990s. Compared with his younger brother, Monte, she said, "is a much more easygoing, caring individual, almost to a fault. But intensely loyal. The people who work for him have worked for him for ever. He's extraordinarily generous."

The image of good-natured excess seemed to typify Dominion's performance. Dominion Stores' slogan was "It's Mainly Because of the Meat," and beefy Monte could have been its spokesman. One person close to the Blacks said Monte had "hedonistic fun" on the job, but critical management issues had not been addressed at Dominion for years. Monte "went to all the food shows, he was photographed with Charlie's Angels and flying around on the plane, and he spent time redecorating it," said the friend.

"Monte was no worker," agreed another executive who knew both Blacks. "Monte is an extraordinarily capable person with numbers and stuff, but has never really been challenged," said Band. "And Conrad's just way ahead of him, in terms of tactical moves."

The role Monte Black's personal style played in the decline of Dominion is debatable, but it would be another episode that suggested the Blacks were better at financial engineering than business building. In the year ended March 31, 1981, Dominion earned a modest $28 million on sales of $2.772 billion. The following year profits slipped to $16.7 million, a level they roughly remained at between 1982 and 1984 while sales slowly diminished to $2.208 billion. In the six months ended September 30, 1984, the company reported a loss of about $24 million, its worst performance in its sixty-six-year history. Once again a Canadian corporation under Conrad Black's watch was going off the rails. He contended that Dominion was "already in steep decline" when he and Monte acquired Argus in 1978. Yet it was one of the first companies over which the Blacks shored up their control, and it was a fixture of their various corporate reshufflings. What began as a food retailer when the Blacks took it over in 1978 was by 1984 also a holding company for their resource holdings and their 50 per cent interest in Standard Broadcasting.

"Everyone thought that Dominion was doing well," said a Black insider. "Remember, those were the great inflation years. I remember saying at times to Monte: 'Dominion Stores had $300 million worth of inventory. At the end of the year, your inventory is worth $337 million, instead of $300. That's basically the whole profit.'"

In 1980 Dominion had some 25,000 employees and 376 stores, many of them ramshackle, small, and losing money. An analysis of each store was conducted, and a wave of sell-offs and closures ensued. In 1981 Dominion sold eighty-six Quebec stores to the Montreal retailer Provigo for $95 million, and two years after that its remaining six western Canadian stores were sold to Canada Safeway. Ninety-three stores in Ontario were shut, and thirty-eight of them were converted into franchised Mr. Grocer stores, which ran at lower cost because they avoided hiring from the ranks of the Retail, Wholesale and Department Store Union.*

For two of the critical years Dominion was under the Blacks' control, 1982 to 1984, the veteran grocer John Toma was president. Toma had started with the company in 1951 as a produce clerk and had worked his way up. The Blacks were initially very bullish about Toma and his abilities, but they ended up firing him just before Christmas 1984, making acrimonious allegations. Toma was forced to sue over his severance, and it took five years to reach an out-of-court settlement. Toma was replaced by the Argus axeman David Radler, which left Argusologists (as the analysts who followed Black were sometimes called) with few illusions as to the company's fate.

Within two months of Radler's arrival, Dominion had sold most of its 133 Ontario stores, two distribution centres, its head office and even its name to the Great Atlantic and Pacific Co. (A&P) for more than $145 million. The once ubiquitous Dominion, later renamed Domgroup, was left with some forty stores and a grab bag of related assets including a dairy, bakeries, real estate, and a food distribution subsidiary — most of which were eventually sold off. "It was a dry rot that had gotten into that company," said Dixon Chant, who was on the board and played a senior role at Dominion. "I guess we grew up a little bit."

There were, predictably, few kudos for the Blacks' performance. Erivan Haub, the West German grocery tycoon who controlled A&P, stopped in Toronto not long after the acquisition. He ventured that in the previous five to ten years Dominion had "become a relatively soft competitor" and its former owners had "neglected their chain for

---

* According to a Wood Gundy report, the return on equity in Dominion's core food business declined from a respectable 16.9 per cent in 1979–80 to 5.4 per cent in 1982–83. Operating profit margins dropped from 3.2 per cent to 2.8 per cent, but so tight are the margins in the food business that each 0.1 per cent reduced operating profit by more than $2 million.

some time." Richard Currie, the president of Galen Weston's Loblaw Companies, gloated to shareholders at that grocery chain's 1985 annual meeting that "your company represents the basic cause of Dominion's decline."

"We had all kinds of people who lost their jobs because of the efforts of Conrad Black, people in their fifties, who had no opportunity of getting another job," remarked Don Collins, head of the union that represented some Dominion Stores workers. "He never did anything for them other than what he was required to do by law, and even then we had to fight in order to get that much."

Increasingly, Black saw himself in the role (as he had once written of LBJ) of "great man much reviled." He argued that blame for Dominion's decline lay not with the controlling shareholders to whom the business was ultimately accountable, but with history and incumbent management. Dominion, he wrote, "was run by an inbred, furtive, overconfident and, in some cases, disingenuous management. It had never made more than one cent on a dollar's sales. Dominion could not possibly repay the huge investments that would have been necessary to reverse that decline." For his efforts in selling off Dominion and other assets, the *Globe and Mail's Report on Business* magazine sarcastically bestowed on Black an award for "the self-inflicted corporate enema of the year." Black later responded drolly: "In commerce, as in matters of mundane physiology and probably journalism too, enemas are sometimes necessary and often invigorating."

Few episodes contributed to Black's rapidly dimming star in Canadian business more than the ensuing controversy over Dominion Stores' pension funds. In Ontario, forty-nine companies withdrew some $187 million of surplus cash from pension plans in the twelve months ended March 31, 1986. Among them was the waning Dominion Stores, which in November 1985 applied for permission from the Ontario Pension Commission to remove cash surpluses totalling about $62 million; it received permission in early 1986. The removal of surplus monies was a long-established practice, and Dominion had similarly withdrawn $16.5 million in 1983. Such actions were based on the principle that employers must honour their commitment to pay pensions when times are bad, and conversely, when the pension is "overfunded," they should have access to the surplus when times are good – so long as pensions are paid and liabilities covered. Overfunding was the order of the day in the mid-1980s. Whereas in the late 1970s pension funds averaged annual returns of 9 and 10 per cent, by 1986 returns were consistently exceeding 20 per cent, leading to a quantum increase in surplus withdrawals.

At Dominion Stores, the withdrawal was greeted by a skeptical, if not hostile, workforce; hundreds had already lost their jobs. Present and former employees, many of whom were given no severance when they were let go, were predictably very wary of what the Black-controlled company was up to. They had received no notice from either Dominion or the pension commission that had given its blessing to Dominion to withdraw the funds. The transaction, however, was no secret. It came to light in Hollinger Inc.'s November 22, 1985, interim financial statement. Conrad Black, Hollinger's chairman and chief executive, concluded his report by explaining that the wholly owned subsidiary Dominion had applied that month for approval to withdraw surplus pension funds that could total up to $75 million. What particularly rankled with some Dominion employees was Black's audacious boast that the surplus recovery was "expected to be offset very significantly by costs related to the winding-down and rationalization of Dominion's ongoing activities," including "employee termination costs." In other words, the surplus derived from the fund whose primary purpose was to assist in the retirement of employees would actually be used to help finance the forced retirement of those very same workers.

Six Dominion employees and their union took Dominion and the Pension Commission of Ontario to court over a portion of the withdrawal – $38 million – challenging the commission's authority and demanding the return of the money. In August 1986, the Ontario Supreme Court ruled in the workers' favour.

The decision, written by Justice Robert Reid and signed by two other justices, noted that "Dominion's managers saw the pension funds as a source of succour." Fault was found not with Dominion or Black but with the pension commission for allowing the withdrawal to go through. And since the commission declined to file an affidavit in its defence in the suit, its justification for giving Dominion access to the funds remained a mystery. "In my opinion, the commission failed in its duty of fairness and its decision should not be allowed to stand," the judge wrote.

Bob Rae, leader of Ontario's left-leaning New Democratic Party, seized on the opportunity to argue that surplus withdrawals constitute "legalized theft from pension plan members." Rae rose in the Ontario legislature and declared: "I have a question for the premier, who I am sure will be aware that the most symbolic representative of bloated capitalism at its worst, Conrad Black, the owner of Dominion Stores, skimmed off $62 million from the pension fund under the open eyes and ears of the government's pension commission.

"At the same time, Dominion Stores is refusing to pay severance pay to the 400 employees who were laid off as a result of a decision by Dominion Stores to shut down several stores. What does the premier intend to do about that to assure the workers of this province that there is some industrial justice in Ontario in 1986?"

Black quickly responded to Rae's attack, calling the New Democrat leader "a symbol of swinish, socialist demagoguery." Rae, said Black, was a "coward and a liar" hiding behind parliamentary immunity and trying to "foist upon this society the utter, defamatory falsehood that I have been enjoying blowing workers out the door while stealing their pensions."

"I never said that anything that Mr. Black has done was illegal. I said it should be illegal," Rae told reporters. "This goes beyond the question of Mr. Black's ego to the question of what's morally right."

Rather than defuse the tension, Black escalated. In an interview with the *Globe and Mail*, he contended that unscrupulous Dominion Stores employees were stealing millions of dollars of food from the chain each year. "We had $30 million in produce stolen by employees every year," Black stormed. Losing a job "is a sad thing," he told the *Globe*, "but it's sometimes difficult for me to work myself into an absolute lachrymose fit about a workforce that steals on that scale.

"I'm sorry for honest people who are out of work, I honestly am. And to the degree that we can, we have helped them. But on the other hand, we are not running a welfare agency for corrupt union leaders and a slovenly workforce."

About a week later, Dominion issued a three-paragraph statement that said it regretted that "certain recent statements made to the media" about the closing of several stores had been "in some cases misconstrued." The statement said of the loss of inventory through theft at Dominion stores: "While some employees obviously abused their position in a very serious way, the majority of Dominion Stores employees carried out their duties in an honest and responsible manner."

Years later, there was little ambiguity about Black's feelings toward the grocery chain and its workforce. Recalling the latter days of his ownership of Dominion in his autobiography, Black wrote: "I recommended that a scythe be taken through the ranks of the lowlives at the warehouse, and it was."

In any event, the pension dispute was eventually settled in 1987, with Domgroup retaining about half the $62 million it withdrew and giving the rest back to the unions. Pension laws were subsequently changed and the Pension Commission of Ontario was overhauled that year. "The overhaul really should have been done two years ago," John Kruger, a special adviser to Premier David Peterson who oversaw the reforms, commented in the *Financial Post*. "But now, everything at the commission is dated BC or AD – Before Conrad or After Dominion."

Black was happily rid of Dominion; the role of Produce King had never suited him anyway. By the time the pension dispute was resolved he was already into a new venture, this one far more to his liking, an ocean away.

Chapter Nine

THE HOUSE THAT
BLACK BOUGHT

On New Year's Eve, 1984, Conrad and Shirley Black stayed at home. Forgoing the glitzy party circuit in Palm Beach, they spent a quiet evening with Peter Atkinson and his wife, Stephanie. It was a warm, clear night, and the Atkinsons volunteered to cook a dinner of scallops, washed down with a few bottles of Puligny-Montrachet.

An interruption to the occasion was a telephone call from Brian Mulroney, who was spending his first New Year's Eve as prime minister of Canada schmoozing prominent people like Black, who had helped elevate him to that office four months earlier.

Not long after midnight, Shirley and Stephanie said good night. Black hoped Peter would stay up with him, and he did. They strolled along the beach running adjacent to the Breakers, the posh resort not far from Black's house, occasionally catching the wafting voices of New Year's revellers. Later, the lawyer and his client sat outside the house with drinks and talked some more.

New Year's is typically a time for reflection and resolution, but Black was in a particularly philosophical mood. He had had some low moments over the past couple of years. And as his lawyer and friend, Atkinson was one of the few with whom Black could share his private thoughts.

Black had now spent nearly seven years relentlessly restructuring Argus. While his efforts had made him a richer man at age forty – a $100 million man, by his own count – Black had become a magnet for controversy. This was a guy, his critics charged, who built nothing but his own ego and private fortune. The media spotlight that had heralded Black as a young corporate dynamo now held him in a wary glare. "I am just trying to do my job," he complained. "I know that sounds terribly humdrum but I am consistently astounded by the facile typecasting that has gone on. I don't regard myself as a source of entertainment."

As much as Black considered himself a patriotic Canadian, he was beginning to feel as disenchanted with the entire country as he had been with the province of Quebec a decade earlier, and the indications were that the feeling was mutual. Moreover, during his tenure at Argus, Black had learned that he had a limited appetite for most of the businesses he oversaw. And so Black decided it was time to propel himself into a much more appealing sphere of operations and influence. That night with Atkinson, he explained exactly what he wanted to achieve over the next year or eighteen months, including the terms under which he would dispose of what remained of Dominion and other assets. Black figured that the money he raised would enable him to buy out most of the partners who had supported him through the Argus escapade, and to move into a new phase in his career. As his own man, there was no telling what might come up.

It was a sign of things to come that Montegu Black was less and less publicly visible through the sale of Dominion's assets and the subsequent pension controversy. "The end of the line was coming," Monte later recalled. "The company didn't have much left, and there wasn't really room for both of us. So he was the logical one to carry on, and I was very happy to move on." As Monte recalled it, the decision to split took place over lunch in the dining room at 10 Toronto Street during February 1985, at which point Dominion was selling off its assets and plans to sell Standard Broadcasting were in the wings. "Quite clearly there wasn't enough work to go around," said Monte, "and it was at that lunch that I said to Conrad: 'Well, why don't you buy me out?' And so he and I retired to my office which was across the hall."

Black also began to buy out most of the remaining Ravelston shareholders, some of whom were grumbling that they had not received dividends for most of their time as investors. Dixon Chant, the Blacks' surrogate father, and Conrad's long-time partners Peter White and David Radler would remain as Ravelston shareholders. Ravelston's main asset, in turn, became its roughly 50 per cent interest in a new company. In one last corporate restructuring, Black amalgamated Hollinger Argus, Labmin Resources (as the holding company for Norcen and Labrador Mining was now known), and Argcen Holdings (the latest depository for Dominion). Black selected the name Hollinger for his new flagship.

Conrad agreed to pay Monte $22.4 million for his approximately 17 per cent interest in Ravelston, an amount that valued the company at roughly three times what the Blacks had paid to gain control of Argus seven years earlier. The parting of ways was also motivated by the fact that Monte was in the midst of a bitter divorce battle, which raised the spectre that his wife, Mariellen, might end up as a significant Ravelston shareholder as part of a divorce court decision.

Conrad Black was and remained intensely loyal to his brother. Some say he was loyal to a fault at Argus, but on the other hand he could not have done what he did without Monte's backing. And there was little doubt to associates of both Blacks that it was tiring for Monte continually to hear about his "smarter" younger brother. Monte would pursue his own investments and later join Hollinger's board, and, until Monte's death in 2002, the brothers would remain linked through their family foundation, which Monte described thus: "Conrad and I put in money each year and we sit around and throw it away. It is terrific. Some of the best humour of the year."

The tip that would lead to Conrad Black's big move on his own came to him out of the blue in Arrowwood, New York, on the weekend of May 10–12, 1985, at the annual Bilderberg meeting. Black was no fan of broiling on beaches or of physical activity; his idea of a good time was to schmooze with "thinkers" like himself, particularly business magnates and former political dignitaries. Black had been a member since 1981 of Bilderberg, a high-level, invitation-only group which takes its name from the Dutch resort where its first meetings were held in the 1950s. The composition of the assembly of 120-odd people at Bilderberg meetings closely resembles the membership of NATO, with Americans being the largest contingent.

With so many giants of business and statesmanship gathered, and the inclusion of spouses frowned upon, some of the best networking takes place outside the regular program. Such was the case when Black chatted with Andrew Knight one evening and suggested they have "one more fiery little Armagnac." As editor of the *Economist* since 1974, Knight was one of Britain's most esteemed journalists. Five years Black's senior, he is a slim, handsome man with a cool, distant bearing, which is amplified by piercing grey eyes. Knight had first met Black five years earlier at the Massey-Ferguson-sponsored conference in Toronto where Henry Kissinger had spoken. They had kept in touch, especially after Black joined Bilderberg and its prestigious steering committee, and they occasionally dined together when Black was in London. Once, with their wives, they had attended the musical *Evita*, although Knight was slightly unhappy that the best seats he could come up with on short notice for his visitors were at the back of the house.

In Arrowwood, as the night wore on and one Armagnac became several, the conversation turned to newspapers. Black told Knight about how he had attempted to buy the *Globe and Mail* newspaper in Toronto several years earlier but had been outbid by the Thomson group. He mentioned his nascent interest in Southam, Canada's largest newspaper chain. Black expounded on his plan to buy out most of his partners and told Knight that the two men with whom he was continuing were the ones with whom he had started in the newspaper business nearly two decades earlier. Then the conversation turned to the possibility of Black's one day owning a British newspaper.

"As it happens," Knight said, "the *Daily Telegraph* looks somewhat unstable." Black was attentive as Knight explained that the Telegraph company was spending a large amount of money on a new printing plant, and its owners, the Berry brothers, were both septuagenarians with no clear successors.

The news intrigued Black; the *Telegraph* was the British paper Black read and appreciated the most. Indeed, he was an unabashed fan of Margaret Thatcher and her right-wing policies, and the *Telegraph* was the traditional organ of Conservative middle England. He did not dwell on the matter that night, though; it was a friendly conversation not unlike dozens Black regularly had.

On arriving at Heathrow Airport a few days later, Knight picked up a copy of the *Times* and read in an article by the City columnist Kenneth Fleet that the *Telegraph*'s owners had been trying to raise money but its investment banker, N.M. Rothschild & Sons, and its broker, Cazenove & Co., were having difficulty drumming up investors.

Knight quickly rang Evelyn de Rothschild, chairman of the namesake firm and also chairman of the *Economist*. Rothschild confirmed the story – the pressure was on, institutions were willing to invest £20 million, but another £10 million had yet to be found. Knight said he could think of at least two people who might be interested in putting up the extra money. (His first candidate was Black, but he also had in mind Katharine Graham of the *Washington Post*, who had been a close friend of Telegraph chairman Lord Hartwell's late wife, Pamela.)

Knight asked for a copy of the private placement document and, after perusing its contents, decided he should call Black. Finding him proved to be difficult, but through Donald Macdonald (another Bilderberg alumnus who later became Canadian high commissioner in London), Knight secured Black's unlisted home phone number.

It was lunchtime in London, Monday, May 20. Knight misjudged the time difference and overlooked the fact that it was a holiday, Victoria Day, in Canada – although in any case, the chances of Black being awake at seven a.m. were not great. Black asked if Knight would ring back in a couple of hours. When he did, Knight told him about the offering memorandum and that he had spoken to Rothschild, who had also met Black through Bilderberg. Knight asked Black if he wanted him to send the document by courier. "They are indeed having some difficulty, and the position is quite strategic."

"Sure," said Black. "Send me the stuff."

The first edition of the *Daily Telegraph and Courier* was published on June 29, 1855. It was around this time that Conrad Black's great-great-grandfather, Thomas Riley, moved to London and was said to have purchased a "fractional interest" in the paper.* The notion of Black investing in the paper was not quite young Bolingbroke reclaiming his family's estates, but the ancestral link added the whiff of destiny that seemed to surround Black's exploits.

The *Telegraph*'s founder, Arthur Burroughes Sleigh, a recently retired colonel, began the venture as a vehicle for a vendetta (the details of which are long forgotten) he had against the Duke of Cambridge as the Crimean War's nominal commander. Like many newspapers of its day, the early *Telegraph and Courier* ran to a scant four pages, but the colonel had trouble from the outset covering his printing bills. If Riley was in fact an original investor in the paper, it was not a shrewd move on his part. Joseph Moses Levy, a printer and for a short time the owner of the *Sunday Times*, agreed to print the *Telegraph and Courier* with the proviso that if the bills were not paid, the paper would become his – a scenario which materialized within a matter of weeks.

A year after Levy took over, the words *"and Courier"* were dropped from the title and Levy set out to build "the Largest, Best and Cheapest newspaper in the world." Growth was spearheaded by Levy's son Edward, who changed his surname to Lawson and later became Lord Burnham. Within six years the paper's circulation was almost equal to that of all other London papers put together.

One aspect of the paper's appeal was its wide-reaching coverage: By the end of 1857 it included a weekly letter from Toronto. By 1876, the paper boasted the largest daily circulation in the world. It had ups

---

* Thomas Riley did go on to invest in other publishing ventures, including papers called the *Maritime Gazette* and the *Tower Hamlets Gazette*.

and downs over the next four decades, and by early 1928 circulation had slipped to 84,000 from 240,000 in the 1880s.

It was then that the paper changed hands again, for £1.2 million. The buyers were Sir William Berry, Gomer Berry, and Sir Edward Iliffe. The Berry brothers were originally from the town of Merthyr Tydfil in the mountains of South Wales, where their father was the agent of the Gwaelodygarth estate.

Along with Iliffe, they were well-known publishers and the *Telegraph* was their first foray into quality papers. Over the years, the empire they founded embraced the *Daily Telegraph*, the *Sunday Times*, the *Financial Times*, *Comic Cuts*, *School Friend*, *Advertising World*, *Boxing*, and some hundred other publications.

When Duff Hart-Davis described the takeover of the *Daily Telegraph* in January 1928 for his book *The House the Berrys Built*, he might well have been writing about 1985 and could have substituted Conrad Black's name for William Berry's: "The paper William Berry and his two partners bought was thoroughly run-down. Its premises were decrepit, its presses out-of-date, its staff old and eccentric, its readers both elderly and dwindling in numbers."

Berry, who became the first Viscount Camrose, rose to be one of the most successful, if least mythologized, proprietors on Fleet Street, the centre of the British newspaper world, with a personal style that formed the basis for the character Lord Copper in Evelyn Waugh's 1938 satirical novel, *Scoop*. Lord Camrose, along with his brother, who became Lord Kemsley, re-equipped the plant and revived the paper. In the 1930s the trio split their interests, with Lord Kemsley taking the *Sunday Times* and Lord Camrose focusing his attentions on the *Telegraph*, and Iliffe taking the remaining pieces.

Thanks to Lord Camrose's unstinting emphasis on hard news, by 1939 the *Telegraph* was selling 700,000 copies daily and was the dominant national quality daily. In 1954, control of the paper passed from Lord Camrose to his two sons: Seymour, the second Viscount Camrose, as deputy chairman and Michael, who later became Baron Hartwell, as chairman and editor-in-chief.

Some of this information was covered in the obligatory company history section of the April 24, 1985, private placement memorandum sent to Black from London. But those sections pertaining to the present day told a more cautionary tale.

As he read, Black was struck by the huge risks to which Lord Hartwell had exposed the company by commissioning new printing plants at a cost of £130 million without arranging financing or having agreements in advance from the powerful Fleet Street unions on job reductions that would justify the expense. "It appeared very odd," Black later commented, "that a man who had operated so conservatively for so long had embarked on such a hazardous course."

Perhaps the simplest explanation for the path taken could be found on page 13 of the prospectus, under the description of directors and senior management: Lord Hartwell, chairman and editor-in-chief, aged seventy-three; Lord Camrose, deputy chairman since 1948, seventy-five; H.M. Stephen, managing director since 1963, sixty-nine; and R.J. Holland – "the baby of the group," in the words of one board member – financial director, sixty-six. Indeed, with an aging executive team and a business adrift, it was not hard to draw comparisons between the Telegraph company and the old Argus.

Whatever the *Telegraph* had become, good and bad, it owed to Lord Hartwell. His life was his newspapers. After studying at Eton and Oxford he had become editor of the *Glasgow Sunday Mail* by the age of twenty-three and managing editor of the *Financial Times* a few years later. After serving in the war, he gradually took command of the *Telegraph*. By 1985 he was a remnant of a bygone era, the last of the "personal proprietors." Although the *Telegraph* was as much a staple of English life as the BBC or the *Times*, average Britons did not know about Lord Hartwell the way they knew about the other press barons: Lord Beaverbrook or Lord Northcliffe, Rupert Murdoch or Robert Maxwell.

Lord Hartwell was a shy man with a stammer, but through the efforts of his glamorous wife, Pamela, theirs had been one of London's liveliest salons. After her death in 1982, Lord Hartwell had become even more remote and singularly devoted to overseeing the daily content of his newspapers. Six full days a week he went to the office, Saturday being the day on which he would don a tweed suit so ancient it had leather patches not only at the elbows but also at the knees. A profile in the *Observer* described the proprietor's typical arrival at 135 Fleet Street.

"His first endeavour is to sidle into the lift without attracting the attentions of the bemedalled commissionaires. Old and sometimes crippled though they may be, they are usually too quick for him. Salutes are given, buttons pressed, and Lord Hartwell is escorted to the lift. His next terror is that someone else will be ascending with him. To meet this conversational emergency, he has devised a question, 'What do you think of the canteen?', which can happily be batted to and fro even, if necessary, until the lift reaches his pine-panelled suite on the fifth floor."

Once inside, Lord Hartwell would rarely emerge from the private apartment, complete with butler and gardener (an avid horticulturalist, Lord Hartwell maintained a small fifth-floor garden adjacent to his office). He communicated with staff primarily via an ancient intercom on his desk that would later evoke comparisons from Conrad Black to the systems in Second World War battleships. But Lord Hartwell's eccentricities and outdated trappings were well earned: the *Daily Telegraph* was the undisputed leader in arguably the fiercest newspaper market in the world. Between October 1984 and March 1985 daily circulation averaged 1,226,359 – more than the *Guardian*, the *Times*, and the *Financial Times* combined.

But now it was in a worrisome decline. In the previous five years the paper had lost 300,000 readers while the *Times* and the *Guardian* shared gains of almost exactly the same sum. Even less encouraging were the figures for the *Sunday Telegraph*, which Lord Hartwell had launched in 1961 and considered his crowning achievement; its circulation, at 695,056, came in at third place behind the *Observer* (754,986) and the powerful *Sunday Times* (1,271,393).

Internal marketing surveys at the *Telegraph* showed that much of the slippage was attributable to a rejection by younger readers of the *Telegraph*'s staid, old-fashioned layout and approach. Only 20 per cent of the *Daily Telegraph*'s readers were under thirty-five; the paper had the most elderly readership profile in Fleet Street, but also one of the wealthiest.

A key measure of a newspaper's attractiveness to advertisers is the average number of readers per copy. In this respect, the *Daily Telegraph* had declined over the past decade from 3.6 to 2.8, and the profile of its readers had also grown steadily older. New presses would allow colour, more flexibility, and the ability to produce papers of more than forty pages. (The limited length of the paper often led the *Telegraph* to refer advertisers to competitors because it could not accommodate their business.*) Thirty million pounds had already been spent on the printing operations in Trafford Park, Manchester, and West Ferry Road on the Isle of Dogs in East London before the refinancing difficulties became critical. A jittery banking syndicate composed of Security Pacific International Leasing (Europe), Wardley London, and National Westminster Bank agreed to provide £80 million in loan financing for the facilities, subject to the private placement raising new equity of £30.1 million.

At this time, 96.9 per cent of the paper was owned by the Telegraph Newspaper Trust, set up by Lord Hartwell and Lord Camrose in 1978, with the balance held by Lord Hartwell's Cowley Charitable Trust. At the conclusion of the proposed private placement, the Berry trusts would own 59.8 per cent and new shareholders, 40.2 per cent. Another sentence on page 13 of the prospectus noted that "it is hoped that the eventual successor to Lord Hartwell will be a member of the Berry family." Lord Camrose had no children, so this was clearly a reference to Lord Hartwell's sons, Adrian, forty-seven, and Nicholas, forty-two. Neither had been involved in *Telegraph* management, although Nicholas had been a City writer before becoming a book publishing executive, and Adrian, whose career had included a stint at *Time* magazine, was a science writer at the paper.

Black discussed the situation in a series of phone calls with Knight throughout the week of May 20. He didn't see much point in investing in the paper for a mere minority interest. Perhaps, they hypothesized, some kind of option on future share issues could be

---

* The strict work practices of the unions limited the number of pages to thirty-six in any case.

arranged, which could potentially lead to control down the road, particularly if the company's projections turned out to be as over-optimistic as they appeared.

Black arranged a lunch in Toronto with John Tory, vice-chairman of Thomson Corp. The late Roy Thomson had owned the *Times* of London and the *Sunday Times* for more than two decades,* but his son Kenneth had sold them to Rupert Murdoch in 1981, after they had produced nothing but losses for two decades. It was not surprising, then, that Tory told Black that he felt negative toward investments in British national newspapers – particularly minority investments. "Stay away from it," said Tory.

The warning didn't dissuade Black, but it firmed up his resolve to cut a deal only on his terms. When Evelyn de Rothschild phoned to ask if he would come immediately to meet Lord Hartwell, Black said he would be happy to come, but not on such short notice. He didn't say so, but Black didn't see why he should drop everything to fly to London over what he considered to be a "casual investment."

When Rothschild suggested they meet in New York instead, Black agreed. "I would have had to be fairly unobservant not to notice that they were under some pressure," he recalled later. "I didn't try to exploit that."

Word was conveyed to Lord Hartwell that an investor might have been found, and his first reaction was that he hoped it wasn't the flamboyant financier James Goldsmith, a man he detested. He was reassured that it was in fact a Canadian, a Mr. Conrad Black. "I've never heard of him," said Lord Hartwell, satisfied.

On Saturday, May 25, Black phoned Rupert Hambro at his country home and asked if he would help out. Hambro, the debonair chairman of London's Hambros Bank, had met Black while working in Canada in the early 1970s. Both young men had been invited one weekend to the farm of Dodie Dale-Harris, daughter of the film star Leslie Howard, and her husband. ("They were making hay or

---

* Roy Thomson bought the *Sunday Times* in 1961 from Lord Kemsley, to the shock and dismay of Lord Hartwell, who thought he and Lord Kemsley held informal first rights to each other's papers. Soon after, Lord Hartwell launched the *Sunday Telegraph*.

something," recalled Hambro. "I don't think Conrad spent much time helping make hay.") Over the following years, they would get together whenever Hambro visited Canada and "always had a laugh." Hambro was happy to assist but admitted he knew little about the *Telegraph* or its predicament. It was the start of a bank holiday weekend, but Hambro managed to get hold of Michael Richardson, a senior Rothschild partner, who sent over a package of documents.

The earliest Black was able to go to New York was Tuesday, May 28, and arrangements were made for Lord Hartwell and his group to arrive that morning on the Concorde. A suite was reserved at the JFK Airport Hilton. Lord Hartwell, managing director H.M. Stephen, deputy managing director Hugh Lawson, and Patrick Docherty, a junior Rothschild representative, prepared for the day trip. R.J. Holland, the finance director, was unable to attend because he couldn't obtain a U.S. visa on the bank holiday Monday.

Separately, Rupert Hambro made his way to the British Airways VIP lounge at Heathrow and ended up on the aircraft sitting beside a man who he quickly realized, although they had never met, was Lord Hartwell. Hambro says, "The trouble was I introduced myself, but I had his deaf ear. He was on the window and I was on the aisle. And the Concorde makes a filthy noise anyway. So he couldn't hear me anyway. He read every single word of that day's *Daily Telegraph* – the lot."

Some four hours later, around nine a.m. New York time, the group settled into the hotel suite to await Black. Black flew from Toronto on his corporate Challenger jet, a flying cocoon of mahogany and leather, its tail emblazoned with the Black/Argus logo of an eagle devouring a snake.

Chapter Ten

"GOOD MAN,
CONRAD RITBLAT"

No one among the *Telegraph* contingent knew what to expect from the potential investor. Little was known among them about Conrad Black, except that he was fairly young and some sort of financier. It was later suggested that the holiday Monday in England had prevented their making routine inquiries about Black – which, if true, was emblematic of the managerial sclerosis at the Telegraph group.

Black's plane was delayed, and he arrived about nine-forty-five. The meeting was informal and relaxed, in the sitting room of a nondescript suite where the windows vibrated each time a plane flew over. The only heated moment took place in negotiations with room service over procuring some coffee.

Lord Hartwell dominated the conversation, talking to Black about completing the issue that would finance the plants and ensure the *Telegraph*'s prosperity. To Black, the Telegraph chairman seemed a charming and elegant figure, who was wrestling with problems he wasn't equipped to handle and was deflecting detailed questions to his team.

After a general discussion about the finances, trade unions, and position of the paper, Black got down to business. Nothing he had heard at the meeting altered his plan. "Look," he said to Lord Hartwell, "I've read the prospectus and, subject to a little more investigation, which could be done very quickly, I suspect I can make the investment to top up the equity part."

This was what Lord Hartwell wanted to hear. But, added Black, he would have to have a pre-emptive right on any issue of new Telegraph shares or any sale of the Berrys' shares. Any prudent person in his position would have to make the same condition, given the speculative nature of the investment.

Lord Hartwell replied without hesitation. "I don't think we can resist that."

Lord Hartwell had not anticipated Black's terms, but he didn't see any harm in them and didn't want the search for equity to come up dry again. The Canadian seemed to fit the bill – at one point he told Lord Hartwell of his $200 million in cash flow, and that "all he had to worry about was which pocket it was coming from."

It had not dawned on Lord Hartwell, as it had on Black and Knight, that the *Telegraph* might need more money at some later stage. This might have been naive of him, but the company had not issued shares in nearly six decades of Berry ownership. "I didn't think it meant very much," Lord Hartwell said much later.

Shortly after the key exchange, Black and Hambro went for a walk outside to discuss the details. Black's share would be £10 million, or about $17 million, for 14 per cent. As airplanes roared overhead, they deduced that in the worst-case scenario Black might lose half his money. In the best case, he might make five times his money, and with his pre-emptive rights he might even achieve control in five years.

When they returned to the room, both sides confirmed the deal, shook hands, and went their separate ways. No papers were drawn up or exchanged, and Black announced that Hambro would deal with Rothschild & Sons and his solicitor would handle the legal side. A waiting car hired by Black drove the British group to the terminal, then swung back to whisk him to his plane. He was back in Toronto in time for a late lunch.

Before they parted, Black asked Hambro to retain on his behalf the services of Daniel Colson, a partner in the London office of the Canadian law firm Stikeman, Elliott. Dan Colson had met Black during the late 1960s in Quebec City, where both were studying law at Laval University. Although his law career had since taken him from Montreal to Hong Kong and then to London, Colson stayed in close touch with Black: Colson is godfather to Black's children. When Black called his friend a couple of days later to tell him he planned to invest in the *Daily Telegraph*, Colson replied, "Lie down until the feeling passes."

Through the summer and early fall of 1985, an uneasy peace prevailed among the new and old shareholders of the Telegraph company. On June 11, a small item appeared in the *Daily Telegraph* announcing "Mr Conrad Black of Toronto" as a 14 per cent shareholder and director through Ravelston Corporation, but it made no mention of the side agreements. Those were revealed two days later in a *Wall Street Journal* article quoting unnamed sources, but the *Telegraph* maintained that Black's investment was "purely passive." Unease within the *Telegraph* about a new, mysterious investor was not alleviated when one of the staff thought he heard Lord Hartwell say, "Good man, Conrad Ritblat."

A carefully worded memorandum of agreement was drawn up under Colson's supervision and signed June 13, at a meeting of the principals of the 140 Trustee Company, which controlled the Telegraph Newspaper Trust. The Right Honourable William Michael, Baron Hartwell of Peterborough Court of Fleet Street in the City of London, and his brother, the Right Honourable John Seymour Thomas, Viscount Camrose of Hackwood Park of Basingstoke in the County of Hants, signed on the bottom line.

Meanwhile, emotions were running high within the Berry clan. Both of Lord Hartwell's sons, Nicholas and Adrian, had recently joined the Telegraph board, but neither had been apprised of Black's pre-emptive agreement with their father. Nicky Berry was not pleased to learn about it in the *Wall Street Journal*.

Back in Canada, Black's investment in the Telegraph company was viewed as a curious development for a conglomerateur on the wane. Black was deluged by requests for interviews from British and Canadian publications. Usually a ready source of florid comment, he maintained a cool silence. For one thing, it wasn't clear to him how things were going to work out with the *Telegraph*. For another, as Black said in his spacious chairman's office in the Isle of Dogs almost nine years later, "I'd gone all through that instant baptism with the media in Canada and I didn't want to go through it again. I'd do it if it was going to serve my interests but it wasn't going to.

"My impression is that in things like that, observers . . . tend to resent and be suspicious of people who suddenly emerge and get a great deal of publicity and appear to be enjoying it. I had been through that, and I didn't think it was in my interest to go through it again."

In a similar vein, it seemed curious to some that Black was in no hurry to fly to London to see at first hand the business he had invested in. But the tangible aspects of being a business owner never interested Black – he'd conducted no plant tours and glad-handed no employees at Argus. Like his father, Conrad Black believed the telephone was a perfectly fine way to conduct business and that it worked just as well from home as from the office. Rupert Hambro, his representative on the Telegraph board, was in constant touch. So was Colson, whose work drafting the key agreements between Black and Hartwell was becoming more relevant daily as the Telegraph company's finances deteriorated.

Befuddled *Telegraph* employees resented that they were learning more about Black's investment from rival newspapers and were puzzled that Lord Hartwell had not fulfilled his pledge to write an editorial introducing his new partner.

Black eventually surfaced in the British media when he responded to an article about Ronald Reagan in the July 20, 1985, issue of the weekly *Spectator*. Under the headline "Living with a Dying President," Christopher Hitchens had argued that Ronald Reagan's recent cancer treatment belied a greater illness and that Reagan ought to resign. Even if Black's published letter to the magazine was not intended as a taste of what to expect from Fleet Street's newest investor, that was the message received.

"I have generally been disappointed by the lack of integrity and serious analysis in British (and most foreign) reporting of American affairs," Black wrote. "This was one of the lesser reasons why I recently purchased a sizeable interest in the *Telegraph*, as it is . . . one of the few British publications whose reports on the United States are not habitually snobbish, envious and simplistic.

"There is ample room for debate over Mr Reagan's performance as president, but no one in his right mind could dispute that he has been an effective statesman and as a cancer patient, he deserves better than Hitchens' nasty, macabre, vulgar, and insolent claptrap."

Black flew to London twice in the fall of 1985, the first trip lasting three days in late September. Now he could see at first hand the antiquated environs of 135 Fleet Street. On September 24, Lord Hartwell hosted a post-board-meeting dinner in Black's honour at his home on Cowley Street, a cordial but somewhat sombre event. A more portentous gathering took place two nights later in the dining room atop the *Economist*'s building.

In the four months since Black had bought his stake in the *Telegraph*, he and Knight had spoken frequently. Knight had made it known that after more than a decade as editor of the *Economist*, he thought he should begin looking for new challenges. Should Black take a greater role in the *Telegraph*, Knight said, he would like to get involved.

The son of an air force officer, Andrew Knight worked at the merchant bank J. Henry Schroder Wagg after graduation from Balliol College, Oxford. After two years there he spent two more as a scribe at *Investors Chronicle*, before joining the *Economist* in 1966. He spent time in the magazine's Washington office, then became assistant editor in 1970 and editor in 1974.

Whatever was to happen, he thought that Black might benefit from a meeting with Frank Rogers. One of British publishing's elder statesmen, sixty-five years old at the time he joined Black and Knight for supper, Rogers was chairman of the magazine, newspaper, and printing group East Midland Allied Press. His had been an impressive career, including, at one period, a stint running the Daily Mirror Group.

Politically astute Knight thought Black could benefit from having in his corner someone like Rogers, who knew his way around Fleet Street. Rogers had been predicting the financial collapse of the *Telegraph* as a consequence of its outdated printing arrangements since the mid-1960s, and he and Black got along from the start. Toward the end of the dinner Rogers said, "This most convivial occasion brings together a potential proprietor of the *Daily Telegraph*, a potential managing director of the *Daily Telegraph*, and a potential director of the *Daily Telegraph*. Let us delete the word 'potential' and decide what *we* are going to do with *our* newspapers."

Rogers joined the Telegraph board in October, filling the second seat granted to Black under his shareholder agreement. When Lord Hartwell commanded the *Telegraph*, he didn't believe in having directors from outside the company, but as part of the June private placement, two other new board members – in addition to Black and Lord Hartwell's sons – were added: Lord Rawlinson, a former attorney general, and the merchant banker David Montagu, a former chairman of Orion Bank and, at the time, deputy chairman of J. Rothschild Holdings.

By the time Black attended his first board meeting in late September, it was brutally obvious that the rosy financial projections presented to investors during the June private placement would not be realized. Before the meeting, Black, David Montagu, and Lord Rawlinson lunched at Rupert Hambro's office. The men agreed that the Telegraph company needed a new chief executive. Knight was discussed as a candidate, as was Ian Irvine, who had recently stepped down as chief executive of Express Newspapers.

As chairman of a newly formed audit committee, Montagu (who later became Lord Swaythling) subjected the Telegraph company's accounts to unprecedented scrutiny. Horror stories of non-existent or archaic accounting systems surfaced daily while profits slipped away – in part because of the recent imposition of a value-added tax on ads and the rising cost of the new plants. No one felt the books were deliberately doctored; it was simply that they didn't have the right information, and senior managers had not wanted to burden Lord Hartwell with bad news.

In October, the auditors Saffery Champness were dismissed and replaced by Coopers & Lybrand. From then on, the company faced one monetary crisis after another. "A nickel and dime store in Parry Sound is run better than this place," Black was heard to say, sending puzzled Fleet Street journalists to their atlases in search of the reference. After the first board meeting he attended, just to see how a potential customer would be treated, Black telephoned the classified advertising department at the *Telegraph*. "I was told I could wait for several weeks and I was referred to the *Times*," he later recounted, "and actually given the telephone number of the *Guardian*."

When, at David Montagu's urging, he returned to London for the October board meeting – a twenty-four-hour round trip on Concorde – the situation was grave. Lord Hartwell agreed quite readily when Montagu and Black suggested that a new chief executive officer would send a positive signal to the banks, and the board decided Lord Hartwell would offer the post to Knight.

The onset of the grey London winter was a cheery contrast to the mood among Telegraph management. The board was informed by Coopers & Lybrand that unaudited results for the six months ended September 30 showed a loss of £14.4 million against a projected profit of £5.5 million. Dan Colson was now working almost full-time on Telegraph business and was in daily contact with Black, usually phoning him late at night London time and several times on weekends.

A new game was afoot, one that involved plenty of finger pointing. Nicholas Berry wanted to know how this "predator" Black had persuaded his father to give away the Berry birthright, and why Rothschild & Sons had allowed it. The institutions and banks wanted to know how Rothschild & Sons could have underwritten a rights issue not five months earlier that was based on inaccurate information. Lord Hartwell was confounded that the situation was this grim so soon after raising the money he thought would put the newspapers on solid footing. He enlisted the help of Nicholas, who was willing, to try to find a new friendly investor who would buy out Black and salvage the situation.

Rupert Hambro recalled, "Many of us felt we should sue Rothschild & Sons, actually, because it had been such a faulty prospectus. But in the end it was Conrad's call, not our call. And Conrad said, 'Well, fine. What am I going to achieve? I bought into this business. I like the business. We're going to make it work. I sue Rothschild and I get a bit of money, that's not going to help me very much. We'll just make sure they do an awful lot of work for not very much fee for a long time to come.'"

Indeed, Rothschild would prove very useful to Black in what was to come. Rothschild countered criticism of its conduct by laying the blame on the auditors and Telegraph management, and pointed out that it was brought in at rather a late stage to help Lord Hartwell out of the urgent financial bind he had got his papers into.

Actually, Black was excited to find that the scenario he had envisioned perhaps two to five years down the road was becoming reality mere months after investing in the paper. Certainly there was the sense that in the Rothschild firm's view the best outcome was for control of the paper to pass to Black. The fact was, to Nicholas Berry's growing dismay, that Rothschild had been hired to represent the interests of the Telegraph company, not Lord Hartwell personally. "I didn't get the advice," Lord Hartwell later lamented. "Perhaps I should have asked for it. I should have known more about whether we would ever require more money, but I was told it was going to be all right. I didn't ever reject any advice; it's advice I didn't get which I regret not having."

Indeed, as David Montagu put it, Rothschild & Sons had "handed the Berry family's balls to Conrad Black on a silver salver."

The disarray of the previous six months was just a warm-up for the chaotic tragicomedy that began to unfold in mid-November. The Telegraph company was now technically in default on its bank financing and Black's options were the key to keeping the company out of receivership. While few people seemed initially to grasp the significance of Black's rights, Nicholas Berry actively sought a way to keep the paper in his family's hands, or at least out of Black's. He arranged a dinner at the swish Boodles club with executives from the Australian John Fairfax Group, who, according to Lord Hartwell, were more "our kind of people." The Fairfax people didn't bite.

At another point, Lord Hanson, one of England's wealthiest industrialists, approached Rothschild & Sons with the intention of making a bid, but he too demurred after perusing Black's June 14 shareholder agreement. The crucial article of the agreement read: "In the event the

Company proposes to issue further shares of any class, the Trustee hereby agrees that if possible under the terms of the issue, Ravelston shall have the right, but not the obligation, to subscribe and purchase any or all the shares being offered by the company to the Trustee (or its nominee) in addition to any shares which Ravelston may be entitled to subscribe for and purchase in proportion to its own shareholding."

Speaking with Colson on the telephone from Toronto on Thursday, November 14, Black firmed up his position: he would inject up to £20 million more into the Telegraph company but would insist on at least 51 per cent of its shares. Given the parlous financial state of the paper, the stock would have to be sold at considerably less than the £1.40 per share Black had paid in May for his 14 per cent stake. Montagu told Colson the new shares would likely be priced at no more than 50p, given the high risk involved and the likelihood that the company would produce no dividends for at least three years.

The next day, Colson relayed Black's position to Lord Hartwell. Black would insist on control but hoped Lord Hartwell would stay as a minority shareholder and editor-in-chief and that Nicky Berry would remain on the board. Lord Hartwell responded by saying he didn't seem to have much time to find another buyer, and he expressed concern that the low price of the planned rights issue would look like a "rescue." Colson decided not to point out that this was precisely what it was.

When the directors met again on November 21, Coopers & Lybrand's latest figures delivered another shock. Revised forecasts for the next three years now showed a meagre aggregate profit of £300,000, as opposed to £55 million at the time of the May private placement and £22 million at the time of the audit committee meeting several weeks earlier. Projected cash flow to March 1988 now showed a £10.2 million deterioration, meaning the banks might have to be asked for an additional £10 million in working capital financing, or the crucial printing plants might have to be scaled back.

The banks rang Montagu to tell him they would not be making a £4 million payment due on the West Ferry Road plant at the end of the month. Lord Hartwell was still quibbling with Knight over the level of stock options he would receive as the new CEO. Colson heard through Coopers that a senior executive of NatWest, the Telegraph company's long-time clearing bank, had called the accounting firm to see if it could act as receiver.

On another front, the Coopers auditors had discovered about 300 more staff working in production at the papers than the Telegraph corporate accounts had indicated. That might have been a bizarre joke if it hadn't meant that more money would have to be found for redundancy payments.

On three separate occasions, Lord Hartwell dipped into his family trusts to produce emergency loans totalling more than £4 million so that his newspapers could avoid receivership. Colson accompanied Montagu on endless rounds of meetings with the banks to make sure they knew there was a shareholder ready to rescue the company by putting in the necessary equity. All that was needed was a little time and pressure on Lord Hartwell to firm up the details. At one particularly grim session with officials from the Security Pacific and NatWest banks, Montagu phoned the governor of the Bank of England, Robin Leigh-Pemberton, to discuss how bad it would be were this "national institution" to fall into bankruptcy. The banks caught Montagu's unsubtle drift and a reprieve was granted.

As they left the meeting with the banks, Montagu explained to Colson that the governor had not been available and he had in fact been speaking to an underling as if he were the governor. "I told the then-governor afterwards," recalled Montagu. "He roared with laughter."

Back in Toronto, Black was less amused when the November 23 issue of the *Spectator* hit the stands in London. In it, the Canadian author John Ralston Saul presented to the British audience the harshest views of Black in his native country.

"He has the abstract talents to make money out of paper, the animal talents to take over other people's companies with or without their co-operation and the intellectual qualities to engage in aggressive public debate on almost any subject at an extremely high level. He has also written a 700-page political biography," Saul wrote.

"There is only one disappointing side to his achievement. While Mr Black personally grows ever richer, some of his companies seem to grow ever poorer."

The article ran through Black's 1978 takeover of Argus and its aftermath, focusing first on Black's controversial extrication of control of Massey-Ferguson from Argus and on more recent sales of chunks of Dominion Stores. It skimmed over the Ontario Securities Commission investigation into his affairs ("In the end no action was taken") and then described Black's state of affairs at the time he bought into the Telegraph group in June 1985: "With nothing left to reorganise, he turned on his partners – including his own brother – and restructured them out, leaving only himself, a solitary, rich young man with his reputation severely undermined in Canada."

In conclusion, Saul observed that "one searches for the spirit of sacrifice in Mr Black's career and finds self-help. Nevertheless, the driving force of his personality and his brilliant sense of applied historical perspective will impress all who meet him. Only with time may they feel that the driving force deforms the perspective so that his masterful conclusions are often wrong."

For the second time in four months, Black penned a letter to the *Spectator*, printed in its December 7 issue. Black wrote that Saul's article, "which purported to be about me, contains several assertions that were so dishonest and malicious that they should not be allowed to pass without comment. An absolute majority of the sentences in the piece were false and a detailed refutation would require a more extensive exposé than is deserved by so crude and transparent a smear." Black ended the letter with this comment on Saul: "Those who would retain his services should confine him to subjects better suited than this one was to his sniggering, puerile, defamatory and cruelly limited talents."

The duel continued the following week, when Saul replied in the magazine that "the enduring impression" of Black's rebuttal "remains that of a maddened corgi yapping at one's heels." Saul retracted nothing and concluded that, "in short, it is difficult to imagine how the odours of what has been cooked in Canada can be prevented from wafting across the waters to England."

Others in Fleet Street took up the anti-Black cause, including the *Times* in an article by Kenneth Fleet which described him as "Genghis Khan" and the *Daily Mail* in a piece which noted, "In the somewhat suffocating provinciality of Toronto, he is no doubt a large fish in a very small pond."

The skirmish with Saul was, of course, a sideshow to the main event. Of greater concern to Black were Colson's warnings of impending disaster at the *Telegraph*. At the Telegraph board meeting on November 28, Colson was relieved to hear Lord Hartwell announce, in the presence of his son Adrian and his brother, Lord Camrose, that he had agreed in principle that control would be ceded to Conrad Black. Under Black's proposal, he would increase his equity to 39 per cent but hold the majority of the company's votes.

A few minutes later the elderly peer collapsed and fell sideways from his chair. Shock and alarm gripped the board – Lord Hartwell has had a stroke! – but Adrian, although concerned, knew better; his father had a history of fainting at moments of great stress. Lord Hartwell was carried from the boardroom to his office, where he quickly revived. After summoning the company nurse, Lord Hartwell's long-time secretary, Eileen Fuller, seemed determined not to let her attend to him. "No ordinary medic is going to touch Lord Hartwell," her voice rang down the corridor, insisting now that his personal doctor be summoned.

Colson suggested that this might be a good juncture for the meeting to adjourn. Suddenly, gentlemanly Lord Camrose spoke, the rarest of occurrences during the endless meetings of the past weeks. "What exactly is it you want my brother to do?" he asked. Colson took a deep breath, maintained his composure, and recited the terms of the agreement he had just finished explaining minutes earlier, and to which Lord Camrose's brother had already acceded.

Back in his office, at about six p.m., Colson was preparing to relay the day's peculiar events to Black in Toronto when Montagu rang. Lord Hartwell had called the audit committee chairman claiming he had not understood the deal. Contradicting what he had said hours earlier, Lord Hartwell had told Montagu he would never agree to give Black voting control with less than 50 per cent of the equity.

On Monday, December 2, a revised investment proposal from Black was delivered by hand for Lord Hartwell, his trustees, and his family to consider. Colson issued a warning through Rothschild's Michael Richardson: the time for negotiation and delay had passed. If there was no response by Wednesday afternoon, he would ask for a meeting with the banks – a subtle way of saying he would seek the banks' assistance to force out Lord Hartwell.

Lord Hartwell mulled over the proposal for a day and called a meeting in the *Telegraph*'s heavily panelled boardroom for Wednesday morning. Lord Camrose, Nicholas Berry, David Montagu, and Lord Hartwell's lawyer and financial advisers attended. Colson brought a telex from Black stating that Lord Hartwell should remain chairman and editor-in-chief for life, and once again Lord Hartwell seemed to agree to Black's offer.

The next day, Colson attended another key meeting with Rothschild's in the firm's boardroom in St. Swithin's Lane, only to find Nicholas Berry and his personal adviser there too. Colson considered Berry uninvited; Berry said he was there at his father's request and demanded that the trusts' loans to the Telegraph company be repaid immediately. The meeting went downhill from there – it was, said Colson, "a screaming match" – until Berry was ejected, but not before accusing Colson of being "Conrad Black's colonial mouthpiece." Berry resigned from the board soon after.

That night, around midnight, Colson received a call from David Montagu with Lord Hartwell's latest demands. Among them, he again wanted Black to buy his shares, but at £1.00, not the 50p previously agreed on, and he wanted the loan repayment made immediately. Colson talked to Black at around one a.m. London time, and Black agreed to repay the £3.3 million no later than September 30, 1989, but he said he would definitely not buy shares at £1.00 then and there. It was Black's final concession.

On Wednesday, December 11, confirmation was received that there would be no referral to the Mergers and Monopolies Commission by the secretary of state. It followed a more crucial ruling from the Panel on Take-overs and Mergers that Black would not be obliged to make a takeover offer to all shareholders, "in view of the serious financial position of the *Telegraph*."

Lord Hartwell retreated to his office to prepare a "personal" statement about the financing which appeared in the next morning's *Telegraph*. "Details will be disclosed on Friday," he wrote, "and I very much regret that readers and staff have so far had to rely on incomplete reports in other newspapers." Lord Hartwell explained that as a "main result" of complex arrangements, Black would own 50.1 per cent, and his own family's holding would be reduced from 60 per cent to a minority. "I remain the chairman and editor-in-chief and I still remain responsible for the editorial policy of the newspapers."

Black went to sleep on Thursday night sensing a victorious conclusion to his British foray. Early the next morning, an urgent outraged phone call from Colson roused Black. A press conference announcing the deal and introducing Andrew Knight as the new CEO had been scheduled for that afternoon, but Knight had not yet signed a contract.

The difficulty of coming to agreement with Knight during the past weeks had been overshadowed by the more crucial wrangling with Lord Hartwell and the banks. Black had already agreed to give Knight options over 5 per cent of the Telegraph company's equity, but they were still arguing over other details. Now Black was listening to Colson's charge that Knight was trying to "blackmail" him.

It had been widely rumoured in the press that Knight would be the new CEO at the Telegraph group, but he was taking a hard line on his contract, often accompanied at negotiations by his brother Timothy, a lawyer. Colson had spoken to Black about Knight's demands several times the previous day, but no agreement had been reached.

While as editor of the *Economist* he had no particular executive experience in a situation of the magnitude or disarray of the *Telegraph*, Knight agreed that he was giving up prestige, security, and possibilities elsewhere. Having brought the opportunity to invest in the *Telegraph* to Black, he wanted to be properly remunerated if he was now going to take the lead to turn the paper around.

Black agreed to Knight's terms, and the conference took place at 3:30 p.m. on Friday, December 13, 1985. Under the deal announced,

£20 million in new share capital would be issued, and the banks would provide an additional £10 million in financing. Hollinger would directly buy £14.4 million of new equity and underwrite a £5.6 million rights issue. (In the end Hollinger held 57 per cent of the company after most of the institutions skittishly declined to pick up the new rights.)

Several of Lord Hartwell's aging top executives would retire in the new year, and Andrew Knight would join in early February 1986. Lord Hartwell coped as best he could with what was an obviously devastating loss of control – he maintained that nothing really had changed. In an interview with the Press Association, he said of the paper's new owner, "I do not know him very well, but I get on with him and he does not want to be a newspaper tycoon."

Lord Hartwell would point out repeatedly over the next few years that he never actually sold the *Telegraph* to Conrad Black as many people believed; that what happened was better described as a surrender. Rupert Murdoch was among those who called up Lord Hartwell, asking in perplexity, "Why are you doing this?" Lord Hartwell said, "He couldn't understand it at all. He thought I was doing it on purpose."

When questioned by one of his own reporters, David Graves, about the change of ownership, Lord Hartwell explained it this way: "The trouble is that we are a family with no other outside financial interests. Almost everyone else in Fleet Street has these interests on which to draw when the newspapers need money. Ours was a family situation and we were the last of them."

For Black, it was not a promising beginning. The company that would now be the epicentre of his business empire reported a loss of £16.3 million on sales of £74.4 million in the six months ended September 30, 1985. Would Black follow the pattern he had set at Argus by trading in and out of the Telegraph company for personal gain, or would he actually try to show that he could turn around a faltering business? This was not only a fresh start but a new country for Black – and Fleet Street was legendarily cutthroat. (It was no fluke that no investor from among the world's big media companies, let alone one in England, stepped up.) Outwardly, Black was not daunted by the task. The writer Diane Francis, then of the *Toronto Star*, asked Black about his initial impressions of doing business in England. "The British as a matter of course have concentrated so heavily on questions of ritual and form, and comparatively little on performance and merit, that there's something slightly self-obsessive about their evaluation as to whether someone measures up or not," he said. "This results in a fair amount of dead wood. They lack basic administrative standards and are still dealing with a delusional structure based on the envy of other nations."

Chapter Eleven

DROWNING THE KITTENS

Visitors to Conrad Black's Park Lane Circle mansion in Toronto in the 1980s entered a two-storey entrance hall which led directly to a sprawling living room, where French doors opened onto terraces and gardens. To the right was a large formal dining room, to the left, a sitting room. From the sitting room a hallway led to Black's inner sanctum, his library.

The design of the drum-shaped, domed structure, containing fifteen thousand volumes, was influenced by the Renaissance architect Palladio and by the Radcliffe Library at Oxford. And it was the pièce de résistance of the new home Black erected in the early 1980s on the estate, after tearing down the aging mansion he grew up in.

To design his and Shirley's Georgian manor, Black enlisted Thierry Despont, a young French architect based in New York whose client list included the designers Calvin Klein and Oscar de la Renta and the Wall Street high flyer John Gutfreund and his wife, Susan. Despont was also retained to spruce up the Statue of Liberty. "As Thierry was finishing up here," said Black, "he was just starting to work on the Statue of Liberty restoration, and I felt that in the brief overlap I got at least equal time with the world's most famous monument."

Including the dome, the library measured a full twenty-six feet high and twenty-two feet in diameter. Books were shelved on two levels, and the upper level, three feet wide and with metal railings, resembled a gallery. A secret staircase to it was hidden behind the bookcases, and another passage led to the master bedroom suite. In the planning stages, Black was concerned the structure might look like an MX-missile launcher amid the grandeur of Toronto's ritzy Bridle Path neighbourhood. But he was not disappointed with the result. "I'm not a great sportsman – my idea of relaxation is to go into my library and just start reading, and I find the room quite fool-proof in that respect."

Peregrine Worsthorne found himself in the library on a blustery winter day early in February 1986. Worsthorne was in Toronto for one day and for one reason: to meet the mysterious new proprietor of the *Daily Telegraph* to discuss the position of editor of the *Sunday Telegraph*. Worsthorne had been with the *Daily Telegraph* since 1953 and had held the position of Sunday deputy editor for some years. But any aspiration he had had for a full editorship died after an incident in 1973 when he deliberately set out to say "fuck" on BBC Television – and succeeded. From then on, ultra-proper Lord Hartwell took a dim view of his prospects as an editor. So low were the self-deprecating Worsthorne's hopes that when the CEO-in-waiting, Andrew Knight, invited him to lunch early in 1986, Worsthorne reckoned Knight's purpose was to pump him for ideas about who else might be right for the job.

The Black household was in an animated state, as Shirley Black had just given birth to the couple's third child, James.* As Worsthorne recalled in his memoir, *Tricks of Memory*, "Perhaps because of all the excitement surrounding this happy event nobody had remembered to unpadlock any of the gates into the grounds, and after the airport taxi-driver had despaired of gaining access I had no choice but to climb over the fence and make my own way up to the mansion on foot.

"This was no easy stroll and I spent at least fifteen minutes stumbling through snow-drifts before eventually reaching the front door,

---

* The births of the Black children seem to coincide with key events in his business life. His first son, Jonathan, was born shortly before Black's dramatic 1978 takeover of Argus, and his daughter, Alana, was born in 1982 amid the takeover battle Black was fighting with Hanna Mining.

my shoes ruined and soaked to the skin. Nor was there any time to improve my pathetic appearance because Conrad answered the door himself, distractedly showing me into a splendid library before rushing back upstairs to help with the new baby. By then I had developed a most fearsome headache, almost certainly through nerves, and it was so bad that when Conrad returned in half an hour's time I felt compelled, almost reluctantly, to ask for a painkiller.

"More confusion ensued because the Conrad Black medicine cupboard did not run to such things and one of the estate's security guards had to be dispatched downtown, blue lights flashing, to buy a bottle. No, it was not a good beginning."

Earlier, at Black's office, a far less eventful meeting had taken place with Max Hastings, Knight's candidate for the key title of editor at the *Daily Telegraph*. Like Worsthorne, Hastings was an unorthodox choice. At forty he was a respected and well-known reporter and military historian who had written several books and made a name for himself as a correspondent during the 1982 Falklands War.

Knight had met Hastings the previous summer, when, as Hastings recalls, Knight was "thinking very seriously about some coup being possible toward the *Telegraph*." Hastings, a tall, stern-looking man (dubbed "Hitler Hastings" by the satirical weekly *Private Eye*, in part because of his hairstyle), believed a "complete cleanout" of the staff would reveal a fine franchise underneath.

As Black, too, was a military history buff, it was likely that he and Hastings would get on. As soon as Hastings strode into Black's office he scanned the various military scenes adorning the walls. "Ah, yes," said Hastings, admiring one over Black's shoulder, "HMS *Warspite* entering Narvik in April 1940." Black had read a few of Hastings's books, and although in the ensuing months and years the two men would find they had many ideological differences, Hastings would become a key ingredient of the *Telegraph*'s – and Black's – success.

Before Worsthorne had left London, Hastings had told him that his own meeting with Black had been fairly painless, "except for the proprietor's almost obsessional preoccupation with abstruse points of nineteenth-century British political history." Margaret Thatcher was campaigning for her third successive term as prime minister, and Black had asked Hastings: "If Thatcher wins, when would there have been a prime minister before who won three successive terms in office?" Hastings had deflected Black's quiz, saying that Perry was the expert and he didn't want to steal his thunder.

Sure enough, Black tried the trivia question on Worsthorne, stumping him. (The correct answer was Lord Liverpool.) Worsthorne felt the quiz was not intended either to catch him out or to show off. Rather it stemmed, Worsthorne thought, from a disparaging piece he had written for the *Spectator* about this mystery Canadian taking over the venerable *Telegraph*. Although Black did not mention the article, "I think he was probably anxious to show that although he was a Canadian financier he was also a sort of educated chap," Worsthorne said.

Both editors' appointments were subject to meeting Black in person, but Knight had insisted that the editors-in-waiting keep their appointments secret; the rights issue that would formally install Black as owner of the Telegraph group would take nearly three frantic months to complete after it was announced in December 1985. In the meantime, Lord Hartwell (wrongly) believed he would still call the editorial shots.*

Along with picking the two editors, Black entrusted Andrew Knight with the task of assembling a new management team. Black knew from Knight and others that a showdown was looming between Britain's newspaper proprietors and the powerful Fleet Street unions, and he sensed that, under new management, the paper had the potential to be profitable, although just how profitable was not clear. More than 5,000 *Telegraph* subscribers were dying each month of old age, and Knight did not think this trend could be reversed by perpetuating the Berry formula. But it was a delicate balance: Knight also needed to ensure continuity in order to retain the aging upper-middle-class readers.

---

* Less reluctant to relinquish their roles were *Daily Telegraph* editor William Deedes, seventy-two, and *Sunday Telegraph* editor John Thompson, sixty-five, who both looked forward to semi-retirement, although Lord Hartwell considered them young yet.

Even before the unions could be confronted, the management-in-waiting met opposition from Lord Hartwell and his team, who continued to run the paper in their old-style gentlemanly way. At a meeting on Sunday, December 22, a majority of the board, which was still under Lord Hartwell's control, rejected plans for major cuts at the new Manchester plant where the *Telegraph*'s northern edition was to be produced. Joe Cooke, the consultant (and later the *Telegraph*'s managing director) who came up with the plans, later recalled the message conveyed to him: "They said when I had been in newspapers long enough, I would find out that all the money was made from advertising. You didn't make money from printing plants and I was very foolish to think you did."

Knight and his group did manage to suspend negotiations with the Fleet Street unions, who were by this time operating without a contract. This would prove to be, in Knight's estimation, "the most important single thing" they did in the early days.

Andrew Knight assumed his duties as chief executive officer on February 3, 1986, and quickly moved forward with major changes. Finally, on February 20, the rights issue was completed, albeit not before the directors temporarily retired Lord Camrose from the board, as, apparently, he was in such a state of inebriation that he was unable to sign the memorandum. (Illness was cited in the minutes and Camrose was reinstated soon afterwards.*)

With the rights issue in place, Lord Hartwell was mildly support-ive of Knight but entirely unaware of the coming showdown with the new owner. At a board meeting on the afternoon of February 25, Lord Hartwell was given a letter from Black announcing the two new editors, Hastings and Worsthorne. Lord Hartwell, normally reserved, was livid. "I am still editor-in-chief!" he raged, arguing that he should have been responsible for or at least consulted on the appointments.

---

* As a result of the issue, at a price of 50p per share, the new ownership structure broke down as follows: through Ravelston Black held 8 per cent of the shares, and through Hollinger 49.8 per cent; the Telegraph Newspaper Trust held 21.9 per cent and Hartwell Cowley Charitable Trust 1.1 per cent; the newly created Daily Telegraph Group Pension Fund held 1.1 per cent; other, mainly institutional, shareholders held 18.1 per cent.

He had nothing against Max Hastings, who was then a columnist at the *Evening Standard* and feature writer for the *Sunday Times*, as editor; he just didn't know him and thought he should at least have had the chance to vet him. As for Worsthorne as editor of the *Sunday Telegraph*, Hartwell reiterated his long-held view that he was a gifted writer but not up to the top job.

After retreating to his office for fifteen minutes, where he was joined by Lord Rawlinson and David Montagu, Lord Hartwell returned and suggested the appointments be put to a board vote. H.M. Stephen, Lord Hartwell's loyal managing director, quickly offered his support. Lord Hartwell's son Adrian Berry, who had worked closely with Worsthorne and liked him, said he would not vote against his father and abstained. The half-hearted poll never made its way around the table, and even if it had, it would have held no authority.

Lord Hartwell's attachment to his newspapers was so powerful that he tried to swallow his intense feelings of loss and failure and resign himself to his fate as a powerless director. Although he would step down as chairman and Knight would take over as editor-in-chief in September 1987, he remained a sometimes cantankerous presence on the board for another eight years. "I suppose if I'd had any guts, I ought to have resigned then," he said in 1993 of the editors' appointments, long after the *Telegraph* had moved out of Fleet Street and Lord Hartwell had installed himself in a St. James's Park office that barely contained his antique proprietor-sized desk. He also admitted that the financial benefits for his family from the turnaround that was about to be achieved by the new regime dulled the pain of his loss.

By early 1986, Fleet Street's owners were emboldened by the sense that they could break the iron grip that print unions held over their newspapers. The charge was being led by a wave of brash newcomers, Black among them. The proprietors found an unlikely hero in Eddie Shah, an Anglo-Persian who had set up Britain's first non-union print shop, a small weekly newspaper operation in Warrington, near Manchester. Shah achieved this landmark victory on the back of hard-nosed trade union reforms introduced by the Thatcher government in 1980 and 1982 that banned the often menacing practice of sympathetic industrial action by non-striking workers. When its usual supporters tried to picket other operations linked to Shah or his advertisers, the National Graphical Association (NGA) was fined more than £500,000 – the first time in anyone's recollection that a strike had cost the strikers more than the publisher.

In early 1985, Shah announced plans to follow his triumph at Warrington with the launch of a new national tabloid. *Today* would be printed outside London, by non-union employees. Later that year, as Black edged closer to control of the *Telegraph*, Robert Maxwell capitalized on growing cracks in the unions' resolve and successfully negotiated the elimination of a quarter of his Mirror Group's 6,500 jobs.

Knight, who spoke frequently with Bruce Matthews, the chief executive of News International, also knew of Murdoch's covert plans to shift production of his newspapers to Wapping in east London. Rather than accede to Murdoch's demands for large-scale concessions, the London print unions, the NGA and SOGAT (Society of Graphical and Allied Trades), had elected to strike on Friday, January 24. A few days without papers, they reasoned, would be enough to bring the rambunctious Australian's News International to bay. But Murdoch had other ideas. On the weekend of January 25–26, 1986, he suddenly moved production of all four of his titles, the *Times*, the *Sunday Times*, the *Sun*, and the *News of the World*, from aging premises in Bouverie Street and Gray's Inn Road to the foreboding Wapping compound in London's Docklands area. What the unions didn't realize was that News International had secretly enlisted the electricians' union – which had its own axe to grind with the printers – to operate the machinery that would churn out papers at the Wapping plant.

The News International journalists, most of whom opted not to join the strikers, arrived at Murdoch's new newspaper fortress in armoured buses, passing through massive gates set in high fences topped with razor wire, while security men, surveillance cameras, and floodlights covered the premises. As days passed, the picketers outside Wapping grew more numerous and more unruly, and at times violent, but papers were delivered and their efforts crushed.

By the end of 1986, Murdoch had reduced his print workforce from over 2,000 to 570. The historic Wapping dispute ended with Murdoch employing the full force of Thatcher's new labour laws to pay the strikers less than he would have had to if he had merely laid them off.

The new bosses at the *Daily Telegraph* were certainly encouraged by the developments at Wapping, but as they laid their own plans to move production from Fleet Street to their new plant on the Isle of Dogs in February 1986, Murdoch's gambit was still in its early days, the outcome far from certain. And while aggressive measures might have suited the rough-and-tumble Aussie, who could trumpet his triumph as a victory for all England in the racy tabloids his plant belched out, such behaviour was unbecoming to the genteel *Telegraph*. As Adrian Berry put it, "It's a terrible bore to put barbed-wire fence around the office."*

Black was happy to remain in Canada for most of this period, which suited Knight, as an element of his scheme was to portray Black as the "distant ogre in Canada" who was inaccessible to the unions. Traditionally, the printers had insisted on face-to-face meetings with proprietors when negotiations reached a crucial stage, in effect reducing the management to mere puppets. "Conrad played that role brilliantly, and he also played it vis-à-vis the outside community," recalled Knight. "There were all sorts of people in politics and in the rest of Fleet Street all dying to find out who this new, mysterious owner was. And we deliberately cultivated around him an air of mystery."

Black was also preoccupied with other challenges. Just as he wrote Hollinger a cheque for $47 million for the Telegraph group and crystallized his control over the paper, the Canadian Imperial Bank of Commerce called in a $40 million loan to Dominion Stores and the Supreme Court of Ontario ordered Hollinger to return some $40 million to Dominion's pension funds. This created a cash crisis at

---

* Unlike his brother, Nicholas, Adrian Berry harboured no resentment toward Black, saying that since the 1969 moon landing he had been more interested in science writing than in following in his father's footsteps.

Ravelston, the top private company in Black's hierarchy of holding companies, and brought Black to the brink of financial collapse. (This, despite his early boast to Lord Hartwell of having $200 million in cash flow, and "all he had to worry about was which pocket it was coming from.") The money crunch was particularly surprising given the weight Black carried as a member of the board of directors of the Bank of Commerce, one of Canada's largest banks. He later laid the blame on "lesser echelon" loan managers who had doubts about his companies' balance sheets. "I'm afraid some of the senior managers were trouble as well," recalled Hollinger deputy chairman Dixon Chant. "We needed just a bit of time."

Black quickly visited Bank of Commerce president Donald Fullerton (a future Hollinger director), asking him to "get these guys off my back and I'll clean it up." Fullerton agreed, and the bank executives backed off. Black later acknowledged the episode as a cautionary tale for any borrower who does not happen to sit, as he did, on the board of his bank. "You can't trust these banks once they decide there is a problem," Black said. "I'll tell you what it's like: it's like that mentality I encountered with the police a few years before."

At one point during this cash crunch, Black approached Douglas Creighton, chairman and chief executive of Toronto Sun Publishing, about taking an interest in the *Telegraph* papers. Creighton was interested in an investment not unlike Black's own Telegraph deal, where Sun Publishing would acquire rights that would give it eventual control of the British papers. Creighton, who had launched a string of successful Canadian tabloids, had great entrepreneurial instincts and was given considerable latitude by Sun Publishing's controlling shareholder, Maclean Hunter (which had almost bought Black's Sterling papers a few years earlier). When Creighton raised the prospect of a Telegraph investment alongside Black at a board meeting, the normally acquiescent CEO of Maclean Hunter, Donald Campbell, declared that this would happen only "over my dead body." In the end, Black held onto his stake and got his financial house under control. Had he not worked his way out of the jam by selling assets and toys, his dream of an entree to the storied realm of British press barons would have been over before it began. But he managed to pull through thanks to his influence at the bank and quick, drastic cuts among his holdings, including the sale of the Argus jet and Ravelston's security guard company. The lean times would not last long.

The plan to tackle the unions, called Operation Blackbird, was successfully implemented on March 26, 1986 – and the subsequent transformation was remarkable. In early 1986, the *Telegraph* staff had numbered 3,900, including part-time casuals and about 500 journalists. By 1993, the total staff would be slashed and whittled to roughly 1,000. The greatest number of redundancies – more than 1,500 jobs – came from the transfer of production to West Ferry Road in London's Docklands. The move, in the summer of 1987, of the newspaper's headquarters out of Fleet Street and into gleaming new headquarters at South Quay near the plant brought a further 900 redundancies thanks to the introduction of a computerized pre-press production system; it eliminated the need for 700 compositors who had typeset the articles after reporters had typed them or written them out longhand.

Another key decision taken early on was to relieve the financial burden of the new printing plants by finding partners that would either buy them outright and print the *Telegraph* on contract or join the *Telegraph* in a joint venture. In the summer of 1987, Lord Stevens, chairman of Express Newspapers, flew to Toronto and met Black to hammer out a deal that called for West Ferry Road to be increased from six computer-controlled web offset presses to sixteen and for both sides to own half of the resultant operation, the largest in the world outside Wapping and Japan. The plant became one of the most efficient in the world, with each press capable of producing 60,000 papers per hour, for a total capacity of 2.5 million copies per night, of the *Express*, the *Star*, the *Telegraph*, and *Daily Sport*.

In the oil-splattered bowels of the *Telegraph*'s old Fleet Street press room, only thirty-six pages in black and white could be produced with hundreds more workers. The new Goss Headliner presses could accommodate papers of twice that number of pages, print at twice the speed, and include twenty pages of colour. In the old Fleet Street, the most feared union was the paper handlers, who could elect not to bring fresh rolls of paper into the press room unless their demands were met. That work was now done by twenty-three robot reel-delivery vehicles which played no cards, took no tea breaks, and raised not a murmur of complaint about their seven-day working week.

Black arrived in London in April 1986 and applauded the Telegraph team on its early success with Operation Blackbird. It was only his third visit since investing in the paper and his first since the previous October; he had been busy in Canada with the arrival of his third child, James, with sorting out the remnants of the Argus empire, and with back problems, all capped by a severe bout of bronchitis. But it was time to reap some of the rewards his new acquisition had bought him. One of his first appointments was to travel with Knight to Chequers – the prime minister's country home – for lunch with Margaret Thatcher and her senior foreign policy adviser, Charles Powell. It was, said Powell later, "love at first sight – in a political sense."

Thatcher was relieved to find not only a forceful personality behind the paper that had traditionally been the flagship of Conservatism but somebody whose instinctive ideas were close to her own. Black spent large portions of the meal regaling the prime minister with his encyclopedic knowledge of nineteenth-century Tory history. "It became evident during the lunch that Conrad knew far more about the history of the Tory party than she did," said Knight. "Far more. And he didn't do it in an overbearing way, but the conversation was fascinating because, you know, there she was, the leader of the party that he knew more about the history of than she did – certainly than I did too."

Black was unrelentingly flattering. As he departed, he told Thatcher, "The revolution you have wrought in this country is more important by far than the episodes in British history that usually enjoy that description. After all, what are the decapitation of Charles I and the deposing of James II, particularly as described by that egregious utilitarian and Whig mythmaker Lord Macaulay, compared with what you have done?" As Black later recalled, "Mrs. Thatcher is not particularly historically minded. When I described Thatcherism in such epochal terms, she blinked at me twice, demurely, patted me most considerately on the shoulder, and said, 'That is very good, Mr. Black. Do come back.'"

Black made a similar impression after being invited to Highgrove to have lunch with Prince Charles, at the initiative of the Canadian financier Peter Munk, who thought Black might be able to help Charles with the bad publicity he was suffering because of his relationship with Camilla Parker Bowles. The men travelled by helicopter from Canary Wharf and were served the Prince's usual lunch of only organic foods, whose virtues he explained at length. Black, who up to this point had not said much during the lunch, told Charles that his food preferences weren't that different from his ancestors'. "In what way?" the prince asked, and Black went into a lengthy history of organic dining and vegetarianism through the ages among royals. "Prince Charles listened intently," recalled Munk. "It says a lot about Conrad. There was nothing he didn't know, it didn't matter what subject."

Black's relations with his new editor, Max Hastings, got off to a shakier start. The previous December, before he was offered the editor's job, Hastings had set out his vision for the paper in a memorandum to Black and Knight. It was, recalled Hastings, a "sort of blueprint of what I did thereafter. And I said, 'Although the *Daily Telegraph* always would be and should be a Conservative newspaper, in my view it should be an independent Conservative newspaper, and it should clearly be perceived not to be a house magazine for the government, and we should simply judge issues on their merits.'" This was a significant shift for what was known as the "*Torygraph*," and Hastings knew it was essential if younger staff who would inject new vigour into the paper were to be attracted.

His first few weeks were difficult. In the days before the American bombing of Libya in the spring of 1986, some of the staff suggested the *Telegraph* send a reporter to Tripoli to monitor the U.S. air base there. Hastings was anxious to save money and didn't – and later admitted he had made "a bad call." It got worse when the *Telegraph* published an editorial condemning the U.S. action, and a similarly negative opinion piece by Ferdinand Mount. Black was irate and called up Hastings; he told him both items were "seriously fallacious analyses of what really happened." The episode made Hastings deeply uneasy, but it turned out that tongue lashings from the new owner were infrequent – although Black would ring Hastings at all hours to discuss the paper's contents and coverage. Although Black held strong ideological views and clearly favoured editors who shared them, his guiding principle was that he would let his editors run their own show – so long as they delivered commercial success. Black soon grew to appreciate Hastings because he was, as Black put it, "good at drowning the kittens."

To try to make the paper appeal to younger readers, Hastings had put on his best war correspondent's demeanour and set about sacking staff members and making key hires. One member of the features staff who Hastings felt did not fit with his revitalization plan for the *Telegraph* was Carol Thatcher, the prime minister's daughter. Hastings approached her and suggested she might like to look quietly for a job elsewhere. This particular kitten roared. "Well, you've sacked lots of other people – if you really want to sack me, sack me," she told Hastings. "But I'm not going to make it easy for you."

Hastings did indeed fire her, and the prime minister was livid. Margaret Thatcher believed it was a mean-spirited act by a new editor seeking to distance himself from the *Torygraph* label. She was skeptical anyway of Hastings, whom she viewed as a proponent of tweed-suited, hunting-and-fishing, old-style Toryism, not the hard-edged Conservatism she championed.

Indeed, Thatcher would not speak to the editor of the Conservative Party's flagship newspaper for as long as she was prime minister. Hastings said, "Given Conrad's devotion to her, I greatly respected the fact that Conrad never, as far as I know, gave any encouragement at all to those around Thatcher who would like to have seen me go." Black said he "took a fair bit" of heat, but Thatcher accepted his position. "You have to defend your editor. She defended her daughter and I defended my editor. We agreed that we had different roles to play in that case."

Key people Hastings added to the journalistic staff were Veronica Wadley, John Keegan, Robert Fox, Neil Collins, Trevor Grove, and, not least, Hugh Montgomery-Massingberd, whose idiosyncratic style transformed the *Telegraph*'s obituaries page into a must-read. The changes spearheaded by Hastings soon produced results. Circulation at the daily increased in 1987, despite the launch in October 1986 by three former *Telegraph* journalists of a new broadsheet, the *Independent*. As it happened, the circulations of the *Times* and the *Guardian* suffered worst from the *Independent*'s competition. In the same year, Worsthorne's *Sunday Telegraph* gained almost 50,000 subscribers.

In Black's view, the paper's success was a result of cutting non-editorial costs and returning to the formula perfected by the first Lord Camrose, which Black described in a 1991 speech in Toronto: "This consisted of a good, informative newspaper, concise, fair, and covering all the news, but enhanced in its appeal to the British middle class by heavy emphasis on bourgeois sports and pastimes, and a relentless truckling to the Royal Family. I scarcely recall an edition of the newspaper in the nearly six years of my association with it when there wasn't a flattering photograph of some member or other of the Royal Family. Not for the *Daily Telegraph* the lurid propagation of vapid gossip about every aspect of their sex and marital lives."

It seemed to Black that one of the paper's great traditional strengths, along with "recitations of life's quirky episodes," was its "practice of presenting Britain's gamiest, kinkiest, most salacious, and most scatological news with apparent sobriety, but with the most explicit, almost sadistic, detail, including carefully selected extracts from court transcripts. Middle-class commercial travellers from Manchester and Birmingham may still be seen on the verandas of the Victorian railway hotels, in Russell Square, as they were fifty and a hundred years ago, reading in our newspaper unashamedly of the indiscretions of deviant clergy, the activities of paid flagellators, and the rest of the vast English supermarket of unconventional sexual titillation."

In 1987, Black added the 160-year-old *Spectator*, the prestigious but money-losing weekly British magazine, to the Telegraph group. Several *Telegraph* scribes also freelanced for the *Spectator*, and Black reasoned that owning the magazine would ensure the paper had access to a talented writing pool. The *Spectator* acquisition was all the more intriguing because Black had been criticized in the magazine on more than one occasion, including in a piece by its editor at the time, Charles Moore.

"He brought a sinister reputation in front of him," recalled Moore. "We'd heard stories about business dealings in Canada that made him sound very ruthless. Also, we heard that he had very strong political views. Of course, if a journalist hears that about a proprietor, he gets nervous. And when you first meet Conrad, that impression can be confirmed: because he's so full of views, and he expresses them so forthrightly, you think, 'Christ, he's going to trample all over us.'

"But in fact you quickly discover two things. One is that he's professional in the way he runs his organization. He knows that he's not a hands-on chap anyway, and he knows it's ludicrous to come into the office every day and tell everyone what to do in detail. It just doesn't work. It's not good journalism, so he never tries to do that. The other thing is, though he likes holding forth, he doesn't make you feel a worm. I think one of the things Rupert Murdoch does – though he's a very charming man often – is that he uses conversations with journalists in a manipulative way. He tries to make one journalist feel small in order to make another one feel big, and it's all a great big complicated game. You don't feel that with Conrad. Though he can be an intimidating presence when you meet him, you actually find that if you have a conversation it's pretty relaxed. You feel that he wants to have the conversation just because it's a conversation, rather than in order to lay down the law."

Black's ownership of the *Spectator* did not curb his habit of writing letters to the editor for publication. In October 1991, he fired off a missive against an "unbalanced attack" by the *Telegraph*'s Washington correspondent Stephen Robinson against U.S. president George H.W. Bush; the item reminded Black of Christopher Hitchens's "demented ravings against Ronald Reagan" in the magazine, which had prompted a letter from him six years earlier. He also took exception to an article by Edward Whitley. "In recent years," Black wrote, "the *Spectator* has published an error-riddled cover piece on the Reichmanns and Canary Wharf and a gratuitous sketch of Lord Carrington [Paul Reichmann and Lord Carrington had become directors of Hollinger and the Telegraph company respectively].

"Lord Carrington and Paul Reichmann would have the right to expect to be treated fairly by the *Spectator* even if they were not directors of the companies that ultimately owned it and friends of its proprietor. It is not normally the duty of the proprietor to distinguish between intelligent controversy and bile." A year after that, Black added a new element to his letter-to-the-editor repertoire by partially recanting his previous letter, given that Bush had lost to Bill Clinton and Canary Wharf's financial woes had led to the spectacular bankruptcy of the Reichmanns' main company, Olympia and York. A new *Spectator* letter ran under the headline "It Takes a Big Man": "While I continue to believe that President Bush's conduct of foreign policy was quite successful and that the articles about the Reichmanns and Lord Carrington were unnecessarily snide, subsequent events demonstrate that Stephen Robinson was not mistaken in taking the Democratic quest for the presidency seriously and Edward Whitley, the author of the Canary Wharf piece, was essentially correct in his financial prognosis for Canary Wharf. I would like to retract those aspects of my letter of 12 October and apologise to Mr Robinson and Mr Whitley for them."

This prompted a surfacing of the long-simmering feud between Black and Christopher Hitchens, who took to the *Guardian* to publish an open letter to Black. "From my observation of you," Hitchens sniped, "I would say that you knew at least as much about the American presidency as you do about the delicious world of Canadian real estate. So what's the use of an apology when all can plainly see that Bush and the Reichmanns have lost out? Do you mean us to understand that until last week you thought Bush was fine, the Democrats washed up and the Reichmanns on the level? If your reporters followed your example, there would be room for nothing but grovels, Canossas and *mea culpas*. And by the way, since you don't mention the Carrington editorial again, are we to suppose that you think he retired with honour from the former Yugoslavia? Can we expect a tortured rethink about your recommendation of John Major?

Of Brian Mulroney? I would say – stop now before you kill again. Think of the apologies *before* you write the letters, or the editorials."

Black's first public speech in London was before the Canadian Club on July 1, 1987, Canada Day. The Canadian high commissioner in London at that time was Roy McMurtry, whom Black had labelled a "cockroach" during the 1983 police investigation into his affairs while McMurtry was Ontario's attorney general. McMurtry declined to attend, citing the club's male-only membership policy, which Black allowed was a plausible excuse. "The last time Roy was invited to a dinner at which I was speaking," Black quipped, "he declined my invitation because, he said, he would be studying penal reform and the humane interrogation of detainees, in Pakistan."

The comment was typical Black – an inside joke delivered in sufficiently colourful language that much of his audience might chuckle despite being unsure what exactly they were laughing at. Among those attending but looking rather bored was Robert Maxwell, owner of the Mirror Group, who had printing interests in Quebec.

In his speech, Black launched into a defence of Ronald Reagan and an attack on much of the British press's coverage of the Iran-Contra affair. Black had already banished the use of the word *Irangate* from the *Telegraph*'s pages, in a rare corner-office edict. He also took time to express "a few words of gratitude" for the recent re-election of Prime Minister Margaret Thatcher, "a social and political champion of unheard-of determination.

"There is, in Mrs. Thatcher's policies and in her demeanour," Black gushed, "not only the triumph of Victorian middle-class values but also a hint of the grandeur of Elgar, and even of Kipling." Black praised Thatcher for promoting the concept that the honest accumulation of wealth is admirable. "It is not," he noted, "an indecent ambition to seek material wealth, and the ranks of those who achieve that status in this country should not be confined to the most fortunate inheritors and the most ingenious outsiders, such as my ineffable friend Bob Maxwell."

Spending the summer of 1987 in London in a rented house with his family, Black was gradually shedding the mystique of being the shadowy man in the back of the 1958 Rolls – a car Ravelston had purchased from Massey-Ferguson and Black had shipped overseas. Slowly, Conrad and Shirley Black began to make the rounds of British society. When Queen Elizabeth visited the *Telegraph*'s new offices on the Isle of Dogs after the opening of the Docklands Light Railway, the Blacks were there, although in the photo that ran in the next day's *Telegraph*, Andrew Knight was most prominent; Black's head was obscured by the top of the monarch's hat. Meeting Sarah Ferguson, the Duchess of York, on another occasion, Black was so enamoured that he sent her a copy of *Duplessis*.

In September 1987, Black assumed formal control of his British newspaper when he became chairman of the Telegraph company. In an interview with the *Financial Times*, Black revealed that "my greatest pleasure beyond the satisfaction of basic appetites is to sit at home with my family and my cats and read my books." But it was clear that Black was far from content. "I want to build a first-class international newspaper company," he allowed, "and I think the omens are favourable." Indeed, Hollinger's cash flow increased from a deficit of $7 million in 1986 to a positive figure of $45 million in 1987, $99 million in 1988, and $106 million in 1989.[*] "A company's cash flow is like a dictator's army," Black explained to another interviewer. "You've got to do something with it. You can't just stand around like Franco's Guardia Civil, waiting for something to happen."

Black's appreciation for the editorial product was secondary to his affection for the cash and influence the Telegraph group's success brought him. From a pre-tax loss of £8.9 million in 1986, the Telegraph company earned £620,000 in 1987, then £29.2 million in

---

[*] Along with operating-profit margins, cash is the benchmark typically used to judge the performance of media companies. Cash flow relates to the actual amount of cash coming in and going out of the company, while net profit figures include depreciation, amortization, and other non-cash charges that can have more to do with accounting methods than the state of the business. For companies like Hollinger that borrow money to make acquisitions, comfortable levels of cash flow are essential to cover debts.

1988, and £41.5 million in 1989. In retrospect, rival publishers were astounded at the mere $67 million Black paid for control in 1986. Black called the Telegraph takeover "not the sort of deal you get two of in a lifetime." In 1987, Robert Maxwell put it even better when he said Black had landed "history's largest fish with history's smallest hook." In the early 1990s, Rupert Murdoch opined that if sold, the Telegraph group could fetch £1 billion.

Having the Telegraph flagship would provide Black with not only wealth but the cachet to live the kind of life he had always envisioned for himself among the international elite. He seemed especially warmed by the archaic term *proprietor*, which was still commonly used in the United Kingdom to describe newspaper owners. No longer just an attendee of lofty international conferences (Black was a regular not just at Bilderberg but at the Trilateral Commission and World Economic Forum), he would be able to draw the bold-face names to a court of his own making. When he was younger, Black had confided to friends an ambition to "internationalize" himself. Now, it was all tantalizingly within reach. As he noted, "No one snubs the owner of the *Daily Telegraph*."

Hollinger's board of directors in the late 1980s began to reflect both the company's growing stature and Black's affinity for celebrities; in addition to Carrington and Reichmann, Henry Kissinger and the Canadian moguls Peter Bronfman and Robert Campeau were enlisted. Black also decided to raise the profile of his annual fete for the great and the good, the Hollinger Dinner. The dinner had been around since 1929, when the original Hollinger – a man known as Benny, whose first mine was in Timmins, Ontario – founded it as a gathering for his rough-and-tumble mining crowd. Through the Argus era of E.P. Taylor and Bud McDougald, the event became more of a Toronto society gathering, and after Black took over Argus he decided to update the evening by bringing in speakers and inviting more politicians and foreign guests. One dinner in the early 1980s featured a political debate between the Conservative parliamentarian John Crosbie and the future Liberal prime minister Jean Chrétien.

The first big international speaker was Kissinger in 1983, who along with Black and David Rockefeller stopped for the dinner en route to a Bilderberg meeting in Montebello, Quebec. Kissinger later became a fully fledged Hollinger director.

Black set a high standard for speakers that he worked hard to maintain. On June 21, 1988, during a meeting of the leaders of the Group of Seven industrialized countries held in Toronto, Margaret Thatcher was Black's guest of honour at the Toronto Club for the dinner. In attendance were Canadian prime minister Brian Mulroney, Governor General Jeanne Sauvé, and Kissinger, whom Black introduced to the black-tie crowd as "the only director in our history not to appear at our annual meeting because of a long-standing prior engagement with the king of Morocco." Black's panegyric on the British prime minister ran for eight minutes but seemed, to some guests, considerably longer. Black praised her for reducing corporate tax rates, championing privatization, increasing general productivity, and for bringing about "the abstract renewal of British greatness . . . the revival of Britain's capacity for moral leadership."

Thatcher began her own lengthy remarks by jesting, "I really don't think you've left very much for me to say . . .

"Of course, we're used to Canadians in Fleet Street," she continued. "Lord Beaverbrook and Lord Thomson – and Conrad Black is continuing a great tradition." It was a triumphant moment for Black – a ruling British prime minister praising him at his own dinner before a glittering crowd in his hometown of Toronto. At the end of Thatcher's speech, described by one jaded guest as "her Cheltenham Women's Garden Club Address No. 3," the guest of honour was thanked by Henry Kissinger.

"I must say I listened to Conrad Black's beginning with mounting panic," Kissinger deadpanned. "Because I thought, 'If this is what is being said before the prime minister has spoken, what can I possibly say after the conclusion of her remarks?'" Of course it was usual that the owner of the *Daily Telegraph* – the traditional pipeline between the Tory party and the lawn-mowing classes – should enjoy some sort of relationship with the prime minister. But it was clear

Black had a special affinity for Thatcher, and she in turn remarked that Black made her feel like a "wet."*

"The *Telegraph* was not always a strong ally to the sort of Conservative government that Mrs. Thatcher was running," observed Sir Charles Powell, who served as her senior foreign policy adviser. "But on the crucial moments – I mean, (a) election times, (b) some sort of international crisis – it generally was. And Conrad saw to that."

As he became more visible in London, many of the old Canadian myths about Black re-emerged, including the notion that Black was a Napoleon fanatic. This misconception (according to Black) may have been aided by the way Black often employed Napoleonic analogies to describe his business dealings, or by the fact that he hung a portrait of the emperor in his office, alongside various naval battle scenes, or maybe by the bust of Napoleon that he put in his library in London, or by the fact that he even acquired a chair once owned by the famous commander that he sat in to ponder weighty decisions. "His [Napoleon's] talents as a military commander are, to say the least, rather impressive," explained Black. "His career was just so prodigious. His origins were so obscure and his impact on Europe was so great that he's automatically an interesting phenomenon. And to add to all that, he obviously had enormous skill as an administrator to maintain some sort of authority over so great an area. And, finally, his talents as a mythmaker, as a self-romanticist, are astonishing. How he managed to persuade the French public to become nostalgic about him, after all the carnage for which he was largely responsible, is an amazing thing. Selling glory is a little hard when the sole beneficiary of the glory is yourself – I mean, selling it to the people who give up their lives and limbs for you. But all that said, I've never found him an attractive personality, just a great talent. I wouldn't go so far as Clarendon's statement of Cromwell, 'He was

---

* Before another dinner, in London, Black arranged for Hollinger's entire board of directors to meet the prime minister at 10 Downing Street. "We all sat in the Cabinet Room and she gave us a nice chat, answered questions," Black recalled fondly. "She was sitting there under the painting of Walpole and she was very generous with her time."

a great bad man.' I don't think Napoleon was bad, but he had psychopathic tendencies. He was indifferent, I think, to the misery that arose at least partly in consequence of his policies. In certain areas he was surprisingly unimaginative. As a statesman, he had no policy really except making war."*

One day, a London auction house announced that it was selling a cache of exotic Napoleonic memorabilia including, it was whispered, Bonaparte's preserved penis. A rumour swept through media circles that Black had purchased the body part. Francis Wheen, writing for the *Independent on Sunday*, phoned Black's office to ascertain whether there was any truth in the rumour. Rosemary Millar, Black's stoic assistant, said she would speak with the chairman about this matter. She soon rang back with a prepared response: "The proprietor of the *Daily Telegraph* would like to go on the record to say that he does certainly *not* own Napoleon's penis."

---

* Black identified his greatest hero as Abraham Lincoln. "Now there was a man associated with a terrible war, but whose solicitude for the victims was very real. And yet he made the conscious and no doubt the difficult decision of pursuing the war to absolute victory in the name of a just cause."

PART TWO

THE WORLD'S FASTEST-
GROWING PRESS EMPIRE

Chapter Twelve

"NEWSPAPERS WANTED"

I n his Argus days, Conrad Black liked to compare his business strategy – or the apparent lack of one – to the military historian Sir Basil Liddell Hart's "expanding funnel" theory, which was based on "the unpredictable downhill course of water in ways that were unforeseeable." By the time he snagged the *Telegraph*, Black had poured a lot of water down a lot of hills. In late 1984, a full half-year before the notion of investing in the Telegraph company came to light, Black's partner David Radler had been running a small advertisement in the back of *Editor and Publisher*, the American trade magazine, under the heading "Newspapers Wanted." It read: "Well respected, growing Canadian daily newspaper with cash seeks to purchase smaller newspapers (5000–10,000 circulation). Write or phone Arthur Weeks, Sterling Newspapers Ltd., PO Box 10079, Pacific Center, Vancouver B.C. V7Y 1B6 (604) 682-7755."

Soon after Black took over the *Telegraph*, Radler's ad led to the purchase of a group of thirty-four small-town papers in the United States for $106 million. Small newspapers were, after all, Conrad Black and David Radler's original business. They named their new subsidiary American Publishing. Combined with their continuing ownership of nine small Canadian papers in the Sterling chain, the new acquisition gave them a foothold in three countries. Ambitions to build an international newspaper company began to take shape.

"Conrad is the master opportunist," Peter White explained during these heady times. "I used to compare him to a spider sitting in the middle of a web, and the spider receives messages from all the far-flung corners of the empire as to what is going on and then rushes off to see what is happening." By 1995, Black, in large measure thanks to his partnership with the frenetic deal-maker Radler and the growing involvement of his old friend and lawyer Dan Colson, would preside over a press empire of more than 500 newspapers and a combined circulation of 4.7 million. At its peak, Hollinger's total would be surpassed only by the number of newspapers owned by Rupert Murdoch and by the U.S. chain Gannett, both of which had been in the game much longer. But alongside the dramatic corporate transformation came an unexpected period of personal turmoil for Black and a resulting phase of reinvention – complete with a new soulmate who was well suited to the new path he had embarked on.

Black viewed the prospects for buying up small-town American newspapers with his usual historical perspective. "My associates always essentially believed in Reaganomics. We always believed in the economic recovery of the so-called Rust Belt, and we knew that daily newspapers could be profitable down to 4,000 circulation or even less." For American Publishing's official motto, Black asked a classics scholar to translate into Latin the phrase "In rust we trust."

Following a strategy similar to Roy Thomson's in his early news-paper days, American Publishing focused on papers with a circulation of 4,000 to 25,000, and there were plenty to choose from. Changes in U.S. federal tax laws on the treatment of capital gains, introduced by the Reagan administration, were inspiring long-time owners to sell. Between 1986 and 1992, the Radler-led group would spend US$302.1 million acquiring 288 titles. In all, over a decade, Radler closed one hundred separate deals – a pace of almost one per month – to create American, which was initially run out of a small, drab office off the main street in West Frankfort, Illinois.

With every deal, Radler would send his lieutenant, Sterling general manager Arthur Weeks, ahead to scout the newspaper property. But Radler – in this respect and others the polar opposite of Black – would never complete a deal without checking out the premises himself. At some point during the inspection, he would invariably turn to his colleague and say, "Arthur, count the chairs." Radler's Sterling experience told him that the number of chairs – not official head counts (which might not include part-time and contract staff) – told the true story of a paper's labour costs. It also told him that often fully half those chairs could be thrown out without a noticeable decline in quality or productivity. Following American Publishing's first purchase, the *Wapakoneta Daily News* in Ohio, Hollinger quietly but steadily bought up such papers as the *Morocco Courier* in Morocco, Indiana (circulation 1,400), the *Hawaii Pennysaver* in Honolulu (circulation 22,500), the *Punxsutawney Spirit* in Punxsutawney, Pennsylvania (circulation 6,000), and *Stamps Magazine* in Hornell, New York (circulation 14,000). In 1988, the group bought a 40 per cent interest in the *Caymanian Compass*, the daily journal of the Cayman Islands. Black liked to joke that it featured "a swimsuit issue every week."

Although he was effectively barred by Black's U.K. executives from playing an active role at the Telegraph group, Radler would play as great a part in Black's coming triumphs and trials as anyone in his life. He held the titles of president and chief operating officer at Hollinger and chairman at American Publishing, but Radler was never one for ceremony. He described the Hollinger style as "probably closer to an American-style brokerage company where guys have their own kinds of deals" than to a hierarchical corporation. The rule of thumb was that whoever "did the deal" within Hollinger looked after that particular business. The Telegraph company was Black's deal, while American Publishing was Radler's creation.

With a personal style that fit in as easily at the Kiwanis Club as at the Vancouver Club, Radler was well tanned from regular sojourns in Palm Springs with his wife, Rona, and their family. Flip and sarcastic, he, like Black, enjoyed a good verbal joust, and he called negotiations a "grind." An admitted worrier and hypochondriac, Radler hated to fly, even though he was constantly on the road meeting publishers and advertisers in specks across the American map. To add emphasis to his statements, Radler often transformed them into questions, usually ending with "okay?" or "all right?" Some who have worked closely with Radler found him to be argumentative and to possess a deeply cynical view of human nature. One former colleague described him as "the *Simpsons'* Montgomery Burns played by Dustin Hoffman."

During the expansive early 1990s, there was a glint in Radler's narrowed eyes and a sense of whimsy in his manner and in the decor of his comparatively shabby office, which was situated well off Vancouver's beaten path in a nondescript building. Radler's lair contained an old Dominion Stores toy truck, baseball caps and fighter aircraft models, and a Terence Gilbert print of Queen Elizabeth and Ronald Reagan on horseback at Windsor. He could sometimes be found behind his massive desk sucking loudly on a candy or digging into a box of gumballs. At five-thirty one Friday afternoon, Radler was on the phone when his secretary popped her head around his door to signal that she and the other office staff were leaving. "Where are you guys going?" Radler asked in mock astonishment. "We've been so successful, *is that it*? It's been a good day, *is that it*?" Radler paused a moment for effect, then shrugged. "We fired three and didn't hire anyone, so I guess it is a good day."

From time to time it seemed that Black's affinity for the limelight kept Radler from receiving his due, but Radler derived most of his satisfaction from his family and seemed to be not a little awed by Black's intellect and eye for a deal.

As uncomplicated as Black was Byzantine, Radler saw no great mystery in their quest to assemble one of the world's biggest newspaper groups. "What do you think motivates any one of us? You go out and you try to make a living for your family; pre-marriage you try to make a living just to have a family. And these are basic desires, *okay*? The desire to eat, the desire to have things, the desire to accumulate, those kinds of things. It's not terribly complicated."

Like Black, Radler once suffered from anxiety attacks, but he used no historical analogy to explain them. It was in the early 1980s, when the Sterling offices were in the Pacific Centre in Vancouver. "I remember one day I was walking up Granville Street and suddenly I felt faint," Radler said. "I had to sit on a bench. And I never felt the same. I got back up, it was like you were afraid you were going to fall. Then of course I couldn't sleep. I kept on going to the doctors and they kept saying there's nothing wrong. So then I thought, 'I've got cancer.' One day I had a nightmare that my wife knew and I didn't, that kind of stuff. Finally, I couldn't take it any more and I went to one doctor and said, 'I can't function.'" This time, the doctor prescribed a "nerve pill," and Radler spent a month in Florida. Three weeks later, he tapered off the dose and was fine, and he has been fine ever since. "This is not unusual," he said in a 1994 interview, pointing to the stress of running big companies as the root of his, and possibly Black's, anxiety-related difficulties. "I think you pay a toll, remembering everything. Our styles are similar: remember everything in your head, never write anything down. I think it does come from something, and I suppose if you go under deep psychoanalysis you might know." But Radler had no interest in knowing such things. "One of the things I learned is that every once in a while you've got to take a pill."

In Ravelston, the private company that controlled Hollinger, Radler was the second-largest shareholder with 14 per cent, compared with Black's 67 per cent.* Although the two men were usually separated by thousands of miles, Radler has said, "I know what he thinks and he knows exactly what I think. We run on a certain wavelength." That was not always apparent to those who knew both men. "Black and Radler are like day and night," contended one Hollinger director. "They have absolutely nothing in common. David is a small-town newspaper guy. Black never gets involved in the nitty-gritty. He's a big-picture guy." Black himself admiringly dubbed Radler "the Refrigerator," because he was hard and cold.

The acquisition of Quebec's UniMedia, in the summer of 1987, was Peter White's deal.** The third member of the original triumvirate

---

* The other shareholders in Ravelston, as of mid-2004, were Peter White, Jack Boultbee, and Dan Colson.

** Although he was a partner in the first newspaper they bought, the *Sherbrooke Record*, White pursued other interests in business and politics and played a significantly lesser role than Black and Radler. Fluent in Spanish, he was in charge of searching for acquisitions in Latin America, which led to a $2 million investment for 51 per cent of *La República*, a tabloid-format paper based in San José, Costa Rica. The only catch was that its shares had to be held in a trust because foreigners were barred from owning Costa Rican media companies.

that bought the *Sherbrooke Record*, White had known the company's majority shareholder and CEO, Jacques Francoeur, for more than two decades – indeed, a·Francoeur paper, the *Granby Leader Mail*, at one time printed White and Black's first venture, the *Eastern Townships Advertiser*. UniMedia owned three daily newspapers, twenty weeklies, and four printing plants. Since it operated three French-language dailies, most notably *Le Soleil* in Quebec City, the notion of selling to any anglophone, let alone Black, was controversial. Hollinger bested the offers of established Quebec media players, including Paul Desmarais's Power Corp., which owned the Montreal daily *La Presse*, by representing a diversity of ownership. But in order to complete the $50 million buyout, Hollinger had to give the Quebec government an assignable right of first refusal should Hollinger propose to sell either *Le Soleil* or the group's third-largest paper, *Le Quotidien* of Chicoutimi, to a non-resident of Quebec, or should a non-resident propose to acquire control of the whole company. Protecting the paper from the clutches of non-Quebecers was a somewhat ironic gesture, given that Black and Radler were both born in Montreal.

Less than a year after the deal, the Hollinger operating style was evident: a ten-week strike closed Ottawa's *Le Droit*, the second-largest of UniMedia's dailies, after the new owners revealed plans to convert the paper from a broadsheet to a tabloid. From more than 300 employees at the time Hollinger took over, the staff was slashed by more than a third by 1991. One of the lesser-known assets acquired in the UniMedia deal was Novalis, a publisher of Catholic periodicals in French and English. Under a licence agreement with St. Paul University in Ottawa, Novalis delivers more than two million copies of its religious periodicals in Canada and the United States via parishes, congregations, and subscriptions, including the publication *Living with Christ*.

In the summer of 1986, a year before the UniMedia acquisition, Black had converted to the Catholic faith. Raised an Anglican, he had never been particularly religious, but his interest in Catholic figures such as Cardinal Paul-Émile Léger in Quebec and Cardinal John Henry Newman in England and his close association with Toronto's Cardinal Emmett Carter were well known.

In describing Maurice Duplessis's Catholicism, Black had written a decade earlier that the former Quebec premier "had nothing against Protestantism; it just didn't mean anything to him. It was indistinct, full of compromises, and not sufficiently uplifting . . . Catholicism to him, apart from all its institutional importance in Quebec, was the link between the mundane and the celestial and was to be embraced with fervour."

In his own case, Black posited that either one believes in the basic concept of Catholicism "or you don't. And there's nothing wrong with it if you don't and I eventually came to the conclusion that I did – but by a fairly narrow margin. And I'm not a zealous or pious person and I don't make all sorts of displacements involving religious matters."

Not long after his conversion in June 1986, Black described the occasion to the author Ron Graham. It took place in Cardinal Carter's private chapel. Apparently Black told the cardinal that he was ready to join the Church, and Carter said he would be welcome.

"Ah," Black replied, "but would I be invited?"

"All right," the cardinal responded, "I invite you."

A debate ensued over the Truth. Eventually, an agreement was struck. "Then Emmett called for champagne, to celebrate," Black recalled. "So I didn't exactly go to them on my knees."

It's not difficult to imagine that the grandeur of Catholicism appealed to Black's sensibilities. Writing in the *Spectator* several years after his conversion, Black noted: "Those who find trendy and undignified the Anglican tendency to agonise in public deliberations over every contemporary moral issue, and who detect a tendency to strip the faith down to feel-good, love-thy-neighbour handclapping as our pal God jogs along beside us, may find Rome more appealing."

Black had long been interested in the venerable but perennially money-losing monthly *Saturday Night*, a general-interest magazine that focused on cultural and political matters. He had first looked at buying it in 1973, when he even wrote to William F. Buckley seeking advice on transforming it into a Canadian emulation of Buckley's right-wing journal, the *National Review*. Norman Webster, scion of a wealthy Montreal family and editor of the *Globe and Mail*, and two of his siblings had purchased the magazine in the late 1970s through a company called Dascon Investments. Throughout Webster's eight years of ownership, the magazine never made money, although it reaped more critical acclaim and awards than any other Canadian magazine. With a paid circulation of only 135,000 in 1987, however, the magazine remained unviable. Webster liked to point out that on a per capita basis, that level of circulation "would have made us a champion in the United States," a country with ten times the population. But such were the realities of publishing in Canada that, as *Saturday Night* marked its centenary, the Websters had lost millions on the venture and were losing money at an accelerating pace. They wanted out, and Black was a willing buyer.

In June 1987 a deal was struck with Hollinger, but a dispute threatened to scuttle it. Under the terms Webster negotiated with Peter White, Hollinger agreed to buy the assets of the magazine but did not want an associated publishing services business, nor was it willing to take on the magazine's debts. Webster had assumed Hollinger would be picking up the debts. "There was a hitch," recalled Webster, "because the initial agreement had been drafted loosely, and the lawyers on the two sides looked at it and said, 'Well, what was our intention?' The intention on both sides was to close clear [of debts]. So we went ahead on that basis. They bought it for $1.4 million, but they bought the assets of the magazine; i.e., they did not buy all the debts the magazine had. We had to eat those." He would not say how much the debts were, but both seller and buyer deny the story that went around at the time contending that Webster actually ended up paying Black to take the magazine off his hands.

Toronto was abuzz with talk that *Saturday Night*'s new owner would turn the magazine into a tout-sheet for his well-known conservative views. Black invited Robert Fulford, the magazine's eminent editor of nineteen years, to lunch at 10 Toronto Street. Fulford possessed no animosity toward Black, and, unlike many journalists, he believed in the principles of capitalism and supported neo-conservatism. Besides, Black was not the first flamboyant tycoon to take a stab at owning the magazine. But the editor reckoned even before meeting Black that his departure from the magazine was likely.

"When I arrived at Toronto Street I was inspected by a secretary and a security guard and then taken upstairs to a sitting room," Fulford recounted in his book *Best Seat in the House*. "A woman in a maid's costume came in, said we were having steak for lunch, and asked how mine should be cooked. I said 'medium,' a serious mistake – it was close to inedible when it arrived. Indeed, the cuisine at Hollinger was in all ways a disappointment. Truman Capote once said, 'The real difference between rich people and regular people is that the rich people serve such marvellous vegetables. Delicious little tiny vegetables . . .' By Capote's standards, Black is not a rich person."

Fulford waited for twenty minutes before Peter White came in, and after a while Black finally joined them. Fulford wrote, "In the conversation that followed he seemed particularly interested in telling me about his friend Andrew Knight, the former editor of *The Economist*, who was now running Black's *Daily Telegraph* and *Sunday Telegraph* in London. I mentioned that I'd never met him.

" 'The amazing thing about Andrew,' Black said, 'is that he knows everyone.'

" 'It's true,' White said. 'I do believe Andrew Knight knows every important person in the whole world.' Suddenly it occurred to him – his face is like that electric sign on Broadway that gives the news in giant capital letters – that he might have insulted me, a wretched fellow who had reached the age of fifty-five without once shaking the hand of Andrew Knight. 'Sorry, Bob, I didn't mean that . . .'

"Black went on, 'Everyone asks about him. When I saw Katharine Graham the first thing she said was, "How's Andrew?" And when I was speaking to George Shultz he asked me, right away, "How is Andrew?" And so did the Aga Khan. And Henry Kissinger, when I saw him, he said [here Black went into a German accent], "Howss Undrew?" '

"He sat back, well satisfied. He had dropped the names of Katharine Graham, George Shultz, the Aga Khan, and Henry Kissinger, all in one paragraph. It occurred to me that I might never see this feat equalled in my lifetime."

The lunchtime discussion was amicable, but Fulford felt uncomfortable. He was particularly put off when White and Black each pulled out copies of the magazine's payroll list and asked the editor to go through it and grade employees as excellent, good, or fair. Despite their expressed hope that he would stay on, Fulford resigned the next day but agreed to continue until a successor was named and to contribute to the magazine thereafter. Fulford's lingering impression of his lunch was that the magazine's new owner was "an extremely uncommon millionaire, not so much in the content of his conversation as in his manner. He was more theatrical than any other businessman of my acquaintance. His personality had a staged, directed feel to it. It was also oddly familiar. Where had I seen it before, a large, handsome man with a supercilious and condescending manner and a baroque vocabulary? Of course: Orson Welles in *Citizen Kane*. I was talking to Citizen Black."

Black's choice to succeed Fulford as editor was John Fraser, his former classmate from Upper Canada College and, since the summer of 1984, London correspondent for the *Globe and Mail*. Fraser accepted Black's job offer on the proviso that Black sign an addendum to his employment contract ensuring him, Fraser, full editorial independence. In drafting the clause, Fraser borrowed some heavy phrasing from a volume on the correspondence of William Pitt during his term as prime minister of England. "He was talking about the role of the monarch and the executive, essentially a system in which the cabinet was only emerging, and I used a bit of his language," recalled Fraser. "Conrad caught it. He said: 'I know where you got that from – and George III was mad at that time.'" Fraser was not surprised that his new employer identified the reference. "It was put in there partly for amusement and partly as a test. But I had to look it up – he knows this shit off the top of his head!"

For a time, the two men enjoyed a good working relationship, and Black was finally the owner of a respected national publication in his own country. However, he was not always happy with Fraser's story selection; he was dismayed, for example, when the magazine ran a controversial cover story purportedly exposing the existence of American "death camps" under Eisenhower. One of Fraser's favourite tales from his term at the magazine was about the time he told Black that the cover story in the May 1989 issue was going to be a profile of MP Svend Robinson, who was then rumoured to be a federal leadership hopeful for the left-wing New Democratic Party. The story was entitled "Canada's Gay MP." Fraser informed Black of the story a couple of weeks before publication. "What, that faggot?" Fraser recalled Black saying. "Yeah, you know, the NDP guy." Black was floored to hear that Fraser was putting the story on the cover, mustering only a "Wow." As he often did, Fraser handled the situation with cheek. "Conrad, you know you're going to sleep easier knowing you did your bit to help Svend Robinson get the leadership of the NDP." Black replied, "I can use that line."

Though it represented only a small fraction of Black's expanding publishing interests and continued to lose money, Black regarded *Saturday Night* as a good investment that bought prestige and journalistic legitimacy in his native country at a bargain price. Black continued his 1987 buying spree by acquiring a 15 per cent interest in the *Financial Post*. The $6.9 million investment was made after Black suggested to Toronto Sun Publishing chief Doug Creighton that Sun Publishing buy the eighty-year-old weekly from its parent, Maclean Hunter, and turn it into a daily. Black believed the paper could be a strong competitor to the *Globe and Mail* and its daily "Report on Business" section, then the only widely read business report. He also brought in London's *Financial Times*, which took a 25 per cent interest in the venture.*

---

* Hollinger and the *Financial Times* later adjusted their stakes to own 19.9 per cent each,

Chapter Thirteen

ISRAEL

The *Jerusalem Post*, purchased by Hollinger in 1989, was David Radler's deal. Radler is Jewish, but he is not a terribly religious man, nor was he then well known in Israeli circles. But, as he said, "You're going to send the Italian guy to Rome, aren't you?" He had travelled to Israel a number of times on holiday, and on one trip during the Argus years he had bought a subscription to the *Post*'s international edition. Later, he gave a *Post* subscription to Black as a gift.

In 1988, while in Jerusalem with his wife, Rona, and their two daughters, Radler proposed, as a major Canadian publisher, to call on Prime Minister Yitzhak Shamir. He was not available, so Radler instead met with Shamir's political secretary, Arye Mekel, at his office. In the course of their conversation, recalled Mekel, "He told me about the fact he owns a few hundred newspapers in Canada. He said that he was a conservative himself, and that he supports the policies of Mr. Shamir, and, as I recall, he may have mentioned the fact that maybe he would want to buy a newspaper in Israel." One story going around Jerusalem was that Radler had asked what he could do for the right-wing Likud Party, to which Mekel replied something to the effect of: "Buy the *Jerusalem Post* if it's ever for sale, because every morning when Shamir reads it his blood pressure goes up." It's a good story for those who came to believe Hollinger's interest in the

Post was mostly politically motivated, but neither Mekel nor Radler confirmed it. Nevertheless, such stories are part of the folklore that surrounded Hollinger's acquisition of the *Post*, and indeed it is a jarring case where Conrad Black imposed his right-wing ideology on one of the world's best-known newspapers.

Founded by its editor Gershon Agron on December 1, 1932, as the *Palestine Post*, the journal's first edition ran to four pages and sold 1,200 copies. Agron's *Post* was first and foremost a Zionist Labour paper, and the commercial imperative took a back seat. "The aim of this paper," he once said, "is not to lose money, but not to make a penny at the expense of the staff. The staff come first, not profits. If we can make our way, preserve our reputation, and serve the country, I and the board of directors will feel ourselves well rewarded." Chances are that Agron would not have fared well in Black and Radler's employ.

In 1950, two years after the creation of the state of Israel, the paper was renamed the *Jerusalem Post*. In 1959, it introduced a weekly overseas edition, precursor to its influential international edition, which sells largely in the United States and is credited with shaping overseas perceptions of Israeli affairs. In the mid-seventies, the *Post* came under the stewardship of co-editors Ari Rath and Erwin Frenkel, who established and maintained the paper as the thoughtful voice of liberal Israel. As the country's only English daily, it had a limited audience but enormous influence. By 1989 the *Post* had achieved a daily circulation of 25,000, rising to around 45,000 on Fridays, and the weekly international edition sold a further 60,000 copies. The paper was controlled by the ailing Israeli conglomerate Koor Industries, which was ultimately owned by Histadrut, the Israeli labour movement.

Radler heard that the *Post* was for sale from Yehuda Levy, a retired Israeli Defense Forces colonel who lived in Vancouver and ran a business that operated tours to Israel. Radler thought it had potential. Black's London lawyer, Dan Colson, who had handled the Telegraph deal, was brought in to draft the formal bid. Colson recalled first hearing about it on a Sunday afternoon, in a phone conversation with Radler. Colson and Black had been to Mass at the Brompton Oratory, near Colson's Kensington home. There was, he says, "a certain irony [in that] after being at High Mass, we walked over to our house around the corner and then we proceeded to have a chat about buying the *Jerusalem Post.*"

Radler and Colson were mainly concerned about whether the business could be made viable; by their criteria the paper was overstaffed, with some 450 employees, but it was unclear whether Israeli labour laws would allow Radler to lop jobs. It was on its way to losing $2 million in 1989, and was not a typical North American–style paper – a much higher percentage of its revenue was generated from circulation than from advertising. Also, the *Post* was perhaps unique in that, through its international edition, its largest readership lived outside its home country. Moreover, as the bombings of the past and the rain of Scud missiles during the coming Persian Gulf War would demonstrate, the region's political events could have a sudden and dramatic impact on revenues.

On the other hand, the paper was internationally renowned. It also derived a larger proportion of its profits than other Hollinger papers from commercial printing and held a potentially lucrative twelve-year contract to print the Golden Pages (Jerusalem's equivalent of the Yellow Pages). Alan Rawcliffe, the *Daily Telegraph*'s printing press guru, flew to Jerusalem to assess the operation, and eventually Hollinger would invest $10 million in new presses, giving it the only commercial printing plant in Jerusalem.

The paper attracted six or seven serious offers. One rival bidder, Robert Maxwell, cobbled together an offer with the Canadian distillery magnate Charles Bronfman, who at the time was funding *Jerusalem Report* magazine. It seemed that wherever Hollinger turned, Maxwell was there. The previous year, Hollinger had tried to buy the *Age* of Melbourne from the Australian John Fairfax Group, only to have Maxwell top its bid by a considerable margin. A public outcry against potential ownership by the controversial Czech-born publisher prompted the Australian government to make it virtually impossible for any foreigner to own the paper. The *Post*'s editors published a front-page article making it clear that Maxwell was just as unwelcome in Israel.

Hollinger outbid its rivals by paying US$17.5 million for 78 per cent of the *Post*.* A year later, it spent another US$4 million to buy most of the rest of the shares.

According to *Post* editor Ari Rath (who himself had tried but failed to put together a "Jewish liberal consortium" to bid for the paper), when the Hollinger bid envelope was opened by Koor in April, the amount enclosed was so much greater than the nearest bid that "they thought it was a typo." Maxwell put out the word that he and Bronfman had bid only US$3.5 million, which fuelled suspicions that Hollinger had an ulterior motive. Few in Israel had heard of Hollinger; one theory had Black and Radler as a front for the Hollinger director Paul Reichmann and another blended Black's ownership of *Encounter* magazine and friendship with Henry Kissinger into a rumour that the CIA was somehow behind the purchase.

Black dismissed these theories in his usual thumping manner when he paid his first visit to the paper almost a year after its acquisition: "It wasn't that our bid was higher than it should have been; the other bids were lower than they should have been." Black contended that the other bidders were trying to have a controlled auction and keep the price down. "This part of the world is most historically prone to discussions of conspiracies, hidden agendas, and esoteric motivations," Black offered. "In this case, these tendencies were undoubtedly inflamed by the sour grapes of the defeated bidders. Crestfallen after the breaking up of their closed auction, they confected the theory that we had been taken completely over the barrel by the vendors. But, on our record, we seem too astute for that. So they spread the rumour that perhaps it was just some heinous plot to produce a Likud propaganda sheet and bring Israel to extreme Orthodoxy – the whole male population would have to go around in peyot and phylacteries."

Black went on: "I consider Bob to be the main author of those wild rumours. Bob Maxwell is a sort of friend, and he put out the story that we overpaid, because he was particularly horrified at having

---

* Hollinger was later refunded US$1.15 million in a "clawback" arrangement implemented after the financial statements on which the bid was based were audited.

his bid topped. Also, there was some lack of enthusiasm around here about working for Bob, because for all his merit – and he has a lot of merit – he is known as an overbearing proprietor. Not everyone at the paper was enchanted at the thought of coming to work here like happy little elves singing, 'Heigh-ho, I'm working for Bob Maxwell.'"

As Black told it, Maxwell capped the escapade by quietly offering to take the paper off Hollinger's hands for more than it had paid, while at the same time telling everyone Black had overpaid. Black then asked Maxwell to join the paper's board of directors, and he agreed. "I think it was to shut him up," Colson said later.

After the deal closed in June, Radler met Frenkel and Rath, the editors, and said there would be no dramatic change in the paper's direction. There would, however, be greater emphasis on running it like a business: staff would have to be let go. In interviews, Radler had said earlier that the editors would retain their jobs and would continue to dictate editorial policy. But at the same time, he made no secret of his vision of the role played by newspaper publishers: "They have a responsibility to be aware of what they're publishing and to influence it. They can't hide behind the concept of 'journalistic independence' and pretend that they are not aware of what is going on in their paper." Radler and the co-editors looked casual and chummy in their open-necked shirts at a *Post* photo shoot. But, as happens so often in the Middle East, peace was short-lived.

What followed soon after Radler took over command of the *Post* has been portrayed by former *Post* journalists as nothing short of the imposition by Black and Radler of a right-wing agenda on what had been the bastion of Israeli liberal journalism. The *Times* of London billed it as a fight "over the soul of Israel." No one disputes that there was a sudden and dramatic shift in the paper's editorial direction. Radler argued that it was merely a case of repositioning the paper to reflect the readership more accurately and to make some money. "Let's not play games," Black huffed. "It was universally perceived to be a very left-wing paper before. Well, the far left isn't the only game in town."

For Yehuda Levy, whom Radler anointed publisher despite his lack of media experience, it was really a tale of office politics, a struggle for power. Rath and Frenkel's suspicions were piqued when they discovered that Levy was taking Radler to meet right-wing figures like Yitzhak Shamir and Ariel Sharon at the latter's farm. As Frenkel later told the *Independent*, "I knew it was over a few weeks after Levy joined. I had a sick feeling in my stomach." Added Rath, "I said, 'I smell a rat here.'"

Levy soon told Rath, who was sixty-five, that it was time for him to retire – as Radler recalled it, he thought Rath should stay but never expected him to retain the editor's post. To Radler's desk-counting mind it was absurd that a paper the size of the *Post* should need two editors.

Rath sent an urgent fax to Radler asking whether he knew about this development, to which Radler responded by phone, telling him to do nothing until his next planned visit in a few weeks to take over as chairman of the paper. Before Radler's arrival, Rath called a friend in London, the *Times* columnist Barbara Amiel, who knew Conrad Black and was linked romantically to Rath and Black's mutual friend the publisher Lord Weidenfeld. "Ari, if anything is happening, I can talk to Black," Rath says Amiel told him. "Better still, George Weidenfeld can talk to Black. This is ridiculous."

But by the end of 1989, just six months after Hollinger bought the paper, both editors had been pushed out of the paper, and there was open revolt in the newsroom. On the morning of January 2, 1990, Yehuda Levy arrived in his office to find resignation letters from thirty journalists on his desk. Each letter was identical, citing "a substantial deterioration in the terms of my employment," leaving the writer "no alternative but to ask to be relieved of my duties at the newspaper" and giving thirty days for the publisher to respond. Just two days later, after consulting with Radler, Levy accepted all the resignations. He ordered that power to the newsroom's computer terminals be shut off and that all those resigning vacate the building within two hours.

The official version of events, given in the 1989 Hollinger annual report, noted: "As editorial ranks had swollen from roughly fifty to one hundred since 1986 without any corresponding increase in editorial product, this was not an altogether unwelcome development. The departing personnel used their contacts in the international press to stir up an unwarranted volume of overseas comment, some of it, especially in Canada, rather uninformed and tendentious."

Joanna Yehiel, a feature writer who had worked at the paper for twenty years, sued the *Post* for severance pay in an Israeli labour court and ultimately won. The forty-six-page ruling by Judge Elisheva Barak, delivered on April 25, 1993, concluded that Levy's interference in the workplace made it impossible for Yehiel to carry out her duties. Barak ruled that the mass resignation was not a resignation at all, but that the resigning employees had hoped the management would make changes and ask them not to leave. From a Western journalistic perspective, it was a remarkable judgment, basically saying that the editors and writers' freedom of expression superseded that of the owners and publisher.

Two years after Frenkel's departure, Levy made editorial writer David Bar-Illan the *Post*'s editor. A native Israeli and concert pianist known for his renditions of Franz Liszt's compositions, Bar-Illan had lived in the United States for many years and was a veteran commentator on Israeli affairs in American newspapers and magazines. A self-described hawk, earlier in his career he had written speeches for Yitzhak Shamir. "Generally speaking," said Levy of the hiring of Bar-Illan, "I knew we were standing more or less with the same views on the most important issues, and I knew he was a very good writer." But Levy insisted it was not a conscious turn to the right, and that neither Radler nor Black tried to dictate any change in the paper's political line. The only push was to make more money. Said Levy: "They wanted results, period."

Radler said, "This is not a left-right bullshit thing, okay? The reason David Bar-Illan is there is not because he's right-wing, it's because he's probably the greatest editorial writer I've ever seen – it does tend to be right-wing, but it's good."

It is indisputable that the paper took a 180-degree turn from dovish to hawkish during the four years Bar-Illan led the paper, and it has maintained its stance through several editors since.*

---

* Bar-Illan went on to be communications director for Israeli prime minister Benjamin Netanyahu; he died in 2003.

David Horovitz, a London correspondent for the paper who moved to Israel in 1989 and was among those who quit over the new direction, said the story of the *Post* is as complex as the country in which it operates. In his case, he couldn't stomach the *Post*'s new line advocating the continuing occupation of Gaza and the West Bank. "It's not just a job and it wasn't just a power struggle – although that was part of it," he said. "The fact was that these are existential issues for people who had come to live in this country with certain beliefs. The paper was no longer representing why they were here."

As far as David Radler was concerned, the *Post* was an unqualified success. While it would not produce profits on the scale of comparable American Publishing titles, the operation did begin to generate profits after the 1991 Persian Gulf War. The number of journalists was cut from 130 in 1989 to 62 in 1993, and overall staff was slashed to 210 from 450. The printing plant was upgraded, which made for a better-quality paper and more commercial printing work. Radler was proud of the role he was playing in Jewish life, but the true measure of success was always the bottom line. "Has the *Post* been a headache?" Radler reflected five years after buying it. "Yes. Would I have done the deal? Yes. We're talking about an operation that makes a lot of money."

Fast-forward nearly ten years. The former *Post* journalist David Horovitz found a home for his brand of journalism as editor of the magazine *Jerusalem Report*, only to see Hollinger buy it in 1998. This time, however, there was no new direction or interference from above despite the *Report*'s "liberal, pluralistic" editorial position, which ran quite opposite to the *Post*'s. "Radler, I think, relished the fact that he owned a title that would have confounded people's expectations about him," said Horovitz. Even though there was plenty of debate about political issues with Radler, Horovitz said, he never interfered. "He enabled us to maintain a separate editorial operation, which is not the most cost-effective way to own these titles. There was definitely respect for what we're doing," Horovitz said in 2004.

For his part, Black became increasingly supportive of Israel's right wing in his own views over the years. Ironically, one of the few times he seemed genuinely unnerved by criticism against one of his publications occurred when the October 29, 1994, issue of the *Spectator* included an article on "Hollywood's New Jewish Establishment." The *New York Times* reported that "few in Hollywood could recall such an anti-Semitic article in a mainstream publication," while the Simon Wiesenthal Center said the writer, William Cash, "plagiarized a page from the playbook of Julius Streicher and Joseph Goebbels." Letters of complaint were sent to Black by such luminaries as Steven Spielberg, Barbra Streisand, Kevin Costner, and Tom Cruise. Jack Valenti, head of the Motion Picture Association, called Black and demanded a full-page apology. *Telegraph* editor Max Hastings, who was in Black's office when Valenti chewed him out, said, "It was one of the few moments in my time with Conrad when I saw him look seriously rattled." "You don't understand, Max," Black told him. "My entire interests in the United States and internationally could be seriously damaged by this."*

---

* Nonetheless, Dominic Lawson, then the editor of the *Spectator* and now of the *Sunday Telegraph*, noted that Black shielded him from the furor. "Advertisers threatened to withdraw their business across the length and breadth of Conrad's empire," recalled Lawson. "But he never gave me any sense of the pressure he was under; still less did he rebuke me."

Chapter Fourteen

MINDING THE KINGDOM

he guest speaker at the Hollinger Dinner in Toronto on June 29, 1989, was Ronald Reagan, whom Black once praised as "one of the most important and successful presidents and one of the most formidable political leaders in U.S. history." In the early days of Black's ownership of the *Telegraph*, a colleague told the cartoonist Nicholas Garland, "Black once said that he was prepared to let his editors have a completely free hand except on one subject. He forbade attacks on American presidents in general and Ronald Reagan in particular." For the Hollinger event, Black hired a local tenor, John McDermott, to sing a stirring a cappella rendition of "Danny Boy."

During the after-dinner drinks, Black chatted with a group that included Toronto Sun Publishing chairman Doug Creighton and *Financial Post* editor John Godfrey. Witnesses observed a curious scene. Earlier in the day, Black had filed a column to run in the *Sun* and the Sun-controlled *Financial Post*. In the article, in one of his more memorable outbursts, he described investigative journalists as "sniggering masses of jackals" and in particular blasted the *Globe and Mail* reporter Linda McQuaig as a "weedy and not very bright leftist reporter." Black had asked Creighton to ensure that the column ran unedited, and Creighton had left those instructions with the various editors. The column ran intact in the *Sun*. But Godfrey had problems with some of the language and, after consulting the *Post*'s libel lawyer, thought the phrase "weedy and not very bright" ought to be taken out, along with the word "mendacious."

"So did you receive my column?" Black asked at the dinner.

"Indeed," said Godfrey.

"Is it running tomorrow?"

"Indeed."

"Is it running without changes?"

"No," Godfrey replied, explaining that certain references were removed on the advice of the *Post's* libel lawyers, and that, as editor, he didn't think it appropriate to attack a journalist personally. Black's expression darkened. He had already run the copy by his own libel lawyers, he complained, which was why the instructions were to run it unedited. As a result, Black, for a time, stopped writing for the *Financial Post*, a paper he partly owned.

For her part, McQuaig was amazed at Black's animosity toward her, which dated back to her coverage of the regulatory and police investigations into him in 1982. "I thought Ms. McQuaig should have been horsewhipped," Black once commented to the radio interviewer Peter Gzowski, "but I don't do those things myself and the statutes don't provide for it." McQuaig said she was initially hurt by Black's denouncements, but that feeling quickly passed. "The kinds of attacks are so extreme and kind of bizarre," said McQuaig. "When you get over the initial hurt, you end up thinking, 'Wow, that's kind of interesting. He's made me into a character.'"*

The evening with Reagan and the swipe at McQuaig were Black's final goodbyes to Toronto and to being a Canadian resident. After renting a house and spending the previous three summers in London, Conrad and Shirley had decided to make London their primary residence, although they would keep their homes in Toronto and Palm Beach. They took with them their children Alana, seven, and James, three; the eldest, Jonathan, eleven, chose to stay at boarding school in Canada.

---

* When Black launched his *National Post* newspaper in Canada nearly a decade later, McQuaig was among its columnists, although Black had nothing to do with her hiring

From a business perspective, Black reasoned that the *Telegraph* was by a large measure Hollinger's major asset, and that he ought to take a more active role in its affairs. "As a Canadian, I wish I could sit here, hand over heart and tell you otherwise," he said. "But the fact is, London is more interesting than Toronto. It's an endless sequence of sumptuous lunches and dinners with terribly interesting people from all over the world."

Black did not attempt to contain his delight at his membership in the exclusive club of British press owners. "Do you realize that anyone who owns the *Telegraph* has access to anyone in the world? Even Gorbachev passes through here. It's remarkable," he said. London's social round suited Black well. On a typical day he would sleep until mid-morning, have lunch, work at his Docklands office until the evening, then go off to a function; in London he discovered a fondness for opera and ballet. "He loves the atmosphere over there," observed his old friend Peter White. "He absolutely adores being a newspaper tycoon, and that's the place to do it. He's lionized over there and that's very much to his liking."

Prominent Londoners were initially interested in Black because he owned the *Telegraph*, and Black played the part of proprietor well. "He charmed an enormous number of people in this country by sitting next to them at dinner or by talking," said his friend Rupert Hambro.

"In the early stages, not many people knew a lot about him, and I think, yes, quite a lot of people were inclined to laugh at him," Max Hastings recalled a few years after Black's relocation. "First of all, he himself has changed. He was quite nervous and unsure of himself . . . when he first came here. Now he's much more relaxed, he's much more sure of himself and his own position."

Conrad and Shirley's new home in Highgate, north London, sat on two acres of land and was somewhat smaller than their Toronto house. As was often the case with Black acquisitions, it soon expanded. He added a conservatory, which could serve as an extra dining area for entertaining – at first the house could accommodate only sixteen for dinner or twenty for a buffet – then bought the house next door and tore it down in order to add a library. "Conrad needs, I think, to have 'big' around him," observed a friend.

Black's arrival in London in 1989 came at a time of upheaval and unease at the *Telegraph*. The paper was undergoing a restructuring to introduce seven-day publishing and a five-day working week. Unlike North American newspapers, Fleet Street broadsheets operated under a model where Sunday papers had entirely different staffs and personalities than their daily siblings, and openly competed with them. In *Quaynotes*, the internal *Telegraph* newsletter, Black made it clear that he was not content with the papers' financial turnaround, and more changes were to come. "We've got to move on to other challenges as a company and as a newspaper," he said. "But they should be rationally conceived and not compulsive and they should not be motivated by obscene ambitions or Napoleonic ideas. I mean, I'm not marching on Moscow – I'm just trying to build our company in an orthodox and dignified way."

Between sips of iced tea, Black also confirmed the well-circulated view that he was no champion of the people who toiled in the offices beneath his. The newsletter quoted him as saying, "I have made all sorts of unflattering remarks about the media in general, and I hold to them. I used to see a lot of journalists in Canada (in the contentious period of the 1960s) and it was in that context that I was commenting. I'm not a particularly great admirer of journalists. A great many of them are irresponsible. They have huge power, and many of them are extremely reckless." Here as on other subjects, Black had a way of making a harsh or outlandish point but then qualifying it in such a way that the listener wasn't sure of Black's true feelings. "But like people in all other occupations, many of them are outstanding professionals, competent and conscientious people. So I would avoid generalisations about them – and let me add that there are very high standards at this newspaper and, indeed, at other quality broadsheet newspapers." It was a strangely mixed message, not the sort that journalists normally hear from their owners, that roughly translated as: The boss doesn't like journalists, except for the ones that he likes.

For most *Telegraph* employees, journalists and others, the interview was the closest they would come to a personal encounter with the proprietor. There were no annual addresses to the troops, no general memos to staff, no strolls through the newsroom to see what the team was up to. "He's very remote," observed Charles Moore, who joined the *Daily Telegraph* as deputy editor shortly after Black's move to London. "There can't be very many people among the journalists who know him at all well. I think if you were a normal journalist, you wouldn't expect to go see Conrad about something."

This is not to say that Black did not take an active role in the newspaper's affairs after he arrived. By the spring of 1989, after a string of strategic and financial successes in the three years that Andrew Knight had been guiding the Telegraph group as chief executive, things suddenly were out of kilter. There was infighting among the management team, and Rupert Murdoch was rumoured to be courting Knight to work for him at News International, effectively the *Telegraph*'s main competitor. Much of the tension stemmed from Knight's demotion of Peregrine Worsthorne as *Sunday Telegraph* editor and the plan to move to North American–style seven-day publishing, with Max Hastings in charge of all the editions.

In August 1989, Knight visited Black at his home in Highgate and told him, "I actually think I ought to step aside." "You'll stay on the board, won't you?" Black asked. "Would you like to be deputy chairman?" At first, Knight reluctantly agreed that he would, but he was uneasy about it; a few weeks later he changed his mind about becoming a director, saying that, having once been in charge, he would have difficulty merely coming in for board meetings. In September, Black announced that he would be taking the role of executive chairman and that Knight would be standing down as CEO. "We have created a kingdom," proclaimed Knight. "Now it's time the king took over."

One of the king's first managerial tasks was to resolve a festering debate over the seven-day operation. Under the compromise Black worked out among his executives, the *Telegraph* announced thirty-three layoffs and a new five-day workweek. "That may be good for him," complained Lynne Edmunds, a features writer, "but what about the quality of the two newspapers?"

The move prompted a thirty-six-hour wildcat strike. Black saw the scattered pickets in front of the *Telegraph*'s South Quay offices as "a rather picturesque illustration" of "the penchant of many journalists to masquerade as a learned profession while behaving like an industrial union."

Black later recalled sardonically, "I brought my hobnailed jackboot down on the necks of our journalists by proposing the Dickensian Bleak House of a five-day workweek. The *UK Press Gazette* instantly reverted to being an NUJ [National Union of Journalists] tout-sheet. Serious financial journalists, with whom it is usually possible to have a sensible conversation, became hysterical muckrakers, febrile with righteousness, as if they were exposing the most repulsive abuses of the Victorian sweatshop. On that occasion the widely retailed theory of my implacable hostility to journalists was noisily revived."

In late December, Black received a note from Knight saying that Murdoch had made him an offer he could not refuse – the executive chairmanship of News International, overseeing Wapping's five newspapers. Black was angry, claiming that Knight had only three days earlier denied the latest rumours. The financier Lord Cayzer expressed "great surprise" that Knight had sold to his family's Caledonia Investments two million of his Telegraph shares just a few months earlier, without letting on that he was planning to step down. "If you lose one of your best managers it is bound to make a difference," he told the *Sunday Correspondent*.

Throughout the months of planning his departure from the Telegraph company, Knight had been concerned that it should not appear as though Black had fired him. But now Black was the one worrying about appearances; the defection of the Telegraph chief executive to his main competitor so soon after his move to London could reflect poorly on him. After consulting with deputy chairman Frank Rogers, Black elected to dispense with his low profile in Britain and to fight this battle on familiar turf – through the press. In contrast to his past public battles in Canada, this time Black had his own papers at his disposal.

Rogers sent the company's correspondence about Knight's defection to the *Observer* and the *Sunday Telegraph*, and Knight later provided his letters to the *Sunday Times* on the proviso that all the letters be published in their entirety. In one exchange, Black wrote: "I advised you again and again to execute your departure without harm to your reputation. You followed your own counsel, and, demonstrably, your reputation has suffered. I didn't provide a 'very jolly story for the newspapers.' You did. In addition to being jolly, it is rather tawdry and disappointing." Knight replied that he had been "deluged with so many calls and notes of outrage at your conduct." The same day as the first letters were published in the *Observer*, a no-byline profile in the *Sunday Telegraph* (written by Worsthorne and a fellow journalist, Frank Johnson) ran under the headline "The Constant Smiler with the Knife." It was accompanied by an illustration depicting Knight, in a suit of armour and with his weapons laid down, embracing a dragon with the head of Rupert Murdoch. It noted of his defection to News International within an "astonishingly short" time after leaving the Telegraph company: "Among quality newspapers, only relatively junior employees would normally make so swift a change."

In the same day's *Sunday Times*, business editor Ivan Fallon described the piece as "one of the most poisonous, score-settling pen profiles seen in journalism in recent years," while Knight dismissed Black's attacks as "the rather sad inaccuracies of a wounded lover." William Rees-Mogg wrote in the *Independent*, "Surely it cannot have been read by the *Sunday Telegraph*'s lawyer, who must know as well as anyone that malice invalidates a fair-comment defence to libel. This profile breathed malice in almost every paragraph."

At Hastings's urging, Black quickly unwound the seven-day newspaper arrangement by installing a separate editor of the *Sunday Telegraph* (although he did leave Max Hastings as editor-in-chief responsible for both titles). Despite the stumble of the seven-day notion, the strategy of moving the colour magazine to the Saturday edition was paying off. By 1990, the *Saturday Telegraph* was outselling the *Sunday Times*, while the *Sunday Telegraph*, despite declining newsstand sales, surpassed the circulation of the *Observer* to move from third to a distant second place behind the *Sunday Times*.

Now physically at the helm of the *Telegraph*, Black displayed a tolerance for some journalists who had crossed him in the past. One was Charles Moore, who joined the *Telegraph* as deputy editor from the *Spectator* and became *Sunday Telegraph* editor in 1992 and later succeeded Max Hastings as editor of the *Daily Telegraph*. Moore's move to the *Telegraph* was intriguing because (even though his plans to join the *Telegraph* were already in the works) he had written critically of Black shortly before Black's move to England. According to his wife, Shirley, this was an aspect of Black's often combative nature. "He's easily riled, and easily placated by flattery," she once said.

Black had also been the target of a much-publicized anecdote involving Moore that the cartoonist Nicholas Garland recorded in his diary, which he published in 1986. It recounted a story Moore told after attending a dinner at 10 Downing Street for the retirement of former *Telegraph* editor William Deedes. "Charles was very funny about Bill's dinner at Downing Street," Garland wrote. "At one stage of the evening the lights were dimmed in the drawing room so that the company could watch the Guards beating the retreat or flashing their colours or whatever they do. Everyone stood spellbound. But Conrad Black's act is apparently to be the one who knows everything, and he completely ruined the spectacle with an interminable monologue about the history of the uniforms and the origins of the ritual before them. Charles gave his spluttering laugh. 'And it was so boring and pointless.'" Yet even after Garland defected to the *Independent* and his diaries were published as a book, Black approved his rehiring by Hastings.

With Knight's rocky and public departure, Black became an object of growing curiosity in a country obsessed with press owners, and he established his own style. "Unlike, let's say, Rupert or unlike a lot of tycoons, Conrad loves to play," Max Hastings observed. "He adores to talk all night. One of the problems can be that his staying power is a good deal greater than mine as regards all this all-night gossiping."

"I wouldn't say Conrad is a hands-on proprietor," said Telegraph director Sir Evelyn de Rothschild. "I think he is interested intellectually in the content of his newspaper. I think he's quick to praise certain areas of good and bad. I think he's very interested in the standard of production, the quality of the paper. I think he's very interested in the type of people who work for him. But at the same time he's also a businessman. He's interested, obviously, in the capitalist system of using funds to the best advantage."

Central to Black's notion of being a captain of industry was being able to bask in the reflected glory of like-minded luminaries. The membership of the board of the Telegraph company began to signal Black's new place among Britain's business elite. In August 1990, he added former NATO secretary general Lord Carrington; the financier Sir James Goldsmith; the chairman of Jardine, Matheson Holdings, Henry Keswick; Sir Evelyn de Rothschild; and British Airways chairman Lord King of Wartnaby. The addition of Goldsmith particularly infuriated Lord Hartwell, who remained on the board and had long despised Goldsmith for a hatchet job on Lord Hartwell's wife, published in a magazine once backed by Goldsmith. "I couldn't and can't stand that man," grumbled Lord Hartwell. These being the years before the term "corporate governance" had entered the business lexicon, Lord Hartwell also saw no need for the new faces around the board. "I don't think non-executive directors are all the shout," he said. "If the company is controlled by one shareholder, there's no point in having non-executive directors. They might come up with some interesting ideas, but as far as I can see they don't."

Another director said that Lord Hartwell was not the only director to be surprised when Black began to expand the Telegraph board a year after his move to London. "Conrad, as is his way, suddenly announced he had a new slate of directors he wanted to add," recalled the director. "I think we have the biggest board in the country!" The same claim may have been true in Canada, where in 1990 the Hollinger board was twenty strong and Black created an additional thirteen-member international advisory board, a star-studded assembly of tycoons and pundits with whom Black could hold his own Bilderberg-style think-tanks. One observer described the board as "a sort of *Almanach de Gotha* of the international right."

The international advisory board brought together Dwayne Andreas, chairman of the U.S. agricultural giant Archer Daniels Midland, Lord Hanson, Sir James Goldsmith, Lord Rothschild, former U.S. assistant secretary for international security policy Richard Perle

(architect of Reagan's Star Wars initiative), former Canadian ambassador to the United States Allan Gotlieb, former chairman of the U.S.
Federal Reserve System Paul Volcker, former assistant to the president
of the United States for national security affairs Zbigniew Brzezinski,
and the well-known American pundits David Brinkley, William F.
Buckley Jr., and George Will. Henry Kissinger and Lord Carrington
moved over from the main Hollinger board as senior international
advisers. Additions in subsequent years included Fiat chairman
Dr. Giovanni Agnelli, former president of Israel Chaim Herzog, and
Dr. Josef Joffe, editorial-page editor for *Suddeutsche Zeitung*. Black's
crowning catch was Margaret Thatcher, who, three years after her
departure from politics, was placed at the top of the list as honorary
senior international adviser. One person who politely declined Black's
invitation was the billionaire Berkshire Hathaway chairman Warren
Buffett.* "Conrad's role to some extent is to ingratiate himself in certain
circles, and this does help," noted David Radler. "Every one of these
guys are pros at putting in off-the-record stuff. They do it for a living."

The international advisory board met once a year, holding round-
table discussions on world political and economic affairs during the day
and a dinner at night. Its members were paid like ordinary directors,
which could be rationalized as a bargain when compared with the sums
they commanded for public speaking engagements on the rubber
chicken circuit: according to *Forbes* magazine, Thatcher commanded
just under US$60,000 for an appearance, Kissinger US$40,000, Brinkley
US$30,000. And as advisory rather than regular board members, they
did not share the corporate directors' liability for such matters as signing
off on prospectuses and other company documents.

At the advisory board's meetings, the discussions, led by Black,
were quite intense, recalled William F. Buckley Jr. "They're almost
too rich, when you put those ten or twelve people in a room,
convene at ten, have a lunch and get through it by three-thirty or
four. A little bit *dizzy*, the amount of talent that can only be given
ten or fifteen minutes each because of the hectic schedule. I guess the

---

* Black ventured that he also would have liked to include Richard Nixon, "if he were
younger and more gregarious."

reasoning behind it is that you can't get people who include Kissinger and Thatcher and Brzezinski and George Will and so on and hang on to them for more than a day, day and a half. As I say, it's a little bit too rich for satisfactory exploitation – that is a little bit frustrating. Otherwise, it's a little bit bracing to run into each other and say hello."

The meetings are held in different venues each year. In 1994, for instance, the advisory board met in Washington, D.C., with the Republican senator Robert Dole as dinner speaker and the Democratic senator Lloyd Bentsen at lunch. "It was an experience, for me, second to none," said former Hollinger director Peter Munk. "To have the president of Israel and Kissinger debating with Volcker and the head of Archer Daniels Midland – I mean, it's spectacular, it's informative, it's just fascinating."*

According to Black, the advisory board was not a vanity collection of celebrities but a key ingredient in Hollinger's corporate success. "Frankly," explained Black, "a lot of the use of these boards is to load them up with important people who can be helpful to you. I'm interested in relationships that can be useful. I'm not interested just in trotting these people around."

One acquaintance on whom Black made an impression was Raymond Seitz, American ambassador to the United Kingdom. The first time they met was at a breakfast at the embassy, at Seitz's invitation. "I liked him," recalled Seitz. "I could tell he was extremely bright, politically engaged, interesting to be with – he had a rather orotund or pompous way of speaking, but he had real substance in what he said."

As an unabashed fan of the United States, Black often came to dinners held at the embassy at Seitz's invitation. In 1994, when Seitz resigned from the foreign service, Black was one of the first people who called, offering him a seat on the Telegraph board, which Seitz accepted.

"The newspaper industry in London has long attracted proprietors of immense ego." So began Black's review of a biography of Lord

---

* Soon afterwards, Munk's Barrick Gold started its own international advisory board

Beaverbrook in *Saturday Night*, which also noted that "megalomania is an occupational hazard." There was always a temptation to compare Black with the famous Canadians who had preceded him on Fleet Street and entered the House of Lords, Roy Thomson and Max Aitken. Like Black, Lord Thomson was devoutly committed to the bottom line. Unlike Black, Thomson had little interest in public life. Max Aitken, who became Lord Beaverbrook, had more surface similarities to Black: he was a financier who moved to London in 1910 after trying unsuccessfully to buy a newspaper in Montreal. In 1917, he bought control of the *Daily Express* and, at age thirty-seven, was elevated to the House of Lords. Like Black, Lord Beaverbrook regarded himself as a historian. Unlike Black, Lord Beaverbrook was known for a frenzied romantic life, for maintaining a "blacklist" of people banned from the pages of his papers, and for his statement that he ran the *Express* "purely for the purpose of making propaganda." Black said Lord Beaverbrook "will always remain a model of the panache and influence an aspiring media proprietor may seek to achieve, and [of] some of the excesses and frailties of character and judgment one would wish to avoid."

Charles Wintour, a former *Evening Standard* editor who worked for Lord Beaverbrook, interviewed Black and found his style to be quite different. "He's very interesting in private conversation, but he's an extremely orotund and boring public speaker," said Wintour. "Whereas Beaverbrook was one of the great platform speakers of his day."

Black did put on a performance reminiscent of "the Beaver" in his staunch speech at the Centre for Policy Studies meeting at the Conservative Party's Bournemouth conference in October 1990. Black cautioned against allowing Britain's identity and currency to be subsumed through its participation in Europe, and warned that monetary union in particular would mean "the British government would have lost all power over the currency, and all the ramifications of that power." Indeed, Black warned, if the House of Commons were to agree to such a thing, "that ratification would be the last properly sovereign act of our Parliament."

It was clear that Black had quickly warmed to his new role as a defender of Conservatism in England: during the course of his

Bournemouth speech he used the words *we, our,* and *us* no fewer than eighty-six times. This performance only added to growing speculation that Black would soon be following his Canadian predecessors into the House of Lords. The gossip was fomented, in part, by Shirley Black's decision to change her name to Joanna Catherine Louise. In fact, this was Shirley's decision and unrelated to her husband's ambitions. She simply had never liked her name.

Black always publicly played down the notion of a peerage. That said, from his earliest days of *Telegraph* ownership he privately ran through the various titles he might like to be called if one were ever bestowed. He had not particularly liked his name to begin with, he joked, and did not wish to be called Lord Black. Perhaps "Lord Ravelston" after his private holding company or "Lord Havenwold" after the name he gave his Toronto estate when he had a Black coat of arms created.* "If Thatcher would have offered it," said a close friend of Black's, "he would have accepted it with enthusiasm." Barbara Amiel, the prominent Canadian journalist who was writing for the *Times,* opined to the Toronto Star, "There's just no way Mrs. Thatcher can leave office without giving [a peerage] to him."

All such musings, both public and private, faded when Thatcher was ousted as Tory leader and replaced by John Major. Black's, and the *Telegraph's,* tepid feelings toward Major forestalled, for the moment, any suggestion of Black's being rewarded with a seat in the House of Lords.

With or without a peerage, the beginning of the 1990s was a prosperous time for Black. Despite warnings of an oncoming recession, the *Telegraph* was performing well, with cash flow approaching $100 million. It had increased its cash in hand by selling shares in Reuters for £35 million and by selling its London office building in South Quay at a £14 million profit as part of an arrangement with Paul Reichmann to move the *Telegraph* into five floors of his struggling

---

* The coat of arms incorporates a book, an eagle, a plumbline (representing the fact that his family had come from abroad), sheaves of wheat for western Canada and a fleur-de-lis for Quebec. The crest was hung above the front door at Havenwold and was replicated on a large gold signet pinkie ring, a gift from Joanna.

Canary Wharf development. *Telegraph* staff who bemoaned the Docklands' remoteness from the City and Fleet Street joked that nearby Canary Wharf was at least "a hundred yards closer to civilization."*

These were heady times. From his new perch in Europe's largest building, Black's horizon for newspaper acquisitions could extend virtually to the ends of the earth. "Our cash flow," Black mused, "is almost entirely available for acquisitions, and my associates and I may even someday be entitled to say, as Roy Thomson famously did when asked why he wanted to buy more newspapers: 'To make more money'; and when asked why he wanted more money: 'To buy more newspapers.'"

---

* A separate office for the City (business) section was opened closer to the action after much protest about the lengthy cab and train rides required to get to interviews and lunches.

Chapter Fifteen

SOUTH PACIFIC

On November 9, 1990, Warwick Fairfax flew from La Guardia in New York to Toronto's Lester B. Pearson Airport, where a car waited. Desperate to salvage his control of a family empire incorporating Australia's most esteemed newspapers, dishevelled, bespectacled Fairfax was on his way to 10 Toronto Street. With him were Bill Beerworth, his Sydney-based adviser, and Luis Rinaldini of Lazard Freres, the New York investment bank.

The drive from the airport to Conrad Black's Toronto office takes about half an hour in light traffic. The small, three-storey building is tucked away on a downtown side street, and behind it, a rarity in the city's business community, is its own ground-level parking lot. Since moving to London in 1989, Black had been an infrequent sight at 10 Toronto Street. But on this gloomy, overcast day, his polished navy Cadillac was stationed in the car park.

The grey-haired, grey-jacketed sentinels who watched over Black Central ushered the three men through the double set of bulletproof doors into the small reception area and upstairs to an anteroom near Black's office. On offer was a stake in Fairfax's storied titles, including the *Sydney Morning Herald*, Melbourne's *Age*, and the *Australian Financial Review*. Fairfax papers boasted a combination of prestige and some of the richest operating-profit margins in the Western world. The problem was that three years earlier, Warwick, then aged twenty-six, had borrowed a crippling A$2.1 billion to take the family company, John Fairfax, private in the largest takeover in Australian history. It had seemed like a good idea at the time.

In search of an investor, the Fairfax entourage had already trod similarly opulent corridors at some of the top North American newspaper groups – the Washington Post Co., the Tribune Co., the New York Times Co., and Thomson. Some were deterred by the Australian government's policy, similar to Canada's, which discouraged foreign control of its media, and so far there were no takers. In fact, Hollinger was one of the few newspaper groups with aspirations of building a global empire. "It didn't seem to appeal to us as an attractive financial opportunity, so we didn't pursue it," said Ken Thomson. "Now Mr. Black is another story."

"I would be a little bit leerier than Mr. Black is about acquiring papers overseas," said former New York Times Co. chairman Arthur Sulzberger Sr. "Papers are rather a personal thing to the community. I'm not sure that we can run a paper in Prague or the *Irish Echo* or whatever else it is going to be. We'll sell them our news service, but I think they have to be pretty homegrown."

A quarter of an hour late, Black made his entrance. He spoke with familiarity about Fairfax's predicament, peppering his remarks with military analogies. Fairfax and his advisers pressed their case; Black's expression was stony.

But he had been eyeing Fairfax for some time. Telegraph chief executive Andrew Knight was quite taken with the Fairfax papers in 1986, when he flew to Sydney to negotiate the sale of part of the *Telegraph*'s Manchester plant to Rupert Murdoch. In those early days of Black's control of the *Daily Telegraph*, Black suffered badly from jet lag. Half in jest, Knight raved to Black from Australia about how the *Sydney Morning Herald* was bursting with advertisements on the day he was there. "This Fairfax company is unbelievable," Knight gushed to Black over the phone. "It's got the most fantastic classified advertising business I've ever seen in my life."

"Andrew," Black interjected, "I find it hard enough to get on the airplane to come to London. Certainly you *can't* imagine me going back and forth to Australia."

Warwick Fairfax and Black had met before. In early 1988, Warwick Fairfax had visited Black at his Palm Beach home to solicit a bid for Melbourne's *Age*. In April that year, Black bought the *Spectator* from Fairfax, for about £2 million, and bid about A$500 million for the *Age*. The deal dissolved when Robert Maxwell bested Black's offer. This prompted a flurry of anti-Maxwell sentiment among *Age* journalists and prominent Melbournians, and the Australian government tightened foreign-ownership rules. The paper was taken off the auction block, but not before the Telegraph group had completed the *Spectator* deal, which Fairfax had offered as a "sweetener," according to Dan Colson, Black's lawyer and chief deal adviser in London. "In the end we took the bait but not the hook."

Now, two years later, Black wanted to know who else might be interested in Fairfax. One of Warwick's advisers volunteered that Kerry Packer, Australia's richest man and a long-time Fairfax rival, would no doubt have his eye on the *Sydney Morning Herald* and perhaps other properties, despite having potential cross-media ownership problems. "Oh, Kerry Packer," Black nodded, "didn't he take a coronary?" The unusual construction stuck in one of his visitors' minds. "From this, it seemed that Black didn't know Packer, but I suspect he knew him very well," he said. In fact, Black had been introduced to the garrulous Australian five months earlier over dinner at the London home of the financier Sir James Goldsmith, a mutual friend and Telegraph director. Packer's heart attack had occurred a few months earlier while he was enjoying one of his favourite pastimes, polo.

Over dinner, Black and Packer had discussed the deteriorating Fairfax situation and agreed to stay in touch. Not even someone with Black's well-developed sense of destiny would have bet that he would soon be the central character in one of the most vicious and highly politicized takeover battles that Australia had ever seen. By the time it was over, Black would have crossed swords with no fewer than three former prime ministers and with legions of journalists and corporate rivals. For a time, his involvement in Fairfax would boost Black's celebrated status as a globe-trotting media owner, but his best attempts to impose his will on Australia's leaders would ultimately be frustrated.

A month after Warwick and Black met in Toronto, Fairfax was placed in receivership. Kerry Packer phoned Black a few months later, in May 1991, and said that it was time to get serious about Fairfax; a bid gathered shape amid a flurry of telephone calls and faxes over the next few weeks. Black and Packer met twice more in Packer's permanent suite at London's Savoy Hotel. The more Black looked at the numbers, the more he liked what he saw. In the fiscal year 1991, the company had a pre-tax and pre-interest operating margin of 16.5 per cent, which is better than many newspapers achieve in nonrecessionary times. Black knew that Packer would be limited to a 15 per cent ownership in the company because of laws prohibiting cross-media ownership.*

Black set his sights on being Fairfax's largest shareholder, with at least 20 per cent of the company, depending on how much the Australian government allowed foreigners to own. Packer had invited another foreign partner into the deal: the San Francisco–based investment bank Hellman & Friedman, which managed large pools of money and was looking to make its first investment outside the United States. Packer liked what he knew of Black; they agreed on politics, and they had friends in common, including Sir James Goldsmith and John Aspinall. Nevertheless, he knew Hellman better than he knew Black, and he liked the idea of a financial partner whose interest, combined with his own, might give him control of Fairfax down the road.

Every Australian investment house was on the prowl for a piece of the Fairfax fee bonanza. Among the canniest players was Malcolm Bligh Turnbull, a fiery, brainy former lawyer who knew everyone down under. He had once been Packer's personal lawyer, and his firm's merchant banking services had been retained by Warwick three years earlier to elicit bids for the *Age*. Now, Turnbull & Partners was retained as the exclusive adviser of Fairfax's bondholders, who had backed Warwick's ill-fated buyout. Turnbull reckoned he could arrange for the bondholders to be paid at least 30¢ on the dollar in a

---

* Packer owned the Channel Nine Network, the highest-rated of the country's three commercial television networks.

Fairfax sale. His strategy hinged on suing the banks for having earlier misrepresented the company's financial health. Turnbull liked to say this didn't just give the bondholders a seat at the table but nailed them to it. Without their consent to the sale, the litigation could tie the company up indefinitely. Turnbull's view was that an exclusive arrangement with the bondholders could prove a major strategic advantage for one of the Fairfax bidders.

The brokerage firm Ord Minnett teamed up with Turnbull to bring the bondholders into a consortium and underwrite the eventual deal (gaining Turnbull & Partners another success fee). The first formal meetings of the full consortium took place in Packer's lavish suite at the Savoy on Monday, June 3, 1991, with Turnbull, Ord Minnett's Neville Miles, and the Hellman & Friedman executive Brian Powers among those attending.

Partnerships were not Black's style, but in this case, he could see clear advantages to joining forces with Australia's richest man and signing with the bondholders. A lead investment in Fairfax would gain Hollinger even greater stature on the world stage. The Australian newspaper market was carved up neatly between Fairfax and News Ltd., Rupert Murdoch's subsidiary. With its national broadsheet, the *Australian*, major-market tabloids, and smaller holdings, News Ltd. owned 62 per cent of all papers in the country. Fairfax produced 20 per cent, but the prestige and influence of its titles considerably out-stripped Murdoch's.

Under the initial proposal, the *Daily Telegraph* would take a 20 per cent interest in the corporation that would purchase Fairfax. The corporation would be a dormant Australian company called Tourang. Packer would take the maximum 14.99 per cent allowed under cross-media ownership laws, and Hellman & Friedman would take another 15 per cent. From Packer's standpoint, an investment of around A$180 million wasn't a huge amount to fret over. "Okay, guys, we've now done the deal," Packer declared at one point. "You go and fix it, and I'm going to go and play polo."

Black said that his participation in the bid would be handled by Colson, who was no stranger to complicated deals – during a three-year stint in Hong Kong, Colson had done everything from financing duck farms in China to handling major investments in Canada for the Hong Kong billionaire Li Ka-Shing. Fairfax would be his most complicated and acrimonious assignment yet.

Tourang's bid for Fairfax was not yet public knowledge, but Black couldn't resist dropping a few boastful hints at the Hollinger annual meeting at Toronto's Royal York Hotel that June. He had spoken for some years about using Hollinger's cash flow for acquisitions "when economic conditions open up such opportunities."

Black could also not resist noting that the NDP government in Ontario had indirectly encouraged companies like Hollinger to seek better prospects elsewhere. "The government of Ontario appears to believe that capitalists, including average shareholders, are omnivorous and undiscriminating predators who will greedily pursue a 1 per cent return on their investment or gross revenues with just as much ardour as they would forage for a 10 or 20 per cent return," Black said. "The inevitable consequences of these misconceptions are that capital and talented people will avoid or flee Ontario until a more favourable climate returns." An investment like the one he was privately planning would allow Hollinger "to avoid being unduly inconvenienced by exactly the sort of absurd and punitive parochialism that is now being inflicted in Ontario."

Black arrived in Sydney in mid-July for Tourang's official launch and was bemused by the sight of his face glaring from the cover of the *Bulletin* magazine, and advertisements for it, at newsstands around town. Black was whisked through a cluster of reporters at the airport and driven in a white Rolls-Royce to Ord Minnett's Grosvenor Place office. In the lobby, a second media scrum awaited Black. Showing little evidence of jet lag, the Canadian seemed to enjoy his new audience. How would he like to be seen in Australia, asked one reporter. "As the Samaritanly philanthropist that I am," Black quickly replied. "I'm just here to help you, you know that."

On reading the quote in the *Herald* the next day, Hellman & Friedman's Brian Powers asked in amazement: "Conrad, did you really say that?"

"Yes," Black replied with a grin. "I suppose I did get a bit carried away."

Black spent the day after his arrival in Australia in Canberra, meeting briefly with Prime Minister Bob Hawke and Treasurer John Kerin (whose responsibilities included foreign investment) and lunching with Communications Minister Kim Beazley. There was no question that Fairfax was the most politicized prize Black had yet pursued. The Australian government had a large degree of discretion in determining the appropriate level of overseas ownership. "I hope that my arrival," Black told the *Bulletin*, "will dispel the notion that I have cloven feet and pointy ears." In reality, there were few, if any, preconceptions about Black. For once, someone else – Packer – was the lightning rod.

Black flew to Toronto for the summer, satisfied that he had played his part well. He was in daily contact with Colson and less frequently with the other key players in Tourang, and he saw no pressing need to be in Australia working on the cut and thrust of the deal. "If it had been necessary for me to be there I would have gone. But I didn't see the need. You can make a study of command techniques," Black explained. "Someone like MacArthur did both. Some of his greatest actions were right when he was at the front himself, and equally brilliant ones were when he was hundreds of miles away."

Two other serious bidders emerged, one local, the second another high-profile foreigner. The local group had money and was, in theory, politically attractive. Australian Independent Newspapers (AIN) was a blue-chip group of Melbourne-based investors backed by major institutions and headed by former Qantas chairman Jim Leslie.

The other entry, Tony O'Reilly, was a busy man when he decided to go after Fairfax. This was the year the former international rugby player was paid US$75 million as chairman of H.J. Heinz, earning him the title of the world's highest-paid executive. Somehow, O'Reilly also found time to purchase 30 per cent of Waterford Wedgwood, to sponsor rugby's World Cup, and to bid for Fairfax. In his native Ireland, O'Reilly also controlled the Irish Independent group, the country's largest media company, which published about 60 per cent of the country's newspapers. Although Black called O'Reilly a friend, he dismissed him as not in the same league, calling him a "ketchup salesman" and the "world's greatest leprechaun."

It quickly became clear that Packer was going to be "heavy baggage" for Tourang's bid. Former prime ministers Gough Whitlam and Malcolm Fraser — sworn enemies in Australian politics during the 1970s — joined forces with a group of other former politicians to sign a petition against concentration of media ownership and to express concern about foreign ownership of print media. At one point, Fraser charged that Black was "not a proper person to own media in Australia." The battle was escalating, and the efforts of Whitlam and Fraser ensured that the story spilled out of the business sections and onto the front pages of the country's papers. The fax machines at Canary Wharf and at 10 Toronto Street were humming with each day's clippings. Black decided to launch a few intercontinental verbal missiles of his own, and letters from lawyers representing Packer and Black were faxed to four Fairfax journalists responsible for one of the pamphlets criticizing the men that had been handed out during the protest.

Conrad Black whistled "Waltzing Matilda" as he descended the staircase at Brooks's club in London on the evening of October 22, 1991. He had just excused himself from the dinner and drinks that followed a *Spectator* board meeting, having agreed to a live interview with the Australian journalist Jana Wendt ("the rather pulchritudinous interviewer," he said later). Wendt was the host of *A Current Affair*, a top-rated news program that aired on Packer's Channel Nine Network. The Fairfax story had become a prime-time drama. In the Newman Street studio, Black, clad in a grey suit and sporting a navy tie emblazoned with boxing kangaroos, settled into a chair before a fake-looking backdrop featuring London Bridge.

"How do you rate your chances now of taking out the Fairfax prize?" Wendt began.

"I wouldn't put it in quite such predatory terms. I think our chances are quite good . . . I, of course would have to be brain dead to be unaware of the fact there's some political controversy, which I've found somewhat mystifying."

At the interview's conclusion, Wendt asked Black how badly he wanted Fairfax. "It's hard to quantify. Obviously if I wasn't reasonably highly motivated, I wouldn't have put up with even the inconvenience that I've been subjected to," he replied, levelling a serious glare at the camera. "They're fine papers, but I mean, can I live without it? Will I jump off the bridge behind me as I speak if I don't get it? No, of course I won't."

The following evening, Packer appeared on the program with three Fairfax journalists and was instantly testy. When asked why he had looked overseas for a partner, Packer snapped, "Who are you suggesting . . . for God's sake? Conrad Black is used to running a quality newspaper. Are you really suggesting there are better partners to do that here than him? If so, name one. If not, withdraw the question. *Who* is better than Conrad Black at running the Fairfax group?"

Black followed up his TV appearance with a lengthy interview with the *Sydney Morning Herald*'s New York correspondent, John Lyons, at 10 Toronto Street on November 2. The interview ran verbatim over several pages. This gave him ample space to vent against some of the more irksome criticisms of Tourang and himself. He condemned what he saw as an orchestrated effort to thwart Tourang's bid by his rival Rupert Murdoch. (As it happened, Black had seen Murdoch at a dinner the night before the interview and had told him that the way his papers were carrying on wasn't doing Tourang any favours.)

"It is the corporate policy of News Corp. [Murdoch's main company] that they would prefer not to compete with Packer and me," Black told the Fairfax-owned *Herald*.* "Mr Murdoch has not enjoyed competing with me in London and he would prefer to compete in Australia with people who have less background in the industry . . . No-one has ever accused Rupert of erring on the side [of] excessive quality or independence in his newspapers, which makes all this hypocrisy and bile about them purporting to say how best to maintain the standards of the Fairfax papers almost ridiculous and unworthy of any credence at all."

---

* News Corp.'s managing director Ken Cowley issued a statement the following day calling Black's assertion of a corporate policy on the sale of Fairfax "completely false. There is no corporate policy. To suggest any such policy would be followed by our editors is preposterous."

Black's ire was piqued when Lyons began quizzing him about the various controversies that had surrounded him, such as the Ontario Securities Commission investigation a decade earlier. In a scolding tone, Black replied that if an investigation that went on for almost a year "resulting in absolute exculpation" is "deemed to be a blot on the ledger of somebody, then truly you people who are upholders of professional integrity in the press in Australia should engage in some agonizing, and, as Kissinger would say, 'prayerful' self-analysis.

"You give me some concern that this witch-hunting vocation that the Australian media has demonstrated on this issue is not entirely absent from your own thoughts."

By late November, it became clear that the political pressure on Packer's involvement in the Fairfax bid was working. Packer phoned Black and told him he was withdrawing from the group – a positive development for Black, as it put him squarely in the driver's seat. Now it was just the Telegraph company and Hellman & Friedman against Tony O'Reilly and Australian International Newspapers. Black regretted Packer's departure but knew that with him out of the way Tourang's chances for success were improved. O'Reilly intensified the pressure on Black, labelling him "an interventionist, right-wing, pro-Thatcherite owner." The Irish tycoon explained that Black's and his own views of running newspapers were quite dissimilar. "Lord Thomson of Fleet was my hero. He built some of the greatest papers in the world on a totally non-interventionist basis," he said. Black shot back, "We are not talking about selling snake oil, but the future of Australia's leading newspapers."

The final bids for Fairfax were submitted in early December, and Black and Colson were optimistic, especially because they had the backing of the Fairfax bondholders. The last hurdle was approval from the Foreign Investment Review Board, and this seemed a no-brainer. In October, the Labour Party caucus had issued a policy statement limiting foreign voting equity in media companies to 20 per cent. This was the level of investment in Fairfax that the Telegraph group proposed, with Hellman holding a further 15 per cent in non-voting shares. Once the bids had passed the Foreign Investment Review

Board, the whole affair could be wrapped up before Christmas. But, to Black's dismay, the FIRB ended up ruling that his bid was not in the national interest and instead approved O'Reilly's bid.

Black went ballistic and blasted the decision as "sleazy, venal, and despicable." He told the *Herald*, "We have been the victim of sleazy political lobbying. I'm sure the Australian public are shocked and appalled by these tactics." Black said he suspected that "O'Reilly and his pimps" were behind the lobbying, knowing that Prime Minister Hawke had preferred O'Reilly's bid all along. "I have been portrayed as a fanatical right-winger, an interfering meddler, and that is simply not true, not true."

A reconfigured bid was resubmitted, with the Telegraph company's voting interest reduced to 15 per cent. Hellman & Friedman's non-voting interest was scaled back to a mere 5 per cent. This brought Tourang's foreign ownership level in line with O'Reilly's bid. The new treasurer, Ralph Willis, despite being bedridden with the flu, approved the revised structure on December 13, 1991. At three a.m. on December 16, the banks accepted the receiver's recommendation that Fairfax be sold to Tourang for A$1.6 billion. Just before dawn, Colson telephoned Black to relay the news: Fairfax was his. Black wondered aloud to his friend whether his "sleazy, venal, and despicable" outburst had won the day. Colson didn't think so.

Early the next morning, weary from the twenty-two-hour flight but bearing a full grin, Black strode out of customs at Sydney airport, pinstripe jacket slung over his arm, and straight into the first of several media scrums. Breakfast at the Ritz Carlton was followed by meetings with institutions and lunch at the Union club. Everywhere he went, camera crews and journalists pursued him. Black assured them that no Fairfax journalists were earmarked for "busting," and although the Australians were not familiar with that colloquialism, they deduced that no busting must be a good thing. He added, "Contrary to widespread rumours, it is not a plan of Mr. Colson's or myself to erect a guillotine at Broadway and move journalists through it on a random basis." Asked at one juncture to point out the best and worst aspects of Australian media, he said that on the negative side the press seemed rather preoccupied with itself. On the plus side, Black quipped, "There do seem to be rather attractive women in the field."

As soon as the Telegraph company assumed management control of John Fairfax, Black and Colson began planning to increase its ownership position from 15 per cent to 25 per cent. As the largest shareholder, the Telegraph group called the shots and had the support of the institutions that had backed its bid. But its control was illusory and tenuous – reminiscent for Black of his early Argus days.

The Fairfax contest, and some of Black's public comments, had not endeared him to everyone in Australia's governing Labour Party. Still, the new prime minister, Paul Keating, was the person who would ultimately decide whether Black could increase his interest, and Black claimed to get along with him. Black and Colson began complaining publicly and in private about how they had only 15 per cent of the stock in Fairfax but 100 per cent of the responsibility. It was they, for instance, who brought in Stephen Mulholland, a veteran South African newspaper executive, as Fairfax's CEO. Within a year of their listing Fairfax on the Australian stock exchange at A$1 a share, the stock was trading at A$2.02 based on early plans to cut costs and upgrade printing facilities. Black's investment had grown by more than A$100 million. In the year ended June 30, 1992, Fairfax recorded earnings before depreciation, interest, and tax of A$152 million on revenue of A$729 million, despite operating in the worst recession since the Great Depression. Between them, the *Herald* and the *Age* had a stranglehold on classified advertising, commanding more than 80 per cent of their respective markets, against competition from Murdoch's tabloids.

Fairfax's improving results and share price might have led Black to expect a warmer reception when he returned to Australia for the first annual meeting of John Fairfax Holdings, held at the Sydney Opera House on November 25, 1992. But the wounds of the Fairfax contest festered. Among the 800 shareholders packed into the concert hall was Malcolm Turnbull, the banker who had represented Fairfax's bondholders in the company auction. Now Turnbull was spearheading a legal challenge in the Federal Court to a proposed executive option plan that had the appearance of free money being given to top Fairfax executives.

The meeting dragged on for most of the day, with Turnbull filibustering and portraying the option plan – which was withdrawn over a technical error – as a moral victory for Fairfax shareholders and a public humiliation for Black. Afterwards, both men laid claim to the most applause. It was another episode in Black's career that would be defined as much by his irascible style as by what he actually accomplished.

"Normally I take Malcolm fairly light-heartedly," said Black. "He is a fairly histrionic and picturesque character. He does a great deal of to-ing and fro-ing and every now and then gets a little out of control. It's a pity. Malcolm is a talent and an attractive man but he involves himself in these quixotries and renders himself susceptible to really serious questions about both his judgments and his efforts."

Turnbull's impression of Black was equally complimentary. "When he is here, he tends to give very colourful and verbose speeches to all and sundry, most of which are couched in terms that are difficult to understand. Some of the things he said just don't make sense. You sometimes wonder whether he doesn't have a sort of random word selector somewhere in his brain. Words just sort of pop out. It's a bit odd."

Chapter Sixteen

MEDIA MERGER

The thrill of planting his flag in the South Pacific was bitter-sweet for Conrad Black, who returned to Canada to face the demise of his thirteen-year marriage. He and Joanna had been estranged since September 1991, when, after they had spent the summer together in Toronto, she had remained there with their three children and he had returned to England. But Black wanted to maintain appearances and had asked Joanna not to tell anyone of their difficulties, not even the children. Among outsiders and friends, speculation grew that Joanna disliked London and was having difficulty fitting in with society there. "She was just an appendage," said one ·London friend of Conrad's.

The Blacks had grown apart. Bright, lively Joanna did not aspire to being a fixture on the London social circuit. Black's position exposed him to a fascinating array of people and events, but Joanna was not interested in establishing a salon with him. She wanted to spend time with their children, who, she estimated, saw Conrad for only a day and a half a week, on Saturday afternoons and Sundays. Looking back over their relationship some time later, she recalled the qualities that had attracted her to the young *Duplessis* author in 1977: "I was attracted to the *real* Conrad Black – the person that is under there," she explained. "When I first met him I didn't see that real person, I saw this arrogant stuffed shirt. But after a while I realized that underneath that arrogance was a wonderful, vulnerable, very shy man."

Following their move to England two years earlier, Joanna had seen the private Black transforming more and more into his public persona. "Conrad is very quotable because I think he's living in a book," she explained. She thought that her husband had plotted out the life story of a great man and was determined to live it. "Conrad had written his life, and he had it all planned out," she said. "And everything he spoke was quotable. Not to me – he would say, 'Let's get a pizza' to me – but if he was being interviewed by somebody or if he was at a dinner party with people there of interest or influence, he would be very quotable, very colourful."

After they separated, Joanna flew over to London twice, once for a wedding and later for the October 1991 Hollinger Dinner, held at Lord Rothschild's Spencer House and again featuring Prime Minister Margaret Thatcher as the speaker. The guests, including William F. Buckley, Lord Carrington, and Henry Kissinger, milled around one of the house's grand rooms before dinner. At one point, one of the guests touched Joanna Black lightly on the arm. It was Barbara Amiel, the former *Maclean's* columnist who now also wrote for the *Sunday Times* and was a long-time friend of Conrad's.

"Joanna," Amiel said in her soft manner, "you *must* come back to England or you'll lose him."

Joanna returned Amiel's light touch. "Barbara," she replied, "he'll lose me."

Amiel had already made her excuses and left the dinner before Thatcher's speech in order to fulfill an engagement on the television show *Newsnight*, where she gave typically provocative opinions on the sexual misconduct allegations against the U.S. Supreme Court justice Clarence Thomas.

The next month, the Blacks attended the twentieth-anniversary celebration of the *Toronto Sun* newspaper at Toronto's SkyDome, where they were photographed happily chatting to each other and noshing on popcorn. But soon after this event, they told their children and a few friends that they were separating. Black returned to London, then flew to Palm Beach from Australia. In late December

Joanna flew to Palm Beach to join Conrad for the Canadian senator and businessman Trevor Eyton's annual holiday party.

Since October it had been painfully clear to Black that the marriage was over. He whimsically noted later that their house in Toronto had been transformed into a "seminary." His wife's interest in Catholicism (her father was Catholic, her mother Protestant) had been renewed after their move to London but was different from his. Black was dismayed, for instance, by Joanna's preference for the more pedestrian Westminster Cathedral over the grandeur of Brompton Oratory.

Joanna had grown close to a priest who had left the clergy soon after their meeting; following the Blacks' divorce, the couple married. Speaking of the effect the marriage breakup had on him, Black said: "For months after my wife left me, I lived like a Benedictine monk, trying to decide what to do, whether to try to save my marriage."

When news of the breakup began to circulate, one British friend asked Joanna, "How could you leave a man on his way up?" Another friend in Toronto was astonished that she would leave a man who will "eat anything you put in front of him." Of her split with Conrad, Joanna said simply, "I didn't leave him for anybody. I left him for me."

The dissolution of his marriage left Black – who considered himself an "exemplary husband" – wounded, and for a time he was much less visible on the London social circuit. "I can remember Conrad often looking terminally glum and gloomy, and obviously one didn't know why at that stage," recalled *Telegraph* editor Max Hastings. After some dark days of lonely reflection at his Highgate mansion in late autumn – interspersed with Fairfax plotting – Black decided to get on with his personal life. There were any number of attractive female acquaintances whom friends thought he could have pursued: Marie-Josée Drouin (who later married the New York leveraged-buyout king Henry Kravis), Cathy Ford, and Princess Firyal of Jordan among them. According to Black's autobiography, *A Life in Progress*, however, it did not take long for Barbara Amiel to be elevated from "cordial acquaintance" to "the summit of my most ardent and uncompromising desires."

Amiel had made it abundantly clear over the years that Black was her type. In 1990 she called him "my role model." Shortly after he acquired the *Daily Telegraph* she wrote, "I never have noticed how he handles knotting his tie or washing behind his ears, because he handles words with such considerable skill . . . I have always been intrigued by the manifestations of Conrad Black. He understands power." In a prescient article in the Canadian monthly *Chatelaine* entitled "Why Women Marry Up," she observed that "power is sexy, not simply in its own right, but because it inspires self-confidence in its owner and a shiver of subservience on the part of those who approach it."

When Black began pursuing Amiel in mid-November, she was reportedly involved with the screenwriter William Goldman and contemplating a new life in New York. She was so surprised by Black's advances that she suggested he see a psychiatrist. "She was worried that Conrad was not in a sane frame of mind at the end of his marriage," recalled Miriam Gross, a *Sunday Telegraph* editor and one of Amiel's closest friends. He went, at her bidding. Black was diagnosed as sane.

At Conrad's request, Joanna had held off announcing their separation, but now she warned that it "wouldn't be right" for him to take up with Amiel so publicly after the recent news of the split. It would appear, she predicted, that Amiel was the cause of the breakup. But Conrad told Joanna he was "not going to make the same mistakes with Barbara" that he had made with Joanna when he had concealed her pregnancy before they were married. "I'm not going to keep her in a closet."

The Blacks had attended various social events together and had even lived under the same roof at various points during the summer and winter of 1991. But they were not living as husband and wife. When they sat down in May 1992 to finalize the details of their divorce, Black first proposed that the date of separation be set at the previous September, when he had returned to London and Joanna had stayed in Toronto. She had countered that December was appropriate, because that was when their children and friends had been told. After all, she had wanted to leave him in June but had for months maintained the charade that their marriage was intact, at his request.

From Joanna's perspective, her husband had wanted to keep under wraps the fact that she had left him, to give him time to get his personal life in order. Once he had begun seeing someone new, he could appear like a man in control rather than one whose wife had left him. When the bickering over the date of separation began to get heated, they agreed simply to backdate it to May 1991, and to divorce as quickly as possible. Conrad wanted it agreed that Joanna could not change their children's surnames and that, after he paid her a lump-sum monetary settlement, she could not come back for more. Joanna wanted Conrad to agree to the same terms.

By early January – within weeks of the Blacks' children hearing the sad news from their parents – the first reports linking Amiel and Black began to appear in the British, then the Toronto, press. In mid-June 1992, Stephen Grant, a lawyer representing Black in his motion for a divorce from Joanna, submitted his client's affidavit to a Toronto family court judge.

In London, the talk was of what an exciting salon the union of Conrad and Barbara would create. Amiel, the thrice-married neo-conservative, occupied a special place in British newspaper punditry. "She looks like Gina Lollobrigida and writes like Bernard Levin – and do get it the right way round," a friend said in 1988.

In Toronto, the angle was that journalism's femme fatale had snared her ultimate catch. The tabloid *Toronto Sun* reacted to news of the dalliance by featuring Amiel as its daily Sunshine Girl – "beauteous and brainy, right-wing and right on" – trotting out an old photo of her in the skimpy red and black showgirl number and fishnet stockings that she had once donned for a fundraiser.

Although she had not lived in Canada since 1985, Amiel was still a well-known personality, through her columns for the *Sun* and *Maclean's* magazine. Before she went overseas she had left an indelible stamp on Toronto both as a writer and, briefly, as the first female editor of the *Toronto Sun*. "Conrad and Barbara can say big words to each other," commented the Toronto socialite Catherine Nugent, "words that Shirley/Joanna had never heard of." Another sniffed, "They're doing this to spice up their CVs. He needs sex for his image, she needs power."

Amiel professed that she wanted to keep private matters private, but, like Black, she could not allow the barbs to go unchallenged.

"Now, the knives are drawn," Amiel wrote in her monthly column in *Maclean's*. "My marriages and even the cup of coffee I had with a friend become 'an item' in My Past . . . The upside of all the nasty remarks that peppered the Canadian press about my friendship with Conrad Black is that, speaking for myself, happiness is an elusive bluebird and all the screechings in the world can't make its song sound any less sweet."

She and Black shared a similar world view, but in many respects Black could not have found someone more unlike himself. "You couldn't think of two people with more differing backgrounds," observed the financier and Hollinger director Peter Munk, "and yet they really are soulmates."

While Conrad Black was making his name in the realm of corporate conquest in the late 1970s and early 1980s, Barbara Amiel was establishing herself as a figure of comparable notoriety. In those days, Black would send the journalist annual holiday wishes for "an ideologically uplifting Christmas." When Black held a party for Andy Warhol at the Art Gallery of Ontario in 1981, Amiel was on the guest list.*

She was a self-promotion machine who derived obvious satisfaction from rattling the establishment, dispensing potent opinions, and seeing her name in the papers. In 1980, aged thirty-nine, Amiel published her autobiography, *Confessions*. Intended as a journal of ideological self-discovery – her upbringing was British Marxist and she had attended the Communist World Youth Festival in Helsinki in 1962 – it was more noted for chronicling a troubled but adventurous life in sometimes embarrassing detail. *Confessions* revealed the evolution of an uneasy soul, toughened by harsh experience that also left her insecure and vulnerable. Like her new love, Amiel was a night owl. "I've suffered from insomnia all my life," she once explained. "My earliest memory as a child of four was being sedated to sleep."

Amiel was born into a comfortable middle-class Jewish family in east London in 1940. Her father was a lawyer and a colonel, her

---

* Warhol painted a three-panelled portrait of Black.

mother a nurse. They divorced when Barbara was nine, and in 1952 her mother married a draftsman and the family emigrated to Canada. They settled in the steel town of Hamilton, Ontario, where her Anglican stepfather had a difficult time supporting the family of five.

Relations between Barbara and her mother were tense. When she was fifteen, the family moved about half an hour away to St. Catharines, but Amiel remained in Hamilton. She spent the next year boarding with strangers in basements and working odd jobs in drugstores, canning factories, and dress shops while attending school.

After a year, Amiel had a tenuous reconciliation with her family and rejoined them in St. Catharines. Shortly after, she received devastating news from England: her father had committed suicide.

Amiel was remembered by former classmates in St. Catharines as being erudite, worldly, and (despite her own image of herself) beautiful. She read *Punch*, listened to opera, and spent summers with relatives in England. On a bursary, Amiel enrolled at the University of Toronto in 1959 to study philosophy and English. There she met her first husband, Gary Smith, a tall, handsome political science student who hailed from the upper-class enclave of Forest Hill. They dated for four years, but their 1963 marriage lasted less than nine months.

After university, Amiel joined the CBC as a typist. She quickly ascended to script assistant and eventually to on-air interviewer. She was not a great success on television and later deprecated herself as "a lacquered apparition with bouffant hair, glazed smile, and detachment bordering on the unconscious often reinforced by the mandatory dosage of Elavil." Amiel was addicted to Elavil, an antidepressant, for seven years. She began taking pills in university to cope with stress and fatigue and was known to pop as many as twenty painkillers a day. She said that her only experience with marijuana, to which she reacted badly, was in a Times Square hotel room with the poet and singer Leonard Cohen.

At the age of twenty-four, while a script assistant at the CBC, Amiel had an illegal abortion. "I believe it to be morally wrong," she later wrote. "At the time I had my own abortion I believed it to be morally wrong." But rather than waiting four more months for the child's birth, "I chose murder instead."

Amiel's second husband was the motorcycle-jacket-clad poet and journalist George Jonas. With Jonas, Amiel co-authored her first book, *By Persons Unknown*, about an infamous murder in which a Canadian businessman took out a contract on his wife, a model. Her marriage to the Hungarian emigré lasted five years, until 1979, when she left him for Sam Blyth, a travel agent thirteen years her junior. The relationship with Blyth didn't last long, but Amiel and Jonas remained close friends.

One of her career highlights was an account of a trip to Mozambique in early 1981, when she and two male companions were imprisoned for ten days for entering the country without a visa. At one point, Amiel said, she ate her press card to avoid being identified. That year, she became a columnist for the tabloid *Toronto Sun* and then its editor.

In 1983, she met the cable television magnate David Graham, and a year later the Ottawa Valley native became her third husband. The Blacks were among the guests who feted the marriage at a lavish party at Toronto's Sutton Place Hotel. Amiel resigned her editorship of the *Toronto Sun* and moved to England with Graham in 1985, but the marriage was dissolved three years later. She had no children by her three marriages.

Once in England, Amiel pounded the pavement to find a job as a columnist. But her Canadian credentials did not immediately open any doors. One of her earliest interviews was with *Sunday Telegraph* editor Peregrine Worsthorne. "I remember it very well because this was still in Fleet Street," said Worsthorne. "She was sexy, slinky, beautifully dressed, and she was wearing some enormously sexy scent. You had to walk down the corridor in this very old building and scent, therefore, would climb. She stayed about an hour." Worsthorne enjoyed meeting her but did not offer her a job. Conrad Black sent *Daily Telegraph* editor Max Hastings a note about Amiel, mentioning that she was a girlfriend of George Weidenfeld's and an acquaintance from Canada, and proposing that Hastings meet with her. "On the appointed day, a vision of fine cheekbones and huge deep, penetrating eyes surmounted by a mane of black hair swept into my office, swathed in furs," Hastings later wrote in his memoir, *Editor*. "I have seldom been so discomfited." Summarizing the meeting in a memo to Black, he wrote: "I saw Barbara Amiel. I cannot say that I think it was one of my great performances, in that after a 45-minute chat, she told me she found me most frightening. I said that made two of us."

By the time she and Graham split, Amiel had been hired by the *Times* and had established herself as one of its top columnists, dispensing opinions first on the women's page against feminists, gay rights, and state-financed abortions. The magazine *Tatler* dubbed her "Wapping's own Iron Lady," and in 1988 she was runner-up in the Press Association's Best Columnist category. In 1991 she became the lead political columnist in the *Sunday Times*. Around that time Hastings had a further conversation with Amiel about becoming a *Telegraph* contributor, but nothing came of it. Nonetheless Hastings always remembered Black's caution: "I think it is quite in order to proceed with Ms. Amiel, but don't feel that you are being urged to pay her more than you think she is worth."

Despite her blossoming career, Amiel was not universally accepted by the British in-crowd. Just as she was whispered about in Toronto for her thickening Oxonian accent, in London Amiel was often treated as an outsider, neither truly a Canadian nor a Brit. And her outspoken views did not make her universally welcome. "The fashionable intellectual world in English journalism tends to be among those on the left," noted her friend Miriam Gross. "To be ideological is not British at all." Joanna Black recalled running into Amiel in a shop on Sloane Street a few months after the Blacks had taken up residence in London in 1990. Amiel congratulated Joanna on how well she was doing in London and how she must have done the right thing to become so popular. "Everybody likes you," she recalled Amiel telling her. "It's terrible not to be liked."

Amiel refused to discuss her personal life when queried by journalists, yet when it came to her own writing it seemed she couldn't stop talking about it. "I so loathe the permissive promiscuous society and so long for fidelity, stability and monogamy, but it is always just out of my reach," she lamented in *Chatelaine* magazine in 1980. "There is a thing called discipline. I have tried to inflict it on my work. I've tried to inflict it on me. But all that emerges is self-indulgence. Really, I won't talk about my personal life because I am ashamed of it."

In June 1992, Black had other pressing matters to attend to. At Hollinger's annual meeting in Toronto, he took time out from revelling in the Fairfax victory to deliver yet another of his considered tirades against Ontario's NDP government: "Ontario has the distinction of being practically the only jurisdiction in the world except for Cuba and North Korea that officially discourages the incentive system. No serious businessman can coexist comfortably with such a regime."

The next evening, a red rose tucked into the lapel of his tuxedo, Black stood expectantly while a light tapping of silver against crystal silenced the dining room at the Toronto Club. It was the annual Hollinger Dinner, Amiel was his escort, and the guest speaker was Richard Nixon. "As emotionalism has subsided," Black said of the once-disgraced president, "he has been seen to be a profoundly and widely esteemed figure, an elder statesman. I think there has been no American political leader since Thomas Jefferson who has been in the forefront of the country's attention for so long." (Black's views on the former president had clearly evolved from a decade earlier, when Black told the biographer Peter Newman that Nixon was "sleazy, tasteless and neurotic" and "deserves the compassion due to sick people.")

Before introducing Nixon, Black scanned the room, playfully acknowledging some of his high-powered guests. He introduced Dwayne Andreas, head of the giant food processor Archer Daniels Midland, as "allegedly the most politically influential businessman in the United States . . . a man who because he is in the agribusiness masquerades as a bit of a hayseed"; he noted that Cardinal Emmett Carter, his close friend and spiritual adviser, was "dressed tonight in his raiment as the ecumenical chaplain of 10 Toronto Street, as well as the ecclesiastical Toronto stringer for the *Jerusalem Post*"; Lee and Walter Annenberg were recognized for having served as ambassadors to Britain under Nixon. "Above all else," Black said of Annenberg, he was "the man who sold *TV Guide* and the *Daily Racing Form* to Rupert Murdoch for one billion dollars more than they were worth."

Nixon took the podium and, before beginning his lecture on international politics, said he was impressed by his host. "I thought I knew something about American history, but he knows far more. And it was fascinating to hear him recount speeches that he could remember – that even I have made."

Two weeks after the Hollinger Dinner and six days after the uncontested petition was filed, Conrad and Joanna Black's divorce was granted. "You and I wouldn't have a hope of getting [a divorce] as quickly as that," the Toronto lawyer Erica James commented in the *Globe and Mail*. Less than a month after that, on the late morning of July 21, 1992, Max Hastings waited on the steps of the Chelsea registry office holding a bouquet while ignoring the taunts – "Are those for me, love?" – of a vagrant.

Black arrived for his second wedding wearing a dark double-breasted suit, and Amiel wore a green and white dress from Place Vendôme. Black's old friend Brian Stewart, now a senior television journalist with the CBC, flew to London to be his witness; Miriam Gross was Amiel's.

Amiel had recently attended the wedding of Lord Weidenfeld to Annabel Whitestone at the same registry office, and it did not escape her that the brief ceremony contained not a hint of the grandeur one might expect of the nuptials of Conrad Black. Presumably because Black was Catholic and Amiel Jewish, they chose not to wed in a church. And, under section 45 of the Marriage Act, religious references are barred from registry office ceremonies.

Two days before their wedding was set to take place, Black and Amiel met with the Chelsea registrar, Norman Stephens, for a routine prenuptial chat. Warned of the blandness of the ceremony by his bride-to-be, Black asked Stephens whether he and Amiel could not produce "a more resonant rationale for our desire to marry than 'the absence of any legal impediment to do so.'" As Amiel later related in a *Sunday Times* column, Stephens looked puzzled. "I was thinking of God," Black explained.

"Mr Stephens looked very glum at this," Amiel recalled, "and repeated that any cribbing from known ecclesiastical ceremonies such as 'love, honour and obey', was out, never mind God." However, no one tells Conrad Black what to do, and he unleashed a barrage at the hapless civil servant about how Parliament might have the right to dictate how a bureaucrat performs his job, but it had no business muzzling what he and his intended could say at their own marriage. To defuse tensions, Amiel pulled out some words she had written "in perfect samizdat language" for the service and ran them by the registrar, who was satisfied they did not contravene the law. "They were horribly pompous," Amiel admitted of the phrases she had composed, "all about 'human beings are more than blood and flesh and city and state' and ending up with a vow to my future husband of true love in the 'name of my fathers, their fathers, and the faith and beliefs that have sustained us through time.'"

For Black, the Marriage Act was just another obstacle to be intellectually outsmarted. "I, too, should like to add to the ceremony," Black ventured. "I wish to say that, were it appropriate, I would pledge what was normal in a Christian ecclesiastical marriage oath, but as that is not appropriate, I would like it recorded that the sentiments in that oath are the ones I hold."

That night, the newlyweds celebrated by dining at exclusive Annabel's, in a private room. The twenty-odd guests included the Duchess of York, Lord and Lady Weidenfeld, Lord Rothschild, Baroness Thatcher and Sir Denis Thatcher, the broadcaster David Frost, former U.S. assistant secretary for national security policy Richard Perle, and Brian Stewart and his wife. Hollinger president David Radler and his wife, Rona, flew over from Canada.

To some, the event had a showy, "rent-a-celebrity" quality about it, with most of the attendees hailing from Black's new life as proprietor of the *Telegraph*. In the text beneath the photo of the couple looking adoringly at each other on the Chelsea registry steps, the next day's *Daily Telegraph* dutifully noted that "the couple, who have homes in London, Toronto and Palm Beach, leave today for an extended holiday and working trip in North America." Black stopped at his home after the ceremony, to change in preparation for the trip, and found, slipped through his letter box, a couriered handwritten note from Prime Minister John Major wishing him and Barbara well.

The first stop on the trip was New York, via the Concorde, where they dined that evening at La Côte Basque with William F. Buckley, his wife, Pat, and John O'Sullivan, Buckley's successor as editor of the *National Review* and a close friend of Amiel's. "It was a very chirpy evening and they had some political disagreement at dinner," Buckley recalled. "Nothing deep. Decriminalizing drugs. She was pro, he was not. Certainly their conversation suggested that she had by no means been satellized in the twenty-four hours they'd been married." A few days later the pair attended a dinner and concert at the Buckleys' home, and from there they went to a Maine cottage owned by David Rockefeller, where they were joined by Black's children. There Amiel bashed out her weekly column, choosing her wedding as its topic. Black had vacationed at the cottage with his former wife and their children the previous year. The cottage had no television, let alone a fax, and Black played the role of dutiful husband as he drove around trying to find a fax machine in order to send his wife's column to his chief competitor.

Black and Amiel soon took another trip, to Fiji and Australia, and his friends and employees began to notice a marked difference in Black's demeanour as well as in the company he kept. One noted drily that Joanna had kept Conrad's feet on the ground, certainly "more so than his present wife."

"They've become incredibly glamorous as a couple," observed Miriam Gross. "One notices when they come into a room at a party. Everyone knows that they're important including, I think, themselves." Max Hastings, for one, noted that the gloom that had surrounded Black after his first marriage had fallen apart quickly lifted. "Nowadays," he said a year after the wedding, "he's absolutely full of the joys of spring, and terribly happy. I mean, dealing with him on business things is incredibly easy. He's infinitely more relaxed, he enjoys the social rounds terrifically. I think he feels comfortable with himself and the life he's living. You know, he's just a completely different person."

"I think that sex played a very, very big role," said one long-time friend of both Blacks. "He couldn't stop smiling. And Barbara catered to him in a way that really made him a happy boy. I don't know how you define love, but that goes a long way toward love."

Conrad and Barbara lived at the home in Highgate for almost a year, but it was far from Amiel's habitual lunches in the centre of town or coffees at Harvey Nichols. And, Amiel complained to friends, there was a long walk from the house to a waiting car, which ruined her hair. The house was put up for sale and the Blacks moved into a rented home on Chester Square with the Black feline, Max (named by his children and not after Hastings). Friends began to notice that Black was doing things that he had said he would never do, such as living in a row house, contemplating the installation of a tennis court at his Palm Beach home, and wearing shorts. Though she was four years Black's senior, it was almost as if Amiel were making him younger. "They're intellectually very well suited," said Gross. "He has these obsessive interests in Napoleon or Cardinal Newman which she doesn't necessarily share but finds amusing and funny."

Amiel encouraged Black to exercise and to update his wardrobe – and then their home. Several months into their marriage, the Blacks found new digs on Kensington's Cottesmore Gardens, paying about £3.5 million for a four-level nineteenth-century townhouse most recently owned by the fallen Australian tycoon Alan Bond. One of its most alluring features, according to its selling agent, was an "environmental chamber," an upmarket sauna room that blew cold or warm winds to simulate the climate of virtually any locale: "It's an all-round paradise and you can transport yourself to any part of the world." The newlyweds hired the architect Anthony Collett to make major renovations and to collaborate with the designer David Mlinaric, whose work included the Royal Opera House and projects for J. Paul Getty Jr., Lord Rothschild, and Mick Jagger. The property is actually two large homes joined together, and the renovations called for a new grey slate mansard roof (which met with opposition from local council members because it threatened the uniformity of the street) and a single front door. Inside, it featured a gymnasium, Jacuzzi and pool, eleven bedrooms, eight bathrooms, and two elevators. The environmental chamber did not survive the redesign. "I was always skeptical it would work properly," Black said with a shrug, adding, "It's not my style to sit there and try to simulate a South Sea island."

Two years after they bought the house, the renovation was completed and the Blacks moved in. Along the way, their new neighbours had insisted the plans be scaled back, calling them a "folie de grandeur" and "pretentious." Black fired off a sardonic letter saying, "I look forward . . . to reciprocating your helpful spirit of neighbourliness."

For Black, a mahogany-panelled library inspired by the Duff Cooper Library in the British embassy in Paris was filled with books and an 1810 English desk, on top of which sat the requisite bronze of Napoleon. The U-shaped second-floor living room had an international feel with such touches as an eighteenth-century Chinese leather screen and a nineteenth-century Tabriz carpet; portraits by Sir Joshua Reynolds and George Stubbs hung over the fireplaces. One thing that was clear from the renovation, including the massive industrial-scale stainless-steel kitchen, was that the Blacks intended their home to be a salon, capable of accommodating dinner parties for fifty and bigger gatherings of 350 guests. The architects took out part of the second floor to make a high-ceilinged formal dining room. Collett explained, "You walk down the main staircase, through the marble-floored entrance hall and along a balcony at the upper level of the dining room for a view down to the candlelit glamour of the table below. It's like coming into the upper rows of a theatre, seeing a glowing and opulent set on the stage, then descending to be part of the performance. The staircase is deliberately narrow, a bit confining; guests lose sight of the room just before they emerge into it." The second floor also boasted *papier peint* walls with images of trees that took a year to complete and *trompe l'oeil* draperies.

To some visitors, the house seemed less a home than a diorama of how a press lord should live, with all the trappings but somehow devoid of personal taste. In Cottesmore, the Blacks would hold their summer cocktail party and many other events, in honour of various dignitaries and royals. "He had adopted a social profile. It was a jet-setty kind of crowd," recalled one Telegraph director. "Conrad invited and people came. But his social contacts tended to be more of the big business men or the aristocrats. Everything was always heavy-hitter, and that gave him great satisfaction. And, in that sense, he was a generous host." Indeed, the Blacks would entertain guests like the actress Candice Bergen, the playwright Tom Stoppard, Elton John, and assorted dukes and earls. "You go to an English party, and you get some cheap white plonk," noted Taki Theodoracopulos, a columnist for Black's *Spectator* magazine in London. "You go to one of their parties, and you eat and drink to your heart's content."

The Blacks hired a cook and a butler, who would fly ahead to Toronto or Palm Beach to prepare for their arrival. The butler, Werner Jankowsky, had been a fixture at Toronto's Sutton Place Hotel, where around-the-clock butler service had been an advertised feature until the hotel ran into financial difficulties and was sold in 1993.

In a story entitled "Is This London's Most Powerful Woman?" the *Evening Standard* explored the percolating theory that Amiel was a nineties version of Pamela, the glamorous late spouse of Lord Hartwell. Less charitable comparisons were made with Yoko Ono. Friends took up Amiel's defence. After all, she was an easy target – ambitious, brainy, successful, attractive, and decidedly politically incorrect. As her husband saw it, she was "made the subject of all sorts of common tittle-tattle about her private life and how she used, allegedly, her physical attributes to advance her career . . . [Such stories] have had no other basis than the envy extended toward an attractive, intelligent woman."

Black appointed her to the boards of the *Spectator* and *Saturday Night* and made her the head of the private Black Foundation, replacing Joanna. It was around this time that Black encouraged a shake-out of the *Telegraph* newsroom that saw deputy editor Trevor Grove sacked and replaced by Simon Heffer, signalling a toughening of the paper's conservative bent. When asked by a *Maclean's* scribe whether Amiel steered his guidance of the *Telegraph*, Black's eyes narrowed. "I was aware that there was a myth that had floated around – though I thought it had died by now – that my wife was exercising some Mephistophelian influence on my relations with the editor. I can assure you none of that is true."

It was not difficult to discern Amiel's influence on at least one article that found its way into the *Daily Telegraph* on the last day of 1992. Black had written various weighty contributions to the paper since moving to London, including commentary on the Canadian elections and a review of the *Oxford Book of Canadian Military Anecdotes*. But on December 31, the *Daily Telegraph* published what was believed to be the first contribution by a British newspaper proprietor to the fashion pages.

Before Christmas of that year, at a party organized for the newspaper's department heads by Max Hastings, Black had scolded fashion editor Kathryn Samuels for writing favourably about long skirts. Standing her ground, Samuels countered that Black was welcome to write an article arguing the opposing view. Black was reluctant, but another piece in his paper on December 28 that advised "a long, slim skirt is a basic essential" was too much for him. A more autocratic proprietor might have simply had the editor replaced for insubordination, but this was not Black's approach. During a holiday in Florida, Black wrote what he described as "a personal offensive against the efforts of the long skirt brigade to kill off the short skirt." Black wrote, "The frenzied efforts of the long faction to pretend that the short has been exterminated other than among the perverse, the penniless or the reactionary enemies of style is outrageous . . . It is bunk to claim that long is in, short is out and anything above the knee, as the *Daily Telegraph* wrote of the Princess of Wales, is dowdy." The article was accompanied by photos of various women in short skirts, including the princess and Barbara Amiel.

It remained a matter of curiosity that Black had chosen a career journalist as his bride. After all, Black was not exactly a champion of the craft. "Many journalists and most of the more talented ones," Black has said – and more than once, "are happy to chronicle the doings and sayings of others, but a significant number, including many of the most acidulous and misanthropic are, in my experience, inexpressibly envious of many of the subjects of their attention."

The answer may have been that Amiel's regard for journalism was only a few notches higher than her husband's. In 1993, when

Margaret Thatcher's memoirs were England's publishing sensation, Amiel wrote a column condemning the editor of *Harpers & Queen*, Vicki Woods, for deceptively turning a photo shoot with the former prime minister into an article about her comments and actions throughout the shoot. (Woods's article, incidentally, ran in the Black-owned *Spectator*.) Amiel wrote that Emperor Franz Josef "hit the nail on the head when he described journalists as *canailles*. Today that means rogues, but as I understand it he used it in the sense of scum or sewers." Amiel did not buy Woods's explanation that the idea for the article arose only after she witnessed the photo shoot.

"I am a journalist myself and I think we are all made of *merde* and the craft is *merde*," wrote Amiel. "Why, I ask myself, does someone stay in a wretched occupation like journalism? Anything other than straight news reporting often forces us to become courtiers of people we dislike or resort to little ruses even with those we admire to get our copy – a host of smarm [*sic*] and iffy relationships that brings me out in spots half the time. After each profile I write I vow never to play the game again. And then the vow is broken. Why?" Amiel called on one of her favourite references, Adam Smith, to provide the answer, and explained somewhat mildly that while journalists may live in the sewer, they prevent from arising "an even worse sewer, that of star chambers and secret power-holders in high places."

Writing in the *Evening Standard*, the press critic Stephen Glover compared her argument to "one of those brutes who go on the rampage, spraying bullets in all directions, before turning the gun upon herself." Glover argued that just because Amiel's personal circumstances had changed, she was not justified in her attack. "Now that she is rich, Mrs Conrad Black gives the impression she wants to be on the inside. She feels differently about her chosen profession, which is not all that glamorous. Perhaps she looks forward to intimate parties and grand holidays, interspersed with a little gentle charity work."

Echoing her husband's trait of not leaving anything alone, in a subsequent column, Amiel responded that "one of the differences between me and my sisters in the women's movement is that I do not regard my husband's money as my own. Having married very wealthy men before my current husband, I can guarantee that I parted from them leaving both their fortunes and my opinions intact." Amiel said that she had been called a bitch "all my life and did not need the authority of money to be one." Hers was the classic celebrity line that she had not changed, those around her had. "Me, I continue to be moody, opinionated, a bit driven and all the things that rubbed people the wrong way before I met Conrad, and rubbed some the right way which was responsible for my getting a column and other jobs.

"Ultimately, I am a north London Jew who has read a bit of history. That means I know this: in a century that has seen the collapse of the Austro-Hungarian, British and Soviet empires, reversal of fortune is this rich bitch's reality; one might as well keep working and have the family's Vuitton suitcases packed."

Fast-forward to a sunny Toronto afternoon in June 1994: Conrad and Barbara Amiel Black, as she was now known, milled about with shareholders following the Hollinger annual meeting at the King Edward Hotel. By now Amiel had resigned her *Times* column and transferred her allegiance and her writing wholly to the *Telegraph*. Her husband had hired Amiel as vice-president of editorial for all the newspapers in the Hollinger stable, at a handsome salary, and added her to the company's main board of directors. It was Amiel's first annual meeting as a Hollinger director, and a reporter pointed out that she was the first true journalist to join the board.

"Mind you, you were the one who wrote they were *canailles*," Conrad said playfully.

"Yes," replied Amiel, "they are *canailles*, but they're necessary, too."

"Barbara, if I didn't think journalists were necessary I wouldn't employ them. And indeed," he said, placing his arm affectionately around his wife, "our relationship might be quite different."

Chapter Seventeen

THE HUNT

I n the early 1990s, the worst recession since the Great Depression blanketed much of the Western world. It was a time of introspection and retrenching in all industries, including the media business. The legendary investor Warren Buffett, with more than US$1 billion invested in media stocks, ventured that the "media business will prove considerably less marvellous than I, the industry, or lenders thought would be the case only a few years ago." Metromedia chairman John Kluge declared of the marketplace: "It's murder out there."

Yet the *Telegraph* was proving resilient to the downturn, in part thanks to its strategy of cover-price increases. This meant the paper was less dependent on advertising revenue, which was tied directly to the economy. Although the company's budgets would be reduced as advertising revenue fell, the *Telegraph* would prove to be more profitable than all the other quality U.K. dailies combined during the recession. More important to Black than profit and loss columns was cash flow – the amount of actual money available to finance activities in a given year. In 1990 it was holding steady at £32.6 million – enough to cover interest payments on debts ten times that size. On top of that, the Telegraph company had another £40 million in cash on hand.

The *Telegraph*, however, was not Black's only concern. His own fortune was tied more directly to its parent company, Hollinger Inc.

of Toronto, whose financial health was not nearly so robust. At year-end 1991, its net debt was $685 million and its shareholders' equity $348.9 million, a debt-to-equity ratio that Dominion Bond Rating Service said was too high. Black's plan was to sell shares in the Telegraph company and list it on the London Stock Exchange.* For the task he enlisted the blue-chip investment houses Cazenove & Co. and Rothschild & Sons, whose relationships with the company predated Black's. But the market timing for the issue was not ideal.

Robert Maxwell had died in mysterious circumstances while yachting off the Canary Islands in November 1991. There had always been widespread doubts about Maxwell's character and business practices, but few imagined the scale of the massive fraud he left behind. Still, the *Daily Telegraph* ran a respectful obituary of the man, written by editor Max Hastings. Hastings had rung Black, who was in his Toronto office, to tell him the news. "Well, err on the side of generosity," Black said. Hastings recalled, "I think Conrad is sometimes inclined to give the benefit of the doubt to apparently very rich men. And Conrad would sometimes say to me that while of course he knew Maxwell was a rogue, [he didn't] share my view that he was actually a bad man." In any case, it was also Hastings's policy to go easy in obituaries. But on other occasions the two men had tense exchanges over the paper's critical coverage of anyone Black considered a fellow mogul. Such instances included a scathing article about Black's friend Walter Annenberg by the paper's art critic, and the coverage of the arrest in 1990 of the property tycoon Gerald Ronson, who was subsequently imprisoned over an insider-trading scandal involving Guinness. "Conrad felt that the law had dealt uncharitably with Ronson, a view disputed by most of our own pundits," recalled Hastings.

Black may have felt sympathy toward Maxwell, but partly as a result of the massive fraud that Maxwell had committed, Black was assigned what was known as a "tycoon factor." "As a swashbuckling media proprietor who pops up to buy newspapers all over the globe, has a web of companies, heavy debts, a pattern of shuffling assets between his

---

* Black had made a pledge to list the Telegraph company when he took it over.

companies – and a penchant for libel litigation – Black realised comparisons between him and the Maxwell empire are inevitable," the *Sunday Times* wrote. "He tackles them head-on and at length."

The London Stock Exchange imposed an unusual "geographical" separation clause on the Telegraph company's listing, under which Hollinger agreed that Telegraph plc would be Black's sole investment vehicle for the United Kingdom and Europe. Coolness toward the issue was not aided by the fact that existing Telegraph minority shareholders – Black owned 83 per cent of the shares at this stage and the plan was for him to hold 68 per cent – received a letter from the company explaining that an "obscure" London Stock Exchange rule governing minority shareholder approval had been "inadvertently overlooked." As a result, minority shareholders were only now being notified that loans totalling £33 million had been made by the Telegraph company to Hollinger between December 1990 and May 1992.

The "Max factor" and a dismal market for initial stock offerings left the underwriters Rothschild and Cazenove with 10 million of Telegraph plc's 13 million shares issued at £3.25, and the share price proceeded to plummet to a low of £2.22 within weeks of the offering. One disaffected analyst said, "The reaction from institutional investors was either a big 'So what' or an acutely cynical comment about Mr. Black and his bandwagon."

If the critics were to be believed, London investors were not keen on any company that relied heavily on the vision and whim of a single person. No one canvassed the thoughts of David Radler, who was once asked what would happen if a tragedy were to strike Black. "Well, it would be lighter on the payroll," he said with a chuckle. "We'd lose about four club memberships . . . Absolutely nothing would happen, okay? I mean, all of us could be on the airplane when it went down and nothing would happen."

To Black's relief and satisfaction, the share price of Telegraph plc soon rebounded. Stock in the company Black had secured control of at a mere 50p per share six years earlier was soon trading at £3.70, and it was partly on the strength of the company's increasing value that he pursued the Fairfax deal.

There were other prospects. Hollinger held exploratory discussions with representatives of the South African gold magnate Henry Oppenheimer about investing in his Times Media, publisher of South Africa's largest paper, the *Sunday Times*. Those talks fizzled out, as did discussions about joining a consortium with Time Warner to launch Britain's fifth television channel. But participation in a consortium to win one of Britain's breakfast television franchises left Telegraph plc with 5 per cent of Carlton Television. Black had begun to define this strategy as "Micawberism." This was a reference to Wilkins Micawber, the impractical optimist from Charles Dickens's *David Copperfield*, whose credo was that something will always turn up.

Shortly after buying the *Spectator*, Black had also effectively acquired *Encounter*, a right-wing journal once funded by the CIA. Commercially, the magazine was intriguing because, although it was based in Britain, more than 80 per cent of its sales were in the United States. However, Black and his lawyer Dan Colson, who served as a director of the magazine, quickly found its editorial product wanting and the editors unyielding to change. About two years later, Black gave his shares in *Encounter* back to the money-losing magazine, which failed to find another buyer and folded.

Black also made bigger efforts to try to fortify his position in the United Kingdom. At different points in the late 1980s he purchased small stakes in United Newspapers, which published Lord Beaverbrook's once-vaunted mid-market titles the *Daily Express* and the *Sunday Express*, and Trinity International, publisher of the Liverpool *Daily Post* and *Echo* newspapers. But both stakes were eventually sold off – United at a $38 million loss and Trinity at a $13 million gain.

While Maxwell's death had created image problems for Black, it also meant that his newspapers were now for sale. In the United Kingdom, Black was fleetingly interested in Maxwell's Mirror Group Newspapers, but it was difficult to imagine his purchase of a left-of-centre, down-market tabloid going over well either at the Mergers and Monopolies

Commission or, for that matter, with Black's conscience. The New York *Daily News* was altogether a different prospect.

Founded by Capt. Joseph Patterson in 1919, the *News* had once boasted the highest circulation in the United States. Its circulation, at 800,000 when it went into the hands of receivers, was still considerably higher than that of its competitors, the *New York Post* and *New York Newsday*, but down more than 300,000 from the previous year, when it had suffered a debilitating 147-day strike. Before his death, Maxwell had cut the number of employees at the union-fortified *News* to about 2,100 from about 2,700.

Although his home in Palm Beach and ownership of American Publishing gave him a bit of a presence in America, Black was not the player in the New York scene that he had always yearned to be. One evening a few months after Maxwell's death, Black went to a dinner party in London, where he chatted with the American television interviewer-of-the-stars Barbara Walters. While discussing his newspaper exploits, she suggested that he ought to speak to her friend John Veronis, an investment banker specializing in media, about buying the *Daily News*. After a call from the Telegraph company, the managing director of the Veronis, Suhler investment bank, Martin Maleska, flew to London for a long meeting with Black to discuss the New York newspaper market and the *News*'s place in it.

In Black's assessment, the *News* was consistent with his other deals: it had too many workers and was desperately in need of a new printing plant. On the other hand, the New York market was notoriously tricky. "I think Conrad would be very good for the *News*, and he'd be better still for this city," Rupert Murdoch remarked. "It needs a strong voice. I think it would be good all around. I just hope that the financial markets don't punish him too much, because the tabloid wars in New York are a black hole."

Black met with the bankrupt paper's board of directors during a paper-plate lunch catered by the Taste Bud deli on the eighth floor of the *News*'s renowned art deco building on Forty-second Street, where he told editor and publisher Jim Willse, "I have no interest in coming to New York to clasp my lips around an exhaust pipe."

This would be one deal that Black and Radler would oversee together. If they were successful, the *News* would fall under Radler's American Publishing aegis. Radler was no stranger to New York – his father and grandparents on his father's side had been born there, and as an adolescent in Montreal he used to read the *News* for its sports. Talks were held with Peter Kalikow, then the owner of the *New York Post*, and Mort Zuckerman, who owned *US News & World Report*, about teaming up to bid for the *News*. In the end, Zuckerman and Hollinger bid separately and on August 17, 1992, Hollinger's offer to invest US$75 million in the newspaper won the backing of the *News*'s board of directors and management. The deal, which included cutting a further one-third of the paper's jobs, was contingent on coming to an agreement with its unions – which Hollinger failed to do.

The crucial drivers' and pressmen's unions backed Zuckerman's bid, and a third bidder gained the support of the journalists' guild. Though unwilling to raise the ante, Black was clearly agitated about yielding to Zuckerman. "He has given the store away," Black told the *Financial Post*. "He has capitulated to the pressmen and the drivers." He opined that Zuckerman would run the paper as a "hobby." Zuckerman took over the paper in October and calmly responded that as a private individual he did not have to worry about short-term profit objectives in the way a company like Hollinger did. "We have much more of a focus on the editorial product than most people who own public companies," he said. "We have a long-term view." For his part, Black rationalized the loss by pointing out that it proved he was not willing to overpay, and that his bid had increased his profile in the world's media and financial capital. Anyway, he already had another target – this one far more familiar – in his sights.

Conrad Black and Barbara Amiel could hear faint sounds of honking and cheering as they strolled into the grand ballroom of the Royal York Hotel, where Black was to deliver a speech to the Toronto branch of the Canadian Club. Outside, on Front Street, a parade was in full swing marking the victory of the Toronto Blue Jays in World Series baseball. The jubilation at the Canadian team's mastery of the most American of sports contrasted starkly with the mood of uncertainty across the country. On this day, October 26, 1992, Canadians were voting in a referendum to ratify or reject a document known as the Charlottetown Accord, which had been approved by Prime Minister Brian Mulroney and each of Canada's ten premiers, and was intended to quell the nationalist ferment in Quebec. In his speech Black called the accord "far from a solution" and described the federal government as "a beached whale from whose carcass the provinces, and native people in particular, carve chunks of jurisdiction, virtually at their pleasure."

Black went on to deliver a lecture on how Canada's media contributed to a government that spent too much effort pandering to special interest groups. "To read the press of Canada today," said Black, "it would be hard to avoid the conclusion that we are a society composed almost entirely of battered wives, molested children, humiliated ethnic groups, exploited workers, and other groups despised for their sexual preferences or cultural attributes, all festering in a spoiling environment." After the speech, a woman from the audience asked why Black did not enter politics to set things right. Politics, he replied, tends to be "a contest for who can be more compassionate. And while I regard myself as a reasonably magnanimous person, I couldn't win a contest like that. I don't have the impression Canadians want me, and I'm not convinced I want them either."

Black could not resist pointing out, in front of all the journalists recording his every word, that Hollinger's Quebec City daily, *Le Soleil*, was in the midst of an industrial dispute. "My interest in that paper," Black intoned with a wicked smile, "is undimmed by the fact the journalists are momentarily on strike. But we are producing thick, informative, and profitable" – he practically spat these adjectives – "editions, thus proving it's one of the great myths of the newspaper industry that you need journalists to produce a newspaper."

The press of Canada was on Black's mind that day in more ways than one. Earlier, at his office at 10 Toronto Street, he had received a phone call from David Galloway, chief executive of Torstar, publisher of Canada's largest newspaper, the *Toronto Star*. On and off for months, Galloway had been sounding out Black about a joint bid for Southam, the largest newspaper publisher in Canada, in which Torstar already held a 22.5 per cent interest. Ironically, it was during the threat of a hostile takeover, possibly from Black (though he denied it), that Southam had turned to Torstar to become an investor in the first place, back in 1985. Now, even though Black's major interests were outside Canada, his Micawberish outlook would lead to his biggest acquisition so far.

It is easy to compare the Southam print dynasty to Britain's Berry family or Australia's Fairfaxes. There is a sameness in the way many similar publishing enterprises were assembled during the late nineteenth and early twentieth centuries throughout the former British Empire, just as there are similarities in the way many of them were crumbling by the late twentieth century.

William Southam was a hard-working twenty-three-year-old when in 1877, a decade after the British North America Act had established Canada as an independent dominion, he bought a 25 per cent interest in the London Free Press in London, Ontario. By 1944, when a quarter of the company was sold to the public, Southam was well established as Canada's premier national newspaper chain. When William Southam's grandson St. Clair Balfour took over the company a decade later, it owned seven dailies, and over the years Balfour continued to buy major metropolitan papers and smaller trade publications in the east and the west. By the time Southam caught the eye of Black, it was Canada's largest publisher of dailies, including some of Canada's bedrock metropolitan newspapers – the Ottawa Citizen, the Montreal Gazette, the Edmonton Journal, the Calgary Herald, and the Vancouver Sun among them.

Like Lord Hartwell at the Telegraph, Balfour belonged to a fading generation of news owners who viewed themselves as benign caretakers. Every newspaper was run as an autonomous fiefdom by a publisher who subscribed to the family's high journalistic principles and commitment to public service. Most efforts to take advantage of the economies that a national chain of newspapers offered – for purchasing, marketing, or advertising sales – were shunned as infringements on that sacred independence. In 1975, at age sixty-four, Balfour passed the reins to Gordon Fisher, the son of one of his first cousins. Fisher was less tied to the company's newspaper roots and expanded the company into printing, cable television, and broadcasting, as well as into a range of databases, trade shows, and electronic media.

The soaring economy of the early 1980s ensured that the company continued to be profitable and masked the waywardness of many of Southam's diversifications and the impact on some of its most lucrative newspapers of competition from new tabloids launched by Toronto Sun Publishing. Conrad Black's view of Southam was that it gave its journalists "absolute liberty of content and virtual liberty in editorial budgets," and that over time, "this arrangement degenerated, inexorably, into soft, left journalistic pap for the readers and collapsing profits and stock price for the shareholders." Both he and his partner, Radler, viewed the company as ripe for cost-cutting and revitalizing, and Black took no small pleasure in the idea of coming back into Canadian media like a conquering crusader.

In spring 1985, Gordon Fisher became terminally ill with liver cancer. It was the era of the corporate raider, and the Southam family feared that its hold over the company was at risk. The family's once tightly held shares had earlier been dispersed among a wide group of Southams, Fishers, and Balfours, and together these represented considerably less than 50 per cent of the company's ownership.

With Fisher ill, Balfour was brought back to guide Southam, while rumours swirled that the company was being stalked by a predator. Black's name kept coming up as one of the possibilities – he had already acquired a 5 per cent stake in the company. In fact, Black did suggest to Balfour that he take a friendly 25 per cent position in Southam and was "very politely" rebuffed. (Some of the negative press from Black's Argus exploits made Balfour uncomfortable with the idea of Black as a partner.*) Instead, Balfour sought a controversial joint investment arrangement with Torstar.

---

* Balfour and Black were not strangers. In 1937 Balfour had attended Black's parents' wedding in Winnipeg while working as a reporter at the *Winnipeg Tribune*. When Black began establishing Sterling Newspapers in the 1970s, Balfour put prospective sellers of small papers, including the Summerside, P.E.I., paper the *Journal Pioneer*, in touch with him. Balfour said, "When people came to us and we didn't wish to buy them, I'd say, 'There is an alternative to Thomson who I'm sure will buy it. There's Conrad Black.'"

But by 1991 that partnership had not been as fruitful as either Torstar or Balfour had envisioned; Torstar had become frustrated. CEO David Galloway was looking for a way out: he wanted either to put Torstar's stake toward an outright buyout of Southam or, preferably, to trade it for some of the company's titles, perhaps papers in Ontario or Alberta. But when he called Black on the day of his Canadian Club speech to talk about their joint bid, Galloway raised a new option: "There is a chance that our board may suggest selling our shares."

Black replied quickly, "If you want to sell your shares, I'll buy them." Galloway agreed but added that Torstar's main interest was in getting some newspaper properties in exchange for what amounted to having ensured Southam's independence for the past seven years.

Four days later, on Friday morning, Galloway was in the tony town of Caledon, north of Toronto, for a round of business golf at the Devil's Pulpit course. On the first tee, he was informed that his office had just forwarded a call. It was Black, now in London. "David, I just want to reiterate what I said on the phone. I'm serious about that," he said. "If you people are interested, I just want you to know I'm very serious about that."

The following Wednesday, Galloway laid out the situation to the Torstar board's strategic planning committee (whose members did not include any of the three Southam appointees). In 1991 Southam had lost $153 million on revenue of $1.2 billion; it was on its way to losing another $263 million in 1992. Its quarterly dividend, which had been 20¢ in 1990, had been cut in half, and by early 1993 it would be halved again. The committee voted to sell to Black. The price, a total of $259 million, would not be an issue, as Torstar could accept only up to a 15 per cent premium over the current trading price of the stock without triggering a bid for the whole company.

Eighty-one-year-old St. Clair Balfour sat stunned and silent at the board meeting on the afternoon of November 8 when he heard that Torstar was selling its Southam shares to Black. The deal, which closed in January 1993, left Hollinger as the largest shareholder in Canada's largest newspaper company, whose centrepiece was seventeen daily newspapers with a combined circulation of more than 1.5 million.

In the *Globe and Mail*, editor William Thorsell penned a welcoming editorial about Black's newest acquisition. Thorsell, who, like Black, had been a columnist for *Report on Business* magazine in the 1980s, was on better terms with him than previous *Globe* editors had been. "Businesses do best under the guidance of an informed and engaged proprietor, none more so than newspapers," the editorial said. "Mr. Black is that rarity in Canadian capitalism, a businessman who reads. Besides his evident distaste for many journalists, he clearly loves the craft of journalism – more so than many media barons we could name. He has done much to reinvigorate the newspaper trade abroad, rescuing publications that would almost certainly have gone otherwise. We welcome his rediscovery of Canada."

There were less favourable commentators, such as Tom Kent, the chairman of the Royal Commission on Newspapers, who contended in the *Ottawa Citizen* that "as a multiple proprietor, he will milk many of his papers to the sacrifice of their quality and spend on some of the more important in order to bend them to his ideology." Black rejected Kent's views as a "pompous farrago of nonsense."

Shortly after the Southam deal was announced, Black sat in his office at 10 Toronto Street, munching on a cheddar cheese sandwich, facing a stack of letters commending him on his recent speech to the Canadian Club and his Southam coup. "I'm actually slightly touched by the rather generous response I seem to evoke around here," he said. At the same time, he was mildly fuming over a recent profile in London's *Financial Times*. His friend Hal Jackman, controlling shareholder of National Trust, then serving as lieutenant-governor of Ontario, was quoted as saying: "The problem with Conrad is that he's always looking to the next deal."

"Well, that's absolute crap," Black huffed between bites of his sandwich. "I'm not. In the meantime we manage value into what we have, but when there are opportunities there you snap them up . . . It's all very nice to have a strategy, but if you can't do the deals what use is the strategy? If I announced my strategy is to take over the *New York Times*, but it's not for sale and I can't do the deal, what good is my strategy for me? You've got to go where you think there's an opening."

Black's retort on Jackman was, "What did *he* do with the National Trust Company? You see, Jackman's problem is that he is very suspicious of everything that isn't very slow-moving and very deliberate, following upon his father. They've been working on a fifty-year plan, you see . . . I mean, he's an entertaining guy but as a commentator on how to build a business he has his limitations."

Jackman and Black had been yanking each other's chains for years. "I like to bring him down to earth," Jackman said. "When a Roman general defeated the barbarians, his army would give him a triumph. And he would ride in a chariot, but behind the general they always had a slave who would be holding a wreath over the general's head, whispering in his ear, 'Glory is but fleeting.' So I said, 'I'm the slave that holds the wreath over your head, Conrad.'"

Any plans Black might have had for a warm and fuzzy return to Canada were jolted by a phone call in early March 1993 from Paul Desmarais, the head of the Power Corporation conglomerate. Power, he informed Black, was putting a proposal to the Southam board to buy almost $200 million worth of equity directly out of the company's treasury. Among his diverse holdings, the courtly, debonair financier owned the Montreal French-language daily newspaper *La Presse*, three television stations, and seventeen radio stations in Quebec. A Palm Beach neighbour of Conrad Black's, Desmarais shared Black's fascination with Southam, and over the years the two men had discussed their respective ambitions to own it. Desmarais called Black "a character."

Media businesses were a fraction of sixty-five-year-old Desmarais's interests. In 1993 Power's $27 billion in assets included control of the mutual fund giant Investors Group and of Great-West Life Assurance, numerous industrial ventures in China, and half of Pargesa Holding, a Geneva-based company with wide-ranging interests in European financial services, media, and industry. Over the years, Desmarais had proven himself a shrewd and patient buyer and seller of companies. Following asset sales in 1989, Power Corp. was sitting on close to a billion dollars in cash.

Now it turned out that the Southam board, unbeknownst to Black, had sought out Power to be a counterforce to him. In the weeks since Black's deal, there had been much speculation that it would not be long before he moved to tighten his hold over Southam – in particular, there was fear about what damage David Radler might wreak if he were unleashed on the company's payroll. The company's new CEO, Bill Ardell, had already laid plans to eliminate 1,300 of the company's 7,500 jobs, but the new shareholders were wary of his inexperience in the newspaper business.

Just before Desmarais's move, concerns about Hollinger's intentions calmed down when Black and Southam chairman Ron Cliff agreed to a standstill agreement that granted Hollinger three slots on the Southam board in exchange for an agreement not to challenge a poison pill defence until it came up for renewal in 1995. In order to appease its banks, Southam had also announced that it expected to be issuing new equity, but under his agreement Black was limited to taking up only his pro rata share.

After Power's first proposal was rejected by the Southam board (Black lobbied hard to get enough directors on his side), Desmarais phoned Black. This time, they agreed they would try to work out an arrangement together and present a fresh proposal to the Southam board. Black arrived in Palm Beach on March 13 and met Desmarais that day and the next at Desmarais's home on South Ocean Boulevard. Also present at various times were Southam directors Adam Zimmerman and Hugh Hallward. By telephone, Bill Scott, a Stikeman, Elliott lawyer in London, was handling the drafting of the legal document.

On the third day, Desmarais had to leave Florida, but his son André came to Black's red-brick house on Canterbury Lane. The resultant agreement essentially made Black and Desmarais equal partners, with right of refusal on each other's shares. They even agreed to rotate the chairman's role every year. Desmarais said that he was a long-term player in Southam: the agreement would be good for fifteen years, provided that each side owned at least 15 per cent of the stock. Final details were worked out over the phone, then Black descended the stairs of his Palm Beach mansion and brought out champagne. Black quickly forgave Desmarais for sandbagging him; he had decided that, despite the motives of the old-guard Southam directors who had sought Desmarais out, he and Desmarais could work well together. "There was an awful lot of shilly-shallying and foot-dragging and pusillanimous mealy-mouthed evasiveness going on," Black said. "We were generally aware of who our friends were."

On the surface at least, Black and Desmarais shared the same goal for the company: that shareholders receive an acceptable return derived from improved quality and efficiency at its newspapers. Power invested $180 million in the company, buying almost 13 million treasury shares at $14 apiece, giving it 18.8 per cent of Southam's shares, roughly equal to Hollinger's stake. But the chummy partnership would be short-lived. Over the next two years, Black and Desmarais would grow disenchanted with each other as well as the Southam old guard with whom they shared the board.

Although Power and Hollinger together owned enough of Southam to yield what would be considered co-control in most companies, their influence was limited by the agreements they had worked out with Southam's "independent" directors – board veterans such as former chairman Ron Cliff, Adam Zimmerman, and Hugh Hallward – under which the independents could veto significant initiatives by the major shareholders, such as buying or selling assets. Another agreement Power apparently thought it had was that neither Desmarais nor Black would buy newspapers in Canada without first offering them to Southam. As far as Hollinger was concerned, no such agreement was in effect – yet another instance in Black's career in which the fine print of a deal takes on greater significance than was originally envisioned. In this case, the purchase of nineteen small papers from Thomson in August 1995 was the start of a chain reaction that would lead to Hollinger vaulting, in a little over a year, to ownership of more than half of the country's daily newspapers, igniting a controversy about the unprecedented control by one company – and ultimately one man – over the nation's printed news.

Part of a growing rift at Southam's board was Black and Desmarais's frustration at the slow financial progress of the company, despite the trimming of its ranks and the sale of some assets. Another contentious issue was that some of Hollinger's former Thomson papers effectively competed with Southam properties; for instance, Hollinger acquired the *Cambridge Reporter* in Cambridge, Ontario, whose major rival was Southam's nearby and much larger *Kitchener-Waterloo Record*.

Unable to have the kind of impact on the company that they had in other ventures, Black and Radler soon grew frustrated with the investment, almost to the point of indifference. By 1995 the company's stock had not yet risen to the $18.10 Black had paid for his stake in 1992. According to one Southam board member, on the very day in late 1995 that Paul Desmarais lectured Black at a Southam board meeting for not putting Southam's interests first, Hollinger was quietly putting the finishing touches on another deal to buy papers for its own account. Days later it announced that it was acquiring the remnants of another of Canada's waning press dynasties, the Sifton family's Armadale Co., a total of fourteen papers, including the Regina *Leader-Post* and the Saskatoon *Star-Phoenix*. The deal, for an undisclosed sum, gave Hollinger a daily news monopoly in Saskatchewan, as it already had in Prince Edward Island and Newfoundland.

The Armadale deal did little to improve Black and Hollinger's reputation for heavy-handedness. Forty-eight hours after that deal closed in February, *Leader-Post* and *Star-Phoenix* staffers were ushered into off-site convention rooms. There, 173 of the papers' 650 workers were taken aside and fired. While he defended the cuts as bringing the papers' staff levels in line with industry norms, Black also claimed that what he called the "inelegant" layoffs were executed by the local management and were in the works long before Hollinger took over. "Had we been the domineering meddlers we are occasionally taxed with being," he argued, "the issue would have been handled with more finesse."

The uproar over the layoffs did not position Hollinger for a warm reaction during events that were to unfold next. Southam's independent directors continued to skirmish with both the Hollinger and Power executives who tried to extract detailed financial figures and business plans from Southam managers. At one point, executive committee chairman Ron Cliff wrote to Power and Hollinger that any requests for information from CEO Bill Ardell or other Southam executives must go through him.

By March 1996, the situation had become, according to one Hollinger executive, "untenable." Black and Desmarais, he says, were "like two guys who are after the same girl" – and the girl didn't seem particularly interested in either of them. Finally fed up, Black proposed to Desmarais that Power buy out Hollinger's stock in Southam. Desmarais countered with a proposal under which they would break up the twenty-paper chain. Black agreed, but the Southam directors once again opposed them. His own attentions diverted by other matters, including a restructuring of his European television holdings, Desmarais then told Black that he had decided to sell rather than buy. After all, he had bought his Southam stock considerably more cheaply than Hollinger had bought its, and was already in the black on the investment. As a Southam director put it, "Desmarais didn't want to put up any more money. He could walk away from an unpleasant situation with a $60 million profit." And so he did.

For $294 million, Desmarais was out of Southam, the power-sharing arrangement that had kept Hollinger at bay was dissolved, and Black suddenly was in control of a prize he had stalked for more than a decade. Black installed five new directors to replace the "obdurate rump" of old-guard Southam directors, whom he had blasted at Hollinger's annual meeting a month earlier for standing in the way of Hollinger and Power's efforts to boost the newspaper chain's performance and editorial quality. Now Hollinger controlled 58 of the nation's 104 dailies, putting Black in a position where he had to defend the unprecedented concentration of power he had amassed in the country he had left seven years earlier. Black attempted to calm the uproar by pointing out that even after his spree, only about seven of every hundred Canadians read a Hollinger daily. "Newspapers," he said, "do not have the media market share they did prior to the rise of a practically unlimited variety of television channels and the emergence of alternative electronic media."

By downplaying the significance of newspapers, Black was high-lighting the vulnerability of his strategy of placing ever bigger bets on the industry's future. To help finance the Southam purchase, Hollinger tapped into the U.S. debt and equity markets in mid-1996, raising some $700 million. But alarms were rung by some analysts and rating services about the level of Hollinger's debt, which was now close to $1.4 billion. Such questions would persist until Black could prove that his wager on the future of newspapers – in stark contrast with the ways of Thomson, for instance, and in the face of the threat of price wars with Murdoch – was right.

Within Canada, as Black himself pointed out, no other Canadian appeared keen to expand in the newspaper business. The Thomson, Southam, and Sifton families were all out of the game of buying newspapers, and many media players were wary of the industry's prospects.

Not everyone agreed. Senator Keith Davey called Black's growing dominance "awful" and a "disgrace." Council of Canadians director Maude Barlow warned that Black posed a "clear and present danger to democracy" and unsuccessfully tried to challenge the approval of Black's buyout of Desmarais by the federal Competition Bureau in court. Black took none of it in stride. "It's hard not to impute to [Barlow] the motive of regret that the Southam papers may henceforth be less absolutely reliable and predictable mouthpieces of her feminist, socialist, envious, anti-American views than they have been. In that sense, her fear is legitimate. But that is not an attack on diversity. It's the enhancement of diversity."

Before long, Black began to remake Canada's largest newspaper company by replacing editors at its major papers in Ottawa, Montreal, and Vancouver, while trying to fill in what he considered the missing piece of Southam's puzzle – a paper based in the country's biggest city, Toronto – by attempting to buy the *Financial Post*. Several top Southam executives, including CEO Ardell, would soon depart, and this was one deal for which Black and Radler would share responsibility. Rather than count the newspaper's thousands of chairs, Radler enthused that he needed merely to flip through the company's inches-thick internal telephone directory to size up the managerial and operational fat.

Black was back in Canada, a decade after deciding that his future lay elsewhere, but this time on his terms. Mere days after the announcement of his Southam coup, he played host to one of the super-secret Bilderberg meetings, at a converted luxury resort in King City, just north of Toronto. The four-day event, planned long before Black knew his name would be plastered all over the local papers, brought in carriage-loads of luminaries, including Queen Beatrix of the Netherlands, Prime Minister Jean Chrétien, Henry Kissinger, Andrew Knight, David Rockefeller, George Soros, and Henry Kravis. The European Union, Yugoslavia, China, and Russia were all topics for discussion among the 120 attendees. But, as always, the gathering was off-limits to the press – Southam's or anyone else's. The secrecy, Black explained without irony, "has no purpose other than to allow leading citizens to speak their minds openly and freely." It was a scene that could not have been scripted better had it been in a Hollywood movie about a larger-than-life press tycoon.

Chapter Eighteen

MAN OF LETTERS

Saturday, December 18, 1993, three p.m: In the pre-Christmas scramble at the Eaton Centre in downtown Toronto, shoppers queued in separate lines in two sections of the sprawling shopping complex. In one line, children and their harried parents awaited a Polaroid, a kind word, and a candy cane from Santa Claus. And in a corner of the menswear section at Eaton's department store stood a line of people lured by the promise that Conrad Black would be signing copies of his new autobiography, *A Life in Progress*.

Beside a dais amid racks of blue jeans and corduroy shirts, a grey-haired, bespectacled announcer barked into a loudspeaker that a "special guy" would soon arrive. "This very special guy is, of course, Conrad Black, a special Canadian . . . You are welcome to meet one of the world's most enormously successful financiers . . . Conrad Black will not ignore you today, folks."

Wearing a grey suit and blue tie, Black arrived his standard half-hour late. He was flanked by George Eaton, president of the family-run retail chain on whose board Black sat and which went into bankruptcy protection a few years later. Before Black could sit down, a man in a tuque bellowed out a question about whom he had supported in the recent federal election. Jean Chrétien's Liberals had just trounced the Progressive Conservatives, with whom Black had been closely identified. "I'm just an author, you

know," Black replied with a grin, adding that his company had sup-
ported various candidates. (In fact, Black had voted for the Reform
Party, the Alberta-based right-wing grassroots party led by Preston
Manning.) "I'm astonished and grateful that so many people are here."

Black and Eaton settled behind a table, and for ninety minutes
Black patiently shook hands and signed books for all customers who
laid out $32.95. For years, whenever Black arrived home from what
he considered a particularly memorable encounter or event, he had
written down or recounted into a tape recorder his day's experiences.
This distillation of moments, combined with his legendary memory,
served him well when, in April 1991, he quietly decided to write his
memoirs. It was a chronicle of war that had impelled Black to put
pen to paper. He had recently viewed the PBS television series *The
Civil War*. "They were so good that they inspired me to do something," Black said. He was staying in Palm Springs, on his way to
Tokyo for a meeting of the Trilateral Commission, when he decided
to procure a pad of paper. On his flight to Tokyo, he pulled out his
fountain pen and began writing. No writer's block here – Black spent
the even longer return flight from Tokyo to London at the same task.
By the time he was back at his home in England, he had completed,
in longhand, the first three chapters of his book.

Black was unsure at first whether he should publish his memoirs.
Although Black wouldn't try to squelch other books about him, he
said, "I didn't see why I shouldn't do it myself." And, he added, at
least it would not be "Conrad Black *with*" some writer, like so many
business autobiographies.*

Black had reasons for publishing the book at the age of forty-
nine: he wanted to write about the evolution of his thoughts on his
native Canada and to explain why he no longer lived there; he wanted
to "set the record straight" on the various controversies that had
surrounded him over the years; and he wanted to write about some
of the "obstacles" he had overcome, such as his anxiety attacks during

---

* The writing style was unquestionably his own. For example: "The demure, stylish,
convent-educated young ladies of Lima and their macho, blustery, or esoteric boyfriends
or husbands were elegant and hospitable, but lived behind high walls and moved fretfully,
darting through the congested streets in their unobtrusive automobiles."

the 1970s, so that anyone facing a similar challenge might "take some encouragement from it."

The 522-page book was a best-seller in Canada, generally praised by critics, and nominated as Canada's business book of the year. In his review, the business writer Peter Foster described it as "the work of a man who rejoices in the intellectual and financial status of not giving a damn, of living a kind of Basil Fawlty wet dream in which Basil has not only won the football pools but has also swallowed a thesaurus and somehow acquired another fifty points of IQ."

A Life in Progress was filled with anecdotes and reflections on the various luminaries whose paths Black had crossed, and all the obscure witticisms he had said at the time. Encountering a minister in Pierre Trudeau's cabinet dressed in "some sort of celebratory sash," Black had told him he looked "like Wallenstein on the march . . . you should complete the ministerial dignity with epaulettes the size of fruit tarts." In kicking off a strategy session during the Hanna Mining lawsuit, Black wrote, "I quoted de Gaulle and said 'It has begun as badly as it could, and so it must continue.'" Black's frequent use of obscure words like *fenestrated* and *psephological* ensured that the book's copy editor, Wendy Thomas, kept a dictionary close at hand. She could not always locate the words Black used. A number of the people Black skewered in the book had a similar experience – only it wasn't words that they couldn't find, but memories that jibed with the author's.

The *Maclean's* columnist Allan Fotheringham complained about the way he was depicted in the book, saying that Black's "imagination does run to Technicolor."[*] He accused Black of taking poetic licence even with his reminiscences about his childhood idol, the

---

[*] Black wrote about dropping off Fotheringham in an inebriated state at the Park Plaza Hotel in Toronto several years earlier, and watching Fotheringham collapse "in a heap" at the feet of the doorman. At the launch party for *A Life in Progress* atop the same hotel, Fotheringham sulked in a corner and complained about the "goddamn millionaire who libels me and I have to buy my own Scotch." Black later agreed that the cash bar furnished by his publisher, Anna Porter, was "déclassé" but said that he had contemplated asking Porter to throw Fotheringham out. Trying to defuse the situation, Black's friend Baton Broadcasting president Doug Bassett bought Fotheringham a copy of Black's book, and had it signed by the author. Black wrote, "To Allan. Let peace break out. Conrad." At which Fotheringham muttered, "Peace on you."

Montreal Canadiens hockey star Maurice Richard. Black wrote in his book that it was Richard's "implacable determination" that impressed him most, as when the hockey hero went through a sleeper train on its way from Montreal to Detroit during a weekend home-and-away series, "tearing open curtains to find, and pummel in his berth, one of his opponents." Black also wrote about a time Richard allegedly leaped from behind a pillar in a New York hotel and tried to "strangle a referee who had recently penalized him." Fotheringham declared that if these anecdotes were true, Black had "scooped the entire world of sport." The passages were later shown to Maurice Richard by another journalist. The hockey legend said he did not recall the incident on the sleeper train, and said he had not tried to strangle the referee, but "only took him by the shoulders." This and numerous other minor disputes stemming from *A Life in Progress* seemed at odds with Black's legendary photographic recall, but his ex-wife explained it this way: "I wouldn't call Conrad a liar," said Joanna. "I would call him a revisionist historian."

Laurier LaPierre, who had taught at Upper Canada College and later advised Black on his Duplessis master's thesis, was incensed by Black's characterization of him as a homosexual and "one of the more enthusiastic flagellators" at UCC.* After the book was published, LaPierre delivered his own scathing appraisal of the young Black in a letter to the *Financial Post*. LaPierre wrote that while he was at McGill, Black's "contacts with his fellow students were limited and his arrogance and snobbery prevented him from participating in class with any degree of involvement. I was rather naive in those days and not a good judge of character: Consequently his extreme right-wing views, his extensive homophobia, his disdain of the 'common' ordinary

---

* He added in a subsequent interview with the journalist James FitzGerald, who was researching an oral history of UCC, that LaPierre's indiscriminate canings were "not unlike the Lidice solution, when the Nazis killed all the innocent occupants of a Czech town in reprisal for the assassination of the SS governor, J.R. Heydrich, in 1942. Actually, I don't want to be tendentious in bringing in that analogy. UCC was certainly not a Nazi institution and it's outrageous that I should say so. I am defaming it. I would wish either not to be quoted on that, or if I'm quoted, at least quote my withdrawal of it."

French Canadian, and his reverence for all things British did not point me in the right direction. I dismissed all of these as the affectations of a rather limited personality." (Black wrote a letter to the *Financial Post* apologizing for causing LaPierre any offence.)

Perhaps the most notable aspect of the book was the verbal napalm Black levelled at anyone who had ever crossed him, including some of his supposed friends, such as Paul Desmarais, Brian Mulroney, and Hal Jackman. "Why a millionaire many times over seems so angst-ridden and vindictive toward all those above and beneath him is somewhat puzzling," commented Fotheringham. In particular, the book "infuriated" former prime minister Brian Mulroney. Peter White, who attended law school with Mulroney and served as his principal secretary for a period when Mulroney was prime minister, was caught in the middle. "He cannot imagine why he gave Conrad the membership in the Privy Council, because he considers that his reaction has been ungrateful," White recalled. Mulroney's public stance was that he never actually read Black's book, although he was told about the references to himself. "At an appropriate time I'll have something to say myself," said Mulroney. "You have to understand that I know things about Conrad and his state of mind and what was really going on that he hasn't told anybody, but that I will at an appropriate time. No hard feelings, that's just a fact of life. And I've learned a long time ago that, you know, memory tends to be selective."

From his perspective, Black felt he "was really rather positive about most people" and had accomplished what he had set out to do in Canada. "On the things that I wanted to set the record straight on, nobody has challenged my version," he said. "From Upper Canada right through Massey and Dominion Stores and that farce with the Hanna company and so on, I think I have laid to rest a number of irritating, to use Napoleon's phrase, 'instances of lies agreed upon.' So I think it was successful in those respects."

The publication of his book, in any case, underscored the fact that Black could indeed dish it out. Why then, his critics charged, was he so notoriously thin-skinned? "The fact is I like to mix it up with people," said Black. "I've never minded a good verbal punch-up. I'm not trying to silence anyone and I'm not sensitive to people holding forth about my alleged shortcomings, but I draw the line at serious defamation."

The line that Black drew was said to have contributed to a period of libel chill that blew frostily through Canadian journalism for much of the 1980s and 1990s, adding to the irony of Black becoming Canada's largest press owner. Black maintained that at each of the fifteen times he either sued or threatened to sue for libel, it was only because he was being accused of dishonesty or grossly unethical conduct. All he ever wanted was a retraction, he said, which, without a single case going to trial, he has received every time, often with costs and sometimes a cash settlement on top. "It's a profit centre for me," Black once said, cheerily.*

Black could also point to instances where he had stood behind his journalists when they were being sued. When former *Sunday Telegraph* editor Peregrine Worsthorne was sued by *Sunday Times* editor Andrew Neil for an editorial that questioned Neil's cavorting at the Tramp club with Pamella Bordes, a woman who had been involved in a sex scandal, the *Telegraph* defended the case until, after an eight-day trial, a jury awarded £1,000 in damages to Neil and 60p – the cost of a single copy of the paper – to the *Sunday Times*. The *Telegraph*'s legal bill came to £66,000. "Perry went on TV for night after night afterwards," Black noted, "and we got at least £66,000 worth of PR out of it. It was damn good publicity for the *Sunday Telegraph*."

The first time Black sued for libel was over an article by Peter Newman on the richest Canadians, which was published in the November 1983 issue of the American society magazine *Town and Country*. Black engaged lawyers in New York to serve a demand for a retraction on *Town and Country*'s publisher, the Hearst Corporation. Because U.S. libel law offers some protection to writers and publishers, his demand was generally ignored. But the magazine was also

---

* In a 1988 speech, he said, "Anyone who has witnessed, as I have, both as a media owner and employer and as a litigant, the pitiful spectacle of reckless journalists trying to defend under oath negligent or malicious libels with spurious apologia or glazed prevarication will not soon forget the illustration of how much better the working press often is at dishing out abuse than at answering for its own conduct."

published in Canada, where the law is more restrictive, and Black could argue real damage had been done to his reputation. His legal firm, Aird & Berlis, accordingly served a demand. They also threatened to sue Newman, who only a year earlier had written a favourable biography of Black. "It doesn't matter who you are. If you defame him," declared Black's lawyer Peter Atkinson, "he's going to consider his options."

From the mid-1980s to the mid-1990s, Black served writs on virtually all major media in Toronto – the *Globe and Mail*, the *Toronto Star*, the Canadian Press wire service, and the CBC among them. But once he achieved the status of media mogul, he appeared to follow the advice of friends, which was that he had a public forum through which he could respond to what Atkinson called "Black bashing." One of Black's first major suits was filed in the Supreme Court of Ontario over an article written by the *Globe and Mail* business reporter John Partridge and published in the paper, on July 25, 1987, under the headline "Citizen Black." The fact that Black, at the time, was a monthly columnist for the *Globe's Report on Business Magazine* did not dissuade him from suing the paper for $7 million in damages, claiming that several of the article's passages were "demeaning and scandalous" and that their publication had "exposed him to contempt and ridicule." The *Globe* initially contested the case vigorously but almost two years later, after lengthy and expensive pretrial proceedings, published a comprehensive retraction and apology.

As it happened, two days before the publication of the *Globe's* retraction on June 30, 1989, the *Toronto Star* published a lengthy feature about Black under the headline "Black Sheds His Bad Boy Image." Black sued the *Star*, again seeking $7 million in damages. The *Star* filed a statement of defence denying Black's claims and arguing that the article fell within the parameters of fair comment. One sentence in the article that Black did not sue over read, "It's been a long time since Black got himself into one of his famous tirades against the media."

The *Star* eventually also settled with Black, and an "agreed statement of facts" was published on page 3 of the first section of the paper's July 27, 1992, edition. In his suit, Black had complained about various passages describing his involvements with Dominion Stores and Massey-Ferguson and his friendship with Cardinal Carter. The *Star*'s statement – which settled both that lawsuit and another Black had filed – referred only to the facts of the Dominion Stores pension withdrawal. The article was not headlined as an apology – "Black Settles Libel Suits with *Star*," it read – and it stated, "The *Star* regrets any misunderstanding that may have arisen from the articles concerning Dominion's withdrawal of pension surplus." The next page carried a short article about the settlement. It said the paper had spent more than $180,000 defending itself and that the *Star*'s editor, John Honderich, was "happy" with the settlement. "It should be obvious to our readers," Honderich said, "that we have not published the kind of unctuous and unreserved apology that Black has obtained from other media outlets." In the same article, Black said he was "only interested in setting the record straight. They've now set the record straight."

Only in one instance has Black sued a writer whom he might have, at one time, considered a friend. In November 1990, McClelland & Stewart published Ron Graham's book *God's Dominion: A Sceptic's Quest*. An examination of religious and spiritual life in Canada, the book earned Graham and his publisher a libel writ from Conrad Black demanding $1.5 million in damages and an injunction barring the book from being sold or distributed. The book contained only two references to Black in its entire 452 pages, one of which immediately caught Black's attention. "In the midst of this book," he recalled in a speech shortly after launching his suit, "in a mid-paragraph Damascene lightning bolt of discontinuity, the author announces that having me as an acquaintance taught him that greed and ego add peculiarly to the sum total of human misery."

On receiving a letter of complaint from Peter Atkinson, Graham sent a letter of clarification to the lawyer, in which he said he regretted that Black had taken offence at the passage and noted that the complaint seemed "based upon an unfortunate misinterpretation of a few words." Graham maintained that he meant the rich and powerful have troubles of their own – in effect, the old line that money does not buy happiness. Black found the clarification unacceptable and on November 7 he filed a claim in the Ontario Court (General Division). While trying to resolve the suit without going to trial, Graham offered publicly to debate the passage in question with Black in front of a neutral adjudicator or before a paying audience who would vote on which man was in the right, and the money would go to charity. Even though Graham would be hamstrung by being unable by law to repeat the alleged libel in public, he felt it would be a worthwhile way of airing and ending the dispute. Black did not.

The matter was concluded sixteen months and many thousands of dollars in legal bills later when McClelland & Stewart published, in the *Globe and Mail*, an open letter to Black that was signed by both M&S president Avie Bennett and Ron Graham. "It was never our intention to cause offence to you," it read. "Indeed, we deeply regret that the ambiguity of the passage in question caused you offence. As leaders in Canada's writing and publishing community, we make every effort to be precise in what we write and publish. In this instance, we were not, and for that we apologize."

Bennett felt that the wording of the apology left his company's and the author's integrity intact – and put a welcome end to the mounting legal expenses. For Black, it was yet another success. The way he saw it, Graham's attack on his character stemmed, at least in part, from residual anger Graham felt at not being offered the *Saturday Night* editor's job. Graham denied that he ever wanted the job and has since acquired an equally jaundiced view of his former friend. "Any respect I had for him as an intellectual or publisher or man of letters totally went, and with it my esteem for him," Graham said. "I always liked him and I always defended him. [But] he can flip in a minute from being very congenial and interesting and bright to being all puffed up and arrogant and cold. And I didn't like that side of him and actually felt sorry for him for having that side."

For a while, at least, Black's most litigious days seemed to be behind him. In the spring of 1994, Black travelled from Palm Beach, via Henry and Nancy Kissinger's wedding anniversary celebration in New York, to Ottawa to address the Canadian Association of Journalists. He delivered his usual bombastic dissertation on the media's shortcomings, but the tone was more tempered than it had been in the past. Afterwards, he answered questions and stayed a few minutes to sign copies of his book. "Your speech wasn't good," offered a ruddy-faced, drink-toting blond man in a track-suit jacket. "The questions and answers were good. I didn't understand what you were trying to say in the speech. I mean, what was your point?"

"Well," Black said, pausing for a moment, "it's the only speech you're going to get tonight."

Two journalism students, Dawn and Heather according to their name tags, tentatively approached. "Mr. Black, we heard what they said about how you'll sign books if we buy them, but we're poor students and we can't afford it. So can we just ask you a question?"

"Sure."

"Well, we want jobs. We're in journalism school and there's no jobs out there and what can we do to make sure we get jobs when we graduate?"

Black's lengthy response included a suggestion to travel to Europe – as he had done as a young man – and the opinion that a journalism degree is "better than no degree." Studying one of the name tags, Black added that "all work and no play makes Dawn a dull girl." Later, as he walked out of the hall, he raised his fist at them and bellowed, "Don't be demoralized, girls!"

As he left the hotel ballroom for his jet at the Ottawa airport, a young man who looked every bit the cocky, idealistic journalism student came forward and pumped Black's hand. "You know, I've never been a big fan of yours, Mr. Black," he said, looking very pleased with himself.

"Then why are you shaking my hand?"

Chapter Nineteen

A QUESTION OF BALANCE

An odd side effect of Black's memoir was the bizarre regulatory furor it caused in Australia. In a passage that did not appear in the book's Canadian edition, Black wrote that Australian prime minister Paul Keating had pledged to "entertain" an application from Telegraph plc to increase its shareholding in Fairfax from 15 per cent to 25 per cent in return for assurances of balanced coverage during the March 1993 federal election campaign, which the incumbent Keating won despite being widely regarded as the underdog.

According to Black's book, in early 1992, over dinner at Kiribilli House, the prime minister's residence in Sydney, Keating had explained to him that he couldn't immediately alter the 15 per cent foreign ownership limit imposed on the Telegraph company's investment. Black quoted Keating as saying that it was "shitty and outrageous, of course" and asking Black to "leave him six months for matters to settle, whereupon he promised to put things right." Black and Telegraph vice-chairman Dan Colson had met Keating again on November 27, 1992, at his Sydney office. Although he was heading into the election, Keating had "urged" Black to apply to the Foreign Investment Review Board to allow him to increase the Telegraph company's Fairfax holding to 25 per cent and had said he would "champion" the application.

"If he was re-elected and Fairfax political coverage was 'balanced' he would entertain an application to go higher," Black wrote. Opposition leader John Hewson, he added, had "already promised that if he was elected he would remove restraints on our ownership." Keating was re-elected in March and several weeks later Telegraph plc received permission to increase its stake to 25 per cent, amid protests from some journalistic and parliamentary quarters that its papers had declined in quality since Black's group had taken control. (Black added in the book that Keating "impresses me as a more capable leader than any other current English-speaking government head, as well as a delightful companion.") Black further claimed, in an article he wrote for Fairfax's *Sydney Morning Herald* and Melbourne *Age*, that Keating had told Black he "might be disposed to support" ownership of up to 35 per cent in the future.

In expounding in his book on his Australian experiences, Black achieved something quite rare in the annals of publishing and policy: with a single word, he set off a massive public and political controversy, culminating in a full-blown senate inquiry that would dominate the headlines in Australia for weeks in early 1994.

The word in question, *balanced*, was set by Black in quotation marks. He later said this was not meant to indicate that he was quoting Keating. Rather, he explained confusingly to the senate inquiry, "The word 'balanced' was in quotes by me because that is the word that was used and that is what he meant." Black claimed that in fact *balanced* was his own word, a "fair summary" which Keating "accepted and has used since." The prime minister made it clear, Black said, "that he absolutely was not using the word 'balanced' as a euphemism for supportive or favourable or adulatory or hostile to his enemies, or any such thing."

Six months after the Australian election, Black's book was published and Keating's critics quickly accused him of making sleazy backroom arrangements with the Canadian tycoon in an attempt to influence coverage from the traditionally anti-Labour Fairfax press. Opposition leader John Hewson, in the high-rhetoric Australian parliamentary tradition, said that the Black-Keating pact was "one of the most disgraceful acts in public policy in the history of this country."

"Rarely has such an innocent word," Black wrote in the *Herald*, "been the subject of such misinformed debate." Reflecting later on the controversy, Black ventured that perhaps the Australian publisher, Random House, had been "a bit mischievous" in the way the crucial passage had been edited. "But I guess it helped sales . . .

"The fact is, it could have been better edited in Australia, but it doesn't matter.* It's not unhelpful and it's certainly not inaccurate either."

For his part, Keating denied telling Black that he might entertain an increase in Telegraph plc's stake to 35 per cent, and he brushed off Black's observation that the Labour prime minister had promoted the interests of entrepreneurs "against the excessive appetites of the labour unions."

"Well, that's Conrad," Keating said to one journalist. "Of course I did not say that. Why believe that text? I mean, Conrad is a wordsmith and romantic."

Black made his appearance at the Senate Select Committee on Certain Aspects of Foreign Ownership Decisions in Relation to the Print Media on April 21, 1994. At precisely 2:01 p.m. Black strode into the Jubilee Room at Sydney's New South Wales Parliament House and accepted an invitation to make a few opening remarks – speaking until 2:51 p.m. without notes. He was accompanied by his wife, Barbara, who told him she would wear her "best Mo Dean outfit" (a reference to Maureen, wife of the disgraced Nixon counsel John Dean, who had gazed admiringly at her husband throughout his testimony during the Watergate hearings). Despite the press's portrayal of Black and Kerry Packer as titans clashing over who would eventually control Fairfax, while they were in Sydney the Blacks dined with Packer and his wife, Ros, at their Bellevue Hill home.

By the time Black made his appearance before the committee, he had reviewed all thirty-four written submissions and fifty-one testimonies of previous witnesses. The most extreme of them claimed

---

* The Australian editor had taken the liberty of explaining that Maurice Richard, Black's boyhood hockey hero, was a "basketballer."

that the Fairfax takeover was part of an international conspiracy to plunge the world into a "dark age," and was linked to attempts to destroy the global monetary system. Black was more concerned with less wild and potentially more damaging theories.

Malcolm Turnbull was certainly one witness with whom Black had his differences. When asked by the inquiry to give his view on Black's depictions of his dealings with Keating and Hewson, Turnbull said, "Black is a man who is an extraordinary egoist. I think that is fairly obvious. Truthfully, I do not believe his word can be trusted on matters where his own involvement is concerned. His book is full of misrepresentations and he, in my experience of him, has almost no regard for telling the truth." Black responded that such "allegations emanating from him are, to say the least, bizarre."

Trevor Kennedy, a veteran media executive who had been fired from Black's Fairfax bidding group, proved a helpful witness for Black, telling the hearing he did not think any deals had been made with the government. "He is an urbane character," Kennedy opined of Black at the hearing. "He is not unintelligent. Although for a smart bloke, he has done some pretty stupid things. If he had not opened his big mouth, none of us would be here."

The nastiest stoush (Australian for dust-up) was between Black and Bob Hawke, the former prime minister. Hawke's role in the Fairfax sale had been minor, as he had met Black only once, in July 1991, shortly before being ousted as Labour leader and replaced by Keating. Unhappy with Black's portrayal of him in *A Life in Progress*, Hawke kicked off his testimony to the inquiry by declaring: "At the obvious risk of disadvantaging myself at the hands of Mr. Black, who has made it quite clear that he thinks proprietorship gives him the right to determine the policies of his papers . . . the simple fact is that Conrad Black has the habit of distorting events through the prism of his own self-interest."

Hawke claimed that Black had inaccurately recalled that their only encounter had taken place in the office of Treasurer John Kerin. In his book, Black wrote that he concluded from the meeting that "it was obvious that Hawke and Kerin were not reliable."

Hawke said that the meeting had taken place in his own office. "It's a bit rich . . . for this media mogul to say that Hawke and Kerin are not reliable," Hawke said. "He gets wrong where the meeting was held and then asks to be believed in terms of this self-serving version of what happened."

Hawke's own version was that he "found it a rather boring meeting. I was at the outset not particularly impressed with Mr. Black, who regarded it as relevant and necessary to tell me he was not Jewish. He came having said he owned the *Jerusalem Post* . . . It didn't create a very favourable impression upon me that someone has to make that statement."

When Black had his chance to respond to the inquiry, he levelled a verbal barrage at the former prime minister. Black and his associates were particularly unhappy that Hawke's comments had been reported in newspapers around the world, at a time when two of Hollinger's other subsidiaries, UniMedia in Quebec and American Publishing, were attempting to raise money in the market. Accusations from a former world leader that Black was a liar were no help.

None of the points raised by Hawke was too minute for debate. Black told the inquiry that the references Hawke relied on – articles in the *Age* and the *Herald* – to prove that Black did not know in whose office they had met were in fact published on different dates from those Hawke had recalled. "I was never under the illusion we were meeting anywhere but the prime minister's office," he said. "Indeed, it would have required a person of extraordinarily low intelligence not to realize where we were meeting." Black laid the blame for the erroneous placement on the normally diligent Fairfax scribe who had written the article, and spat, "It is extremely irritating for a man who has held the great office that he has to attempt to magnify an episode derived entirely from his sloppy research." On this point, the senate committee concluded in its report that "both witnesses were dogmatic and even pedantic in arguing that theirs was the more accurate recollection of what happened, particularly at the July meeting. Both witnesses endeavoured to damage the credibility of the other by reference to matters of fine, but irrelevant, detail."

Black was understandably even more outraged by Hawke's recollection of his pointing out that he was not Jewish; Black interpreted that as Hawke suggesting he was anti-Semitic, although it was conceivable that the fact that the *Jerusalem Post* was owned by a Gentile could be relevant in a discussion about foreign-ownership policies in other nations. "I think," said Black, "that his words constituted a degradation of every office that he has held. If he had any sense of shame, he should exercise it on this occasion."

Black offhandedly added that Hawke, "despite being unimpressed with me at our meeting, saw fit to ask my colleague Mr. Colson some months ago whether we would anonymously hire him and pay him US$50,000 to be, and I quote, 'our eyes and ears in Canberra, to keep an eye on the successor.' We did not accept the offer."

"I have my detractors," Black later added, "and they are exceedingly vocal at times but they do not accuse me of lying and they do not, I might add, accuse me of being in any sense racially or religiously bigoted either, as Bob [Hawke] was kind enough to suggest."

At this, Hawke, who had read Black's comments in newspapers while in Hong Kong, flew home and demanded to reappear before the inquiry the next day. He called Black's depiction of his statement about not being Jewish a "grotesque distortion" of what he had said. "How can what I actually said possibly, by any stretch of imagination – even one as fervid as Mr. Black seems to be possessed of – begin to found the proposition that I am accusing him of racial or religious bigotry?" To Hawke, Black's performance was further evidence that "he simply cannot be relied upon." Hawke said what offended him about Black pointing out that he wasn't Jewish was the notion that it would matter. "I regard it as an insult that someone regards me as thinking it to be relevant whether they are or are not Jewish or are or are not Catholic."

As for his purported offer to be a consultant for Black, Hawke said it was Colson who had raised the idea with him. Hawke said Colson had told him Black's people were interested in an analysis of the political field, and that he would raise the matter in London and get back to Hawke.

"I did not hear anything more from him," Hawke recalled. "I made no approach to them. That was the context of what happened.

Out of that . . . we get this preposterous statement from Conrad Black, which has led to this sort of stuff, that I have asked for $50,000 to spy on the prime minister. What do you make of a man who does that?"

Black called Hawke's performance "pathetic." "What possesses Bob Hawke to carry on in this asinine fashion I don't know," Black mused to two reporters from the *Sydney Morning Herald*. "But I would have thought just the dignity of being ex-prime minister would require him to behave with a little more decorum."

While Black was outwardly defiant and visibly enjoying the joust, he and Colson were concerned that the sideshow with Hawke was deflecting them from their objectives in speaking at the inquiry: to quash any suspicions of a deal with Keating and to lay the groundwork for increasing Telegraph plc's ownership in Fairfax. While Black eagerly volunteered to take part in a television debate with Hawke, he also asked Fairfax's CEO Stephen Mulholland to approach the former prime minister quietly with a proposal to end the matter by agreeing to disagree. Hawke agreed. Black personally drafted a large portion of the resulting statement, which was issued on April 26, 1994. "The recent public disagreement between Conrad Black and Bob Hawke has been concluded," it read, "with the acceptance by both of them of the principle that people can sincerely have differing recollections of past meetings. This principle applies to their only conversation in July 1991, and to Mr. Hawke's discussion with Mr. Black's associate, Mr. Colson, in 1993, about a possible corporate relationship between them. All reciprocal allegations of untruthfulness are withdrawn. All disparaging reflections over the venue of the 1991 meeting, over Mr. Hawke's professional activities subsequent to his retirement as prime minister, and over Mr. Black's motives in raising Israeli matters with Mr. Hawke in the 1991 meeting, are also reciprocally withdrawn.

"Mr. Hawke intended no suggestion or implication that Mr. Black had any anti-Semitic attitudes and Mr. Hawke repeats his assertion to the senate committee that he had no reason to believe this to be the case. As mentioned above, it is agreed that it is possible for people to have different recollections of conversations and with regard to the discussion between Mr. Colson and Mr. Hawke, Mr.

Black accepts Mr. Hawke's integrity and the sincerity of Mr. Hawke's statement of his recollection. For his part, Mr. Hawke also accepts Mr. Black's integrity.

"Mr. Black withdraws the statement in Sunday's *Sun-Herald* concerning the term 'official greeter' and Mr. Hawke having retainers with foreign companies to spy on his successor. With these misunderstandings removed, both men profess a reasonable regard and absence of ill-will for the other."

Given the viciousness of the slagging that had led up to the statement, the senators hearing the inquiry were not persuaded by the sudden about-face, concluding the recantations "were simply an exercise in media damage control rather than a genuine change of heart." And if the statement could not be taken seriously, what of the two men's testimony?

As far as Black was concerned, the highlight of the affair occurred when his wife said, during an interview on Australian television, that Hawke's performance made a convincing argument in favour of public flogging. "I thought that was a scream," Black said later.

The committee's first report into the affair was released in June 1994. The opposition majority accepted Black's claim that he was given a "positive indication" from Kerin and Hawke that Telegraph plc could own up to 35 per cent of Fairfax. The committee also concluded that Keating had indeed been attempting, albeit in vain, to influence coverage of the 1993 election in the Fairfax press through his discussions with Black. It was a partial victory for Black. According to the report: "Black's writings and interviews, however much he subsequently sought to disguise the nakedness of the arrangement, made it clear that he was willing to trade at least a promise of proprietorial intervention to enhance his prospects of increased foreign ownership in the Fairfax empire." The report also took exception to Black's observations on Australia's foreign ownership policies, calling his views "indignant and condescending." As far as Black was concerned: "It was not foreigners who put your entire media industry into the tank, you had dinky di Australians to thank for that."

The four Labour senators on the committee of nine authored a dissenting report, containing what was perhaps the most important finding of all. The inquiry, they concluded, was "a pointless and expensive exercise in deliberately misunderstanding the trivia of public life at the taxpayers' expense."

Around the same time, Australia's most powerful media moguls, Packer and Murdoch, were buying into Fairfax, underscoring how tenuous Black's control over the company was, and raising the spectre of their joining forces to oust him. Chatting with Black at a World Economic Forum meeting in Davos, Murdoch blithely claimed that he had bought 5 per cent of Fairfax shares because they were a good investment. He had a way of being charming and polite in public while going for the jugular in business. "I'd rather buy shares in a company that's well run and makes lots of money," he told Black, "than leave it to some money manager in a bank." Black returned the compliment but also made a pointed statement about his feelings toward the money men who owned large swaths of Hollinger stock: "I'd rather have a shareholder like you than an imbecile institution."

Chapter Twenty

PRICE WARRIORS

One of the qualities that made Rupert Murdoch stand out among the deal-driven, chest-thumping moguls of the 1990s was that he thrived on taking on the establishment wherever he set his sights – be it British newspapers and satellite television, the big American TV networks, or the cable news channel CNN. Black's closest head-on competitor in London, Murdoch was a devout political conservative like Black, and his *Times* and *Sunday Times* held an editorial position similar to the *Telegraph*'s. Also like Black, Murdoch had started his empire in a former British colony. "Black was very conscious of Murdoch," recalls a close associate of Black's, "because he had come from Australia yet had transcended his origins and used the U.K. as a stopoff point en route to the U.S."

Murdoch is one person toward whom Conrad Black has normally been respectful, even reverential (and not just while he employed Black's wife). "He's sort of a funny guy," Black said. "He's very friendly and affable on a social basis, but as a competitor he's a real brass-knuckles type." Black's regard for Murdoch, however, did not mean he tried to emulate him. "I don't see him as ever having tried to do the same sort of thing we're trying to do," Black explained. "You see, he was never a big quality newspaper owner. He had the *Times* and the *Sunday Times* and he produced the

*Australian** basically as a hobbyhorse, as far as I could see, but his big effort in newspapers was in down-market tabloids. That's his specialty, whether it's Australia, the U.S., or Britain. And we aren't in that field. We've got another concept here. I'm not saying it's better than his – it isn't."

Black contended that Murdoch was more of a gambler than he was. "He's a plunger by nature, you know, both financially and otherwise, and he falls in love with places and industries . . . He's much more peripatetic and much more courageous than I am. I wouldn't roll the dice like that. As a friend of mine in New York says, 'He's the only guy I know who'll bet a billion dollars of borrowed money to make a point.' Well, I admire it in a way but I don't do that."

For his part, Murdoch professed to be similarly impressed by Black. In a 1992 interview in his New York office, he said, "I'm a great admirer of his. He's done a superb job in London." Curiously, he went on to say: "I like my opposition to be run by competent people. You don't get unnecessary price wars." A subsequent encounter with Murdoch was recounted by Sir David English, the head of Lord Rothermere's Associated Newspapers and publisher of the *Daily Mail*. English ran into Murdoch in the fall of 1993, and English explained that he was reorienting the *Mail*, a mid-market tabloid, to go after the market-leading *Telegraph*. "Don't worry about the *Telegraph*," Murdoch said. "Leave them to me. I'll put them out of business for you."

Indeed, a few weeks later, in September 1993, News International reduced the *Times*'s cover price to 30p from 45p. At the time, it was selling 356,000 copies per day, versus about 1.1 million for the *Daily Telegraph*, which retailed at 48p. Murdoch's public rationale for the move was that the price of British newspapers had increased at twice the rate of inflation; the price of the *Times* had gone up by 80 per cent since 1987, inflation by 40.7 per cent.

Not surprisingly, Black did not buy Murdoch's inflation theory. "While it is entertaining to see Rupert masquerading as the Robin

---

* Murdoch's national Sydney-based broadsheet.

Hood of the media – the frugal consumer's friend – it is scarcely believable," he told the *Observer*. He added: "It does not frighten us and we will not be lowering our price."

Cover-price increases were a major ingredient in the success of all British newspapers, and the *Telegraph* in particular, in the post–Fleet Street years. Without union constraints, papers could add more pages, sections, and colour, and charge more for their product. "The argument that newspaper price increases have been excessive is easily refuted," Black wrote in the *Telegraph* a few days after Murdoch's move, in the first column he wrote for the paper that featured his photo. "Many more pages and improvements in content and production techniques have been proportionately greater than cover price increases. Circulation losses have been generally due to a decline in multiple newspaper purchase as most titles have become more comprehensive."

Although the average circulation of national daily newspapers declined in the United Kingdom from 14.9 million copies in 1982 to 13.7 million in 1991, sales of quality daily broadsheets had actually risen by 14 per cent, largely as a result of the launch of the *Independent* in 1986. And, during the same period, the estimated gross circulation revenue of the quality daily sector increased by 135 per cent – thanks to steady cover-price increases.

When Black first invested in the ailing *Daily Telegraph* in 1985, its cover price was 23p compared with the *Times*'s 25p. Once he had replaced Lord Hartwell at the *Telegraph*'s helm, one of Black's first strategic decisions was to insist that, as the market leader, the *Telegraph* should be the price leader, selling for at least as much as the *Times*. A succession of *Daily Telegraph* price increases followed. And after the successful move to make the Saturday *Telegraph* that day's dominant paper, its cover price rose 160 per cent between 1985 and 1992, from 23p to 60p. The *Sunday Telegraph*, meanwhile, doubled its price to 70p.

By 1993, the *Telegraph* boasted one of the industry's highest ratios of circulation to advertising revenue, with circulation accounting for about 45 per cent. This was a key factor in the paper's ability to prosper during the recession, when advertising dwindled, and a big reason why Black was expanding his interests at a time when other publishers were stumbling.

Murdoch's organization saw the *Telegraph*'s pricing strategy in a different light. Murdoch thought back to the 1920s, when the *Times* had a circulation of 200,000 compared with the *Telegraph*'s 100,000, and both sold for two pennies a copy. Then, on December 1, 1930, the proprietor of the *Telegraph*, Lord Camrose, had audaciously dropped the price of the *Daily Telegraph* to one penny, taking up his predecessor Lord Burnham's vow to make the *Telegraph* "the largest, best and cheapest newspaper in the world."

Competitors had sniffed that a serious paper could not sell for the same price as the tabloids. But *Telegraph* sales doubled to 200,000 in January 1930 and settled into a steady climb toward a million copies per day, from which the paper would never look back. Lord Camrose "took the quality premium away from the price," Murdoch later explained. "He was allowed to get away with that for fifty years and establish total domination of the quality market. We are in the business of taking that back."

Those within the Canary Wharf offices could not deny the logic behind Murdoch's current and Lord Camrose's earlier tactics, but took solace in the notion that the newspaper business – and its consumers – had become much more sophisticated since the first Lord Camrose's day. In editorial positioning, the *Telegraph* and the *Times* were not dramatically different – both were quality Conservative papers – but the *Times* was less consistent than Black's *Telegraph*. Over the years it had been through several editors and related "repositionings," both up- and down-market. By comparison, the *Telegraph* was "big, rich, and serene." As Simon Midgley described it in the *Independent on Sunday*, "The *Telegraph* usually cuts the figure of a *Queen Mary* among national daily newspapers; opulently fitted out, carrying more passengers, displacing more water and maintaining a higher profile than any of its rivals."

In other words, the *Telegraph* was precisely the sort of big, established target that Murdoch seemed most to enjoy toppling. One of his key advisers at News International was executive chairman Andrew Knight, who had captained the Telegraph company as its chief executive during the first three years of Hollinger's ownership, until his resignation and bitter falling-out with Black in 1989. After the price cut, critics railed that the *Times's* real aim was to eliminate the struggling *Independent*, which Knight denied. "The *Times* is the natural competitor of the *Telegraph*," Knight said. "If people want to go on concentrating on what impact it will have on the *Independent*, by all means let them. But the real debate is between us and the *Telegraph* over a ten-year period."

One thing Knight and the strategists at News International predicted when they lowered the *Times's* price was that Black would not respond by cutting the *Telegraph's* price immediately. In their view, Black was a financier first, a newspaperman second – they believed he would not jeopardize his precious cash flow or share price unless he absolutely had to.

Black did indeed stand his ground, though not, ostensibly, for the reasons Murdoch and "his numerous spear carriers and bootlickers" (as Black labelled them) gave. No stranger to things historical or military, Black reasoned it would be better to let the enemy expend resources for as long as possible while the *Telegraph* solidified its financial position. Moreover, like many newspaper executives, Black did not believe cover price was the factor determining why readers chose his paper. "They'll hang in for a while, but I don't think they'll get anywhere," he said after the first month of the *Times's* price cut. "You've got two directly competing theories here. I mean, Murdoch's theory is 'Don't overestimate the intelligence of the reader, keep going down-market and keep it cheap.' And our view is 'People will pay for quality' – so we'll see who wins."

By June 1994, the *Times* had increased its sales to 515,000. "The problem is the future," Black conceded in an off-the-record meeting with investors at the National Club in Toronto on June 10, "if our chief competitor is steadily gaining from far behind us." And Murdoch wasn't just any competitor, he was a colossus. Across all its businesses worldwide, News Corporation generated annual revenues of $10 billion. Hollinger's, by contrast, were $900 million, with the *Daily Telegraph* and its sister paper, the *Sunday Telegraph*, accounting for more than half its revenues and earnings.

Nevertheless, Black's message at the National Club was a positive one. He dismissed the "deeper pockets" theory that gave Murdoch an edge: so superior was the *Telegraph* franchise and cash flow that even if he matched the *Times*'s price cut, losing millions in circulation revenues, it would remain profitable; the *Daily Telegraph* was a better product – it had been named National Newspaper of the Year in the British Press Awards; moreover, Hollinger was in good financial shape, having recently taken its American subsidiary public and sold a tranche of Telegraph shares.

At the conclusion of the National Club gathering, in mocking reference to his reputation for litigation, Black exhorted the lunchers: "Anyone who wants to get something off their chest should do it – *even if I sue you for it.*" No one did.

The following Tuesday, June 14, the Telegraph managing directors' committee held its weekly meeting. The only items on the agenda were the latest Audit Bureau of Circulation and National Readership Survey figures. They showed that, for the first time in more than four decades, the *Daily Telegraph*'s circulation had fallen below 1 million – a key psychological barrier – while the *Times*'s had increased to over 500,000. Moreover, for the first time, readership (the number of people who read the paper as opposed to merely buying it) had declined while the *Times* again showed gains. Black was in New York that day, and spoke by phone separately and at length with his top executives, all of whom now recommended a price cut.

Having just sold 12.5 million Telegraph shares to institutions from Hollinger's holdings, Black was mindful of the public relations problem that would result from cutting the newspaper's price and depressing its stock value. But public relations problems had not stopped Black before.

That night, Black went to the Ritz, where Barbara Amiel was co-hosting what was described as the "high society party of the summer." One hundred and fifty glitterati, including Diana, Princess of Wales, had gathered to celebrate Sir James Goldsmith's election to the European Parliament and his wife's sixtieth birthday.

Two days later, the *Telegraph* finally cut its cover price from 48p to 30p. "Murdoch is a Darwinian," Black declared. "He wants survival of the fittest, and that's what he's going to get . . . If the *Times* wants to cut again they'll just make fools of themselves."

That day, Rupert Murdoch was in New York for a News Corporation board meeting. With very little fanfare, over a dinner, he and his directors decided to drop the *Times*'s price again the next day – to 20p.

On the London Stock Exchange, Telegraph shares plummeted from £5.40 to £3.49. Institutions that had bought Hollinger's Telegraph shares at £5.87 on May 19 were, as expected, furious. The broker that had handled the sale, Cazenove & Co., one of the City's blue-chip firms and one of the most secretive, resigned from the Telegraph account a week later. It made the banner story in the *Financial Times*, which included an unnamed "senior Cazenove official" saying it was "the first time in recent memory that Cazenove had voluntarily resigned as stockbroker to a company."

Black was enraged. "It was an orgy of self-righteous English hypocrisy," he later recalled. "I mean, the fact is, I naturally had them [Cazenove] in and consulted with them the day before we cut the cover price. They didn't offer a word of dissent. You know, it's a bit rich for them to carry on the way they did. I don't think they did themselves any favours in this thing. I gave them a pretty good shot on the way out which they richly deserved." The "shot" Black gave was to tell the *Financial Times* that Telegraph plc had in fact been planning to fire Cazenove because it had mishandled the May 19 share sale in the first place. "This famous firm just scuttled out the back door into the tall grass," sniffed Black.

A London Stock Exchange investigation into the timing of the share sale cleared Black of any impropriety. Nonetheless, analysts who followed Telegraph stock now declared Black would never be able to raise money in the City again. "The credibility of the management is somewhat suspect and their reputation has been severely damaged in the eyes of the City," said Richard Peirson, investment director at Framlington Group, a small but long-time Telegraph shareholder. The newspaper broker Hylton Philipson of Pall Mall Ltd. put it more plainly: "He has pissed off the establishment on this one." As usual, Black was unrepentant. "You can't make war and peace at the same time, you can't suck and blow at the same time," he said. "If you're going to regret an escalation of hostilities by an adversary who has already declared war on you, you might as well have flown up the white flag in the first place."

The price war became a fact of life in British newspapering, and Black responded in part by reducing his dependence on cash from his U.K. flagship through his globe-trotting diversifications, and by reorienting his financial base toward the United States. Still, the effect of the price war on the Telegraph company's financial statements was undeniable – a £23.5 million reduction in circulation revenue in 1994. Throughout the fall of 1994, Telegraph shares continued to trade well below what they were before the price war began.* In some respects, the price war set off a chain of events from which Black would never fully recover.

Black never hesitated to claim victory in the price war; even though it reduced the *Telegraph*'s profitability, he noted that it was costing the *Times* millions in losses and the *Telegraph* remained England's top-selling broadsheet. Black dismissed Telegraph executives who raised concerns about the long-term impact of Murdoch's apparent determination to keep up the pressure as weak and cowardly. "You shouldn't listen to the propaganda of our rivals," Black would say. "We have our foot on the windpipe of our principal competitor."

---

*In October, with Telegraph stock at around £3.05, the company began buying its own shares back, which the law allowed it to do at the rate of 5 per cent per year. Despite the controversy surrounding Hollinger's sale in May of 9 per cent of its Telegraph holdings at £5.87, Black was not going to miss a chance to buy back shares on the cheap, regardless of what people thought. The sale had raised about $150 million; the October purchase of 5 per cent was expected to cost about $50 million. "We're basically buying dimes for nickels," Black said. "What's wrong with that?"

Chapter Twenty-One

CHICAGO

In the quarter century that Conrad Black and David Radler had worked together, Radler had played the role of the fixer and axeman who relishes the art of the deal for its own sake. For example, in the 1990s, in addition to overseeing his side of Hollinger's publishing interests, Radler continued to run Western Dominion, the former Black family company that, under Radler's direction, had become the operator of Slumber Lodge Motels in western Canada and several Jessop's jewellery stores in southern California. His oversight of the *Jerusalem Post* gave him more prominence in the media world, but by late 1993 he was working on a deal that would elevate his profile even higher and, in the process, steer Hollinger's base of operations toward the United States.

The *Chicago Sun-Times*, the ninth-biggest daily newspaper in the United States by circulation, began as a morning paper in 1950 when Marshall Field III, a member of the legendary department-store family, bought the *Chicago Daily Times* and merged it with his *Chicago Sun*. In 1984, the Field family sold the paper to Rupert Murdoch. The two years Murdoch owned the paper are remembered without fondness by most Chicago journalists, who watched as the mid-market paper took a turn down-market. In 1986, when the Federal Communications Commission forced Murdoch to choose between owning the paper and owning a TV station in the same market, he chose the latter. An investor group, which included the New York investment bankers Adler & Shaykin, bought the paper and soon expanded its operations by acquiring sixty-three weekly and biweekly papers distributed in the Chicago suburbs.

Several months after buying the paper, Sun-Times company chairman Leonard Shaykin was invited to lunch at the Four Seasons in New York with Conrad Black, new owner of the *Daily Telegraph*. Black explained that he was trying to build a global newspaper group. Shaykin explained that Adler & Shaykin were financial buyers, not operators. "If you ever decide you want to sell, give me a call," Black told him. "That's a telephone call you will get," Shaykin replied.

Shaykin phoned Black in 1991, tracking him down in New York in the midst of Black's pursuit of the *Daily News*. "After you lose your enamour of the *Daily News*," Shaykin told him, "come back and let's talk." Around the same time, one of Radler's newspaper connections suggested the time was right to buy the *Sun-Times* and that he should contact Sam McKeel, its publisher. Radler was flying from Vancouver to board Hollinger's jet in Chicago and make one of his periodic whirlwind tours of American Publishing newspapers. He and McKeel agreed to meet at the Butler Aviation terminal at Chicago's O'Hare Airport. The remote location and clandestine atmosphere made Radler sure that the tipoff he'd been given was accurate. "We were in this kind of nondescript boardroom, thirty miles from the centre of Chicago," recalled Radler. "And McKeel said, 'The *Sun-Times* is not for sale.'

"And all I could think was, 'What the hell are you doing in this stinking boardroom thirty miles from the centre of Chicago?'"

Radler eventually received the answer he wanted, but it took two more years of lunches and phone calls – usually about baseball – with McKeel and Shaykin before they agreed to sell to Hollinger. With a circulation of 523,000 in 1993, the *Sun-Times* boasted the largest sales in the city of Chicago; the problem was that the mighty *Chicago Tribune* commanded 70 per cent of the advertising market. With a circulation of 697,000, it was the preferred paper in the suburbs, where most people lived. The population of the city was declining, and the *Sun-Times*'s circulation with it – between September 1991 and 1994, circulation was down 3.6 per cent during the week and 11 per cent on Sundays.

Moreover, as a leveraged buyout under the Shaykin group, the Sun-Times company had lacked the resources to invest in the paper when the economy had worsened in the early 1990s. With heavy financing costs, the newspaper's management was always strapped for resources, and Adler & Shaykin was not about to put more equity into the business. In fact, the fund that had bought the paper was being wound down in 1993 – and the *Sun-Times* was one of two assets left to be sold.

Radler was still interested in buying the paper, but he and Shaykin could not agree on price. At the same time, Shaykin did not want to hold a full-fledged auction for the paper. He wanted to sell to a committed newspaper owner who would slug it out with the *Tribune*. He also felt that newspapers were "delicate things," and having prospective bidders traipsing through the newsroom kicking the tires should be avoided. "Conrad was the logical buyer and the perfect buyer," said Shaykin. "He knew that, I knew that, Radler knew that. All we really had to deal with was the timing of the issue and the appropriate price."

In autumn 1993, some of the smaller banks in the Sun-Times syndicate became nervous about their exposure to the paper and offered to sell their debt at a discount to newspaper and financial buyers they thought might be interested, including Hollinger. Black and Radler declined to buy any of the debt, but the fact that it was being offered signalled declining confidence in the company. Shaykin brought his asking price down from US$240 million into Hollinger's range. After all, argued Radler, if the banks are selling at a discount, why should Hollinger pay full price? Over drinks at the Four Seasons on Michigan Avenue, the basics of the deal were agreed on and recorded on a cocktail napkin.

In December 1993, American Publishing bought the *Chicago Sun-Times* group of papers for US$180 million. The *Sun-Times* brought a weighty new dimension to the American Publishing group. Until its purchase, the largest title had been the Texas *Port Arthur News*, with a daily circulation of 23,900.

Black now owned a major American newspaper. A tabloid and traditionally Democratic in its editorial bent, it had the film reviewer Roger Ebert to the *Tribune's* Gene Siskel. Black was quick to point out that, in contrast to its Murdoch days, the *Sun-Times* was now a fairly sober mid-market paper. Rather than being a second paper in the market, there was so little overlap between it and the *Tribune* that he reckoned the papers were actually quasi-monopolies.

There was plenty of room for operational improvement in the *Sun-Times*: in 1993, it generated US$136 million in revenues, but only US$2.6 million in operating income – a mere 2 per cent margin. With 2,200 employees, Radler would find much to cut. American Publishing set aside US$10 million for voluntary layoffs when it took control, and Radler set about scrutinizing in his usual laser-like way every spread-sheet and department. Among the first people to leave were four vice-presidents and the company's treasurer, and then, in July, publisher and chief executive Sam McKeel. As far as Radler was concerned, the resignations were a predictable result of a new owner coming in and proclaiming that the results the company had been achieving were no longer good enough. "Then there's the style thing," said Radler. "Some of my American Publishing executives are a little rough around the edges, okay? I mean, they come from a background of entrepreneurship, okay? They don't have the style or the presence – *presence* isn't the word, there's probably too much presence – that these kind of people are used to."

One such person who would agree is Dennis Britton, who resigned as the paper's editor soon into the new regime. "The most interesting example of Radler to me was when he came into an executive meeting once and threw a sheaf of papers down and said, 'I want 100 people laid off,'" recalled Britton. "We said, 'What are you talking about?' He said, 'See this sheaf of papers? There were 100 people off work last week and we got the paper out without them.' That's the kind of guy he was. He was ruthless."

After Britton's departure, Nigel Wade, the *Daily Telegraph*'s foreign editor, was brought in as editor. Wade put less emphasis on the paper's sports coverage and gave its news pages a more serious tone.

Within six months of buying the paper, Radler had taken an apartment in Chicago and was doing things like clipping the colour advertisements out of the *Tribune* that he reckoned the *Sun-Times* could get if only it had presses capable of proper colour. Twenty of the group's biweekly papers were printed by a contractor, and Radler visualized major cost savings by producing them in-house. Eventually, he took the position of *Sun-Times* publisher for himself, but, true to his retiring nature, he did not make much effort to schmooze with the movers and shakers in America's third-largest city. Sometimes he would conduct business while on the terrace outside his office, sunning himself, or he would invite his top executives out there for lunch with him.

In December 1994 the company bought a local community paper with a circulation of 60,000, the *Daily Southtown*, from Pulitzer Publishing. The *Southtown*'s assets included a modern printing facility that had long-term contracts with the *New York Times*, *USA Today*, and the *Wall Street Journal*. Analysts hailed the purchase not only for bolstering the *Sun-Times*'s regional presence against the *Tribune* but also for laying the groundwork for a new printing facility. It was just the first in a series of additions Radler made to the group between 1994 and 2000, building up what came to be called the Chicago Group. Anchored by the *Sun-Times*, the group eventually grew to include more than one hundred papers in the Metropolitan Chicago area with a combined weekday circulation of more than 700,000, even surpassing the vaunted *Tribune*, at least in that one respect.

Black first visited the *Sun-Times* five months after its purchase, sporting cufflinks with Franklin Delano Roosevelt's head on them – his way of allaying fears that the paper's Democratic bent was in jeopardy. He sat in on an editorial conference and met senior department heads. "For such an architecturally well-endowed city, it really is a terribly humdrum building, isn't it?" Black observed of the offices. "I wouldn't say it's ugly. It's just sort of pedestrian."

The *Sun-Times* was not exactly the prestige flagship that Black might have wanted for the United States, but it was a start. By 1995 American Publishing, which had not existed nine years earlier, ranked as the twelfth-largest newspaper chain in the country based on circulation, and second-largest when measured by the number of newspapers operated.

As had happened with the *Jerusalem Post* under Radler, before long the editorial voice in this most traditionally Democratic of American cities took a decided rightward turn. In the October 26, 1995, edition, the *Sun-Times* readers were forcefully reminded of who the new owners were with a peculiar spread of stories covering that night's Hollinger Dinner, held in Chicago. The paper printed the full invitation list, which included the former president of Israel, Chaim Herzog, and Margaret Thatcher along with David Brinkley and Gerald Greenwald, then the chairman of Chicago-based United Airlines, plus a smattering of *Sun-Times* employees, including Roger Ebert. As they hung on the straps of the El on their way to work, *Sun-Times* readers were treated to a recounting of the dinner menu of roast loin of veal and "autumn vegetables," washed down with either a 1993 Horton Viognier or a 1989 Château Talbot St. Julien.

Chapter Twenty-Two

ALL OVER THE MAP

The acquisition of the *Chicago Sun-Times* was the catalyst for a series of huge strategic changes for Black's newspaper empire that would shift his financial interests to the United States and have fateful consequences a decade later. After Murdoch lowered the *Times*'s cover price, Black waited nine months before joining the price war by dropping the *Telegraph*'s cover price in kind. Although some questioned whether he had waited too long, the delay did buy him time, during which he fortified Hollinger's finances by raising money in the debt markets, selling some of its Telegraph shares, and issuing stock to the public in his American subsidiary.

Hollinger raised $121 million through a debenture issue linked to the price of its Southam stock, and another US$144 million through an issue of notes. The public issue of American Publishing in 1994, however, was the most critical strategic move. Initially, the idea was to sell the stock to investors as a way to invest in all the community newspapers Radler had acquired over the years, but with the addition of the *Sun-Times*, a major metropolitan daily, the issue was now marketed as an American newspaper company with broader horizons. The issue successfully raised another US$98 million, but it also quietly opened up some enticing new avenues for Black: American Publishing was sold as a company with two classes of shares, while its Canadian parent Hollinger had only one class of stock. That meant that if Black wanted to use Hollinger shares to make acquisitions, he would be diluting his controlling stake in the company unless he kicked in money of his own every time to buy more stock.

Many Canadian companies and media businesses used dual-class voting structures like American's. (Even E.P. Taylor and Bud McDougald's old Argus was controlled through Ravelston via such a construct.) As American's majority shareholder, Hollinger would be the sole owner of the company's Class B shares, bearing ten votes apiece, while Class A shares with a single vote would be sold to the public. As a result, at the end of the issue, Hollinger owned 67 per cent of the company's equity but 95 per cent of its votes. For Black, the financial engineering possibilities of this structure were virtually limitless, and the pedigree of being a player in the world's media and financial capital was doubly alluring. Indeed, within months of American Publishing's May 1994 listing on the NASDAQ market, Black hatched a plan to bring the rest of his interests in Canada, the United Kingdom, Australia, and Israel under the aegis of the U.S. company.

On August 25, 1994, Conrad Black turned fifty. He spent the evening quietly with his wife, in part because Amiel had recently undergone surgery. Black reflected that he was now "too old to be called a 'whiz kid' but too young to get any respect." For some time, the Blacks had been looking at apartments in New York City, and now that they had a publicly traded American company to look after, they settled in December 1994 on a co-op on Park Avenue at Sixty-sixth Street. The price was US$3 million, which, together with "customary transaction costs and expenses and needed capital improvements and furnishings," was paid by American Publishing. Black would be able to use the apartment rent-free. The reason for the purchase, according to American Publishing documents, was "to facilitate the rendering of management and advisory services" and "to enhance the business interests of the corporation with the financial community, the newspaper industry and otherwise." Although Hollinger executives may have thought they were doing the right thing by disclosing the purchase, rather than renting out fancy hotel suites that shareholders would never hear about, the purchase – and that of a US$1 million apartment for Radler's use in Chicago – raised eyebrows after they were mentioned in *Forbes* and *Business Week.*

Even before the proposed shift of Black's power base from London to the United States, he and Amiel had been spending more and more of their time in Manhattan. Despite the cut and thrust of the price war in London, it seemed to some of his friends that Black was growing restless, even bored. "No, not a bit," said Black. "In my position I move around not exactly according to what municipality I most like the public parks in, the theatres or the skyline. I go where my essential economic interests lead. I like London and I like New York. So I'll be a good deal in both of them." Another theory was that Black was growing disenchanted with the political scene, particularly with the prospect of a Labour government turning the Tory *Telegraph* into an opposition paper. Black vehemently denied this speculation: "That's all a load of bullshit. God knows where that nonsense comes from. In the first place, it is well known that we've been highly critical of the government here. In the second place, my relations with the leader of the opposition are perfectly cordial. In the third place, I never particularly care who the government is anyway, unless it's some completely oppressive regime . . . You don't pack up and leave like a dung beetle moving from one place to another. If you're the head of an international company you might choose to have residences in more than one of the countries that you do business in. And that's all I'm doing."

Two days before announcing the reorganization, Black spent much of his evening at home in London, participating in a Fairfax board meeting in Australia via telephone, and the following night he spent even longer on the phone with associates and advisers in Chicago and Toronto running through the reorganization. At one point, Amiel said, "You always have a military analogy for what you're doing. What is it now?"

"Aha!" Conrad replied, "I will show you."

Black later said, "So I got out General Fuller's life of Julius Caesar and I opened it to a map of the battle of Alesia. This was in the suppression of the revolt of the Gauls, you see, and Caesar chased his enemies into this town and laid siege to them. But then a much larger enemy force came and laid siege to him. So you had two lines, a line of *circumvallation* and a line of *contravallation*, and I said, 'There he was – he was between those two lines. He was keeping the inner group in and the outer group out, but it was making for an awful lot of fighting all the time.'

"She said, 'Did he win?'

"I said, 'Oh yes, he won.'

"So that's my little analogy. I was thinking about it. It always struck me as the most astonishing military map I had ever seen, along with its description of Caesar himself charging around in his red cape for weeks on end. He'd be in the east and he'd be in the west . . . I'm joking. I'm not saying I'm in that kind of position. It's just that there's a lot going on at once."

On January 16, 1996, American Publishing was rechristened Hollinger International and floated on the New York Stock Exchange. To mark the occasion, Black had breakfast with exchange chairman Richard Grasso and bought the first 100 shares from the floor of the epicentre of global capitalism. Soon after, despite five years of publicly proclaiming that he was close to approval to increase his interest in Fairfax above the 25 per cent legal threshold, Black finally gave up and sold his interest in the Australian company, taking a $300 million profit for his troubles. ("The proceeds," Black sniffed, "will be better applied in jurisdictions where foreigners are not treated with official bad faith and insurmountable suspicion.") He still had to battle Murdoch in London, turn around Southam, and continue to expand his tentacles and influence in the United States, the country that mattered to him most. But, for a while at least, it seemed like invincibility was within Black's reach. Whatever he did next, he proclaimed, he would not risk what he had built. "If you want to be rich, you've got to do it once," he said, suggesting that the several million dollars he had inherited from his father in 1976 did not fit his definition of rich. "In essence I did it twice, but I would never do it again. Never. Absolutely not. Never bet more than you can afford to lose. No matter how enticing the prize is, don't do it. Don't bet the company."

Over the years that he built Hollinger into one of the world's largest newspaper companies, it became more difficult to distinguish between Black the person and Black the caricature. When he appeared on the BBC Radio program *Desert Island Discs*, on which guests are invited to play songs they would choose if confined to a desert island, Black's eclectic selections included Beethoven's "Emperor" piano concerto, Paul Robeson's version of "Londonderry Air," the Mormon Tabernacle Choir's rendition of "The Battle Hymn of the Republic," and General Douglas MacArthur's 1951 farewell address to the United States Congress.

Charlotte Corbeil, the television interviewer, once asked Black how he wanted his epitaph to read. Just his name and dates, he replied. "Oh, come on," Corbeil said with mock disappointment, having expected something more grand, given Black's fascination with historical figures and world leaders. Black explained that the more exalted a person, the less is written on his or her tombstone: Charles de Gaulle's has just his name and dates, Winston Churchill's has the same, Otto von Bismarck's has only his last name, and Napoleon Bonaparte's has only the letter N with no dates at all. "By those criteria," Black intoned, "I suppose I should aspire to have an absolutely blank tombstone, because I'd be so well known, no explanation would be necessary."

Such proclamations notwithstanding, Black contended he had been falsely typecast by the media "as a sort of blustering, Henry VIII, predatory tycoon. That's essentially bullshit. To the extent that I'm that, that's a very small extent." He was the first to admit that not all his public pronouncements should be taken at face value. "Most of what goes on is a bit of a game," he admitted. "You've got to enjoy the game."

That his style and views did not make him universally popular, especially in his native Canada, was fine by Black, who was always suspicious of overly popular people. The historical figures that fascinated him were often autocratic, frequently beleaguered, usually misunderstood – Duplessis, de Gaulle, Napoleon, Nixon. "I'm not interested in popularity. I just don't want to be synonymous with something that is a magnet for public hatred," he explained.

A 1994 profile of Black in *Time* magazine described him as a billionaire, but nobody checked with him. "In French francs, yes," he quipped later, "but in Canadian or American dollars or pounds, no." He added: "I have run up a profit every year for a great many years." Black dealt in large sums, to be sure, but his fortune did not place him among the world's or even Canada's most moneyed individuals. When asked why he received so much attention, Black responded, "That is a perfectly legitimate question I often put myself. I mean, I'm a well-to-do person but there are lots of wealthier people around."

The financier and former Hollinger director Peter Munk suggested that Black might find the answer in the mirror. "He does seem to lead a lifestyle that would match people who belong to the international world of the heavyweight financiers – which he's not," said Munk. "As long as I have known him, he seems to be attracting attention. He does not particularly seem to mind it: he does drive around in one of the finest old Rolls-Royces in England. You can be Rupert Murdoch and drive around in a black Ford."

By 1995 it was clear that the progress of Hollinger would depend on how Black navigated the realm of tycoons with ambitions at least equal to his and with financial means far outstripping Hollinger's. "In an ideal world maybe I would have no peer," Black said one day in his Canary Wharf office, sitting beneath battlefield paintings of Wellington and Trafalgar, renderings of a couple of cruise liners, and a framed photograph of the Queen reading the *Telegraph*. "I'd own everything I wanted to own and there wouldn't be anyone else to have the effrontery to have a different view or a different interest. But that's not the way the world works, so you've got to deal with who's there. It creates issues, but, you know, what the hell am I paid for? I've got to do something for a living."

The world was changing, and Black could not remain still or satisfied. Despite his happy new marriage to Barbara and his homes in London, Toronto, New York, and Palm Beach, Black was not yet where he wanted to be. The foundation was laid, but America had yet to be conquered. The bull market was starting to charge, the buzz about digital technology and its effect on established media was becoming a roar, and Black seemed poised to ride the heady days leading into the millennium to dizzying new heights of wealth, power, and influence. One way or another, he was going to be titanic.

PART THREE

TITANIC

Chapter Twenty-Three

"THE GREATEST CORPORATE FRIEND CANADIAN PRINT JOURNALISTS HAVE"

On the humid late afternoon of June 30, 1997, Conrad Black suited himself up in a dark, high-collared military coat and broad red-striped pants and sword to assume the role of honorary colonel in the Governor General's Foot Guards at Rideau Hall in Ottawa. Black had always professed to be a fan of military pageantry, and here he had a chance to strut his stuff as a host of Queen Elizabeth and her husband, Prince Philip, in Canada on a royal visit. Showing no signs of discomfort from the thirty-degree swelter, the seventy-one-year-old monarch inspected the troops while Black – sporting a jaunty cap instead of the tall, plumed bearskin hat of the regular Foot Guard – hovered behind. The photo of Black and the Queen ran prominently in the Ottawa *Citizen* and other Southam papers, the attentive Black looking out of place and vaguely like the chief doorman at the Château Laurier. The Queen told Black that she wasn't accustomed to seeing him dressed this way, to which he quipped, "I'm always representing the *Daily Telegraph.*" The *Citizen's* lengthy story neglected to mention that Black was the paper's owner, but it did point out that "Mr. Black got his chance at pageantry and appeared to perform admirably."

The *Citizen* was one of the first newspapers where Hollinger had made its mark after taking control of Southam. The paper was widely regarded as competent but a grey, dull read, and the new regime had committed $50 million to sprucing it up and talked about making it the *Washington Post* of the north, a paper that was respected and read beyond its home market because of the vigour with which it covered federal affairs. "We want the *Citizen* to have more credibility as a forum for intelligent, but not humourless, discussion of major public policy issues and international questions," Black said. "We want to liven it up a bit and make it a more literate, exciting read."

Under its new editor, Neil Reynolds, whom Barbara Amiel had championed for the slot, the revitalized *Citizen* had a bigger news hole and a new weekly Sunday magazine, with lengthy book reviews and essays. "Hollinger poured a lot of resources into the paper, and it certainly shows," noted Peter Calamai, an editorial-page editor who was fired by Black in 1996. "Prior to Hollinger, I had two editorial pages – an editorial page and an op-ed page. Now they have five editorial pages every day." Politically, Reynolds acknowledged that the paper "definitely swung to the right [on the editorial page] from where we were before. But overall, we're trying to provide a broad spectrum of views." Similar revamps would take place at other big Southam dailies including the Montreal *Gazette* and the *Vancouver Sun*, but, ultimately, none of these big "metros" would give Black the satisfaction he derived from owning the *Telegraph*, even though Canada now represented roughly half of Hollinger's revenues. "I don't go around trying to stir up foreign wars," Black said. "I want to be identified with a high-class operation, professionally and financially high-class. It's not so much influence but a low-level, un-jarring notion of prestige."

A paper that Black had thought would at least partially fit that bill was the *Financial Post*, of which he had owned 19.9 per cent since 1988 when he had helped Toronto Sun Publishing transform it from a weekly broadsheet into a daily business tabloid. In September 1996, a management buyout led by Sun Publishing chief executive Paul Godfrey acquired the newspaper chain from Rogers Communications, and Black believed he had a deal with Godfrey to acquire the *Post*. When Godfrey declined to sell, Black, in a snit, sold Hollinger's stake in the paper. "Conrad's version of this is different than mine, but he was under the impression that I had agreed to sell him the *Financial Post* and after the deal was done he came and offered to take the *Post* off my hands," recalled Godfrey. "He was disturbed that I didn't want to sell, but I had investors who thought the newspaper had upward mobility."

The rejection crystallized Black's determination to start an entirely new national newspaper built on the backs of Southam's existing newspapers and resources. Although he called Southam "a national chain without a national newspaper," equally critical to his decision was the fact that the new newspaper would be based in Toronto, Canada's financial centre and biggest city, where the country's two other national publications, the *Financial Post* and the *Globe and Mail*, were also headquartered, but where Southam had no presence. "We don't doubt our ability to produce at least as viable a product as the *Financial Post* relatively easily," Black huffed.

For the task, Black enlisted as the new paper's editor-in-chief Ken Whyte, the Winnipeg-born, thirty-seven-year-old editor of Hollinger's *Saturday Night* magazine. Through a series of phone calls and a brunch with Black and Barbara Amiel at the King Edward Hotel on Good Friday, 1997, the philosophy about the paper began to take shape. Whyte was an unconventional choice in that he was a magazine hand with no daily newspaper experience, but he shared both Black's conservative outlook and a cool ambition to create something distinctive, sophisticated, and lively. It should be not only a flagship for the newly refurbished Southam fleet but an alternative to the smart but sober and vaguely governmental *Globe and Mail.* And, perhaps closest to Black's heart, it would be his organ for trying to challenge the Canadian spirit of left-of-centre liberalism and supposed complacency that he had been railing about for years. As Amiel, who enthusiastically agreed, put it, "For years I've personally loathed the homogeneity of the Canadian media and its closed-minded approach to ideas." As their vision took shape, Whyte dined with the Blacks at their Toronto mansion, struck by how optimistic Black was about the paper and its commercial prospects and how pessimistic Amiel was.

For months, Whyte and a team of top Southam people, with occasional input from some Telegraph group cousins, planned a paper that was to be called either the *Canadian* or the *Times of Canada.*

Whyte hired as deputy editor the *Daily Telegraph*'s Martin Newland, whose newshound sensibilities and daily experience would fit well with Whyte's keen conceptual eye. Donald Babick, the seasoned Southam president who had successfully overhauled the chain's Pacific Press newspapers in Vancouver, would be the *Post*'s publisher. Media executives at the newspapers this upstart was intended to compete with remained skeptical that Black would actually go through with his plans. For a country of Canada's size, it was hard to fathom how the marketplace could support a third national newspaper beyond the *Globe* and the *Post* (which was a niche title, targeting investors and managers). And those papers would not be the only competition. Most North American cities of the same size were now down to a single daily newspaper, but Toronto's news racks boasted four dailies: the market-leading *Toronto Star*, the *Toronto Sun*, the *Globe*, and the *Financial Post*. Adding to the skepticism was the simple fact that, despite his past successes in buying and running newspapers, Black had never before started anything – an endeavour that might require a decade or longer of heavy investment before it turned a profit. The betting was that Black was doing the business equivalent of dressing up in his colonel's uniform, marching missiles through city thoroughfares or running war exercises in an attempt to intimidate the owners of either the *Post* or the *Globe* into selling to him. Indeed, he and David Radler again approached Godfrey about the *Post* and made overtures to the Thomson family, owners of the *Globe*, during this period. Hollinger had already bought twenty-four newspapers from Thomson Corp. during the past few years as it exited the newspaper business, but Ken Thomson insisted he would not sell the *Globe* (at least not to Black).* According to Black, Thomson did offer him a 20 per cent stake in the *Globe* as a way of getting him to call off his new paper.

Black finally acquired the *Financial Post*, and in classic Black fashion – as the unanticipated result of his drawing together all the black-tied

---

* Thomson Corp. did end up selling a majority stake in the *Globe* to the telephone giant BCE Inc. on very good terms in order to combine it with the CTV television network and other media interests, but the Thomson family retained a significant oversight position and Ken remained chairman.

luminaries he could squeeze into a room. It was actually one of Black's oldest and not especially glamorous Toronto friends who made it happen, his doctor, Bernard Gosevitz. As the medical adviser to many of Toronto's elite, Gosevitz for years kept his family practice office at the *Toronto Sun* offices, where he dispensed helpful advice, medical and otherwise, to moguls and hacks alike. As recounted in Chris Cobb's 2004 book *Ego and Ink*, Gosevitz was staying at the Blacks' house in Knightsbridge and was scheduled to return to Canada on the eve of Black's June 1998 Hollinger Dinner, attended by the likes of British prime minister Tony Blair and his predecessor Lady Thatcher. But Black's friend Henry Kissinger had fallen ill, and Black asked Gosevitz to help look after him. He then invited Gosevitz to the dinner, even providing one of his shirts and a bow tie for the doctor. After the dinner, Gosevitz and Black sipped white wine in the Cottesmore Gardens library into the early morning hours. The subject of Black's rancour toward Paul Godfrey for allegedly reneging on a deal to sell the *Post* came up. Gosevitz, who is godfather to Godfrey's daughters, offered to make a call to try to make amends, and soon both sides were talking again. Black and Godfrey never spoke directly, but David Radler and Hollinger's general counsel, Peter Atkinson, met with Godfrey and his representatives to hammer out a deal.*

Godfrey recognized that the *Post*, which was only slightly profitable, was much more susceptible to the impact of a new daily on the marketplace than the *Globe*, bankrolled by Canada's wealthiest family. But he insisted he would not sell the *Post*, and in the end he didn't – he traded it for Southam's daily newspapers in Kitchener, Hamilton, Guelph, and Cambridge plus $150 million in cash. The deal, announced on July 20, valued the *Financial Post* at around $110 million and gave Black's new baby, now christened the *National Post*, an instant subscriber base of some 90,000 each weekday and double that on weekends, a top-flight business section, and a roster of well-known

---

* Radler never particularly backed the idea of the *National Post*, but at least acquisition of the *Financial Post* would allow the new paper to build on an existing title, a type of deal that Hollinger had some experience with.

scribes, including David Frum and Diane Francis.* The inclusion of the *Financial Post* meant that the *National Post* very quickly became more ambitious than originally envisioned, and more squarely aimed at the *Globe and Mail*. The *Post* now targeted a circulation of 300,000 for a start-up investment of $150 million.

Now that the existence of Black's national paper was assured, some questioned whether there was a real business case for it or whether it was just an ego trip the press baron wanted to embark on at his shareholders' expense. In its favour, the company already had printing presses and trucks to deliver the paper across Canada, and in Toronto the *Financial Post* deal brought with it use of the *Toronto Sun's* presses. Once the *National Post* moved off the drawing board, it piggybacked on Southam's thirty-three daily newspapers by cherry-picking the best people and stories – a strategy that drew the enmity of publishers and editors from Southam's dailies. Whyte criss-crossed the country, luring some of the best journalists in the business with the promise of better pay and more adventure. John Cruickshank, who was then editor of the *Vancouver Sun*, had admired the way that Black and Radler had eviscerated the plodding middle-management ways of the old Southam. But he was outraged by the corporate edicts regarding the *Post*; out of his paper's staff of 140, his top seven reporters and editors were poached by the *Post*, and not only was he not allowed to counter-offer but they would now effectively be competing against him. "They took all of the best people, and budgets froze up," Cruickshank said. "It was outrageous."

Black envisioned the *Post* as a kind of creative destruction machine that would cannibalize Southam's local papers in the short run, but in the long haul the company overall would be stronger for it and more valuable. "I don't think Conrad ever saw the *National Post* as a business thing first," Martin Newland said. "It was a movement of the heart and a movement of the soul, and only then was a business model drafted on." Ken Whyte assessed Black's motivation this

---

* The $110 million did not include the remaining 20 per cent of the paper, which Hollinger went on to buy back from Pearson.

way: "My overarching impression of him is of a man who was doing something that he thought was grand and important. He was undertaking it with the best of intentions and the highest of hopes. There was a great deal of romance and idealism behind it. He felt that if the product was there, the business case was there – and that was a bit of a nineteenth-century way of thinking."

One of the last big daily newspapers to launch in the twentieth century debuted on October 26, 1998, after eighteen months of busy preparation. That evening, Black and his wife strode into the spotlight first by attending a small book party at Massey College hosted by his friend John Fraser, and attended by other long-time friends, including Fred Eaton, the former high commissioner to London, and Hal Jackman, the former lieutenant-governor of Ontario. Also on hand were many of the key people in Amiel's life, including her former husband George Jonas and her former boss at the *Toronto Sun*, Peter Worthington. The occasion was the re-release of Black's 1977 biography of Maurice Duplessis, now retitled *Render unto Caesar: The Life and Legacy of Maurice Duplessis* and published by Anna Porter of Key Porter Books, which had earlier released Black's memoir, *A Life in Progress*. It wasn't clear that the world was clamouring for a new version of *Duplessis*, but Black edited the book down and added a new introduction. After the fete, Black and his entourage went to the *Toronto Sun*, where the *National Post* was to be printed.

For the first time in his career, Black played the role of expectant father of a new business. He pressed the button to start the presses and paced the floor while his wife and guests stood by, waiting for the first edition to roll off. Then he was photographed proudly holding up his creation before heading to the *Post*'s office in suburban Don Mills for a party in the paper's first-floor cafeteria. Black signed copies and posed for photos. It was a triumphant moment. Regardless of how the paper performed, its debut proved that despite his own ups and downs with the media, a paper funded by Black could attract some of the country's top journalists to join his crusade. To Black, it validated his retort to critics of his domination of the newspaper business that Hollinger was "the greatest corporate friend Canadian print journalists have."

The next morning, Black left a long congratulatory voicemail for Whyte. The first edition of the *Post* carried a big photograph of the astronaut John Glenn, who was returning to space at age seventy-seven. This resulted in some angry letters bemoaning the trumpeting of an American in the debut issue of Canada's new national newspaper. The author Mordecai Richler took up the cause in a column, saying that he'd spoken to Black and Whyte, and all foreign news in future editions would be banished from the front page. Richler volunteered such examples as "Boris Yeltsin, a Russian politician, threatens to launch missiles tomorrow, not one aimed at Ontario, according to reliable sources. Page 76" and "Non-Canadian scientists discover cancer cure. Page 84."

Black's *Post* had much to offer, from the way it covered arts and sports to its comprehensive business coverage to its Fleet Street–inspired tendency to find any excuse to decorate the front page with photos of sexy women (which Jim Travers, an editor at the *Toronto Star*, memorably dubbed "tits and analysis"). The *Post*'s debut lead story, about a plan to unite the right by combining the Reform and Progressive Conservative parties to form a bloc against the powerful Liberals, sent a blaring message that not only did the paper have an ideology but it saw itself as the unofficial opposition. Of course the *Post* newsroom had the usual infighting and intrigues, but above all Whyte's paper soon proved fun to work at and its daily contents reflected it. "Whether you love Conrad Black or hate him, you have to give him this much: he knows how to make a splash," the magazine *Canadian Business* noted. "In less than a year, his *Post* . . . developed a reputation as a newspaper with a distinctive voice. Editorially, it's aggressive, unabashedly right-wing, and obsessed with tax cuts and Reform leader Preston Manning's plan to unite his party with the Conservatives."

As H.L. Mencken wrote of William Randolph Hearst's contribution to journalism, Black's *National Post* "shook up old bones, and gave the blush of life to pale cheeks." Within just three months, the *Post* claimed to have achieved circulation of 272,778 and a readership of 750,000, coming close to the *Globe*'s circulation level of 308,000. But the *Globe* quickly rose to the challenge, importing the veteran British-born executive Philip Crawley, who had run newspaper companies in New Zealand and Hong Kong, to lead it through a newspaper war that quickly became characterized as a British invasion. Before long, *Globe* editor-in-chief William Thorsell was replaced by Fleet Street hand Richard Addis, who had edited the *Daily Express*; and Alberta-born Chrystia Freeland, thirty, a rising star at the *Financial Times* who had worked in its Moscow bureau, was recruited as deputy editor. Addis's flightiness and lack of knowledge of (or, it sometimes seemed, interest in) Canadian life was offset by his fierce competitiveness and much-needed knack for livening up the newspaper's pages.

The *Post* had its own cadre of imported firepower from the U.K., the world's most cutthroat newspaper market, including Newland, former Vancouver *Province* editor-in-chief Michael Cooke, and, not least, British-born, Canadian-raised Barbara Amiel. Throughout the *Post*'s launch, she played the role of loyal owner's wife, but one who had quite a few ideas of her own about how things should be done – she was, after all, the only journalist on the board of Hollinger and its vice-president of editorial. "I am married to the chairman of Southam Inc., which is launching a new national newspaper in Canada later this month," she wrote in a deadpan column in *Maclean's* shortly before the paper's launch. "I may also write a column for said paper, and if that paper is a financial success, I'm hoping my husband's income from it will subsidize my obscene dress bills. (Of one thing you can be sure: someone will take that last sentence out of context.)"

Amiel had plenty more substantive things to say about the paper, and she helped make recommendations for new hires. She also kicked up a major fuss in the days just prior to launch when she complained that the design of the paper was too radical and vertical and needed to be scrapped. Whyte held his course, the paper's design was heralded as one of its best innovations, and Amiel conceded that in her pre-launch jitters she had erred.

Amiel had built up a storehouse of ideas and clippings over the years, some of which she put together in a binder and handed out to editors. She was knowledgeable, but unpredictable and moody. Whether dealing with butlers or newspaper chiefs, Amiel was not above screaming to make a point. "Barbara has not the greatest people skills," said one executive who dealt with her. "When she wants to be, she can be the most charming person in the world, and she can melt you. But she would turn around in a minute – if she read one line in the paper in one issue that bothered her, she would indict the whole paper. Her style got in the way, because quite often she was right." Michael Cooke, who also worked for the Blacks in Chicago, liked to say, "You just never know what you're going to get with Barbara. It's either chocky or Rotty" – which was apparently Brit-speak for "chocolates or Rottweiler."*

Despite the garden party, and other lunches and dinners for fifteen or twenty that Black would host at the Toronto Club for executives from the big banks or Harry Rosen, General Motors or eTrade, the *Post* was unable to attract much advertising, a major sore point for him and a point of pride for his rivals at the *Globe*. Advertising, after all, typically accounts for two-thirds or more of a big daily's revenues; the concept is predicated on the simple notion that once you build an audience of smart readers, advertisers will want to reach them. While both the *Post* and *Globe* would claim that the other's strong circulation and readership numbers were fudged by massive giveaways, discounts, and gimmicks, there was no hiding the fact that the *Post* was getting far less than its share of advertisers. Black later explained this failing as a rejection of his persona, rather than of the *Post*'s business case. "The fact is that Canada is not only a smug country but a fearful country, very afraid of change and particularly afraid of it if the change, as it was portrayed in this case, is something that, if adopted, would accrue to the benefit of a controversial individual. And the degree to which it was my paper, and therefore something many people wouldn't wish to support, was a problem for it."

There were other explanations for the shortcomings, but not ones that Black and his executives may have readily acknowledged. One was that in buying the *Financial Post*, they didn't build on the true strength of that franchise, which was a weekend business newspaper with a circulation of 200,000 and a following among readers and advertisers that stretched back decades. Another was that the new paper might have

---

* Cooke credited Martin Newland with inventing the phrase.

achieved its financial goals sooner if it hadn't pursued the ambitious and expensive circulation objective of surpassing the *Globe*, which aggressively responded to the challenge. Probably the biggest conceptual flaw was that the *Post* could not escape its advertising overlap with the Southam dailies. Black and Babick argued that the market share they would build would come from the *Globe* and even from other forms of media, but the reality was that many big national advertisers were already in the Southam dailies in major centres such as Vancouver, Calgary, and Montreal. While it was true that Southam had lacked the ability to offer Toronto to these advertisers, there was little reason for them to buy space in both the *Post* and the rest of the Southam dailies, since they'd only be reaching many of the same readers twice.

Black could rationalize any situation, and the *Post* was no exception. Even if the start-up costs were far greater than he had figured – and they were – Black argued that a fast-growing and prestigious upstart could still command a premium price if sold, regardless of its losses. But given that Black would abandon the *Post* far sooner than the viability of any new publication could be determined, the question of whether the *Post* was a commercial folly or a triumph became moot.

Chapter Twenty-Four

FLYING HIGH

The *Post* was born in a period of high optimism. Black recorded in Hollinger International's 1997 annual report that the year was "the most successful in our history but was, we are confident, only a foretaste of what is to come." By the following year, the company's revenues approached US$2.2 billion, producing an operating income of US$282 million and net income of US$196 million. Aside from the *Post*, Hollinger was gearing up for a US$100 million upgrade of the printing plant for the *Chicago Sun-Times* and in the midst of efforts to buy out the remaining minority shareholders of Southam. To fund these initiatives as well as the *Post*'s start-up while managing the company's US$1.4 billion in debt, Hollinger International began selling off the small American papers that Radler and his team had assembled over the previous dozen years. In January 1998, eighty papers were divested for US$310 million, and the magazine *American Trucker* and some other publications fetched US$94 million. A year later another forty-five papers fetched US$475 million. To the media caught up in the *Sturm und Drang* of a Canadian newspaper war, the sale of nearly US$1 billion worth of small newspapers merited little public notice.

While it may have looked as if their company was shifting its focus away from these small-town newspapers, Black and Radler weren't. Instead, some of the papers were being sold to a new company they set up in 1998 called Horizon Publications, led by Todd Vogt, a Hollinger executive based in Chicago who had worked for Radler. Black and Radler each initially purchased 24 per cent of the equity for roughly US$1.5 million, with the rest held by former and present Hollinger employees including Vogt, who became Horizon's president and CEO. Although the formation of Horizon was presented for approval by Hollinger International's board of directors in November 1998, it would eventually become a source of controversy and accusations that Black and Radler were selling company assets to themselves for less than their worth, and that they were even using Hollinger International unwittingly to fund their side venture. (Black and Radler would deny the allegations.) As Black later wrote to a potential Horizon investor: "We have bought and sold hundreds of these little American newspapers in public companies and have never failed to make handsome profits on them."

Black's confidence in his prospects fuelled the propulsion of his and Amiel's opulent lifestyle into the mesosphere inhabited by the New York–centric moguls they now seemed to prefer the company of: the Kravises, the Taubmans, and various members of what Hollinger International executives began to refer to as the "Oscar de la Kissinger" crowd. In 1996, Black had passed along Hollinger's Gulfstream 2 jet to David Radler to use for zipping among the various dots on the map that housed clusters of small-town newspapers, and to commute between Chicago, Vancouver, and his vacation home in Palm Springs.* For its CEO's use, Hollinger upgraded to a state-of-the-art Gulfstream IV, a US$25 million marvel which, unlike the previous jet, was capable of shuttling the Blacks nonstop on their transatlantic journeys. (Hollinger executives later claimed that Amiel had complained in another of those sure-to-be-taken-out-of-context moments about having to take "British public transport," also known as Concorde. She also reportedly said, "It's always best to have two planes because however well one plans ahead one always finds one is on the wrong

---

* The Gulfstream 2 was later retired in favour of a Canadair Challenger 601, purchased for US$12 million in 2001.

continent." Amiel denied saying this.*) Leased from the First Security Bank of Utah, the new G-IV jet underwent an extensive US$3 million remodelling that involved the installation of impossibly plush leather seats in an impossibly blond shade and repositioning the aircraft's galley from the rear of the plane to the front. Private jet travel is a prime perquisite of tycoonery, and Black had relished it for much of his career – on one trip to California in the mid-eighties for a meeting of the Trilateral Commission, he had his pilots dip the plane and circle over the Hearst Castle in San Simeon so that he and his family could take it in. On a more recent journey, the new G-IV encountered white-knuckle turbulence. While the other passengers held on for their lives and the Christofle silverware rattled, Black barked in mock impatience to the buckled-in steward: "The *wine* is flowing like *molasses!*"

The destinations that the G-IV ferried the Blacks to and from were also upgraded. In Toronto, the Blacks renovated and redecorated the estate on Park Lane Circle, adding an indoor swimming pool and expanding the library in order to house more of Black's volumes and memorabilia. Across a courtyard from the library, a small chapel was built, consecrated by Black's friend Cardinal Carter. Since the 1980s, Black had owned a Georgian colonial home on Palm Beach's quiet Canterbury Lane, a short walk from the ocean. But whenever he and his first wife, Joanna, drove around the island, one spread in particular, a majestic property on South Ocean Boulevard, always caught Joanna's eye. In 1997, Black was speaking to his ex-wife about their children and mentioned in passing, "Oh, you'll never guess what house I bought. I bought our dream home."

Black paid US$9.9 million for the 17,000-square-foot estate at 1930 South Ocean, then the thirteenth-highest price ever paid for a property in Palm Beach County. The marble-laden palace had a tragic history. It was originally designed by the architect John Volk and built in 1973 for Hans Fischer, a self-made Cleveland millionaire whose holdings included American Monorail and Mayfran. Fischer's fortunes

---

* "Apart from the fact that such a comment makes no sense in real life or fiction," Amiel said, "I have never seen or been on Hollinger's second company plane and would have no occasion to even refer to it."

took a turn for the worse after a disgruntled butler reported tax shenanigans to the Internal Revenue Service. After pleading guilty in 1978 to filing fraudulent tax returns, Fischer retreated to his Florida home and shot himself in the head. "He died looking at the house he loved so much," said Lillian Jane Volk, John Volk's widow and archivist.

The German tycoon Siegfried Otto purchased the estate for US$6 million in 1989. Otto made his fortune at Munich's Giesecke & Devrient, one of the world's largest currency printing companies. In the early 1990s, however, the octogenarian was arrested by German tax authorities for allegedly hiding millions in earnings from a Swiss company he controlled. Otto settled the matter and put the house up for sale, but it spent years on the market before Black bought it.* Hiring the designer David Mlinaric (who had done the Blacks' London townhouse) and the New York–based architects Fairfax & Sammons, Black sank millions more into renovating the property, including the additions of a $4.4 million elevator and a $2.5 million fountain.

The home featured a dramatic stairwell over which Black showcased an American flag that flew over the White House under Franklin D. Roosevelt during the Second World War. The soft yellow living room featured lofty pillars that offered ample space for paintings, including an Andy Warhol portrait of Marilyn Monroe. Visitors described the home as "Arabesque," "not very lived in, but grand," and meticulously, though impersonally, decorated. The Blacks' master suite was equipped with his-and-hers bathrooms, a nearby library, and a movie theatre.

Up a small spiral staircase was Amiel's private suite, comprising a bedroom, dressing area, and office. A new pool house was added alongside the pool and tennis court, and a ceramic tunnel ran under the A1A highway to access the property's private oceanfront. The back of the house faced the intercoastal waterway, and here Black talked about adding a wharf to bring down the *Ravelston*, the fifty-three-foot mahogany cruiser that was built by the Canadian tycoon Nelson Davis and previously owned by Monte Black. To make it all

---

* Black sold his old Palm Beach house to Izzy Asper, the founder of CanWest Global Communications, who also bought the lot next door.

run smoothly in grand Palm Beach style, the Blacks hired Domenico, an inscrutable butler who once worked in New York for the society doyenne Jayne Wrightsman. While giving a tour to a close friend, Black seemed to acknowledge that it was a bit over the top. "If you want to be in the game," he explained, "you need a place like this."

The year after buying the South Ocean Boulevard property, Black also bought a garden-level three-bedroom apartment in the same building on Park Avenue at Sixty-sixth Street that housed the Hollinger-owned apartment purchased for his use in 1995. The idea was that Hollinger International executives could stay in the garden apartment whenever they were in town, but according to a Hollinger executive Black also used it to bunk his domestic help while he was in residence on the third floor. Two years later, Black effectively swapped the properties by buying the bigger unit that he occupied and selling the garden apartment to Hollinger. Again, Mlinaric was enlisted to decorate. The overall impression was that of a titan to watch. "Poised for a U.S. move, the Canadian billionaire keeps two Park Avenue apartments and regularly visits – by corporate G-IV jet – his world headquarters in Manhattan," gushed a heading on a puff piece in short-lived *Talk* magazine.

The process of assembling the Blacks' refulgent, super-sized life was complicated, lengthy, and costly, involving contractors, architects, designers, painters, draftsmen, butlers, maids, chefs, gardeners, drivers. Unlike many rich people, Black was not coy when talking about his money and contended that he possessed hidden resources beyond his newspaper holdings.★ Bluster or not, what is clear is that his expanding lifestyle didn't correspond to any lasting improvement in the stock price of Hollinger International. The stock, which had sunk to as low as US$8 in 1997, made one of its periodic run-ups, hitting US$18.60 the following year – but Black blamed the stock's rapid slide backward to nearly US$11 by early 1999 on arbitrageurs and market conditions. "The nadir of this activity occurred at the end of last

---

★ "I have just been obliged to make some calculations about the current state of my own financial affairs, Max, and I must say that the numbers achieved a heartwarmingly satisfactory consummation," he once told former *Telegraph* editor Max Hastings.

year's annual meeting," he noted in Hollinger International's 1998 annual report, "when a representative of a large New York house po-facedly asked me if we would lend him stock so he would short sell our stock further. Robust capitalist though I am, I found this sort of reckless neanderthalian avarice distasteful."

Black did not acknowledge that Hollinger International's debt load, or his own unpredictability, may also have played a role in the company's share performance. Several months before the *Post* launched, in June 1998, Southam paid $18 million for a 5 per cent stake in Livent, the live theatre company run by the buccaneering Toronto media executive Garth Drabinsky, on whose board Black had sat since 1993. The "attractive diversification opportunity" came as something of a shock to some Southam directors and investors, given that the only connection between Livent and Southam was that news-papers advertised its productions and also reviewed them – but similar things could be said about a lot of companies. "There are some of us who would say to Mr. Black that you are mixing your private amusement with your corporation," said Southam director Stephen Jarislowsky, who resigned from the board a short time later after spar-ring with Black over the price Hollinger would need to pay to buy out Southam's minority shareholders.*

Black arranged the Livent investment following a rough period for Livent that resulted in Drabinsky ceding control of the company to Michael Ovitz, the former Hollywood super-agent and, briefly,

---

* According to Jarislowsky, as a member of the independent committee of Southam directors assessing the fairness of Hollinger International's bid to buy them out, he obtained an independent opinion that the shares were worth between $32 and $36 a share, while Black had an opinion that said they were worth $26. They settled on $32.50, which was roughly $70 million more than Black had wanted to pay. "When the company went private he was angry at me. He told me, 'You're not staying on the Southam board and you're going to get off the board of the *Daily Telegraph*.'" Black did offer Jarislowsky, whose daughter had also worked at the *Telegraph* as an intern, a slot on a subsidiary board that oversaw Hollinger's Quebec papers, but he declined. "I said, 'Well Conrad, I think it's better for me to resign because I don't think you and I would be happy campers. However, I trust our friendship will be intact.' He said, 'Yes, absolutely.' I haven't talked to him since."

president of Walt Disney. Ovitz had viewed his Livent involvement as something of a comeback, but the situation rapidly turned into a fiasco, with allegations of financial fraud by Drabinsky and his partner, Myron Gottlieb, and their ouster from the company in August 1998, just two months after Black made his investment. Soon afterwards, Livent filed for bankruptcy protection, and a firestorm of legal action was directed at Drabinsky and Gottlieb, including a $100 million lawsuit from the company and criminal charges from the U.S. Justice Department. Drabinsky spent the next few years fighting the charges and the lawsuit, and avoiding extradition to the States. Although Black had lost $18 million of Southam's money almost overnight in the debacle, he stayed loyal to Drabinsky, who before Livent's meltdown had served as a director of Hollinger Inc., the Canadian parent company. Black even contributed money to cash-strapped Drabinsky's legal criminal defence, even though he was a director of the company that was suing Drabinsky. Black explained that he was only contributing to Drabinsky's fight against the criminal charges, and he had the "word of honour" of his friend and Drabinsky's lawyer Edward Greenspan that the money would be used only for this purpose. "In my view he did not commit a crime because he did not intend to commit a crime," explained Black. "Garth doesn't belong in jail and I'm not in favour of any move to try to put him in jail."

Black further supported Drabinsky by later enlisting him to work as a marketing consultant for the *Post* and to produce ads that would run in movie theatres (in the 1980s Drabinsky had been the CEO of the Cineplex Odeon chain). Drabinsky approached the task with the kind of zeal it would take to win an Academy Award.

Even though it had a Web site, Black's *National Post* was more evidence of Hollinger's contrarian play as a believer in newspapers at a time when electronic media and so-called convergence among different media were all the rage. Over the years, Black had made bold statements about diversifying into other media, especially television, yet he stayed resolutely mired in ink and paper. A telling comparison is that as Black was gearing up his plans for the *Post*, his U.K. rival Rupert Murdoch was launching the Fox News channel in the United

States. Similar in one respect to the rationale Black applied to the *Post*, Murdoch's belief was that there was room on the airwaves for a conservative alternative to his rival Ted Turner's CNN, and he battled fiercely to get his new creation carried into homes by cable operators around the country. As with many of Murdoch's assaults on the media establishment during his career, Fox News would fight hard and succeed brilliantly as the Clinton era gave way to the Bush regime, eventually capturing the post-September-11 *Zeitgeist* and overtaking CNN in the ratings.

Print was no longer Murdoch's main focus. Influential Murdoch papers such as the London *Times* and the *New York Post* actually lost money – but their support of his overall media machine by honing public opinion was considered invaluable. What Murdoch recognized was that although new technology offered all kinds of opportunities for newspapers, it was also a major cause of their decline. No matter what a newspaper publisher did on the burgeoning Internet, the view among many investors was that the new-media ventures were merely defences against well-heeled rivals, such as Microsoft and Yahoo, siphoning off their classified advertisers, rather than new business opportunities. Black's serene views on the subject made him sound, typically, as if he had just stepped out of a time machine. "Intermittently, there is fear that we are in the buggy-whip business," he admitted. "Why is it at the end of the twentieth century we are still delivering news . . . through crowded city streets on stripped tree bark? In one sense, it seems a primitive process."

But at first Black believed it was "not in the interest" of Hollinger to be on the "cutting edge" of technology. "We fear that over the next few years the information highway may turn out to be more like the 'highways' of pioneer days – corduroy roads and mud sections with many bumps and places to get stuck." Although he maintained "there's a lot of absolute bunkum uttered about multimedia by a lot of faddish airheads," when the dot-com revolution took off, Black, like everyone else, wanted a piece. The *Telegraph* had actually been the first British newspaper to put its editions on-line, and, like many publishers, Hollinger ensured that all its main titles had a place on the burgeoning Web.

But the on-line versions of newspapers were not where the big, fast money was to be made. Matthew Doull, a stepson of Black's brother, Montegu, who had been working at the *Telegraph* in different roles since he graduated from Brown University in 1991, was by the mid-1990s working on corporate development. After a trip to Silicon Valley, he brought back a proposal for Hollinger to invest US$4 million in the software company Netscape, for a small minority in the company in advance of its public offering. At the time of the issue, Netscape was valued at US$100 million. Black told Doull that he didn't know much about such things, but if he could convince David Radler and Dan Colson to make the investment he would approve it. Neither executive went for it, and the matter was dropped. Several months later, Netscape shares jumped 108 per cent on their first day of trading, valuing the company at US$3.6 billion, and continued skyward; it was eventually sold to America Online for US$9 billion. At its peak, the stake Hollinger had passed on could have been worth US$200 million.

It was the beginning of Internet mania. Doull, who had left the *Telegraph* to work for *Wired* magazine in London, received a call from Black several months later. Black told him that he'd been cleaning up some old files and had come upon his Netscape pitch. Acknowledging the missed opportunity, Black hired Doull back to work on developing a unit for Internet investments. Black also enlisted as his company's unlikely cyber-guru Richard Perle, the Washington power-broker and Hollinger International director who was a chief architect of Reagan's Star Wars defence system. Perle became the division's new chairman and chief executive officer. The newly christened Hollinger Digital opened its digs in a loft space in the section of Manhattan's SoHo that was then known as Silicon Alley, and partly under those auspices Hollinger International made some forty investments outside of the newspaper business over the next few years, most of them Internet-related.

The investments ranged from a few successes (trip.com, Interactive Investor, vault.com among them) to a far greater number of flops (including handbag.com, freesamples.com, wheresfrankie.com). There were some non-media oddities in the mix, including a US$2.6 million interest in a blood storage company called Hemanext (a write-off) that Perle championed and, through the Telegraph company, a US$2 million investment in the coffee and tea merchant Whittard of Chelsea (later sold at a gain). Overall, Hollinger International probably did no worse or better than a lot of media companies that took punts amid Internet mania, losing an estimated US$65 million by the end of 2003 on investments of US$189 million.* Although dot-com riches eluded Black, he and Hollinger's top executives allegedly still thanked themselves for their efforts via an unusual "incentive plan" that the board approved. The plan would reward them for individual Internet investments that were later sold for a profit without penalizing them for the far greater number of eventual losers.

As a result, despite the company's overall losing track record, as the Internet bubble peaked in 2000 and 2001, a total of US$15.5 million was paid in profit distribution to the Hollinger Digital executives who managed them, including Perle and Doull, but roughly a third of that went to Black, David Radler, group financial architect Jack Boultbee, and Telegraph CEO Dan Colson. The so-called new economy may have added a new dimension to their game, but the bonus scheme was consistent with the business philosophy that Radler once explained to a colleague as "I got a piece, Conrad got a piece, and the shareholders got a piece."

---

* The publisher who probably profited the most from the technology bubble – ironically, through a print magazine – was Canadian-born Mortimer Zuckerman, who had once beat out Black for the New York *Daily News*. Zuckerman bankrolled the magazine *Fast Company* and then sold it at the boom's peak to Bertelsmann for some US$300 million.

Chapter Twenty-Five

PEERLESS

The Canadian newspaper war raged on, but there was time to collect accolades and honours away from the battlefield. During the spring of 1999, Black was inducted into the Canadian News Hall of Fame and the Canadian Business Hall of Fame. Then came a curious report in the *Globe and Mail* that Black might finally have entry to his ultimate hall of fame, Britain's House of Lords, following in the tradition of the former Canadian press barons Lord Beaverbrook and Lord Thomson of Fleet. "I do not really know anything about it and I am not directly or indirectly negotiating with anybody about any such thing," Black said through his London assistant on June 8. But Black had been put forward for a peerage by William Hague, the head of Britain's opposition Conservative Party. Black may have objected to the term "negotiating," but on May 10 the British government had requested confirmation from the Canadian government that there was no impediment to Black's receiving the peerage.

There was no straightforward answer to the question, as Roy Thomson had had to relinquish his Canadian citizenship in order to take up his peerage in 1963.* Technically, that was because of an

---

* The Order of Canada, of which Black was a member, was established on Canada's centenary in 1967 in part to bestow the kind of recognition on accomplished citizens that, previously, they could get only from foreign governments.

obscure eighty-year-old House of Commons resolution asking the British Crown not to confer peerages on Canadians; more broadly, it was because, although the British monarch is still Canada's head of state, many Canadians resent any pretension to aristocracy. What made Black's situation different was that in the thirty-six years since Thomson received his peerage, dual citizenship between the two countries had been allowed.

On May 24, Black spoke with Roy MacLaren, the Canadian high commissioner in London. According to Black, MacLaren told him that the Canadian government's Honours Committee, the body that handled such questions, had advised him that indeed there would be no problem with the peerage so long as Black became a dual citizen of both countries.

Four days later, Black met with Prime Minister Tony Blair at 10 Downing Street, and Blair confirmed that so long as he became a U.K. citizen and did not use the title in Canada, he could be in the House of Lords within weeks. Blair received a written confirmation of this from the government of Canada on June 9. Black became a U.K. citizen "on an expedited basis" on June 11. Three days later, Blair wrote to Black confirming that his nomination was being forwarded to the Queen, and that he was one of thirty-six distinguished citizens who would become peers on June 18.

On June 17, Blair phoned Black to say with some embarrassment that he'd been advised that Prime Minister Jean Chrétien had "intervened with the Queen," citing "contravention of Canadian law." Apparently there had been some bureaucratic bungling in the approval of Black's honour on Canada's side, and the Canadian prime minister's objection had only just been registered. In requesting that Britain hold off the honour, Chrétien cited the Nickle Resolution, the obscure House of Commons rule. Black was struck from the honours list. He phoned Ken Whyte at home, awakening him. "Do you know what that bastard has done?"

Black, who was on his way to Bonn, Germany, also called Chrétien. The prime minister returned the call to Black in Bonn and coolly brushed off Black's demand that he drop his interference within forty-eight hours. He wasn't saying no definitely, he explained, but news of the peerage had come as a surprise and the Prime Minister's Office needed time to study the precedents. It would not be working to either Black's timetable or that of the U.K.'s second chamber.

As far as Black was concerned, this was just payback for the heat the *National Post* had been putting on Chrétien. For months, the newspaper had been hammering at him with a series of investigative stories about taxpayer dollars being funnelled into the hands of a businessman in Chrétien's Quebec hometown of Shawinigan. The businessman was using the money on a hotel next to a golf course in which Chrétien himself had once invested.

Black claimed that after one early story ran, Chrétien had called him at three a.m. while he was in Vienna (Black was awake, as he often is in the middle of the night) to rail against the "Shawinigate" coverage.* As usual, Black backed up his editor. He then telephoned Whyte and said, "I don't think the prime minister is too delighted, but it's up to you. Just don't make any mistakes."

In the midst of the peerage imbroglio, another prize was suddenly snatched from Black's grasp. For months, he had been negotiating to buy the *New York Observer*, an irreverent but money-losing weekly that was in those respects similar to the *Spectator* when Black had purchased it. Owning a magazine in New York was important to Black, as he and Amiel wanted a greater presence there, and the *Observer* would lend cachet. Although the New York market was notoriously tough, Black had toyed with the idea of turning the weekly into a daily, possibly by creating a hybrid by bundling it with the London *Financial Times*, which had recently begun an aggressive expansion in the United States. (Both were salmon-coloured broadsheets aimed at moneyed people, though they didn't have much else in common.) The *Observer* was founded and bankrolled by Arthur Carter, a New York financier and real estate mogul, and the deal was that Carter would take cash and shares totalling some US$20 million for the 50,000-circulation title and remain as co-CEO while joining

---

* "I thought we hammered it a little too hard, and beyond a certain point I had some sympathy for Chrétien," Black later said. "He was hypocritical and corrupt, of course, but he had a right not to be harassed on the point every single day."

Hollinger International's board. The announcement of the deal was set for Friday, July 16, but late on the Thursday it was called off. Black contended that Hollinger had just obtained the *Observer*'s tax returns, and they showed a bigger loss than expected. Another executive involved maintained Carter just exercised the founder's prerogative to change his mind after news of the sale leaked on Businessweek.com. Carter was annoyed and denied that there was ever a deal to walk away from. "They know what our numbers are – they've had them for six months," Carter said. "That is a total bunch of malarkey." Black, according to his colleague, was "apoplectic" at losing his "passport to the social scene in New York."

Although Black claimed to have different ambitions than his chief London rival Rupert Murdoch, he was acutely aware of how the Australian had used the United Kingdom as a rallying ground prior to conquering the United States. "By the late 1990s, it was clear that the operation had moved to a grander level – with things like Palm Beach and the advisory board," said one Hollinger International director. "I always thought that Conrad, though pro-Canadian, was always slightly pissed off that he had been born a Canadian. He had a sense that he was bigger than Canada can hold – he needed a bigger stage. That stage, of course, was the United States. He was very successful in terms of social contacts, but he wasn't influential. He found a compromise country in the U.K."

In that country, Black had begun acidly referring to himself as "the Great Commoner," and back in Canada he went on the offensive. On August 9, 1999, Black, the most powerful press owner in Canada, sued Jean Chrétien, the most powerful man in the nation, in Ontario Superior Court, citing "abuse of power." Black's lawyers laid out several grounds for Chrétien's "misfeasance," including the arguments that the Nickle Resolution was not actually a law, and that the Canadian parliament had allowed other foreign honours to be bestowed on dual citizens by such countries as Belgium, France, and England. For instance, Black pointed out that knighthoods for Sir Graham Day and Sir Neil Shaw had been conferred by the Queen without a peep from Ottawa. The complaint also noted that when Black heard the peerage had been blocked and phoned Chrétien, the prime minister complained about his coverage in the *National Post* on "the third occasion in six months." In asking that the courts halt Chrétien's alleged abuse, Black also asked for a token sum of $25,000 in damages for the "considerable public embarrassment and inconvenience" the episode had caused him.

Black relished the opportunity to get Chrétien on the stand in a courtroom to explain himself. "Chrétien has no chance in this," he said. "He has no defence. All he can do is use his position to string the thing out. The longer he does that, the more enjoyable it will be when we finally have him at bay." Chrétien insisted it was not a personal matter and that he was just following "long-standing Canadian policy and custom."

Among the 30 million who constituted Canada's untitled classes, almost everyone had an opinion. On the one hand, there was no question the prime minister was coming off as petty and vindictive; on the other, there was little sympathy for Black's vainglory. Black tried to argue that, its pomp and elitism aside, the House of Lords was a place where he could make a legitimate and serious contribution to public policy, for instance furthering his pet crusade that Britain should forge a free-trade union with North America. And it was fact that every head of the *Telegraph* before him had been made a peer. "Vanity invites the jester's scorn," noted Roy Greenslade of the *Guardian*. "For a man who has espoused the values of the United States and wants Britain to join North America's trading group rather than Europe's, his lust for a feudal favour which most modern Britons are keen to abolish doesn't make sense." Black played down his own desire to become a peer and, in an interview with news anchor Peter Mansbridge on CBC's *The National*, acknowledged that he wasn't expecting much support in Canada. But, he said, he was suing on a point of principle, given that he had followed the government's advice. "Do you think the public cares about this?" asked Mansbridge.

"No, and I don't see why they should," Black said.

"Or does it have any impact on the way the public sees you?"

"I can't judge that," Black replied. "If you'll pardon the ghastly expression, my image is of a Frankenstein monster that's been lurching about for twenty-five years, and I have absolutely no idea what

animates it at times." (A few months later, Canadian papers prominently featured a photo of Black and Amiel, grinning and dressed
in full costume as Cardinal Richelieu and Marie Antoinette, as they
arrived at a themed pre-revolutionary France picnic for 500 thrown
at Kensington Palace by Prince and Princess Michael of Kent.)
Black continued, "I think a good many people see this as a case of
an individual abusing political office for petty reasons and over-
reaching his jurisdiction."

Patrick LeSage was not among Black's sympathizers. The Ontario
Superior Court chief justice ruled against him in March 2000. The
case never went to the full trial Black had hoped for, as LeSage preemptively ruled that Chrétien and his government were immune from
liability for negligence because these were "policy" decisions – and to
allow them to be challenged would invite lawsuits over anything the
government said or did. The plaintiff was ordered to pay a portion of
the $170,000 in legal fees the government had rung up in its defence.
Black could have just taken his lumps and waited for Chrétien's
inevitable retirement from office in a few years, but bowing out
quietly was not his style.

These days, Black was in unusually combative form. On March 3,
2000, twelve days before LeSage released his decision, Black strode
into the Westin Hotel in Calgary for the annual meeting of the
Canadian Imperial Bank of Commerce, where he was a director. For
nearly four months, some 200 recently unionized editorial and other
employees at the *Calgary Herald* had been on strike, and no sign of a
resolution was in sight. Hollinger International's latest earnings,
released two weeks earlier, showed a decline in profitability, but the
company had pointed out that the financial impact of the walkout on
the company "has been, and is expected to continue to be, negligi-
ble." Now Black was confronted by a small group of strikers, among
them Andy Marshall, local president of the Communications, Energy
and Paperworkers Union. Under the glare of TV cameras, a nose-to-
nose grudge match ensued. Marshall claimed the strike and a union-
sponsored boycott had resulted in as much as a 25 per cent plunge in
Herald circulation, which Black denied. "It's profitable as ever, it's
better than ever, it's better without you," Black spat back. "Three per

cent loss of circulation despite massive union intimidation and massive defamation." He dismissed the numbers Marshall cited as a "bought survey made up by a bunch of crooked union leaders who couldn't add up a column of figures if their lives depended on it."

"Sir, what are these insults?" countered Marshall. "How are they going to help resolve the strike when you insult us in this way?"

"This strike is going to be resolved either by coming to an end after two years, by decertification, or by you people coming back to work," Black replied. When Marshall told Black the *Herald* workers wanted protection from "indiscriminate firing," Black said Southam was doing nothing of the sort. "We're amputating gangrenous limbs," he added. "If, by the grace of conversion, they want to function as employees instead of staging an NDP *coup d'état* in the newsroom, they'll be welcome." In an interview in the next day's *Herald*, Black added that the union members "are trying to swaddle themselves in the clothes of oppressed workers seeking respect for their rights. They have no grievance."

Black's typically pleonastic comments drew the ire of F.B. Henry, the outspoken Roman Catholic bishop of Calgary, who objected to Black's use of the terms *grace* and *swaddle*. "Even the devil can quote Scripture, so I am not impressed," Bishop Henry told the *Globe and Mail*, which had been covering the Calgary strike closely. "It is a misuse of those terms and what they really do mean. I object to him wrapping himself in the garments of religiosity when he doesn't understand the social teachings of the church, or at least he is not prepared to live it." Henry penned a lengthy article castigating Black in the *Catholic Register*. Black, who had converted to Catholicism fourteen years earlier and in 1994 had bought 20 per cent of the U.K.'s *Catholic Herald*, returned fire with his own article in the pages of the *Calgary Herald*: "If your jumped-up little twerp of a bishop thinks I'm not a very good Catholic, I think he's a prime candidate for exorcism." Black also added that Henry was a "useful idiot" and "pinko Commie," which drew condemnation from several Church leaders. Henry considered suing Black for defamation but turned the other cheek. "For any offence Mr. Black has caused me," said Henry, "I forgive him."

Darlene Quaife, a former president of the Writers Guild of Alberta, was probably not the only person who wrote to Black to criticize his outburst. But she was surprised to receive a two-paragraph reply from him, with one of the paragraphs asking her not to write to him again. Black instructed Quaife that "people should be judged by their peers" and appended a letter from the author Tom Wolfe (who had been invited to speak at one of the Hollinger Dinners) recommending him for membership in the Century Club, the venerable New York literary hangout:

Ladies and gentlemen,
Conrad Black has done more for the lively, provocative, and sane discussion of the important social, political, and intellectual issues of our time than any newspaper publisher of the past decade. He is also a delightful, charming, congenial gentleman. He is not merely a GOOD candidate for the Century – we NEED him.

I might add that his wife, Barbara Amiel, is one of the greatest Canadian journalists of all time and is a wonderfully engaging person. We should simply CONFER full membership on her.

Yours, Tom Wolfe.

Outside the annual meeting of Hollinger Inc. the following month in Toronto, members of the Communications, Energy and Paperworkers Union chanted: "Spineless, useless, has no tact! What's his name? Conrad Black!" Inside the meeting, Black now struck a conciliatory tone in response to a shareholder question and said it had been late at night in London when he inserted the word *twerp* into his article, and if he had to do it again he would not have used it. Several weeks later, after eight months on the picket line, the ninety newsroom employees at the *Herald* who remained on strike disbanded their union and went back to work. Black had won.

Meanwhile, Black confidently continued to forecast that the *Post* would break even by the fourth quarter of 2000 and be profitable in the following year. Nonetheless, Hollinger International's stock price was in yet another slump and Black announced that the company had hired Morgan Stanley Dean Witter to accept bids for Hollinger's small newspapers, some 350 in all, with circulations under 100,000, as part of a plan to reduce debt. At the Hollinger Inc. annual meeting in Toronto, one shareholder asked about Black and Radler's involvement in Horizon Publications, the private company that had already bought some smaller Hollinger newspapers. Black said neither he nor Radler played an active role in Horizon. "I own a few shares because they needed a balance of sale but I have nothing to do with it." Across the range of business conducted at the meeting, there was no hint of anything to suggest the imminent unwinding of the world's fastest-growing press empire.

Indeed, while the company was shopping its smaller papers, the *Chicago Sun-Times* was preparing for its new printing presses to come on-line. Plans were being made to spruce up the paper's content and perhaps do something dramatic and unexpected with the newspaper. One notion the Blacks were keen on attacking was that quality broadsheet newspapers were an anachronism, and that the future belonged to image-heavy, sound-bite-filled tabloids and television. The Blacks thought that they might be able to challenge this conventional wisdom in Chicago just as they had with the *Post* in Canada, by turning it into a broadsheet alternative to the *Tribune*, which Conrad viewed as a "big whale, spouting profits." In 2000, the *Sun-Times* was selling 471,000 copies during the week and 391,000 on Sunday; weekends were its major liability – the *Tribune* sold over 1 million. Revamping the Sunday paper was the most pressing business, and the Blacks reasoned that the Sunday edition could easily become a broadsheet as it was not read by commuters.

On the idiosyncratic Hollinger flow chart, the *Sun-Times* was the purview of David Radler, who held the title of publisher as well as those of president and chief operating officer of Hollinger. So it was Radler who first approached the editors of the Southam-owned Vancouver *Province* and *Vancouver Sun*, Michael Cooke and John Cruickshank, and invited them to come to Chicago to assume the slots of editor and vice-president of editorial. *Sun-Times* editor Nigel Wade, the former *Telegraph* foreign editor with whom Radler had had his battles – including over Wade's insistence that the *Sun-Times* endorse Bill Clinton in the 1996 election – was moving on. Cruickshank knew Radler a little because of their Vancouver connection but got to know Black and Amiel only through discussions of the opportunity in America's third-largest city. For Cruickshank, those talks included a lunch with Amiel outdoors at Vancouver's Pacific Centre. Amiel ordered her hamburger and said, "I'd like that very rare." The waiter replied, "I'm sorry, health regulations prevent us from serving rare meat." She was affronted. "*Ugh!* My God, I get my blood changed four times a year. I'm not going to be killed by a hamburger."

Cooke and Cruickshank took up their new posts in the Windy City, but then toward the end of 2000 the economy quickly turned for the worse, and advertising took a dive. From 2000 to 2001, *Sun-Times* revenues fell from US$240 million to US$224 million, and operating profits fell from US$32 million to US$25 million. Instead of the promised expansion, it was time to cut – and Radler was the master of downsizing. Among other things, he ordered the paper's newsroom staff shrunk by 20 per cent and eliminated the paper's marketing department.

One of the criticisms of Amiel was that once she became Barbara Black she had a way of looking through people from her "old" life and pouring on her charm for heavyweights whom she now considered more worthy company. One person who disputed that image was the *Telegraph* columnist Mark Steyn, who remembered Amiel sitting at a table with himself, Cruickshank, and other journalists at a lunch held in Washington in mid-2001 on the eve of the Hollinger Dinner. "I thought Barbara Amiel was like Frank Sinatra at parties, when, instead of gravitating to the A-list movie stars, he'd shoot the breeze with the musicians," said Steyn. In this case, however, she wasn't exactly shooting the breeze, but instead shooting darts at the Chicago paper the British Columbian transplants were a year into running – the paper was "shabby" and "a mess," she said, with not enough editorial and too many ads crammed in the front.

According to someone present, Cruickshank walked up to Radler and told him that he should know that his partner's wife and the company's vice-president of editorial had just publicly dressed him down over things that, while true, were a direct consequence of the cost cuts the paper was undergoing. "What do you want me to do?" Cruickshank asked.

"Tell her to fuck off," came Radler's blasé reply.

"That really is not one of the roles that I had signed on for," said Cruickshank, but Radler was unperturbed. "She talks that way," he explained, "but she and Conrad are the first to squeal when the money doesn't come."

Later in the event, Black approached Cooke and Cruickshank and told them not to worry about it. Over the following weeks, the two editors continued to work on their proposal for a revamped Sunday *Sun-Times*, which they finally submitted to Radler, with copies to Amiel and Black. The relaunch never happened, and the editors of the *Sun-Times* never heard from either of the Blacks again.

Chapter Twenty-Six

GOODBYE, CANADA

Part of Black's mystique, dating back to his days running the old Argus, stemmed from the sense that he could make a run on any company at any time, and just as unpredictably could sell anything without warning or remorse. This was the case when, on July 31, 2000, Black struck a deal with Izzy Asper, the media mogul whose family controlled CanWest Global Communications, to sell almost all of Hollinger's Canadian newspapers and half the *National Post* to CanWest. As announced, the unexpected deal would bring Hollinger cash and CanWest securities valued at some $3.2 billion, much of which would go toward paying off the US$1.7 billion debt Hollinger International had amassed over the years, and would perhaps finally put some fizz in the company's stock. As described by Black, the sale would also bring him a degree of personal relief and satisfaction. "Do you remember that cartoon character, Scrooge McDuck?" he mused. "Do you remember how he used to get into his little bulldozer every morning and plow back and forth over his gold coins? Well, maybe I will just sit and look at it for a while." More philosophically, he added: "It was time in the history of my country, and time in my own history, to make things shipshape, to get rid of the debt, to get a bit of a cash box to work from, to enjoy life a little more."

Black portrayed Asper's unexpected offer for Southam, and his insistence on 50 per cent of the *Post*, as simply too good to refuse. He was adamant that he would retain editorial control over the paper – he even became its publisher a short time later, the first time he'd held the title since the *Sherbrooke Record* in 1968 – and he also had a five-year option to buy CanWest's stake back if Asper decided to sell it. But Asper's bid came at a time when Black was increasingly pondering the future. From a business point of view, he was as frustrated with Hollinger International's stock price as any shareholder; his Canadian holding company, Hollinger Inc., relied on dividends and fees from Hollinger International, and as at the old Argus, his wealth was at the top of the food chain in Ravelston, the private company that controlled Hollinger Inc. The task of funnelling money up was increasingly a challenge.

In the wake of the convergence mania that was forging (mostly ill-fated) unions between such companies as AOL and Time Warner, and between Seagram and Vivendi, a compelling argument could be made that the newspapers were worth more – at least in the eyes of investors – in the hands of a multimedia giant, such as CanWest aspired to be. As far as where his company ranked in the pantheon of newspaper giants: "He wasn't going to be able to go from number three to number one for a long, long time," noted one executive who worked closely with Black. "He's a big deal guy, a big fix guy, so there was really nothing left in it for him."

Looking back on the sale years later, Black contended that it was a "myth that I aspired to an ever-larger media company and failed to learn the lessons of Napoleon. In fact," he said, "I lost faith in the newspaper industry in 1998 and 1999 as a growth industry and set about an orderly withdrawal from the business, apart from a few specialized situations."

Black was also thinking a lot about politics; his attempts to influence Canada's political agenda through the *Post* were enjoyable and important to him, but it wasn't clear they were getting anywhere. He had been sounded out as a prospective leader of the new Alliance Party (essentially the renamed Reform Party) and of the Progressive Conservative Party, but he maintained his long-standing position that he was not suited to elected office. The House of Lords was a different story, and he wondered whether someday he might actually find his way into cabinet through it. Through such contacts as the financial support he provided for the Washington magazine *National Interest*, his business relationship with the Republican heavyweight Richard Perle, and his presence within such groups as Bilderberg, it was even conceivable that Black could see his way to some kind of presidential council appointment in the United States. Black was also gathering material about his long-time hero Franklin Delano Roosevelt as the subject of his next book, which would also raise his profile stateside.

As he approached his fifty-seventh birthday, Black calculated that since you don't count the first twenty years, he was just past half and entering the third quarter of his life. One of the people Black had looked up to the most in life was the billionaire-cum-statesman-cum-philanthropist Walter Annenberg, who had lived into his nineties, playing a variety of roles on the world stage until close to the end, and Black didn't see why he couldn't do the same. Even though he was intent on gaining his peerage, Black was increasingly focused on the United States as his "spiritual home" and the place where he wanted to spend most of his time, and he still harboured ambitions of commanding a prestigious American flagship paper. Whether he owned one paper or 100 in Canada had no effect on his standing in New York, where he was still a relative nobody. "One intuits that he has a gravitational pull to the U.S.," said the Hollinger advisory board member William F. Buckley.

Black may have preferred to focus on the possibilities the future held, but the hard commercial reality behind the sell-off of Southam and the *Post* suggested strategic failure and retreat. A simple retracing of Hollinger International's share performance during the greatest bull market in history laid the story bare. Hollinger International had sold its first shares in May 1994 at US$13, when it was called American Publishing and housed the small-town U.S. titles and the *Chicago Sun-Times*. Even after it changed its name to Hollinger International, moved from the NASDAQ to the NYSE, and folded in Black's main worldwide newspaper assets, including the *Telegraph*, Southam, and the *Jerusalem Post*, the stock spent much of the time hovering at or below its issue price (although it did pop above US$16 on news of the deal with CanWest).

Between the initial public offering and August 2000, the stock generated a total return, including dividends, of 6.9 per cent per annum, less than many bond funds returned in the period. Meanwhile, the Standard & Poor's newspaper index was up 15 per cent per annum – before dividends. Key newspaper groups such as the New York Times Co. and the Washington Post Co. were up 20.5 per cent and 12 per cent per year, respectively, also before dividends. And Central Newspapers, a group that included the *Arizona Republic* and was also trading at US$13 a share in May 1994, when Black floated his company at the same price, was acquired for US$64 a share at nearly the same time as Black sold his Canadian papers to CanWest. Black was correct that there was money to be made in the newspaper business, but his shareholders weren't the ones making it. "On occasion, I mused about taking the company private since our status as a public company was accomplishing almost nothing useful for anyone," Black said. "My impression was that after several years of such inveighing, I was running some risk of seeming to be King Lear, becoming progressively less credible in threatening unspecific reprisals for an unsatisfactory (but far from dire) condition."

What Black viewed as a sage and opportunistic deal was not praised as one by much of the news media. The *Wall Street Journal*'s story was headlined "Debt Catches Up with a Media Mogul" and quoted Hollinger president David Radler saying what his partner Black would not – that this was a "retreat." "Conrad Black is licking his wounds, or, as he might put it, brushing restorative balm onto his psychic lacerations," ran an editorial in the *Globe and Mail*. "He has been forced by circumstances and the bargaining strength of CanWest Global to sell 50 per cent of his beloved *National Post*, only two years after creating it, along with the former Southam newspapers, only four years after Hollinger acquired them. The money is good; it will pay down debt and enable Hollinger to invest in electronic media. But the sale puts the seal on the Canadian adventures of Mr. Black."

Black took to the pages of the *National Post* to deliver a 1,700-word raspberry to his critics. Selling a bunch of newspapers, Black noted, "is not the sort of activity that would normally lead, as it has done, to an explosion of journalistic joy on the scale of VE Day, accompanied by an avalanche of denigration of a fervour and tawdriness that only a journalistic lynch mob can achieve. Our company has been disparaged as debt-ridden, although its debt will now be eliminated and replaced with sizeable cash resources. My own net worth has substantially increased in the last week but I have been reviled by journeyman journalists who divine that I may have been less wealthy than certain popular vocalists* or show business impresarios, as if this, if true, were a shaming failure and as if they were qualified judges.

"Competing journalists have imputed to me a variety of motives for a business decision whose commercial logic is obvious to anyone of the slightest business acumen. These range from an incurable illness of my wife's, through a lack of avocational zeal on the part of my children, to a rich variety of my own shortcomings, from the onset of slothfulness to a desire to strut about foreign watering places in ridiculous costumes as a hedonistic court jester to international café society. (My wife's health is satisfactory and stable; my children are blameless, and my own ambitions are somewhat more exalted, though not because I have an inordinate admiration for Napoleon or am a Rupert Murdoch 'wannabe,' two other worm-eaten chestnuts that were shopped around yet again last week.)"

Black painted the sale as a prudent thing to do in light of his company's debts, his estimation that the newspaper market was near its peak, and the fact that CanWest had simply made a good offer. "I do not choose to reply to those who in the last week have likened me to a jackal, claimed that I have left no legacy in Canada and that I stripped little newspapers to feed large ones, declared that I have never added value to any company I was at the head of, or am guilty

---

* An article in the *Globe and Mail* had pointed out that Céline Dion was probably richer than Black.

of the vast catalogue of Kafkaesque shortcomings that have been alleged against me by my self-declared enemies in the Canadian media. The authors of these lies and smears illustrate perfectly (especially the several disappointed seekers of employment with us among them) all the weaknesses of the country and of the journalistic craft that I have often addressed before. To my friends in Canada, who are more numerous than a consultation of the local media would indicate, your support is more gratefully appreciated than ever. To my enemies, some of whom have claimed they will miss me, your nostalgia is premature and completely unrequited."

The finishing touches on the deal with CanWest had been worked out over the last week of July. As it happened, on July 27, a glittering party was held to celebrate the sixtieth birthday of Montegu Black. The black-tie event was held at the York Club in Toronto and featured limousines full of establishment figures with whom the Blacks had come into prominence, including former prime minister John Turner (whose wife, Geills, was George Black's goddaughter); Hollinger director and former Canadian ambassador to the U.S. Allan Gotlieb and his wife, Sondra, a journalist; top executives and fellow directors from the Toronto-Dominion Bank where Monte sat on the board; the Blacks' old Argus allies Douglas Bassett and Fred Eaton; the Blacks' cousin Ron Riley; and Conrad's first wife, Joanna, and their children, including their older son, Jonathan, who flew in specially for the occasion from California. Monte's second wife, June, his four children, and his two stepchildren were also there.

Conrad had told his brother that he would be unable to make it because of a conflicting commitments.* But because of his typically non-committal approach to such events, Monte and others had figured there was a chance that his famously tardy younger brother would turn up to toast his only sibling, with whom he had a close and by all accounts happy relationship. As the night wore on it

---

* "The invitation came in late," Black said later. "I had long-standing commitments to be in Europe, and I spoke to him at length on the day, August 6, 2000. It was never raised as a subject between us."

became clear that Conrad was a no-show. He and Barbara were far away, in Bayreuth, Germany, contemplating the imminent sale of his Canadian interests and indulging his fondness for Wagnerian opera. "It was probably the saddest party I've ever been to," recalled Joanna. "The York Club was jumping, the A-list was there, it was a lovely, lovely party. Then Monte got up to speak and he started to talk about his life – giving a speech that should have been given by somebody else. And who best to give a speech like that than your brother?"

Chapter Twenty-Seven

HELLO, CROSSHARBOUR

Despite Black's repeated public insistence that the *National Post* was approaching profitability and his private contention that Izzy Asper and his son Leonard would grow bored with their half-interest in the paper and he would have the opportunity to buy it back, the paper was not profitable and the Aspers showed no sign of selling. And, as if to underscore how ineffective Black's crusade for the Canadian right wing had been, Chrétien's Liberals handily swept the November 2000 federal election, despite the *Post*'s endorsement of the Canadian Alliance. Hollinger continued to shop its remaining Canadian dailies, including the *Sault Star*, the *Peterborough Examiner*, and the *Kingston Whig-Standard*, finally selling them to the media executive Michael Sifton's Osprey Media.

By the turn of the millennium, which Conrad and Barbara spent at Oscar and Annette de la Renta's Casa de Campo in the Dominican Republic, there was still no progress on his peerage. Then, in May 2001, came the Ontario Court of Appeal's unanimous support of the earlier ruling that Black could not sue Chrétien for denying him his peerage. "Unlike the refusal of a peerage, the refusal of a passport or pardon has real, adverse consequences for the person affected," Mr. Justice John Laskin wrote on behalf of the other two judges on the panel. "Here, no important individual interests are at stake. Mr. Black's rights were not affected, however broadly 'rights' are construed."

Black, who three months earlier had already taken steps toward renouncing his citizenship, went ahead to finish the process. "Having opposed for thirty years precisely the public policies that have caused scores of thousands of educated and talented Canadians to abandon their country every year, it is at least consistent that I should join this dispersal," he said. For the third time in his life – the first when he left Quebec to return to Ontario in 1974, the second when he moved to London to take the helm of the *Telegraph* newspapers – Black was effectively resigning from a place the way most people would from a job.

Meanwhile, his contention that the CanWest deal would eliminate Hollinger International's debts and leave him among piles of gold coins was proving to be a chimera, from a corporate perspective. In the Black chain of companies, he controlled the publicly traded holding company Hollinger Inc. of Toronto through a web of private companies built around Ravelston. Hollinger Inc. (or just Inc., as it will be referred to from here on) in turn controlled Hollinger International (which will be referred to as Hollinger), the operating company listed on the New York Stock Exchange that housed Hollinger's newspapers. In fact, Inc. owned only 32 per cent of the shares in International but retained 72 per cent of the votes over the company's affairs because it owned all of its Class B shares dating back to the American Publishing public offering. Although there had been plenty of criticism in business and regulatory circles about the potential abuse of companies that employed multiple-voting, or super-voting, share structures, they were quite common in the newspaper business, with companies from Torstar to Dow Jones to the New York Times Co. and the Washington Post Co. using them. In those companies' cases, the multiple-voting structure was in place to preserve the control of trusts that represented a fairly wide group of family owners, and to ensure that no external financial forces could influence the papers' editorial mission. In the case of Hollinger, which Black liked to refer to as an "airplane assembled in the air," it was a way for the company to expand its capital by raising money in the stock markets without jeopardizing his control. None of those other companies had the idiosyncratic circular financial structure that Black's companies did, in which money made at

International's level would make its way up to him via fees paid to Ravelston for management services, or via dividends paid to Inc.

The sale to CanWest may have eased the financial pressures on the group of companies, but it had by no means eliminated them. In early 2001, Inc. began to disclose to shareholders that it was experiencing a shortfall between the dividends it was receiving from Hollinger and its operating costs – which consisted mostly of debt payments – and that Ravelston had been loaning Inc. money "on an informal basis" to avoid a default. Black was scrambling to raise money and refinance Inc., the Canadian company being closer to where his fortune directly resided. A key part of the refinancing effort centred on plans by Hollinger to sell a financial instrument called a "participation trust," based on US$500 million worth of debentures that had been received from CanWest. The terms of the CanWest debentures said they could not be sold by Hollinger for several years, but the participation trust was a way around that; Hollinger would retain the debentures but effectively sell an "economic interest" in them. However, when the Aspers caught wind of the planned financing, they sent Hollinger a letter threatening to sue over it. As part of the negotiation that followed, Izzy Asper conceded that he would allow the issue to go ahead in return for various things, including Black's turning over the other half of the *Post* to him. From Asper's perspective, it had become increasingly clear to his managers that they would take a different approach to running the paper than Black had. "There was intense discussion at the partnership level about the *Post*'s strategy, and it became a natural chip in a discussion about how we could resolve a dispute," said CanWest CEO Leonard Asper. Specifically, it was becoming clearer that one side or the other should take full ownership of the paper, because with Black managing the *Post* and CanWest owning only half, the incentive for other Southam papers to play ball with the *Post* editorially or otherwise was dwindling.

Around this time, the Hollinger board and shareholders also became more aware of the fine print of the CanWest deal. When the deal was consummated in November 2000, $80 million was allocated to an agreement that Ravelston, Black, Radler, and others in their group would not compete with CanWest in Canada in the future.

Before his death in 2003, CanWest founder Izzy Asper said the non-competition agreement was his idea. In a letter to Black, he wrote, "It was of foremost importance to CanWest that if we were to do the deal, we would want an ongoing relationship with you, David Radler and others in the Ravelston group – both in a board as well as an advisory role." However, the Aspers did not ask that any money be paid for these non-compete agreements. The $80 million figure, which Black and his associates came up with on their own, would be paid out of the purchase price and therefore made no difference at the time to CanWest. "We paid 100 per cent of the purchase price to Hollinger International and how they distributed it afterwards was up to them," said Leonard Asper. Consequently $18.4 million apiece was paid to Black and Radler, $40.9 million was paid to Ravelston, and Atkinson and Boultbee each received $2 million. ("I wouldn't be so concerned if Peter Atkinson decided to open up a newspaper in Vancouver," Asper said. "But I would be if David Radler did.") Nothing was paid to Hollinger, the ostensible corporate seller of the Southam papers.

There was more. Southam had been paying Ravelston roughly $18 million a year in management fees, and as part of the CanWest sale Ravelston also negotiated an annual $6 million ongoing management fee from CanWest. CanWest would have to pay Ravelston $45 million to terminate the fee, and if Ravelston were to end the arrangement, CanWest would still have to pay it $22.5 million. None of these arrangements were revealed in the company's documents filed with regulators immediately following the deal, but they surfaced as part of the due diligence related to Hollinger's financing activities in spring 2001. Once Hollinger's auditors, KPMG, and some of its own executives became aware of the payments, they insisted that they be properly approved and disclosed.

Thus in May 2001, seven months after the Hollinger audit committee had approved the terms of the non-compete payments under the CanWest deal and five months after the sale had closed, Radler and Black sought and received new approval from the audit committee on these and other terms, saying the failure to disclose them earlier was "inadvertent." However, the belated disclosure of the

CanWest non-compete payments in Hollinger's annual report to the SEC referred to the $80 million payment as being "in addition to the purchase price," which obscured the fact that the money actually came out of Hollinger's proceeds and was not extra money paid by CanWest. What's more, it would later be alleged, the terms of these payments, like other non-competes, were structured to be tax-free under Revenue Canada rules. Additionally, the terms of the payments required that they accrue interest between August and November, which added another $1.7 million to the amounts Black and Radler received. In the context of what was originally termed a $3.2 billion deal, these figures seemed like rounding errors. If they had been presented as bonuses for a brilliantly handled deal and sold as such to the board from the start, they might not have ended up appearing as controversial and suspicious as they did in the months ahead.

On the morning of August 24, 2001, Black travelled the short distance from his Bridle Path estate to the *National Post*'s offices in Don Mills to say goodbye to the staff and hold one more press conference praising the newspaper he had spawned. Some *Post* (female) staff members gave Black teary hugs, while others felt betrayed and scoffed at his claim that the sellout was not linked to the renunciation of his citizenship in pursuit of his peerage, which, it had been reported, was once again imminent.*

Telegraph CEO Dan Colson, Black's friend since their days at Laval University, had never seen Black agonize as much as he did over the *Post* sale. Editor Ken Whyte, who understood that it was primarily a business decision for Black, visited the Blacks on Park Lane Circle over the Labour Day weekend. They had coffee (Amiel drank instant) and the mood was very gloomy. "They were both very upset by it, generally physically unhappy and distressed," recalled Whyte.

---

* Black emphasized that Roy Thomson had set up structures to continue to own newspapers in Canada despite foreign-ownership regulations after giving up his citizenship, and Black had a year to explore similar options, such as putting his interests in the names of his children. He also said that he might reclaim his citizenship in the future, when Chrétien was out of office.

"They didn't want to sell it." (Indeed, Black harboured hopes of buying the paper back from Asper under Hollinger's five-year right of refusal – until a reorganization of its top management in May 2003, after which both Whyte and deputy editor Newland left.) The Blacks told Whyte that various Toronto establishment figures had been calling all week to say what a loss it was that Hollinger had sold the *Post*, and how great the paper had been for Canada. If they were so concerned about the *Post*, Amiel lamented over her Nescafé, they should have bought more advertising.

On the morning of Tuesday, September 11, the Blacks had been slated to travel from Toronto to New York, where Amiel had several appointments for private showings at various couture houses during the city's annual Fashion Week. Black's flagship, the *Telegraph*, memorialized the terrorist attacks with an eight-page special supplement; the front page carried a huge colour photo of the World Trade Center collapsing and the headline "War on America." For Black, who was quickly in touch with his top editors, Charles Moore at the *Daily Telegraph* and Dominic Lawson at the *Sunday Telegraph*, the attacks revived his fervour for stronger bonds between Europe and America. On its editorial page, the next day's *Telegraph* called for Europe to stop ridiculing America's activities in the Middle East and to rally behind it. "What we saw in America yesterday was an attack on the freedom and order and peace that are essential to all of us, no less of an attack because it took place thousands of miles away."

At Hollinger's New York office, some of the shocked and grieving executives and administrative staff took it personally that while Radler and other executives had telephoned soon after the attacks, Black did not call until Friday, three days later, to check in on them. They were similarly put out when Amiel phoned in the days and weeks after the attacks to pursue such matters as rescheduling her fashion appointments and finalizing the details of new cashmere throw blankets she had ordered for the Gulfstream from the super-luxe Madison Avenue linen shop Leron. When the Blacks next came to New York, on September 24, Conrad was irate that because the Hollinger aircraft flew under a Canadian flag, it was required by the Federal Aviation Administration to land in White Plains, New York, rather than at the closer and more prestigious private jet airport in Teterboro, New Jersey.

The mood was darkening. Of course the terrorist attacks left much of the Western world in the grip of uncertainty, anger, and fear. In the business world, this only exacerbated the anxiety that had begun when the technology and Internet stock bubble had burst in March 2001. Across the business landscape, fissures were starting to appear in the reputations of some of the most respected companies in corporate America, led by the spectacular collapse of a Houston energy company called Enron. It would soon be followed by scandals at Tyco International, MCI Worldcom, and others.

The worst of it for Hollinger was that newspaper advertising was evaporating by the last quarter of 2001. The operating income of its Chicago-area papers, including the *Sun-Times*, fell from US$36 million to US$10 million; the *Telegraph* and its sister publications saw theirs drop from US$89 million to US$31 million; the division led by the *Jerusalem Post* lost US$3 million. Meanwhile, the CanWest stock that Hollinger held as partial payment for its Canadian newspapers plummeted in value, and so did the debentures. For example, $425 million worth of CanWest stock that had been ascribed a $25 "fair value" per share in the deal was sold for $10 per share. All this meant that Black's attempts to get rid of debt were thwarted, even though he had been able to pay down US$1 billion in loans with the cash from the CanWest sale. But at the end of the year, Hollinger International's remaining debt stood at a precariously high level for a company of its suddenly diminished earnings. Its share price tumbled from about US$16 to less than US$9.

On October 16, 2001, Hollinger's directors received a letter from the fund manager Tweedy Browne, which owned 10.9 million of the company's Class A common shares, representing 12.7 per cent of those shares and making it one of Hollinger's biggest stockholders. Browne's letter pointedly asked the directors why they had approved a tenfold increase in fees and salaries to Black and the company's top executives via Ravelston between 1995 and 2000, payments that had jumped from US$4.1 million to US$40.98 million. "And what have we, shareholders of Hollinger, received in return for that US$154 million?" the letter asked. "The stock of our company has sagged about 30 per cent from the IPO price."

Black batted Tweedy Browne's query away the next day, writing back that Hollinger's board would determine payments based on "whatever criteria its members judge appropriate." He concluded: "Given your evidently aggrieved baronial references to me, you will be relieved to learn that when I am inducted into the House of Lords at the end of this month, that will not dilute my profound commitment to egalitarianism, in shareholding as in other matters."

Two months after selling the *Post*, and two weeks after receiving Browne's letter, on the afternoon of October 31, as Amiel sat in the visitors' gallery with Henry and Nancy Kissinger, Black donned a red ermine-trimmed robe and walked into the House of Lords flanked by Lady Thatcher and Lord Carrington and became Lord Black of Crossharbour. (Crossharbour is an area of Canary Wharf, where the *Telegraph* is based. Neither Canary Wharf nor Isle of Dogs, where the development was built, had a suitably majestic appellation.) Before the induction, a celebratory lunch for twenty guests was held in the Barry Room, the semi-private dining hall in the Lords. Other guests on hand were Lady Thatcher's husband, Sir Denis; the Kissingers; former Conservative leader William Hague, who had originally nominated Black; the Conservative leader of the House of Lords, Lord Strathclyde; Lord Deedes, a former editor of the *Daily Telegraph*; Lord and Lady Hanson; and Lord and Lady Weidenfeld. The only Canadian guest there – along with the journalist Linda Frum, who was invited to record the event for the *National Post* – was Black's friend and Telegraph CEO Dan Colson. Black sat at the head of the table between Nancy Kissinger and Lady Thatcher. Later, he explained the relatively small size of the celebration: "Unless you're going to take a private room and engage in what are considered to be gaucheries for a new member, you can't make a luncheon any larger than what we had."

After lunch, Black entered the chamber with Lady Thatcher and Lord Carrington; Black pledged his oath and then, with a slight bow, walked forward to shake the hand of the Lord Chancellor. The peers in the chamber shouted the traditional hurrah. One friend of Black's whispered to Frum, "Take that, Mr. Chrétien." Black later said that Chrétien had been the last person on his mind: "Obviously, when you're walking in, and shaking hands with the Lord Chancellor, it's not a very pensive moment. But, moments before, I was thinking that I was standing only a few feet from where Walpole, Pitt the Elder, Russell, Disraeli, and Salisbury stood. And then, what an improbable and provident thing for me to be there. And I was thinking of my mother, who was a great anglophile. I thought she would be pleased. I had no thoughts whatsoever of the government of Canada." Across the ocean, the news of Black's conferment was mocked in the House of Commons by some Liberal MPs and the prime minister, whose barbs included pointing out that it was Halloween, that Black had sold his citizenship cheaply, and that he had gone to a lot of trouble to be able to get decked out in a "woman's dress."

More affecting for Black than the sale of the *Post*, the petty squabble over his peerage, corporate financial pressures, unhappy shareholders, or the economic and political aftershocks of September 11 was the news that his brother had cancer. Montegu Black was diagnosed in the spring of 2001, and the prognosis was not good. For the previous few years, the brothers had seen each other mostly during the Christmas holidays, in either Toronto or Florida. Friends who were disappointed in Conrad's absence from Monte's sixtieth-birthday celebration the previous fall now noted in the latter half of 2001 that he was spending increasing amounts of time in Toronto with his brother. Monte's illness was particularly devastating for his four children, as their mother, Mariellen (who had divorced Monte in the mid-1980s), had been diagnosed with cancer almost at the same time. In his final months, even while weak from chemotherapy, his hair fallen out, Monte would put on a suit and make his way slowly down to the kitchen of his house on Elgin Avenue, where he would await his younger brother. Tragically, Montegu and his ex-wife ended up two doors apart on the same corridor of Toronto's Sunnybrook Hospital and died within two days of each other in January 2002. On hearing of his brother's death, Black arrived at the Elgin Avenue house to grieve with Monte's children and widow, June. Giving her an awkward hug, Black said, "I hope we're going to be very Anglo-Saxon about this and not get all emotional."

Conrad, who had visited his brother daily in his final week, delivered a moving eulogy at the funeral, concluding with the words, "I was, and remain, proud to have been his brother." After Monte's burial in Mount Pleasant Cemetery, a wake was held at Conrad's home on Park Lane Circle, the house where the Black brothers had grown up.

Chapter Twenty-Eight

THE A-LIST

Shortly after her husband's induction into the House of Lords in 2001, Barbara Amiel confided to someone, "I don't know how to be addressed. I know my husband wants 'Lord Black' everywhere by everyone, but I feel rather ill at ease about 'Lady Black.'" Soon she decided that, depending on the situation, people could call her Barbara, Barbara Amiel, or Lady Black, but "never Mrs. Black." For his part, Black was fine with his closest employees and people outside the United Kingdom still calling him Conrad, but on invitations or at public occasions, regardless of the country, the couple made it known that they were Lord and Lady Black. When the Blacks, through Hollinger, pledged US$300,000 to the Metropolitan Opera in New York to become one of its Golden Horseshoe patrons, a bronze plaque was added in one of the opera house's galleries: "Hollinger International, Inc., Lord and Lady Black."

Although a title can make North American eyes roll, it is a perfectly normal part of the system in the U.K., and every previous head of the *Telegraph* had held the honour. Yet in the Blacks' case, the phrase "Lord and Lady Black" was also a creation that mirrored their ascension to their new social stratum and a growing detachment from Black's business, old friends, and family. "The people they most wanted to be with seemed to be rich Americans with a sprinkling of political

Americans – more New York than Washington," said one long-time associate in London. "It did feel a bit disengaged."

Where Lady Black was concerned, the influence she had on Black's newspapering endeavours was also changing. "Broadly speaking, it started off as a plus and became more negative. The plus is that Barbara is a good journalist and very bright and very alert to the way journalists see things. But I think it became much less good because she got onto this thing of thinking it was important to be with the social X-rays in New York. And so she started to see journalists more as sort of rather a nuisance."

If this was how others saw her, it was not how Amiel saw herself. "In her professional life she never stopped being a journalist," said her friend Krystyne Griffin. "She took great pride in her career. She never stopped working."

Aside from the company they mingled with, part of their disengagement may have been the hours they kept. The Blacks lived in their own time zone, which was roughly seven hours ahead of wherever he happened to be. As far as anyone could tell, Conrad and Barbara stayed up most if not all of the night, and Conrad would sleep through the early part of the day (while his insomniac wife preferred afternoon naps). Black remained in daily contact with his executives by e-mail and telephone, but appearances in his offices, especially in London, became less frequent. He began work on his book on Franklin Delano Roosevelt in late 2000 but really set his mind to finishing it within the year 2002, writing into the early morning. The only constant in Conrad's life was Amiel, from whom he was inseparable. To varying degrees, old friends blamed Lady Black for unhealthy changes they detected in her husband, or at least for her failure to moderate them. Although there was no person on earth who could take Conrad Black where he did not want to go, it was clear that she was not going to be the one to keep his feet on the ground.

Most critical were some of Black's prominent Toronto friends, who grumbled that over the years since he had married Amiel they barely saw him except at the Blacks' annual Christmas cocktail party on Park Lane Circle. One exception was the black-tie dinner Black hosted for fellow directors of the Canadian Imperial Bank of Commerce at his home in high style after the bank's annual meeting on February 27, 2003. "Conrad and Barbara hosted an unbelievable dinner at their house," recalled one director. "They put a hard mahogany floor over the swimming pool, everything was perfect. It was really like dining at Windsor Castle. There was a butler behind each chair." During the course of the evening, Black took his friends to his library to show them a cache of Franklin Delano Roosevelt papers that he had obtained. Lady Black remained impossibly glamorous for a woman of her (or any) age; when Lord Black sent out invitations in 2000 for a surprise sixtieth-birthday party for her at Le Cirque in New York, friends assumed her age was a typo. To his executives, Black admiringly referred to his wife as the "little woman" and would boast over drinks, "She has the body of a thirty-five-year-old." Black doted on his wife, indulging her whims and taking an active interest in her expanding and increasingly lavish wardrobe. "He doesn't seem to be able to say no to her," said one of Black's closest friends. One of his favourite dresses was a slinky Alexander McQueen number made of tiny copper scales, which neatly fitted her five-foot-eight, 120-pound frame. "The little panels of metal make the most agreeable rustling sound, like I imagine Richard the Lionhearted sounded going forth to the Crusades," said Black. "She's got this flair for getting really unusual things. I mean, how many women go around in chain mail, and how many look fabulous doing it?"

Amiel had acquired a "semi-royal" aloofness in society settings, according to one long-time director of Black companies who knew her in London. During the late 1990s, even before Conrad's peerage, the director recalled, "her manner was certainly changed . . . There was a kind of arch-graciousness – she 'received' people, whereas Conrad was outgoing, gregarious, and quick. He rarely fumbled." Indeed, one of Amiel's apparent contradictions was that while she was credited with infusing Black's persona with glamour, particularly in London, her erratic behaviour also suggested insecurity and social discomfort, especially at family gatherings. Few second wives have a smooth time with their husbands' children, and Barbara, who had no children of her own, was no exception. Black's children, Jonathan,

Alana, and James, adolescents when he remarried, did not hit it off with her and found that their father would abide no criticism of his new wife – even when, shortly after their wedding, she designated the Black children's playrooms at their homes in both Toronto and London as her new offices.

There are some who claim to have once been charmed by "Babs" Amiel only to be snubbed by Lady Black. One of them was David Wynne-Morgan, a public relations executive based in London, who had received a note from his client Peter Munk in the late 1980s asking him to help Amiel establish herself in London after her divorce from her third husband, David Graham. "I took her to lunch and she told me what she was going to do," recounted Wynne-Morgan. "I then gave a dinner party for her at the Mark's Club for about twelve of the great and the good. I then took her to lunch with Mark Burley [owner of the Mark's Club and Annabel's, the Mayfair nightclub], at Harry's Bar. Once she got in the pond, she swam, if you know what I mean. She then met and married Conrad. Years later there was a big charity event in Toronto. Barrick [a company controlled by Peter Munk] had one table and Conrad had a table beside it. When Peter went over to speak with Conrad I went to say hello to Barbara. She acted as if she had never met me. I looked at her and laughed. It was almost as if life didn't exist before Conrad. She was busy being Lady Black."

The hairstylist Robert Gage, who has known her since her days at the *Toronto Sun* and considered her a personal friend, also discerned a change. "She was always a snob, but she could get down and enjoy the underbelly of the city," he recalled. "One time I came to do her hair at her house in the Bridle Path. I went into the kitchen and said to the butler, 'Is Madam about?' The chef and the butler said, 'She's breakfasting in the dining room.'

"I went right in. She was sitting at the dining table having breakfast by herself. The sideboard had food on it – in chafing dishes, all rather extravagant.

"'Do you have house guests?' I asked.

"'No, Conrad likes to come down and browse.'

"She didn't offer me anything, no eggs. Finally, she said, 'Would you like a coffee?' I said, 'Yes.'

"The butler came in and said, 'I have it all set up for you out here in the kitchen.' The message was very clear: I was help. She basically said to me, 'I had to do this because of how it looks to the servants.'"

Sometimes, Amiel's outbursts at household staff or Hollinger employees left the recipients wishing they'd been ignored. Once, she flew into a fury when she tried to call her husband in his office in New York but her call rang through to voicemail. "You're all fired – every one of you, fired!" she raged when she finally raised one of the assistants. Paul Healy, Hollinger's vice-president of investor relations, approached Black and told him that the staff was upset and worried about their jobs. "My wife is not well," Healy recalled Black sternly telling him. "No one here is being fired. Now, Paul, can we put a sunset on this?"

Amiel suffers from a rare auto-immune disease called dermato-myositis, which is related to lupus and can cause muscle inflammation and degeneration. Black explained in 2000 that regular blood treatments take her "out of commission for three to four days every two to three months – which is a nuisance, but it's a stable situation, not a deteriorating one." One Hollinger executive says that one day she would appear frail, wearing sunglasses indoors, but the next she could be warm and energetic. The same person who terrified the New York staff sent a sweet note to another Hollinger executive on hearing that Black's three assistants, Rosemary Millar in London, Jan Akerhielm in New York, and Joan Maida in Toronto, were coming to Palm Beach after a round of refinancing for the celebratory junket for company executives at the Ritz-Carlton Hotel. "We would love to have them over for a lunch if it were possible or a dinner but I don't want to ruin their shopping time or fun-time in PB," Amiel wrote, adding that perhaps they could stay with the Blacks if they preferred. "This is a pleasure for them, not a chore . . . can you see what might work for them."

A former Southam editor who experienced Amiel's unpredictable sting reckoned that her position and title didn't change her so much as it changed everyone else around her. "When she was screaming as Barbara, nobody really gave a shit," the editor said. "When she was screaming as Mrs. Conrad Black, that was a different thing."

Bret Stephens, the twenty-nine-year-old editor of the *Jerusalem Post*, raised Amiel's ire in September 2003 when he agreed to appear on an editors' panel at a conference on the Middle East in London, hosted by the *Guardian*, the *Telegraph*'s left-leaning rival. When Barbara got wind that Stephens had agreed to participate, she was incensed. Hoping to smooth things over, Stephens, who had joined the paper as its editor in early 2002 from the *Wall Street Journal Europe*, made an appointment to meet Amiel for the first time while he was in London. Until then, because the *Post* was Radler's purview, he had heard from her only intermittently via telephone or e-mail. "Barbara was like a lighthouse, and her gaze would hit you intensely for a week or month, and then she'd disappear," said Stephens.

Arriving in Cottesmore Gardens at the appointed hour, Stephens was waiting in the library of the cavernous home when a studious-looking woman, looking to be in her thirties, came into the room rustling through a sheaf of papers and arrayed them on the table in front of him. Stephens assumed her to be Amiel's assistant. Without any introduction, the woman levelled her gaze on him and said icily, "I don't know whether you are a fool or a knave. Probably both. I suspect that now that you have grown comfortable with the *Jerusalem Post*, you have come to London to seek fancier friends."

The editor quickly realized who he was talking to and jumped to his feet. He explained first that the best journalists in Israel were at the conference, and he wanted the *Post* represented; second, there was an opportunity through the conference to meet Tony Blair; and third, he added, "This was a chance to meet you." On hearing this last bit, Amiel instantly defrosted into a feline, girlish hostess, and the meeting went smoothly from there.

Stephens had never experienced anything quite like it. "The entire thing had this quality of walking into a room and this curtain goes up, and the light comes on and there's an audience there, and she's reciting her lines and I'm supposed to recite mine," he reflected later.

Investors like Chris Browne of Tweedy Browne and aspiring fashionistas alike read with wide-eyed fascination the full-access tour of Lady Black's wardrobe that *Vogue* magazine – edited by her frequent lunching companion Anna Wintour – published in its August 2002 issue. The article was part of a package on "style setters from 16 to 80," featuring profiles of everyone from Alicia Keys and Reese Witherspoon to Diane Sawyer and CZ Guest. The *Vogue* writer, Julia Reed, found Amiel completely at ease with her roaming around her London dressing suite. "What I found was a woman who is pampered and indeed extravagant, to be sure," recounted Reed. "She has a rolling clothes rack with padded hangers, and around their necks are little pillows embroidered with instructions as to the clothes hanging on them: TO BE IRONED, TO PUT AWAY, ALTERATIONS, TO TRY ON." Amiel explained that as a result of a humiliation she received while wearing a used dress when she was a struggling teenager in Hamilton, Ontario, she had vowed "never again," adding, "I sort of never forgot it. And now I have an extravagance that knows no bounds."*

"She is not kidding," Reed wrote. "In her luxurious dressing suite, two floors above where we're sitting, there are so many closets it takes two rooms (connected by a short hall with big walk-in closets – one for day clothes, one for night) to hold them, and on the doors of each are countless beautifully pressed shawls of pashmina and silk and cashmere and chiffon hanging over thin brass rods. There's a fur closet, a sweater closet, a closet for shirts and T-shirts and a closet so crammed with evening gowns that the overflow has to be kept in yet more closets downstairs off the gym. There are glove drawers, belt drawers, drawers full of beaded camisoles and snowy-white handkerchiefs, drawers containing row after row of panty hose carefully rolled into perfect neat balls. (Boxes of unopened panty hose, filed by color and make – Fogal, Oroblu, Bloomingdale's – sit on the floor beneath the furs.) In one walk-in closet, on a single shelf, I count more than a dozen Hermès Birkin bags, most of which are crocodile; 30 or 40 of Renaud Pellegrino's exquisite jewel-handled handbags occupy the shelves remaining. Across the hall, shelves are stacked with well over

---

* Amiel would later say of the "extravagance" comment: "I have been saying that wryly about myself all my life in every economic circumstance. I think I must have heard it in a bad radio play once. I don't know whether I used it in conversation with Reed in reference to handkerchiefs, hand cream, or handbags, but it certainly was the most ill-timed throwaway comment I could have made."

100 pairs of Manolo Blahnik heels stored in clear plastic boxes; on the floor, Blahnik and Chanel flats are stacked, unboxed, two- and three-pair deep." Another guest at the Blacks' London home opened the closet in the guest room and found it to be an overflow cupboard housing seventeen beautiful dresses, all with the tags still on them.

For years, the Blacks had adorned various annual roundups of "power players" and "must-invite" lists in the U.K., but the *Vogue* article was one of a series that seemed to cement the Blacks' place among the super-elite. In an article she penned for the Canadian magazine *Fashion Quarterly*, Amiel admitted that she had not been much for jewellery until she married Black and "vaulted into circles where, for some people, jewellery is a defining attribute, rather like your intelligence or the number of residences you have." Just as her 1980 book *Confessions* had described her political conversion from left to right, she now described her conversion from agnostic to jew-ellery believer at a party at Annabel's after the jeweller Laurence Graff put a stone of about 100 carats in her hand to hold. "All the stuff I believed about big stones just being vulgar went into the ether," she wrote, going on to note that a natural-pearl and diamond brooch she owned "has stayed in my safety deposit box for about six years, unworn because it is so large that I simply can't carry it off."

Her husband was even less averse to playful self-aggrandizement. Black once said loudly to Henry Kissinger, at a party where the society columnist Taki was in earshot, "Taki never spoke to me until he heard I had the same plane as Gianni Agnelli." The Blacks' growing showiness was a bit of a puzzle to those who had known them both before they were married. "It's an odd thing to say," said Hal Jackman, "but Conrad has all the characteristics of a parvenu. He needs to impress the people he is impressed by; everybody else can go hang. That, I think, is what has brought him down. Very odd, because, you know, he was not born above a shop."

That rich people can live differently, better, and more decadently than regular folk was not the point. What was, in the firestorm that was about to strike the Blacks, was whether their decadence was financed by siphoning more than their share out of a public company that Conrad Black controlled and on whose board Barbara Amiel

Black sat. Black would reject any criticism of his and especially his wife's conduct: "The opulence of my lifestyle is a myth, based on one well-attended cocktail party a year in London, not unlike that given by other newspaper companies in that city; and on one quotation from *Vogue* magazine from my wife, when she was, in fact, referring to handkerchiefs. My wife never liked parties, disliked large houses, and prefers to live with minimum domestic help and make her own dinners or eat out. She does like stylish clothes, but is happy to pay for that from her own earnings. The attempt to portray her as a Marie Antoinette and me as a supine lovestruck spouse, like most comment on the subject, is a complete fiction."

The defining portrait of Lord and Lady Black at the giddy height of their power could well be the photo they agreed to pose for in *Vanity Fair* for a feature on Palm Beach. Amid sun-splashed photos of tanned neighbours like Rod Stewart, George Hamilton, and Leonard Lauder, Black maintained his usual pallid complexion but dressed casually in an open-neck white shirt and blazer. The photo the magazine selected for publication in its February 2004 issue featured Black sitting stiffly in a chair in the middle of a perfectly manicured lawn, with a statue of Poseidon in the background and the ocean beyond. Amiel sits barefoot in the grass at Black's feet in a form-fitting Marc Jacobs skirt and top, resting her hands and head on his knee and looking skyward in a pose suggesting doting wife, Renaissance muse, or affectionate poodle.

The photo shoot had swung into action when Black placed a call to Vicky Ward, a *Vanity Fair* writer who was married to the Hollinger executive Matthew Doull, whose mother was Montegu Black's widow. Since Black's own son Jonathan was not involved in the newspaper business and his other children were still in school, Doull was the closest thing to family working at the company (though London's *Evening Standard* once ran a pointed correction, at the *Telegraph*'s behest, after describing him as Black's "nephew" in a story; the correction clarified that Doull was not a "blood relative"). In February 2003, Ward had given birth to very premature twin sons, and she would remain in the hospital with them for two months. One day in the hospital, her cellphone rang – it was Black. She and Doull assumed he was calling to look in on them, since his only congratulations so far had been an e-mail, and other Hollinger executives knew about the babies' parlous health. But Black didn't mention the babies. "Victoria," he said, "I've just spoken to my friend Leonard Lauder. He tells me that *Vanity Fair* is photographing his house. And I seem to vaguely recall getting a letter, which I never replied to. But if *Vanity Fair* wants to photograph my house too, they'd be more than welcome to."

The photographer, Jonathan Becker, and the *Vanity Fair* crew arrived at the Blacks' estate on South Ocean Boulevard on Tuesday, March 18, 2003, just as the American "shock and awe" bombing campaign against Iraq was getting underway, which only added to the incongruity of the surroundings and their assignment. Both subjects were unfailingly gracious, and although Lord Black had to be goaded into the photo shoot, Lady Black handled him deftly and wittily. She was as dazzling as a movie starlet, and when it came to trying on different outfits or poses, she was eager to please. In her upstairs dressing chamber, Amiel threw off one outfit in order to try on another, as unselfconscious as a runway model as she stood before the *Vanity Fair* journalists in just her underwear. Elsewhere in the mansion, the butler, Domenico, prepared coffee and attended to members of the Lanvin family of fashion fame, who were the Blacks' house guests at the time.

There was probably no more media-savvy power couple alive, and the impression given by the Blacks' public profile was that they were seeking not so much acceptance as acknowledgement. One of the many attributes the couple shared was a kind of self-fulfilling persecution complex that necessitated an aversion to popularity. Accordingly, their individual and shared styles did not always win them friends. Winston Churchill's daughter Lady Soames once told friends that Black was "London's biggest bore unhung."

Liz Smith, the doyenne of New York gossip columnists, refused to mention the Blacks in her widely read column after Lord Black dominated the conversation at a diplomatic dinner she attended with blustery dissertations on world affairs. "He just happens to be the most offensive, chauvinistic, opinionated, and overbearing person I've ever had the misfortune to sit near at dinner," Smith said.

In another well-told tale of the Blacks' wayward hospitality, one day in 1998 *Telegraph* features editor Eleanor Mills was recommended on short notice by the editor at the time, Charles Moore, as a last-minute fill-in at a dinner party – held in honour of Sotheby's –for which the Blacks were suddenly short a woman. Mills, who was at the newspaper, went home and changed before making her way to Cottesmore Gardens. When she arrived, Conrad thanked her for coming, and she began sipping a glass of wine. About twenty minutes later, Black came up and said, "It's very embarrassing, but I'm afraid there's been a bit of a mix-up." Black explained that they had been wrong about the numbers and didn't need another woman after all. "Why don't you finish your drink and skedaddle?"

"Sorry?" Mills asked.

"Right, finish your drink and run along. Barbara will sort you out with a taxi."

Mills found Amiel sitting with the writer Petronella Wyatt, and Mills told her, "Conrad wants me to go and said you'd get me a taxi."

As Mills, who became the news review editor of the *Sunday Times*, remembered it, a housekeeper then led her away from the party and down the stairs, through the dining room and the kitchen, where the chef was frying scallops. The housekeeper then phoned to order a taxi at the trade entrance. Instead of standing there waiting, Mills left by the stairs from the basement kitchen and stormed onto the road. "I really remember shaking my hands at the house, and I thought, 'One day you'll be fucked and I'll be happy.'"

The next day, Mills was summoned to the chairman's office, where an assistant handed her a basket of Jo Malone bath soaps with a note from Conrad and Barbara thanking her for being a "good sport." According to Amiel, Mills was asked to leave because of "a potentially difficult situation that involved the new job she was going to at the *Sunday Times* and two of our guests who were in an imbroglio with that paper . . . I appreciate memory can gild events, but the sequence was straightforward: we were very embarrassed and my husband asked my assistant, Penny Phillips, to arrange a taxi for Ms. Mills. Ms. Mills refused and asked if there was 'a back way out.'"

One person who came to regret dining with the Blacks was Daniel Bernard, the French ambassador in London. A few weeks after Black received his peerage, he and Lady Black hosted a dinner in honour of *Spectator* editor and Tory MP Boris Johnson. As the 100-odd guests gathered their buffet plates and sat at tables set around the Cottesmore drawing room, Bernard allegedly said something to Black about "that shitty little country Israel." "Why," he asked, "should the world be in danger of World War III because of these people?" Black later recounted this to Amiel, who used it to kick off a column on anti-Semitism creeping into London parlours in the wake of September 11. "Recently, the ambassador of a major E.U. country politely told a gathering at my home that the current troubles in the world were all because of Israel," she wrote before reciting the unattributed quote. "At a private lunch last month," she added, "the hostess – doyenne of London's political salon scene – made a remark to the effect that she couldn't stand Jews and everything happening to them was their own fault. When this was greeted with shocked silence, she chided her guests on what she assumed was their hypocrisy. 'Oh, come on,' she said, 'you all feel like that.'" The column became the talk of the chattering classes, not so much on the merits of Amiel's argument – which plenty of people backed up – but because of the questions of high-society decorum it raised. When Lord and Lady Black held a dinner, should guests expect anything they said to be in her next dispatch? In classic London style, the anonymous EU ambassador in the piece was quickly outed by a rival newspaper as Bernard, who through a spokesman insisted his words had been misconstrued. Then Lady Powell, the wife of Lady Thatcher's former private secretary, Lord Powell, wrote to the *Daily Telegraph* denying the scuttlebutt making the rounds that she was the "doyenne of London's political salon scene" to whom Amiel had referred. In the aftershock of the scandal, Bernard was transferred to Algeria, and there is no evidence that the upper crust stopped accepting invitations to the Blacks' soirees – more likely they just watched what they said.

In any event, through the Hollinger International board Black could count on drawing an impressive roster of tycoons, dignitaries, thinkers, and journalists to his table in London. New York was coming along nicely, too. Hollinger's star-studded board now counted such luminaries as Henry Kissinger, Richard Perle, former Illinois governor James Thompson, and former U.S. ambassador Robert Strauss, along with the business bigwigs Dwayne Andreas of Archer Daniels Midland, Alfred Taubman of Sotheby's, Leslie Wexner of the Limited, and Marie-Josée Kravis, who Black liked to point out was the wife of the buyout legend Henry Kravis. The Blacks tried to up their presence in New York through the US$2.5 million Hollinger contributed for a minor stake in the *New York Sun*, a new but largely ignored conservative daily newspaper, which counted the financiers Roger Hertog and Michael Steinhardt among its backers, and by playing a bigger role on the black-tie benefit scene for such institutions as the Metropolitan Opera. As Black's book on FDR neared publication in the fall of 2003, he and Amiel pledged US$100,000 and co-chaired the Literary Lions gala for the New York Public Library that spring. "They're definitely on the A-list," said the Manhattan society chronicler David Patrick Columbia. "He's Lord Black. He's got a title. A title, a private jet, and allegedly millions and millions of dollars is all you need."

The status and invincibility that Black had strived all his career to achieve were finally within his reach, yet for some reason – perhaps battle fatigue, hubris, avarice, the death of his brother, the distraction of his book, or the whims of his wife – he was unable to hear the beating drums of unhappy stockholders and head off the scandal that would turn his friends against him and bring his run as a press baron to an end. To paraphrase Hemingway, the unravelling would come gradually, then suddenly. "I used to say to the kids for years, 'Conrad doesn't really know who his friends are. The minute your father loses his money, these people are dust,'" said his first wife, Joanna. "It never occurred to me that that would happen in our lifetime. In some ways I think it's a good lesson my children have learned."

Chapter Twenty-Nine

INVESTOR RELATIONS

Although Hollinger International was legally headquarterd in Chicago, its main corporate offices were located on the eighteenth floor of 712 Fifth Avenue in New York City, a limestone and granite tower owned by Hollinger director Alfred Taubman's real estate company. The tower rises over the intersection of Fifty-sixth Street and features its own discreet lobby entrance into the chi-chi women's retailer Henri Bendel. When Hollinger took over the space, deep wood panelling and plush tan carpeting were installed, and the company's initial – "H" – was engraved on the suite's doorknobs. The modest-sized chairman's office featured a small sitting area with a small red couch and chairs at one end and a leather-topped writing table for a desk at the other, with a plush brown velvet chair for Black. The most prominent piece of art was a portrait of Lord North, the Tory prime minister of England who, while presiding over the loss of the American War of Independence, famously said, "Let me not go to the grave with the guilt of having been the ruin of my king and country."

Consistent with Black's fascination with history, his efficient assistant, Jan Akerhielm, had worked as a young assistant for Larry O'Brien, who was the Democratic National Committee chairman when President Nixon ordered his phones tapped and his Watergate apartment broken into. On a side table was a "Dear Conrad"–inscribed photograph of Taubman playing golf with the caption "Landlord at

The Black Group of Companies Circa 2002

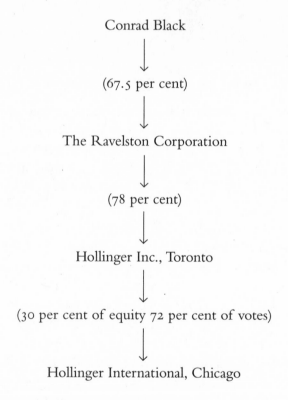

Conrad Black

↓

(67.5 per cent)

↓

The Ravelston Corporation

↓

(78 per cent)

↓

Hollinger Inc., Toronto

↓

(30 per cent of equity 72 per cent of votes)

↓

Hollinger International, Chicago

work." In 2002, when Taubman was sentenced to a year in jail after a price-fixing scandal at Sotheby's, where he was chairman and controlling shareholder and where Black served as a director, Black left Taubman in place on Hollinger's board and also visited him in prison. "His legal problems have no bearing on his utility to our company," Black said. "Other than in cases of legal or moral necessity, which have not arisen here, we do not desert our friends."

Hollinger International's certification of listing from the New York Stock Exchange, dated January 16, 1996, was hung over the toilet in the executive washroom. Black's office and the long, narrow boardroom next to it, where Hollinger's top executives and directors would gather for important meetings, were adorned with framed correspondence from Franklin Delano Roosevelt to his cousin Margaret Suckley. There was also a painting of the battleship USS *Houston* on "presidential passage" through the Panama Canal in 1934 and a small, curiously out-of-place, framed photo and autograph of the Chicago gangster Al Capone, presumably a nod to the *Sun-Times*. Although Black, David Radler, Dan Colson, and the company's other top executives were scattered across several time zones around the globe, the New York office was the principal address and central clearing house for the function known as investor relations. The company's financial reports to investors and regulators were produced and disseminated here, along with press releases whenever there was news.

In 2002, forty-year-old Paul Healy was marking his seventh year as Hollinger's vice-president of investor relations. Healy, an approachable, rosy-cheeked former media banker at Chase Manhattan Bank, was effectively Hollinger's chief emissary on Wall Street. His additional title as head of corporate development meant that he organized the company's financial affairs and worked with the chief legal and financial officers on such tasks as figuring out which banks or financial institutions Hollinger would use, and arranging for presentations to investors. Hailing from an affluent North Dakota banking family and well connected both professionally and socially, Healy prided himself on his straight talk and good relations with the so-called minority investors who held 70 per cent of Hollinger

International's publicly traded shares.* "I'm friends with all my share-holders, and I don't think there's anything wrong with that," said Healy, who taught Sunday school near his weekend house in Roxbury, Connecticut.

Black did not particularly care to be friends with his sharehold-ers, especially the big fund managers, who administered money for such institutions as state pension funds. Nor did Black mix with the professional CEOs who ran publicly traded companies without actu-ally controlling their stock; he fancied himself farther up capitalism's evolutionary scale, in the league of entrepreneurs and owners. "My natural sympathies are with the proprietors, whose own money is at stake," Black wrote in his 1993 memoir. "Too often I have seen non-proprietorial managers focus on keeping others at bay, expanding their companies unwisely and steadily improving their own financial condition irrespective of performance." In Black's view, the dividing line between Conrad Black and Hollinger was opaque, because his control over the company, in the form of super-voting shares, was absolute. Every investor who ever bought a share of stock in his company, dating back to the American company's initial offering in 1994, knew this. They were welcome to come along for the ride, but they were not his partners. If anyone didn't like the way he was running his company – well, they were welcome to sell.

That had been more or less his attitude toward the letter that shareholder Christopher Browne of Tweedy Browne had sent to directors the previous October, although Black did pay a friendly follow-up visit to Browne at his Park Avenue offices the following month and gave him a free subscription to the *Sunday Telegraph*.

Until the eve of Hollinger's annual meeting on May 23, 2002, nothing much happened to alter either Black's outlook or Browne's. Then, on the afternoon of Friday, May 17, Healy forwarded to Black in London an e-mail he had just received from Laura Jereski, a

---

* In business terms, these were "minority" shareholders because Black controlled the majority of votes over the company's shares through Hollinger Inc.'s super-voting Class B shares, which carried ten votes per share, compared with a single vote each for the publicly traded A shares.

Tweedy Browne analyst and former *Wall Street Journal* reporter known for her dogged research. The purpose of the e-mail was to give Healy a heads-up about some questions Tweedy Browne planned to air at the annual meeting. Jereski was not pleased and underscored it by referring to Hollinger repeatedly as "our company." Jereski had scoured the annual proxy statement that Hollinger sent to its public stockholders in March and had two major concerns. The first was the rationale for the roughly US$30 million management fee that "our company" had paid the previous year to Ravelston, the private holding company controlled by Black. The second was the recently disclosed payments from the CanWest transaction, totalling US$15.6 million, sent to Ravelston shareholders and Hollinger executives Black, Radler, Peter Atkinson, and Jack Boultbee. These were "non-compete" payments, fees paid in exchange for the executives' agreement not to start any newspapers in Canada that would compete against the *National Post* or other papers they had sold. "Since your only vehicle for competing in the newspaper business is our company," Jereski asked, "why do you feel it was appropriate for these individuals to pocket the money, instead of our company?"

In the spring of 2002 Tweedy Browne was not considered to be an activist shareholder. Christopher Browne, along with his brother, William, and their partner, John Spears, managed the firm's mutual funds representing some US$10 billion, and the trio have said that they have put at least US$100 million of their own money into their firm's investments. They were known for patient, cautious investing. The company's roots date back to 1920, when it was founded by Forrest Berwind Tweedy as a brokerage; Howard Browne, father of William and Christopher, joined in 1945, and it began managing money five years later. Despite the company's prestige, Browne has said that he and his brother were actually "average Joes" raised in a suburban household in middle-class New Jersey, and that Spears's family were Quakers from outside Philadelphia, "not guys in the Social Register." Tweedy closely followed the value theory of Benjamin Graham, the mentor of Warren Buffett, who advocated buying stocks at a discount to net asset value, and Graham was the firm's largest brokerage customer in the 1930s and early 1940s. Jereski suggested Hollinger International as an investment in 1999 as it neatly fit the company's criteria for investment – a stock then trading at around US$11 per share which Jereski estimated could fetch as much as US$18 if the company were sold privately. Normally, the Tweedy approach was to pick its investments and discreetly apply pressure on company managers, but the feistiness of Jereski's e-mail reflected the changed mood in corporate America in May 2002. "We didn't do much more than get the ball rolling," Browne said later. "There's an old saying: once you see under the rock, you see all the squirlies."

On reading Jereski's e-mail, Black spoke to Jack Boultbee and Peter Atkinson, his top advisers on finance and legal matters respectively. "Laura's letter is nonsense but obviously a number of shareholders are holding hands on this and I accept that the initial appearances are not optimal," he wrote back to Healy. "However, the facts are not embarrassing when explained properly. What dismays me is that you have already been through this with them, but they are back again, unsatisfied. I see it as an opportunity as much as a challenge to present the answers Laura wants preemptively, thoroughly, plausibly, truthfully and courteously. Much as I would like to just blow their asses off, I don't want a sour atmosphere at the shareholders' meeting."

Black said he would gather information over the weekend and assemble a response on Monday for Tuesday's annual meeting. "Could you alert David [Radler] to this issue and ask him if he has any suggestions for how to disarm critics? Could you also make sure he is on the teleconference? I know he tries to avoid all issues implying we are a public company but that won't do this time. If there is a problem, let me know. I will try to send my notes for the House of Lords speech, which I did not consult while speaking but composed in advance and quite faithfully followed."

Even a spirited oration in the House of Lords did not prepare Black for the tsunami of dissent that washed through the stuffy Metropolitan Club at Hollinger's 2002 AGM on the morning of Tuesday, May 23. As part of his statement on the company's performance, Black gave an abstruse explanation of the mathematics and reasoning behind some of the payments Tweedy Browne objected to. On the subject of the non-compete fees, Black said that "in order to remove any possible misunderstanding, these agreements were presented to and approved by the independent directors of this company as equitable after what they considered appropriate analysis . . . The non-compete agreements were requested by the chairman of CanWest who wanted to retain our collaboration and avoid competition with us." Regarding the management fees, he explained that Ravelston was not just himself and Hollinger's top executives but a staff of thirty doing everything from accounting, legal, and treasury work to "general advisory procurement administrative services" for the company.

Jereski went to the microphone to pose the first question at the shareholders' meeting, clearly not appeased by what she heard. "As owners, we are concerned about the level of payment being made by *our* company principally to Lord Black and to David Radler in the form of non-competes. In the past two years, these have totalled US$74 million, of which more than US$22 million have gone to each of Lord Black and David Radler. And my question is, since *our* company is your only vehicle for competing in the newspaper industry, why do you feel that it is appropriate for those payments to go to you and not to *our* company?"

Black quibbled with Jereski's numbers and then reiterated that the non-competes were at the request of Izzy Asper, CanWest's chairman. "We certainly don't depart from industry practice and we don't depart from normal guidelines and we leave the determination of these matters in the hands of disinterested people, who do conduct whatever analysis they think is appropriate. It's not for us to tell them what to do. They're experienced, respected business people and they do what they think is right."

Next at the microphone was Jereski's boss, Christopher Browne, who, in his bankerly monotone, pressed Black on why Hollinger needed a separate company – Ravelston – to perform services that the company itself could handle. Black danced around the question with a variation on his "proprietor" argument. "I realize there are two views on this, but I've always been a member of the school that holds it is a good thing for owners to run their own businesses because no one is going to pursue the interest of those businesses more zealously than the people whose money is involved with them."

Next Lee Cooperman, a Wall Street legend whose Omega Advisors hedge fund managed US$2.5 billion, stood. Cooperman took umbrage at Black's inclusion of advisory services in his description of what Ravelston did for Hollinger. "You're not investment bankers. You shouldn't be getting banking fees . . . The corporation owns you lock, stock, and barrel. That's what you're being paid to do . . . That kind of payment is just inappropriate. The corporation is owed your full faith and fidelity."

"Yeah, well, it gets our full fidelity," replied Black.

"Let me give you a suggestion that you could maybe resolve all of this," Cooperman continued. "Get rid of Ravelston, get rid of all these side deals, get your outside directors to give you an option package so when you prosper, we prosper. But the idea of all these payments being made and our stock is trading at the low end of a range for a decade is unattractive."

The ruckus Black had tried to avoid was in full swing. "I realize that I seem to be swimming upstream here against a current of opinion that this is a complete scam and is just a back-door payoff to the executives of the vendor company. That isn't the case . . . You're not dealing with greed here and you're not dealing with sneakiness. You're dealing with a best-efforts attempt to accommodate to industry practice and do what's equitable as determined by independent directors who are as a group quite a distinguished group."

"You have to eliminate these conflicts," Cooperman persisted. "They never should have existed in the pre-Enron world and they should exist even less now. Warren Buffett and notables like him have talked about the greed in corporate America. You're offended by that term, but this is what the people on the outside look at . . . We all want to be in the same boat, pulling the same direction."

"Yep, yep, yep, good," said Black. "I must object to any reference to Enron in the context of this company. I mean, this is a real business. We buy newsprint, we convert them to newspapers, we sell ads, we hire a lot of writers, we report the news, and it is a business . . . We all know that there are all kinds of scandalous and outrageous examples, even illegal ones, of incompetent managements helping themselves to egregious amounts of money in spurious ways. That has not happened here."

Now sounding like Captain Renault in *Casablanca*, Black added: "I would be shocked, I would be shocked if I thought either you or Chris Browne were trying to suggest there was anything unethical about what we're doing. I take seriously and respect your view that it could be done better and differently. But it certainly has not been done unethically – or even greedily."

With that, a small, pleasant-looking man, Edward Shufro of the money manager Shufro, Rose, came to the microphone. "I've been listening to what my distinguished – and I do mean distinguished – colleagues have been saying to you. They're trying to be polite about it, but what they're telling you is that they consider you a thief, and I can't say that I have any disagreement with that whatsoever."

"Then you shouldn't be here," Black replied.

"Well, I'm here," said Shufro.

"Sell your shares and get out," said Black. "If you think I'm a thief, go. I'm not going anywhere."

"Yeah, well, I thought it would be interesting for you to hear my viewpoint on it," Shufro shrugged.

"If we lived in a country or were now in a country where the civil tort of defamation still existed, my response would be a juridical one," Black added. "Do we have any more intelligent or civilized comments than that?"

At the end of the forty-eight-minute meeting, Black thanked investors for their comments and said he would take them seriously. Barbara Amiel was furious at the attacks on her husband and was led by David Radler to the Blacks' Mercedes limousine, where the driver, Gus, was instructed to take them to the Blacks' apartment.

Another embarrassment for Black that morning was that not one of Hollinger's big-name independent directors had shown up. After the meeting, a directors' lunch was held in Hollinger's boardroom, and several of the independent directors were now on hand. Black mentioned nothing to them of the annual meeting's fireworks, except that the independent directors' absence was noted and perhaps next time they ought to attend. Paul Healy, the investor relations chief, later that day implored David Radler and vice-president of law Mark Kipnis to tell James Thompson – the chairman of the audit committee – that investors had been angry at the meeting. That night, Healy claimed, a furious Black called him at home: "This is my company," he fumed. "I'm the controlling shareholder. I decide what Governor Thompson needs to know and when."

Across the United States, the heat was on company boards. The pressure grew when, a few weeks later, MCI Worldcom announced that it had unearthed a massive fraud – a finding that soon led the company into the biggest bankruptcy in American history. Across a wide swath of corporate America – from Adelphia to Xerox, Global Crossing to Tyco International, star banker Frank Quattrone to home-making queen Martha Stewart – investigations were being mounted and charges laid. With each new debacle, it was as if the signals had gone out at the intersection of public money and private greed. The sexy new catchphrase was "corporate governance," and even President George W. Bush, who had been buddies with the bosses of Enron, could not ignore the news. "Corporate America has got to understand there is a higher calling than trying to fudge the numbers, trying to slip a billion here and a billion there," he said on June 28, and three days later a sweeping new law, the Sarbanes-Oxley Act, was passed by Congress. Under Sarbanes-Oxley, new rules dictating what companies must disclose to their shareholders, how they must compose their boards, and who qualifies as an independent director came into effect. The underlying message was that the age of rubber-stamping whatever was placed in front of them was over, and directors were going to be held accountable.

In private, the new vigilance of his shareholders annoyed Black. A few days after the AGM, Matthew Doull, who was working on the company's Internet and venture capital projects, had a meeting with the chairman. Doull brought Black a proposal in which the company could set up and manage a venture capital fund under a federal government program that would contribute matching funds for whatever Hollinger could raise from outside partners. One of the beauties of the idea, Doull pointed out, was that as the managing partner, Hollinger would receive management fees from the other investors in the fund, and they'd be able to point out to cranky stockholders that this time the company was *receiving* fees, not just paying them out. On hearing this, Black waved his hand dismissively and said, "I don't give a fuck about the shareholders." (Black later denied saying this.*)

Over the course of the summer, Black and Chris Browne continued to correspond. At first, Black told Browne that Hollinger would file an update with the SEC disclosing such things as the company's intention to stop paying insiders for sitting on its board and for signing non-compete agreements. "The transparency you seek will not be long in coming and will not reveal anything startling or discouraging to any reasonable shareholder," Black wrote on June 11. However, Browne sent Black a snarky rejoinder on learning that Hollinger had decided not to file the update immediately but rather to make the disclosure in its regular quarterly 10-Q filing in the fall. Black wrote to Browne, "I'm prepared to offer you a non-competition agreement in the exchange of self-righteous letters, that we cease to exchange such letters, after you've read our 10-Q. And I demand the high consideration of a good lunch, host to be determined by a coin toss."

Behind Black's charm offensive, he was willing to budge only so much. "We have said for some time that [Hollinger] served no purpose as a listed company other than relatively cheap use of other peoples capital," he wrote in an August 3, 2002, e-mail to Atkinson and Boultbee. "We now have an unsatisfactory situation where a number of shareholders think we are deliberately suppressing the stock price, some think we are running a gravy train and a gerrymandered share structure, and we think they are a bunch of self-righteous

---

* "My comment on the venture fund was that I wasn't sure we could sell our expertise in the area, and I was right. I never in my career addressed a directors' meeting in the coarse manner . . . cited, never entertained such opinions about the shareholders, and this story is a complete falsehood."

hypocrites and ingrates, who give us no credit for what has been a skillful job of building and pruning a company in difficult circumstances just ahead of seismic financial events."

By this point, even Black was coming to the conclusion that a company that operated primarily in London and Chicago couldn't justify owning two airplanes. Two days later, he wrote to Atkinson: "There has not been an occasion for many months when I got on our plane without wondering whether it was really affordable. But I'm not prepared to reenact the French Revolutionary renunciation of the rights of nobility. We have to find a balance between an unfair taxation on the company and a reasonable treatment of the founder-builders-managers. We are proprietors, after all, beleaguered though we may be."

Black knew that he was bound to the structure he had created whereby Hollinger funnelled its dividends to Inc. and management fees to Ravelston, both of which went to finance the troublesome debts at Inc. When Hollinger cut its dividend from 11¢ to 5¢ in September 2002, Ravelston once again had to ante up money to cover the shortfall. By the end of 2002, the hard numbers were that in order for Inc. to meet its financial obligations, it used its US$5.2 million dividend income from Hollinger and US$14 million from Ravelston. In turn, Ravelston's main source of income was the management fees it received from Hollinger. "I think we should concentrate on taking steps to keep the management fees as high as possible," Boultbee wrote Black several months later.

But the heat from shareholders and the new Sarbanes-Oxley rules had made Black's corporate construct – Ravelston controlling Inc., which in turn controlled Hollinger – a major problem.

One investor to whom Black did show deference was Mason Hawkins, the chairman of Memphis-based Southeastern Asset Management. Southeastern had become Hollinger's largest institutional shareholder in 2002, eventually buying 20 per cent of its Class A shares. Like Tweedy Browne, it had a reputation for patient long-term investing; but unlike Christopher Browne, Hawkins formed a more collegial relationship with Black. Hawkins proposed that, if Black were to eliminate Hollinger's super-voting rights, Southeastern would combine its stake in Hollinger along with his, ensuring him continuing control. Black thought Hawkins's offer was a "thoughtful proposal" and promised him that if Hollinger's stock did not improve, he'd consider it.

Throughout this period, Black was at work on his FDR book. In January 2001 he had arranged for Hollinger International to buy a cache of FDR papers from the estate of Grace Tully, the president's long-serving secretary, for US$8 million. Over the summer of 2002, because of the new mood of investor vigilance and disclosure, Black's legal adviser Peter Atkinson and investor relations chief Paul Healy pushed for the purchase to be formally approved by Hollinger's board and disclosed to shareholders. Black later explained that the purchase had taken place shortly after the CanWest sale when Hollinger "appeared to be quite a flush company. So it seemed to be a sensible if slightly eccentric thing to do." Rather than admitting that it might look like he was using company funds for a pet project, Black explained that given his expertise on FDR he knew the company was getting the papers at a bargain price. The purchase had been ratified by the executive committee of Hollinger's board in December 2000 – the executive committee being Black and his long-time partner David Radler, since the third executive committee member, Richard Perle, was not present for this telephone discussion. But the FDR purchase was not taken before the full board for approval until October 2002. When it was, Black said, he had offered to pay for the papers himself if any directors objected, but none had. When asked more than two years after the purchase by the *Financial Times* why he hadn't bought them out of his own money in the first place, he replied flippantly, "US$8 million was not something I was prepared to spend."

The purchase of the FDR papers was just one incident that troubled Hollinger's executives and shareholders.* Although he and Black had "had some really wonderful, belly-laughing good times," Paul Healy, for one, had started taking a dimmer view of his boss around the time of the 2002 annual meeting. In addition to the acquisition of the FDR papers, he was rankled by the bonuses Hollinger Digital paid to its executives in 2000 and 2001 based only on investments that

---

* In 2004, Hollinger would accept an offer of US$2.4 million for the FDR papers.

made money – ignoring the far greater losses on duds – as well as the creation of a side company, Horizon Publications, which had purchased some small newspapers from Hollinger. (Healy had declined an invitation to invest in Horizon.)

Because Healy personally owned 300,000 Hollinger shares and options, he shared the discomfort investors expressed at the annual meeting over the non-compete and management fees. The same could be said of the International executives Matthew Doull and Mark Kipnis, and even, to an extent, of Dan Colson (who, although he didn't receive any non-compete payments, held a 3 per cent stake in Ravelston).* "One of the problems that Conrad had is there were a group of people like Paul Healy who were option-holders in Hollinger International who sat there watching while money got siphoned out, and who had a very strongly aligned interest with the rest of the shareholders at International," said one executive who counted himself in this group. "When they started to get restive, they were pushing on an open door."

In his case, Healy had more than his Hollinger options at risk; he had played a lead role in selling Hollinger at investor conferences and during various refinancings over the years, and he felt that the criticisms being levelled at Black, Radler, and the other Ravelston owners could now sully him. Whether lunching at the media power-boîte Michael's or attending garden parties in Connecticut, he had his own reputation to think about. Whenever Black paced Healy's office, telling him what to say to shareholders who had a problem with the way he ran his company, Healy increasingly argued back. Part of it, according to one senior executive, was that Healy resented being "treated like the hired help." More and more, he was like a man caught between two railroad tracks as express trains thundered by him in opposing directions. He thought about quitting, but after a period of agonizing, he decided to stay and become an "agent of change." For a time, Healy thought he was succeeding and that Black was prepared to take measures in response to investor complaints.

---

* Even though he was being paid in other ways, no one had more options in Hollinger than Black.

Healy's dissenting attitude did not escape Black or the other Hollinger executives. In December 2002 Black sent an e-mail to Healy informing him that, for the first time in a few years, he was recommending that Healy receive a smaller year-end bonus than he'd received the previous year. "I hope you will not take it amiss if I add a few other things," Black wrote. "As you know, we fundamentally diverge on a number of shareholder questions. I do not think it necessary or useful to elaborate. David [Radler] and Dan [Colson] and I do not accept that the v.p. investor relations is, as you suggested at the time of the annual meeting, an intermediary between management and shareholders; he is a member, employee and spokesman of the management. There were also a number of other unpleasant developments last year, including the propagation of the theory that I had misappropriated [or] improperly purchased company property in the case of the Roosevelt material. The figure I propose is faithful to the spirit of my e-mail of a couple of days ago in which I promised to put all such unpleasantness out of mind, in what I believe to be the higher interests of the corporation. I hope you will consider my compensation suggestions, in all the circumstances, to be conciliatory, and even generous."

Why didn't Black just fire Healy? "Healy did his job quite well in some other respects, and we thought his conspiratorial efforts were rather amateurish and did not have much impact on the behaviour of those to whom he was betraying us," Black explained later. "I don't know if I would do it differently if I had the chance, but he's an energetic but rather ineffectual schemer."

Besides, Black prided himself that he had had the same group of close executives around him for as much as three decades, but that longevity had made them a dysfunctional, quarrelsome bunch. The odd corporate culture was rooted in the fact that Black and Radler lived nine time zones away from each other. Although he held the title of chief operating officer, Radler was not allowed anywhere near the operations of the company's biggest division – the Telegraph company – and he and Colson openly ridiculed each other to other executives. Only Radler and his tight-knit cadre of executives in Chicago dealt with the *Sun-Times*, the *Jerusalem Post*, and small-newspaper sales and acquisitions. Radler and Colson had little time for "her Ladyship," Barbara Amiel. Jack Boultbee, the financial architect of the group, was a shadowy presence who operated out of 10 Toronto Street, while Peter Atkinson postured as the group's corporate conscience. There was very little turnover among the company's core executives, who, even as they sometimes blanched at Black's pretensions and lifestyle, held him in awe and were like rival step-siblings vying for a father's attention. Black, for his part, parsed out his affection sparingly and could turn prickly when it seemed executives wanted to take credit. In December 2002, for instance, when Hollinger completed a refinancing of its debts, with Radler and Healy winning over investors during a road show in the western United States, Black noted dryly in an e-mail: "We're going to do more than David [Radler]'s old preoccupation of selling the vision."

In a memo to his fellow Ravelston executives on September 6, 2002, Black declared that they "have pretty well won the great battle over the non-competition agreements and a decent interval has passed." He went on to offer a nostalgic view on why he was not about to change. "These companies have always been run in the Argus tradition of proprietary businesses where the controlling shareholders take reasonable steps to ensure their comfortable enjoyment of the position they (we, in fact), have created for themselves. Care must be taken not to allow this to denigrate into decadence, as it did in the old Argus. But nor should we allow the agitations of shareholders, amplified by certain of our colleagues discountenanced at the performance of their stock options, to force us into a hair shirt, the corporate equivalent of sackcloth and ashes."

Christopher Browne, for one, did not think Black had won any battle. The week that Black sent that e-mail, corporate scandal dominated the headlines as Dennis Kozlowski, the former CEO of Tyco International, and his chief financial officer were indicted by a New York grand jury, accused of diverting some US$170 million from the company and using some of the proceeds to support Kozlowski's absurdly gilded lifestyle. Browne began to refer privately to Black as "Kozlowski with class."

Chapter Thirty

HEART OF BLACKNESS

A s Hollinger's 2003 annual meeting approached, the drums began to beat again. Nicolas Sleep, a fund manager with Marathon Asset Management, a London-based investment firm that managed US$12 billion, mainly for American pension funds, wrote to Lord Black on April 29. As other shareholders had done earlier, Sleep argued that the company's underperformance was in part due to its dual-share voting structure and wondered "if it is time to dismantle Hollinger's." Sleep's point was that Ravelston's "look through ownership" – meaning the amount of Hollinger stock it owned through its ownership of Inc. – was around 26 per cent. It wouldn't be hard, Sleep reckoned, for Black to get Ravelston's stake up to 35 per cent, which would give him effective control of Hollinger and enable him to fend off potential interlopers and do away with the "pyramid corporate structure" of the group that was penalizing the stock price. Sleep had a point: other moguls – Murdoch among them – controlled their companies with a single class of shares and around 35 per cent of the stock. Sleep copied his letter to Laura Jereski of Tweedy Browne and Mason Hawkins of Southeastern Asset Management, which may have contributed to Black's prickly rejection.* "I am conducting a peace process

---

* In a subsequent e-mail exchange with Chris Browne, Black wrote that Sleep was "as aptly named as most Dickensian characters, to judge from his letter to me."

with Tweedy Browne," Black noted, "which I hope will bring an end to their unedifying process of denouncing the company in the pages of our competitors, which I assume you will agree is an idiosyncratic method of encouraging a rise in the stock price." He concluded the letter with his usual kiss-off: if Sleep wanted "to exit the company as a shareholder, please let me know, as I believe I could help facilitate that."

Sleep and Browne were not the only twitchy shareholders. Gene Fox of Cardinal Capital Management had been an investor in the company since 1999 and, like Browne, met and corresponded with Black. "Conrad does what Conrad wants to do," Fox said early in 2004. "He has his own agenda, his own rules, he knows what he wants to do and therefore he doesn't really think he has to deal with anything. As a result, you deal with him in forums in which he is not the judge."

Both Cardinal and Browne had enlisted the advice of Herbert Denton, a well-known shareholder rabble-rouser whose small investment company, Providence Capital, had made its reputation in what he called "hairy situations" involving low share prices and entrenched managers. "We tend to seek out situations where there is a lot of hair," explained Denton, a slim bespectacled man with the bemused, distinguished look of a *New Yorker* cartoon figure, "because we feel we might have an opportunity to take some of the hair off and make money."

The "peace process" with Tweedy Browne that Black referred to in his correspondence with Sleep consisted of a new flurry of e-mails between Black and Chris Browne over setting up a special committee to investigate the shareholders' concerns about fees that had been approved by Hollinger's independent directors. Browne balked at Black's insistence that the committee look only at future transactions and not at past fee payments. "Our purpose is in no way meant to impugn the integrity of the current independent directors," Browne e-mailed Black on May 8. "However, the facts known to us do not pass our smell test. Until and unless either the current independent directors, or newly appointed independent directors, address the concerns of your shareholders, I do not believe the market will accord HLR [Hollinger's stock symbol] a valuation commensurate with the value of its assets. Your oft repeated offer to find a buyer for shareholders who do not like the present corporate governance of HLR is arrogant and inconsistent with accepted corporate governance principles."

On May 11, Browne made the move that ultimately led to Black's demise at Hollinger: he sent yet another letter to Hollinger's directors, demanding that they look into the earlier non-compete payments, but this time he also filed it with the SEC as a legal "demand." Written by Tweedy's lawyer, Robert Curry of the firm Kirby McInerny & Squire, the letter demanded that the board "investigate and take corrective action" regarding the more than US$73 million that had been paid to Black, Radler, Atkinson, and Boultbee since the beginning of 2000, either directly or via Ravelston. The salient parts of the letter lay in the legalese that discussed the duties of the board under the laws of Delaware, the state where Hollinger, like most U.S. corporations, was registered. "The acceptance of payments under the agreements by the executives instead of the company constitutes a usurpation of a corporate opportunity belonging to the company," Curry wrote. "Failure to take the action demanded in this letter," he warned the board, "would constitute a failure to act independently, and indeed participation in the diversion of a corporate opportunity to the executives." In other words, the board could be on the hook for Black's money. "We had a very prestigious board who would obviously be concerned about their own reputations," Browne explained later. "And once you waved in front of them the possibility of financial liability, it maybe put them in conflict with Conrad."

This was a calculated gamble on the part of Browne and his adviser, Denton. They had come to see Black's vanity and social climbing as his Achilles heel. Black knew, for instance, that Browne sat on the prestigious board of Rockefeller University with Nancy Kissinger and the Blacks' close friend Annette de la Renta, wife of the designer Oscar, who was one of the hostesses planning the launch party for Conrad's upcoming book at the Four Seasons restaurant. "The question was, Would Lord Black, in effect, remove or replace his entire board?" said Denton. "Our advice was we didn't think he would because he would really slice in half the society that he was aspiring to be welcome in."

In the wake of the Sarbanes-Oxley reforms, Delaware courts were giving more latitude to shareholder claims that boards were liable for breaching their fiduciary duties in cases where they approved transactions. The expanded legal thinking revolved around the "business judgment rule," which is a fundamental tenet of Delaware law. The new interpretation held that boards were not beyond reproach for their actions. Just a week after Hollinger's annual meeting, a Delaware judge issued a landmark ruling that a 1998 shareholder lawsuit against the board of Walt Disney Co., claiming that it had breached its duties by approving a US$140 million severance payout to fired president Michael Ovitz, could go forward.

After receiving Tweedy Browne's letter, Black sent a memo to Hollinger's audit committee, consisting of chairman James Thompson, the former Illinois governor; Richard Burt, the former American ambassador to Germany; and Marie-Josée Kravis, the brainy wife of Henry Kravis. Black was smoothing the way for an internal investigation that, he figured, would focus mainly on audit-committee procedures. "I will certainly go to great lengths to prevent you being subjected to any embarrassment," Black noted.*

In a May 13 reply to Browne, Black was conciliatory but specifically rejected Browne's suggestion that Hollinger hire Bert Denton's firm to conduct the probe of the company's payments to the Ravelston shareholders. Hollinger would not abide "the entry of total strangers with a mandate to run up unlimited legal and accounting bills conducting an antagonistic forensic scavenger hunt through our corporate past, particularly in the manner usually associated with Providence Capital, replete with public allegations posturing in a tendentious media circus."

On the morning of the 2003 annual meeting on May 23, the company's stock opened at US$10.23. It was certain to be another rancorous gathering, but this time Black came ready to spar and bearing some surprising news. Because of all the media attention Hollinger and Black's troubles had been receiving in recent months, the press was out in full force – but the management of the

---

* "He really succeeded here, hasn't he?" Burt said later. "Don't get me going."

Metropolitan Club insisted that it had a policy of "no media" inside its hallowed doors. Several reporters put their notebooks away and donned the guise of shareholders. Lord and Lady Black stepped out of their limousine ten minutes late and cruised into the packed room greeting people, exchanging air kisses with Donald Trump and his girlfriend, the model Melania Knauss. Black's lip curled as he scanned the room. Before beginning the meeting, Black conferred with Mason Hawkins, the head of Southeastern Asset Management, Hollinger's biggest institutional shareholder, and signed some papers.

Trump was there because, in addition to being neighbours with Black in Palm Beach, he was in the midst of finalizing a joint venture under which Trump would erect a ninety-storey tower on the prime riverside site of the *Chicago Sun-Times*. At the Hollinger AGM, in classic *Art of the Deal* style, Trump rose and made a statement that someone close to the real estate mogul (and future reality-television star) later explained was less heartfelt support than savvy buttering-up. "I fully support the company and its management, and in particular I have great respect for Conrad Black and for David Radler," Trump declared.

"Thank you, Donald. And just before you sit down, if it's not an impudence, we'd be happy to hear from Melania, if she wants to tell us anything," Black replied.

Knauss shook her head, but Trump piped up, "She's much better looking than I am. That's one thing."

Trump's valentine to Black stood out among a fresh chorus of criticism from the floor – peppered by applause – that once again put the CEO on the back foot, angrily defending the performance of Hollinger shares in the face of what he described as the epic battles his company had waged against the Tribune Company in Chicago and Rupert Murdoch in London. "You have a right to say whatever is on your mind, all of you – and applaud them if you want to," he said, looking around the room. "You don't know what you're talking about, but you're still welcome as shareholders."

Black had two big announcements, which he hoped would settle things down. The first was the creation of a special committee to look into past payments. As a sign of how seriously the company was taking this matter, audit committee chairman James Thompson, known as "Big Jim," rose in his elegant dark suit and made a classic politician's statement, his fists clenched as he spoke. "First, let me say that I think it is the opinion of all of the members of the audit and compensation committees of this company that they have, in their past decisions on some of the issues raised this morning and in the press, acted appropriately as independent directors, based upon materials that they had and professional advice available to them when it was required in the circumstances." Thompson went on to say that the committee planned to "retain a renowned expert, not only in the areas of corporate governance, per se, but in corporate practice in reality," although they were not ready to announce who that was. The other members of the audit committee, directors Richard Burt and Marie-Josée Kravis, looked on stonily, as did Black.

When he spoke, Black emphasized to the shareholders that he was under no pressure to form this committee, despite the press coverage given to Tweedy Browne, which had escalated its barrage four days earlier by filing a document with the SEC outlining its complaints about Hollinger. "Like all fads, corporate governance has its zealots and its tendency to excess," Black noted. After the meeting, director Henry Kissinger, who rarely attended the company's board meetings, asked Black what the committee was going to investigate, and Black reassured his friend that it was not a big deal and if there were any funds in dispute he would return them to the company. "He mentioned that they might amount to something like, at most, US$5 million," Kissinger said later.

The other announcement was the result of the documents that Black had signed when he had walked into the meeting. He had agreed to a deal with Southeastern whereby he would sell some of Inc.'s controlling stake in International to Southeastern, in exchange for a pledge to eliminate over five years the super-voting powers that Black held over the company. Southeastern would add three directors to International's board, and combined executive salaries would be capped at US$20 million, including limiting Black's take-home pay to US$6 million. Hawkins said at the meeting that in his twenty-eight years of money management he had never seen a company voluntarily relinquish its super-voting share structure. "I think this is not only unprecedented, it's incredible, given the fact that this management team created approximately US$2 billion of intrinsic value from virtually nothing."

Browne and other Hollinger investors were instantly dubious that the deal would ever happen, because under the terms of US$120 million worth of junk bonds that Inc. had issued in December 2002, its shares in Hollinger were held as collateral. Even if Black could figure out a way to sell them to Southeastern, was he really ready to give up control? Indeed, by the time of Inc.'s annual meeting a month later in Toronto, Black was sidestepping the commitment, simultaneously denying that the Southeastern deal was in jeopardy and admitting that he might not cede control after all. "It is a complete myth that that deal is in difficulties," Black said. "It's not in difficulties. It's a difficult deal to do." The deal turned out to be so difficult that, while it was never officially called off, a few months later Southeastern quietly sold its entire stake in Hollinger.

By that time, the sense of siege at the company had worsened as another of Hollinger's largest shareholders, Cardinal Capital Management, in July filed a US$300 million lawsuit against Hollinger's present and former directors, claiming that they had breached their duties under Delaware law. Cardinal demanded the directors be held accountable for money it claimed was usurped by the company and began subpoenaing internal documents to form its case. This new flank in the onslaught was aimed squarely at Black's carefully assembled roster of embossable names: in addition to naming all the current directors such as the big names Kissinger, Thompson, Burt, Perle, and Kravis, it also targeted former board members: Alfred Taubman, Dwayne Andreas of Archer Daniels Midland, Lord Weidenfeld, Limited Brands founder Leslie Wexner, and Robert Strauss, the last U.S. ambassador to the Soviet Union.

The Delaware court put Cardinal's suit on hold pending the outcome of Hollinger's internal special committee investigation, but nevertheless the suit drove deeper the wedge between the outside directors' interests and those of Black and Radler, and their Ravelston partners. At one point in the midst of this turbulence, in his aerie at 712 Fifth Avenue, Black asked Paul Healy what he thought he should do. "Pray," suggested Healy. "I don't believe in mixing ecclesiastical and commercial matters," Black replied.

At least money would solve some of Black's problems with Hollinger Inc.'s debts, and he spent the summer negotiating with private equity firms, including Blackstone Group and Bain Capital, who seemed keen for a while. Although he kept telling reporters that a deal was near – often in a late-night e-mail, a vehicle that he found particularly effective for banter with the press – none materialized. Black would eventually conclude that the special committee he had authorized was spooking potential partners.

By summer, he had assembled a committee to conduct the probe. Black personally phoned Raymond Seitz in July and invited him to join Hollinger's board as a director and a member of the new committee. Seitz and Black were friendly. After he retired as U.S. ambassador to the United Kingdom at the beginning of the Clinton administration, Seitz spent a few years on the board of the Telegraph Group. Having recently moved back to the United and States and settled in Charleston, South Carolina, Seitz was in the midst of a "shambles" of a home restoration when Black rang him. He explained the situation in oblique terms, and asked for Seitz's help. "Like any astute politician, he didn't want to have a committee formed by people he didn't know, or people that would turn out to be rogues or vigilantes," recalled Seitz, an easygoing and erudite life-long diplomat with the manner of the actor Gregory Peck. "He wanted to make sure they wouldn't go off on a wild turkey shoot." After he called several of the Hollinger executives and directors he knew, including Henry Kissinger and Richard Burt, Seitz concluded that joining the committee might put him in a difficult position, so he declined the invitation. Two days later, Black telephoned him again: "Would you please do it as a favour to me?"

Seitz was joined on the special committee by two other new Hollinger directors, the media investment banker Gordon Paris, who would be the chairman, and Graham Savage, a former chief financial · officer at the cable mogul Ted Rogers's Rogers Communications. Paris, an investment banker from the firm Berenson & Co., had just joined Hollinger's board at the May annual meeting as its designated "financial expert" under the new Sarbanes-Oxley rules. As part of his response to Browne, Black had initially asked Paris to evaluate the management fees paid to Ravelston. Because of his independence he was asked to go on the special committee as well. Paris knew Hollinger well, having advised it on various high-yield financings over the years, including during the six years he had worked for the Toronto-Dominion Bank. Savage had come at the recommendation of Peter Atkinson, who served with him on the board of Canadian Tire, socialized with him, and knew him to be a principled if quirky director who marched to his own drummer. "I went into this without a point of view," said Savage. "I had a great deal of respect for Black and what he'd accomplished as a capitalist, and not knowing what we were going to find when we looked under the rug." That said, Savage knew that there was a chance he could end up in a legal quagmire, so he transferred his house and all his assets into his wife's name.

To manage the investigation, Black endorsed the hiring of Richard Breeden, a former Securities and Exchange Commission chairman and precisely the kind of bold-face name Black liked to have around. Breeden had been working as a corporate restructuring consultant since 1996, and the Hollinger situation had caught his attention. In what people now refer to as the "post-Enron" era, Breeden had emerged as one of a dozen top governance sheriffs for hire – someone with powerful presence in the boardroom even though he was neither a company executive nor a shareholder nor a director nor a regulator nor an auditor. In the summer of 2002, Breeden had become the court-appointed monitor of Worldcom (now MCI), the biggest bankruptcy in U.S. history as a result of a US$10.8 billion accounting scandal.

Breeden forced MCI through changes that resulted in its emergence from bankruptcy as a "power-washed, steam-cleaned company." A perfectionist with the cocksureness of a nuclear submarine commander, Breeden brought several esteemed directors to the verge of quitting over what they saw as his constant nitpicking and interference. His efforts earned him the nicknames "Dr. No" and "King Richard." "I don't think MCI would have survived if I hadn't been there," Breeden told the *Wall Street Journal*.

When he heard about Tweedy Browne's letter and the special committee being organized at Hollinger, Breeden pitched his US$800-an-hour services to several directors including Richard Burt, who in turn recommended him to Black. Working with the law firm O'Melveny & Myers, Breeden and the special committee began collecting tens of thousands of files and e-mails from all levels of the company and conducting "bottom-up" research, starting with the lowest-level executives and working higher, at a pace of two per week.

The probe got underway in earnest in August. As it happened, the first binder Savage perused contained three years of his friend Atkinson's e-mails. "It didn't look good for Peter," recalled Savage, who decided the two should stop chatting and socializing. "I've never been able to fully reconcile it since."

Every Monday, the special committee would meet at Breeden's Greenwich office, taking a spiral staircase up to a space filled with pictures and models of sailboats, including his own sloop, *Bright Star.* Over coffee served in giant blue mugs, the committee reviewed the latest findings and interviews. The four committee members started by looking at the CanWest non-compete payments, then decided to examine all non-competes dating back to 1998, when Hollinger had begun selling clusters of small newspapers. Soon they stumbled upon backdated cheques, missing authorizations, and, in one case, an agreement by Black not to compete with a subsidiary of his own company. Most of the payments appeared to have been arranged by Mark Kipnis, the company's Chicago-based general counsel, although the paper trail beyond Kipnis was a bit murky. "Suddenly the flavour changed," Seitz said later. "Rather than personal eccentricity or sleepy corporate governance, suddenly what took shape was the outline of something intentionally meant to mislead or misrepresent or conceal a significant amount of money going to senior figures in management."

What the committee found were payments totalling US$32.15 million made between November 2000 and April 2001, of which US$16.55 million had been made to the parent company, Inc., without any explanation. The other US$15.6 million was depicted as non-competition agreements made in three separate tranches, with the bulk of the funds going to Black and Radler. The first questionable payment related to the November 2000 sale of a group of newspapers for US$90 million to Community Newspaper Holdings Inc. of Birmingham, Alabama. The asset purchase agreement called for US$3 million of the purchase price to be recorded as a non-compete, with US$2.25 million going to Hollinger and US$750,000 going to Inc. The committee found that the closing documents of the deal had been altered to make US$9.5 million in payments to Black, Radler, Atkinson, and Boultbee, with US$4.3 million going to Black and Radler each.

The second set of payments took place three months later, in February 2001, but cheques totalling US$5.5 million had been backdated to December 31, 2000, and paid to Black and the other three executives, with Black and Radler again getting the lion's share. In this case, the special committee could not find a specific deal that the supposed payments related to. Instead, Black and the three executives had signed non-competition agreements with American Publishing – now a small subsidiary of Hollinger – which, like the cheques, had been backdated to December 31, 2000. The committee's findings "moved from the peculiar to the bizarre," Seitz noted, as Black and his team were agreeing to somehow not compete with themselves. A third set of payments in April 2001, consisting of US$600,000 to Black and US$285,000 to Radler, were characterized as non-compete fees for newspaper sales that had been made in autumn 2000, but here again there was no evidence that non-competition payments were part of the asset-sale agreements with the buyers.

The special committee claimed it could find no evidence that any of these payments had been specifically approved by either Hollinger's audit committee or its board, and it noted that Hollinger's 2001 and 2002 annual reports mentioned payments of US$15.6 million relating to sales of newspapers in 2000 and stated that "the company's independent directors have approved the terms of these payments."

The last person they interviewed, in the Chicago offices of his lawyer, Anton Valukas, was David Radler. Like Atkinson and Kipnis before him, Radler wasn't sure about a number of the specific transactions and payments he was being asked to explain. When he was asked about at least one of the non-compete payments, Radler said that it had been initiated by Black. "Why don't you ask *Crossharbour?*" he asked sarcastically. But the committee members never made it up the organization chart to Black. By early November they had determined that the US$32.15 million that had been paid to Black, Radler, Boultbee, Atkinson, and Inc. had not been legitimately authorized by the Hollinger board, and that meant the company's previous disclosures to the stock market were wrong and needed to be quickly corrected.

On October 6, audit committee member Marie-Josée Kravis had resigned from Hollinger's board. "As you know, KKR has expressed an interest in acquiring regional newspapers in the United States, and I wish to avoid any appearance of conflict," she wrote. Black faxed back a handwritten note on his House of Lords stationery, accepting the resignation with regret and thanking her for her services. "You will be missed."

The timing of her departure – in the midst of the inquiry – inevitably sparked questions in the press about whether she was leaving for other reasons. Indeed, in its lawsuit Cardinal Capital would point out that she didn't seem to have a conflict in 1998, when a subsidiary of KKR, the buyout firm run by her husband, bought some publications, including *American Trucker* magazine, from Hollinger. Even Black's close friend Kissinger was by now finding it troublesome to be a Hollinger director. "After Marie-Josée resigned, I told him that I would not resign, but I would like to," recalled Kissinger.

By the end of October 2003, Black was aware that the committee now believed it had unearthed evidence of impropriety by himself and the other top Hollinger executives. He began looking into the payments himself, calling around to his top lieutenants, but he did not behave as though he was especially alarmed by the probe or the special committee. Black may have been preoccupied by how he was going to refinance Inc. and solve its ongoing cash problems, having spent the last several months feeling out potential partners. In early October he began negotiating with Triarc, a conglomerate owned by the financier Nelson Peltz. Peltz had expressed an interest in putting some money into a joint venture that would hold Ravelston's stake in Inc. on condition that Triarc would be in control of the new company until all of Hollinger's legal and corporate governance matters were sorted out. Throughout the fall Black discussed similar deals with various private equity firms and maintained that he was under no pressure. In mid-October, he claimed he was a week or two from sewing up a recapitalization of Inc., and with typical swagger told his old newspaper the *National Post*: "I'll surrender control to the undertaker, but not anyone else."

Black was being very selective about whom he would negotiate with, and when, and why. For instance, Black was less than welcoming on the day after Hollinger's raucous 2003 annual meeting, when he received a fax from Sir David Barclay. He and his identical twin, Sir Frederick Barclay, owned a swath of businesses that generated some US$7 billion in revenue, including the Ritz hotel in London, casino interests in Monaco, and the Littlewoods retail clothing chain. The reclusive brothers, aged sixty-nine, had also been in the newspaper business since 1992 as owners of such titles as the *Scotsman* and the *Business* weekly. The May 23, 2003, fax read:

Dear Conrad

By way of introduction, you may recall we met some years ago with Lord McAlpine and I am the father of Aidan Barclay, whom I believe you know quite well. There has been some recent press speculation, the details of which I need not go into here, suffice to say, I wish to register our interest should you contemplate any serious change in your UK interests.

If however, you feel my inquiry is a little premature and out of order, please accept my sincerest apologies.

A few days later, Black replied:

Dear David,

Thank you for your note. I have indeed enjoyed meeting your son and daughter-in-law. Press accounts of our corporate activities have been even more wildly inaccurate than usual – conditions are quite manageable. No assets are for sale. I would be delighted to see you again, but I doubt that any transaction would arise from such a meeting.

Barclay persisted with a follow-up on September 1, saying, "Further to our recent correspondence, I fully appreciate that you do not wish to sell the Telegraph and I do not wish to be a bore." He had read an article on Hollinger's troubles in the previous day's *Sunday Times* and was wondering if Black would be willing to meet him or his son Aidan to discuss either a sale of the *Telegraph* or the Barclays' becoming investors. The *Times* article had mentioned that Hollinger was looking for potential private equity backers, noting that "Hollinger Inc has come under increasing financial pressure as its various forms of income have been depleted."

The next day, Black replied:

Dear David,

I have the following comments on your letter of yesterday.

It is astonishing to me that a man of your experience would attach the slightest credence to the last sentences in the Sunday Times piece yesterday . . . Since the failed green mail attempt of those who incited the inference that there is an ethical problem in the management of our company, we have been besieged by serious investors wishing to assist us in a range of options, including privatization. Obviously some overtures come from charlatans, but our company is in fact prosperous.

In all of the circumstances, as I have written before, the Telegraph titles are absolutely not for sale and we are not seeking and do not require assistance. I would always be happy to meet with you or Aidan, but if the purpose of it is to sidle up to a phased or disguised purchase of our principal assets, there is no point to such a meeting and you would indeed be transgressing your expressed wish not to be a bore.

On October 30, the same day he learned of the special committee's findings, Black sent an e-mail to Bruce Wasserstein to see if Wasserstein & Co. would be a potential investor in Hollinger Inc. A quintessential Manhattan player, Wasserstein wore at least two hats. He was both a private investor who possessed a range of media assets

(American Lawyer Media and the *Deal* newspaper, and in December he bought *New York* magazine) and also the head of American operations for Lazard Freres, the investment bank. Wasserstein had visited Black at his house in London in May to offer him help, and the two had kept in touch. Apparently the beauty of Wasserstein's position was that even though he did not pursue an investment in Black's companies himself, talks with Black about retaining Lazard to give strategic advice to Hollinger were progressing nicely.

On October 31, nearly two months after his previous fax and the day after Black sent his e-mail to Wasserstein, another letter from David Barclay arrived by fax at 10 Toronto Street. Once again Barclay had read a negative article in the *Times* – the *Telegraph*'s archrival – this one citing a review of Hollinger by Moody's rating service.

I just wish to reiterate that in spite of your letter of September 2, 2003, I am more than happy to talk to you, or your finance director, if you would be willing to meet. It is clear our interests lie in the UK Telegraph, but I would not exclude any part, or whole of the business, or providing equity capital to one of your private companies. Whatever your reaction, please do not take offence because I assure you no offence is intended, in any way, on my part.

Black replied on November 3:

Dear David,

You have made your desire to buy the Telegraph abundantly clear. You may recall that when we actually met we agreed that I would be mad to sell it. In the unlikely event that my views on this subject change, I will not forget your interest.

Please keep in mind how tiresome you would find it if every time I saw a negative article about you in the press I wrote of my unquenchable desire to buy an asset of yours that is not for sale. I'm happy to hear from you, but not on this subject again, please.

By early November, the special committee was ready to share its findings with the other independent Hollinger directors. Gordon Paris and Graham Savage flew to Washington and met with audit committee members James Thompson and Richard Burt at the latter's offices, as Burt was recovering from brain surgery and unable to travel. Also there for part of the meeting was Peter Atkinson, who flew down from Toronto and who, according to an affidavit from Burt, was very contrite. "He said that he had been asked to lie, cover up, that there were documents that were postdated. And it was essentially, he described, a conspiracy. He was clearly a kind of broken man. It was very sad. He and others had been engaging in this process, this cover-up, for years. One of these transactions, one of these non-compete payments, as it was disclosed to us was for a transaction that had never in fact taken place. So I mean we were shocked. We all felt betrayed, really betrayed." (Others involved did not remember Atkinson being quite so confessional, and Atkinson declined to comment.)

Paris, Breeden, and Savage phoned Henry Kissinger in China, which he had famously visited with President Nixon thirty-one years earlier. Kissinger told his callers that their probe's conclusions "came as a big surprise." The two men explained that, as a result of uncovering these unauthorized fees, they would be making a number of urgent recommendations, including that the money be returned and that Black "retire" as CEO of Hollinger but remain as chairman. Kissinger said that before he supported this move he would speak with special committee member Ray Seitz, who had worked for Kissinger in the foreign service and whom he considered "totally reliable." It was two a.m. in Beijing, but Kissinger tracked Seitz down in Hong Kong and woke him to discuss the situation. Afterwards, Kissinger spoke to Paris and Breeden again and agreed to go along with their recommendations on condition that they downplayed any implication of criminal activity by Black and the other directors.

That day, November 6, Black finally heard from the special committee in the form of a letter, which was nearly identical in its contents to ones sent to the Hollinger executives Radler, Boultbee, Kipnis, and Atkinson at the same time. The letters, signed by Thompson, chairman of the audit committee, and Paris, from the special committee, laid out the details of unauthorized payments totalling US$32.15 million. They asked each of the executives to respond within four days. The company was scheduled to file its latest quarterly statements with the SEC on November 14, and the directors were concerned that if they hadn't disclosed the news that money was missing by then, they would be committing a crime.

Black immediately hired Jesse Finkelstein, a top corporate lawyer with the firm Richards Layton & Finger. Finkelstein was in California, but together they drafted a lengthy reply to the special committee's letter. Their letter contained pages of evidence that Black's inquiries over the past week had unearthed evidence which indicated, in his view, that the transactions in question had been approved. Nonetheless, Black acknowledged the difference between approval and "proper" approval, and he expressed regret if mistakes had been made. He proposed a solution that seemed designed both to address the committee's concern for minority shareholders and to set the stage for his own graceful exit from the company. "In the circumstances," Finkelstein's letter read, "it is Lord Black's tentative conclusion that the best course is to seek the approval of the Hollinger International directors for a public announcement that the company will seek and will evaluate proposals for a range of financing alternatives at the Hollinger International level, including the sale of some or all assets, and including solicitation of an offer for all Hollinger International shares, including those owned by HLG [the stock symbol for Hollinger Inc.]." Black subsequently e-mailed over-optimistically to Peter Atkinson: "I think my letter, setting out a possible road map to a satisfactory end of the immersion in this quagmire, has had some effect."

Black did not know Gordon Paris well and had never met Richard Breeden face to face until the urgent pow-wow convened in Hollinger's boardroom at 712 Fifth Avenue on November 13 to discuss the special committee's finding. Also present were Thompson and Jim McDonough, the audit committee's outside counsel. Black was surprised to find Breeden at the meeting. Paris, an athletic, fifty-year-old native of Norwalk, Connecticut, with a tightly coiled, no-bullshit demeanour, took the lead, explaining to Black that the committee had received his letter and canvassed all the directors. All agreed that if Black didn't agree to a number of changes, including his own retirement as CEO, they would go to court to have him removed or even refer the matter to the SEC. They ran though the questionable payments and noted that during the period of these payments, as well as the larger ones relating to the CanWest sale in 2000, it had been learned that Revenue Canada considered non-compete payments to be tax-free income. This suggested to Breeden and the special committee that the US$32.15 million payments were really unauthorized bonuses for Black and his executives from the asset sales, couched as non-competes to make them considerably more valuable.

Black told the meeting that he was shocked and disappointed by these suggestions, insisted that he didn't know that the payments he received had not been authorized, and said he'd relied on company officials to make sure the payments were documented properly. He certainly didn't want the SEC involved and hoped Breeden could help with that. According to Black, Breeden "volunteered that I had been let down by subordinates and professional advisers." The meeting stretched on through the afternoon. It was turning out to be a long, tense, and surreal day. As Black and his accusers strolled by his office – having decided to repair to Le Cirque, where Black had a corporate account, for dinner – Paul Healy joked, "What is this, the Last Supper?"

Over dinner in the garishly decorated eatery, Black talked opera with Breeden, who has a son who is an opera student, and Paris, who has a brother who also studied it. Paris was surprised at how subdued the disputatious press titan was, and the shared sense at the dinner was that together they could fix this mess internally.

The next afternoon, Black retained the additional services of the litigator David Boies, known for such high-profile clients as the U.S. government in its case against Microsoft and Al Gore in his fight for a presidential election recount, and for representing Enron chief financial officer Andy Fastow. When the negotiations with the special committee resumed later that day in the Hollinger boardroom, Boies wandered around Hollinger's office, at one point running into and chatting with Breeden, with whom he had worked early in his career.

Coincidentally, Black had arranged several days earlier for Bruce Wasserstein and his team from Lazard Freres to make their pitch to the board to lead a strategic review for Hollinger, and that meeting went ahead as planned on November 14 – made more relevant now that the company was about to be put up for sale. Lazard was hired for the job, and there was also discussion of the ongoing talks between the special committee and Black. As he had at Le Cirque the night before, Black remained surprisingly composed, a posture that may be explained by the e-mail he wrote that day to Jack Boultbee: "The only advantages of what is proposed are that it seems to head off a real investigation and we get the financial condition of [Hollinger] stabilized to June 1, and Breeden says he intends to finish his process by June 1. Of course it's a smear job, and the audit committee wriggles out by joining in the assault on us on these issues. However, when the smoke clears, we should still have either a functioning business or a good deal of money. We can pick up the pieces then."

One of the first matters Breeden, Paris, and Thompson demanded from Black was the repayment of funds to the company. The US$32.15 million payments included US$16.5 million to Inc., US$7.2 million each to Black and Radler, and US$602,000 to Atkinson and Boultbee. Curiously, Black seemed to have trouble committing himself to come up with – or, as Black would say, "chin for" – the cash. According to one person present, the directors initially proposed that Black pay back his US$7.2 million in US$1.5 or US$2 million instalments, starting at year-end, which was six weeks away, but Black said, "Oh, that's a lot of money to raise." How about US$1 million per payment, he was asked. "That's not very much time to raise that kind of money," Black replied. Finally, they suggested US$850,000 and Black said, "I think I could chin myself to agree to that." (Looking back later, Black said his odd negotiating posture was not because of a shortage of funds. "I was not convinced that the so-called unauthorized payments had not been authorized," he said. "My reasoning was that it might take until June to establish whether the money was really due and so the early payments should be reduced. It was, additionally, an inconvenience for everyone.")

Hollinger's board met on November 15 to approve the restructuring agreement that Breeden and the others came up with after meeting with Black and negotiating with Radler and Atkinson. The only holdout was Boultbee, who refused to pay back the money, was fired, and quickly sued Hollinger for wrongful dismissal. Among other things, the deal that Black signed the next day also called for a renegotiation of the management fee Hollinger would pay to Ravelston from January 1 to June 1, 2004, after which it would be terminated; Radler, Atkinson, and Hollinger general counsel Kipnis would all resign their various posts; and Paris was appointed interim president and CEO. Black's close friend Dan Colson, who had not received any of the non-compete payments in question, was appointed chief operating officer, replacing Radler, and Paris and Black agreed to make a new arrangement for using corporate aircraft.

Where Black was concerned, as well as having to pay back the money and "retire" as CEO, there were several other critical aspects to the agreement he signed. One was the hiring of Lazard to develop a "strategic process" that Black would "devote his principal time and energy to pursuing," and during which Black agreed not to support a transaction involving Hollinger Inc. unless it was necessary to "avoid a material default or insolvency." "Lord Black will retire in writing as the CEO of the company, but will retain the position of chairman to pursue the strategic process. He will continue as chairman of the Telegraph Group," the agreement read.

The board meeting to ratify the deal was held by telephone and was a strained affair. Director Richard Burt said later that Black "was apologetic about the fact this had happened. He said something to the effect, 'I know nobody on this call was responsible for doing this. It is a terrible thing that this has happened.'" Lady Black did not take the devastating news well, defending her husband and calling the proceedings "a kangaroo court." It did strike Burt as odd that Black had for now backed off the claim he made in his November 10 letter that the payments had in fact been authorized. But as Black later explained, he didn't have any other information to go on than the word of Thompson and Paris, whom he then had no reason to distrust. Besides, he was already busy making other plans.

On November 11, the day after Black had his lawyer Finkelstein send his response to the special committee, he had a remarkable change of heart and sent a fax to Sir David Barclay:

Dear David,
    I have had a thought which may be worthy of discussion, based on our previous correspondence . . . I wouldn't want you to think I was trying to avoid you, but I have not, until now, been able to think of a suitable subject for talk.

Many thanks,
Conrad Black

Chapter Thirty-One

UNRAVELLING

November 6, 2003, the same day that Black received the letter from James Thompson and Gordon Paris demanding that he account for the millions in unauthorized payments, was the kickoff of the book tour for *Franklin Delano Roosevelt: Champion of Freedom*. Black strode two blocks north from his apartment on Park Avenue to the limestone-clad offices of the Council on Foreign Relations, where former *Sunday Times* editor Harold Evans led a question and answer session. If he was under pressure from the day's events, it didn't show. Black was commanding and clever, responding to questions from Evans and the audience in his usual rococo style.

Here, and at other book-tour events, people wanted to know why someone closely identified with neo-conservative thinking had nominated the Democrat as not only the greatest of American presidents, but the most important person of the twentieth century, when the prevailing view among the rich of Roosevelt's day – not to mention Conrad's own father – was that he was a traitor to his elite class. Black had no trouble with the paradox. The way he saw it, FDR's New Deal saved capitalism by preventing businessmen from being made scapegoats for the Great Depression; he "made the country safe again for the wealthy." While Black's FDR was a greater president than most believed, "the Great Communicator" was also a complex and duplicitous manipulator, not the man of the people that he portrayed himself as being through his campaign speeches and fireside chats. "He couldn't lie straight in bed," said Black.

Imbued with all the intellectual and physical bulk of its author, *Champion of Freedom* thudded into bookshops with glowing advance praise on the back cover from such Hollinger directors and advisory board members as George Will, William F. Buckley, and Kissinger. It received largely solid praise in reviews around the world, including one in the London *Times* that Hollinger special committee member Ray Seitz penned even as he pressed for Black's resignation as CEO. Seitz called it a "monumental and masterful biography" as well as a "brilliant, scholarly, fluent and stimulating read." *Publishers Weekly* hailed the book as one of the best of 2003 and "not only the best one-volume life of the 32nd president but the best at any length." Among the less admiring critics was the *New York Times Book Review*, which couldn't ignore the confluence of Black's literary work with his day job. "It's hard to avoid a sense of crossover between Lord Black's grand claims for Roosevelt and his grandiose sense of self," wrote Michael Janeway, a professor at Columbia University. "The SEC remains one of Franklin D. Roosevelt's and his New Deal's most signal and durable achievements (alas, it earns one fleeting paragraph in this telling). Lord Black's interest in FDR is longtime. More than two decades ago the SEC successfully litigated a dispute with him over issues of misrepresentation in his American ventures. The SEC has now begun a new investigation of Lord Black's operations."

Connections would later be drawn between Black's literary effort and his role at Hollinger in other unflattering ways, including the suggestion that he was immersed in his book when he should have been focused on company business. "I worked on FDR when others would be golfing or playing tennis," said Black. "It was not in the slightest a distraction. It was helpful in taking my mind off my brother's terminal illness, and I was able to tell him that the first draft of the book, which I had promised to dedicate to him, had been finished, a week before he died. He brightened on the news. It had no impact whatever on my attention to Hollinger matters."

Black was adamant that his American publisher, Public Affairs, not cancel a single publicity event for the book; after all, so far as he was concerned, he had done nothing wrong. On Wednesday, November 12, he jetted to Washington, D.C., for the National Press Club's annual book fair and authors' night, featuring seventy of Black's fellow scribes. Here, Black sat signing copies of his book, occupying a booth across from the Kissinger biographer Walter Isaacson, who had just written a life of Benjamin Franklin. Nearby, Oliver North flogged a new novel and Dr. Ruth Westheimer talked with fans about her new book, *Conquering the Rapids of Life*. On November 17, the day after the news of the unauthorized payments and his "retirement" from Hollinger made sensational headlines around the world, Black was in Toronto for a late-morning book signing at a midtown branch of Indigo, the Canadian bookstore chain, hosted personally by its CEO, Heather Reisman. Stepping out of his Cadillac in a navy pinstripe suit and green tie, his Order of Canada pin in his lapel, Black, flanked by a pair of burly bodyguards was engulfed by reporters.

"Mr. Black, anything to say to your shareholders?"

"Yeah, I hope they're pleased – the stock's rising like a rocket."

Was he forced to resign? "No, the board didn't force me to resign. These people hadn't documented otherwise unexceptionable money transfers, and it's a serious matter, you've got to deal with it. You take your lumps and you move on. But all you fellows who wrote today that I'm 'finished' may not have it right. I'm still the chairman, I'm still the chairman of the parent company, I'm still the controlling shareholder, I'm co-director of the strategic process and I'm chairman of the *Telegraph*. And I made 50 million bucks yesterday. That's a flame-out I could get used to."

Pressing forward, Black gave a slight chuckle. "There's no suggestion of any impropriety. Read the press release."

Had the shareholder activists won? "Yeah, they won. And they deserve to win. A sloppy thing like that, they deserve to win – that shouldn't have happened. Good luck to them. Up to a point the buck stops here. I'm taking some responsibility. I'll write a cheque for 7 million dollars. Don't call me a shirker – I can't stand evasion. I take my responsibilities and so must others – including those who produced filings for years that said all these things had been approved."

Black said he'd been "horrified" when he heard about the un-authorized payments and had insisted on paying the money back, but left the impression that he considered the matter settled. "I founded the company. I built it up from a bunch of basket-case newspapers to one that added 200 million dollars in value in one day yesterday," he said. "Who do you think turned the *Daily Telegraph* and *Chicago Sun-Times* from insolvent properties to market leaders? Who do you think did that: *corporate governance advocates*? Is that what you think?"

As he headed inside, where a crowd of 400 awaited, another reporter asked, "How do you survive?" "I do the job," he said emphatically. "Where's the threat? Show me where the threat is. I do my job, and presumably if I do it adequately, I cast the controlling shareholder vote for myself."

Black's comments were all over the Canadian television news that night and the newspapers the next day, and several of Hollinger's independent directors were enraged. It was as though Black truly believed that nothing had changed, and indeed that same night he hopped the Gulfstream to New York where more book events awaited him.

November 19 was a dizzying day for Black. After a flurry of calls among the directors, he received a terse e-mail from James Thompson with the subject "Aircraft": "The Audit Committee voted unanimously today to halt all flights on company aircraft effective immediately. The aircraft will be terminated." Over the next two weeks, Black also heard from Paris that the more than US$100,000 a year Hollinger was paying toward the costs of his Park Avenue apartment, his car and driver, and his charge account at Le Cirque were now cut off – all of which was reported in the papers, emphasizing that the special committee's investigation was contin-uing and the wayward US$32 million payment was just what had been uncovered so far. The unspoken message to Black was: Actually, you are finished. Also on November 19, Black received a report from the suddenly alert audit committee of Inc., calling upon him to resign as Inc.'s CEO in light of the new developments. A board meeting was set to discuss the report two days later.

These were probably not even Black's biggest worries that day. He also learned that the SEC had served Hollinger and its auditors, KPMG, with subpoenas for company documents relating to the fees and payments in question. Whatever it was that Breeden had said a few days earlier that he might be able to do for Black and the company regarding the SEC had apparently not dissuaded them. Now Black's dusty, twenty-two-year-old consent decree with the SEC over the attempted takeover of Hanna Mining suddenly acquired new relevance. While he had admitted neither innocence nor guilt all those years ago, Black had agreed never to violate the securities rules governing public companies, and a violation could lead to criminal charges.

Black decided to bulk up his legal team, which already included Jesse Finkelstein and David Boies. Normally he would have turned to Paul Saunders of Cravath, Swaine and Moore, the same attorney who had defended him in the Hanna Mining fracas, but Saunders had already been retained to represent Henry Kissinger in the Hollinger mess. So Black hired as his new lead counsel John Warden of the starchy Wall Street firm Sullivan & Cromwell, a burly Indiana native and fierce litigator whose credentials included besting Boies as Microsoft's top lawyer against the U.S. government. Black was particularly drawn by the firm's storied history, which included building the Panama Canal.

At five p.m. that day, Black strode the short distance down the hall from his office and knocked on the door of Paul Healy's office, where his agreed successor as interim Hollinger CEO, Gordon Paris, was meeting with Healy. "Aha," Black said, and asked Paris out into the hall for a moment. Black told him that on the advice of his counsel he was retiring as Hollinger's CEO, effective immediately. The restructuring agreement had stipulated that Black would retire two days later, on November 21, in part so that he could verify and sign off on the company's quarterly financial statements. By resigning now, Black would not put his signature to them and Hollinger would not be able to file them. Under U.S. law, signing financial statements that the signer knows to be incomplete or inaccurate can lead to jail time, and the inference was that Black did not want to verify them. It also sent a message to Paris that, despite the agreement they had struck putting him in charge, Black would continue to do things on his own terms.

The next evening, Black was at a book event in the faculty dining room at Hunter College on New York's Upper East Side. The crowd of cameras, photographers, and reporters was bigger than it had been at earlier events, but it wasn't the literary sensation that was drawing them. "When was the last time you flew commercial?" asked a reporter from the *New York Post*, the Murdoch tabloid that had never taken more than a glancing interest in Black until lately.

"Two weeks ago; it's not such a rarity," Black replied.

"First class?"

"On that occasion, yes."

"What about the book tour?"

"If I don't fly commercial, I will pay for it out of my own pocket."

After answering several questions about his troubles, Black finally said in a woebegone tone, "I ask you to contemplate the possibility that those who benefit from the presumption of innocence may, in fact, be innocent."* A British journalist asked Black about the possibility of being forced to sell the *Telegraph*. "Very distressing, very distressing," he replied huffily. "I am being pilloried as a scoundrel, and I am not a scoundrel."

While the Hollinger imbroglio had developed over the previous months, affairs at the board of the Canadian company appeared to have been proceeding with relative serenity. There had been no vocal dissent from Inc. shareholders or directors – until now. The Inc. board was a fairly cozy group consisting of the insiders Black, Amiel, Radler, Atkinson, Boultbee, and Black's Ravelston partner Peter White** as well as loyal, long-time friends among its independents, including Fred Eaton, Douglas Bassett, and Allan Gotlieb. All of these independents

---

* Of his subject, Black had written, "Roosevelt punished his enemies and rewarded his friends. There is nothing wrong with that, up to a point, but the capricious persecution of those fully entitled to a presumption of innocence is unedifying."

** Dan Colson was also on the board, but as a condition of his becoming chief operating officer of Hollinger in the wake of the special committee's findings, he had to give up his position at Inc. He resigned officially in December.

were on the company's audit committee, which was chaired by Maureen Sabia, a lawyer and governance expert who had recently co-authored a book on the subject called *Integrity in the Spotlight: Opportunities for Audit Committees*. Eaton had been on the board since 1994, and earlier both he and Bassett had served stints as directors after backing the Black brothers' Argus coup in the late 1970s.

Black had called Bassett in September, after a vacancy on the audit committee opened up, and Bassett accepted even though his close friend Fred Eaton had warned him against coming into a tough situation. Like Black, Bassett was deeply loyal and accepted out of friendship with Black, whose oldest child, Jonathan, is his godson. In 1998 Black had been a pallbearer at the funeral of Bassett's father, John, the media baron. Bassett told Black when he joined the committee that he would call things as he saw them, and Black readily and gratefully agreed. Gotlieb, the other audit committee member, also had close ties to Black, having been publisher of *Saturday Night* magazine for several years (back when it was Black's most prominent Canadian media holding) after serving as Canada's ambassador in Washington.

In 1997, after Black made Hollinger International its main operating company, Inc. had been reconfigured as a mutual fund company whose only holding was its controlling interest in Hollinger International, and the Inc. board had come to rely on the idea that the big shooters on the subsidiary's American board had a handle on things. But after the November 16 restructuring deal was announced, Inc.'s audit committee demanded more information from the company and felt it wasn't getting it. (It was Inc.'s audit committee that had earlier brought the US$15.6 million the company had received in unauthorized non-compete payments to the special committee's attention.) Eaton telephoned in from Florida and Bassett flew in from Antigua for the board meeting at 10 Toronto Street on November 21. Boultbee and Peter White were also present in the first-floor boardroom under the portrait of George Black Jr., but Radler was not. Conrad was on the telephone from his New York office, and Barbara from their Park Avenue apartment. It was on the advice of their lawyer, the audit committee members explained, that they were issuing the following ultimatum: Unless a series of changes were made at Inc. similar to those implemented at Hollinger, including the resignations of Black as CEO, Radler as president, and Boultbee as executive vice-president, the committee members would themselves resign. They also wanted the US$15.6 million payment returned to Hollinger. Black calmly said he wouldn't agree because resigning would look as if he were admitting he had done something wrong. He explained that he had a different strategy for Inc. that involved the hiring of former Ontario Securities Commission enforcement chief Joe Groia to conduct a review. The directors then submitted the letters of resignation they had brought with them and, after Peter White chastised them for leaving the company in the lurch, they left. "We should all find it distressing that senior corporate directors are so terrorized by the current governance environment, not to mention by their own lawyers, that they choose to resign rather than continue to fulfill the mandate for which the shareholders elected them," White said later.

Several months after the resignations, Bassett still hadn't heard from Black – despite sending him his family's annual Christmas card – and Black had not taken several calls from Fred Eaton.*

It was back to the media circus a few days later, when Black was the featured speaker at an event at the Harvard Club. Taking the podium in an ancient, book-lined room, Black scanned the crowd and noted that one person had come to the event dressed as Theodore Roosevelt, FDR's distant cousin, who had been shot by a fanatic on the campaign trail in Milwaukee in 1912 but kept speaking after the bullet was slowed by his folded fifty-page speech. "Mr. President,"

---

* In a subsequent court deposition, Black was asked if he thought various former audit committee members had integrity, starting with Eaton.

"Freddy? Integrity, yes. I don't hold it against him [that] his company went bankrupt."

"What about Mr. Gotlieb, man of integrity?" the lawyer asked.

"I wouldn't necessarily stress that aspect of his personality."

"You kept him on as a director for twelve years?"

"It wasn't because of his integrity . . . I'm not suggesting that Mr. Gotlieb is a sociopath, but integrity? In light of what's gone on, I wouldn't bet the ranch on that right now."

"What about Maureen Sabia . . . Did you consider her a person of integrity when you put her on the board?"

"Yes, I think the greatest problem with these people is not integrity, it was judgment."

Black called out, "you famously concluded a speech with a bullet lodged in your chest. I have one in my back."

Indeed, as far as Black was concerned, the grounding of the aircraft and the humiliating cancellation of his perks was just one small way in which the insurgents led by Paris and Breeden had betrayed him; what stung him more was the fact that money had stopped flowing to Ravelston under the services agreement. Breeden and Paris had concluded that Ravelston was wildly overcharging Hollinger for the services it performed, and given that the salaries of the departed executives (Black, Radler, Atkinson, Boultbee) no longer had to be paid out of the fee, they thought US$100,000 a month was a fair amount. This was roughly US$1.9 million a month less than Ravelston had been receiving. Black was so incensed he didn't reply.

If the turnout to the November 24 book party for *Champion of Freedom* at the Four Seasons restaurant was any indication, the New York glitterati were not rushing to Black's side. Although the event had been organized by three of Manhattan society's most prominent names – Annette de la Renta, Jayne Wrightsman, and Marie-Josée Kravis – considerably fewer than half of the 300 people invited arrived to mill around the storied restaurant's Grill Room. Kissinger was there, as was the financier Ronald Perelman and Alfred Taubman, looking svelte after his release from jail in June. Also mingling were Candice Bergen, Joan Collins, Barbara Walters, and Amiel's friend the *Vogue* editor Anna Wintour. Amiel wore a coat with a high collar, not one of her flashier outfits. As it happened, in the Four Seasons' adjacent Pool Room, separated from Black's event by a long hallway, a party for a new book by former treasury secretary Robert Rubin was being thrown simultaneously, and it was rocking. Black's party "was sparsely attended, regrettably," noted Ed Koch, the former mayor of New York, who was invited to both book bashes. "And when I say sparsely, I mean maybe seventy-five people compared with the Rubin party, which was bursting at the seams. I felt sorry for him." Some had seen this coming. At a Rockefeller University board meeting shortly before the party, Christopher Browne had asked de la Renta if she was going ahead with the event. "What can we do?" she replied. "We didn't know he was so greedy." Black's book tour would never make it to

London, where the launch party planned by Lord Weidenfeld, his publisher and a former Hollinger director – now a co-defendant in at least one shareholder suit against the company – was called off.*

Meanwhile, the news that Hollinger had hired Lazard Freres to field bids for all or parts of Hollinger led some fifty prospective bidders to call the investment bank. Among them were David Barclay's son, Aidan, and Andrew Neil, the veteran editor who helped oversee the Barclays' newspaper interests. Simultaneously and unbeknownst to Lazard or anyone else at Hollinger, Black and David Barclay began secretly negotiating with each other via telephone and handwritten fax as frequently, in their tycoonish way, as if they were the bestest teenage buddies using instant messenger.

One of the protections built into many companies with super-voting share structures like Hollinger's is that the multiple-vote shares revert to single-vote status if they are sold or transferred to another owner – the deal with the other shareholders is that they exist to perpetuate the control of the founder only, but no one else. Under Hollinger's certificate of incorporation, if Inc. were to sell its Hollinger shares to the Barclays or anyone else, they would imme-diately revert to single-vote status. (This would have instantly reduced Inc.'s voting stake from 72 per cent to 30 per cent.) But the pyramid structure of Black's group of companies allowed him a clever manoeuvre whereby he could sell control without triggering the conversion: all he would have to do was sell Ravelston's 78 per cent interest in Inc. – rather than Inc.'s shares in Hollinger – and the buyer would inherit command of the whole group. In a memo he sent to the Barclays, Black laid out how much Ravelston would

---

* Around this time it was announced that Black would be included in the second edition of "Wall Street's Most Wanted" playing cards, where he would be joined by such lumi-naries as Martha Stewart, Dick Grasso, Dennis Kozlowski, Frank Quattrone, Sandy Weill, Jack Welch, and – the ace of spades – Kenneth Lay. Parody Productions, the company that made the novelty, made Black the king of clubs, replete with a photo caricature of him with a copy of the FDR book in one hand and the other hand pulling money out of a jar unsubtly labelled "Hollinger Cookies."

expect for such a transaction, including a US$10 million "redundancy payment" for himself and a 20 per cent "premium" on the super-voting shares: roughly US$300 million. This may not have seemed proper for someone who had promised to maximize value for all of Hollinger's shareholders, but as far as Black was concerned he was within his rights to hold simultaneous talks with the Barclays, or whomever else he chose, regarding a deal for Hollinger Inc. "If you want to buy all of Hollinger Inc. and therefore control of Hollinger International and the *Telegraph*, we can talk about it," Black wrote to Aidan Barclay on November 17, three days after Lazard Freres was hired to oversee a sale. Indeed, hours after Lazard had made its presentation to the board three days earlier, Black had met Aidan Barclay briefly in his office. "If you want to look exclusively at the *Telegraph*, Lazard will be calling you."

Even while talking with the Barclays, Black played it cool. As he gloated to reporters, Hollinger International stock was rising on the news that he had been ousted from the company and it was for sale; that in turn fed a 28 per cent increase in Inc.'s share price. On November 20, Black wrote to David Barclay at his office in Monte Carlo: "Our stock is skyrocketing and the special committee process is largely concluded. We don't have to sell anything but will consider it. Ravelston is a rich, debt-free company."

David Barclay considered buying the *Telegraph* to be "a once in a lifetime opportunity" (although his son Aidan was quick to point out that "he says that about a lot of things"). The Barclays wouldn't preclude a deal with Black for either Hollinger Inc. or Hollinger International, or both. If they could buy Ravelston's control stake for less than US$500 million, including the assumption of Inc.'s US$140 million debt, that would give them a great tactical advantage in determining the fate of the Telegraph Group, which on its own was worth more than US$1 billion.

The Barclays were legendary bottom fishers who specialized in buying good businesses from distressed sellers. Whether or not he wanted to admit it, Black fit the bill. Indeed, as business people, the Barclays were very different from Black and came from much humbler beginnings. The self-made identical twins – who can't be told apart either on the telephone or in person, save for which side they part their hair on – were born in 1935 in London's west end. David and Frederick were two of ten children; their father, a salesman, was often unemployed and died when they were thirteen. The boys, who had been promising athletes, left school and started a house-painting business. They saved up to buy several London boarding houses that were being divested by the Church of England, and from there they moved into hotels, then into a swath of industries, from retailing and casinos to newspapers. Largely self-educated, both were said to be keen readers of political philosophy, and David has written on the subject. Although they lived grand lives, commuting between their Gothic-style castle on the tiny island of Brecqhou in the English Channel and their yacht in Monte Carlo, the brothers almost never appeared in public.

In tight negotiations, they were known to employ a "good twin, bad twin" technique, and Frederick has described himself as "the more aggressive half." In pursuing the Telegraph Group, the brothers deliberately decided not to get embroiled in the accusations against Black and his feud with Hollinger's board. Instead they stayed at such a remove that they never actually met Black face to face. "Some of this stuff was a mystery to us because it was never fully explained and we never sought to really understand it all," said Aidan Barclay. As for where Black stood: "I always assume that what he says and what he does are two different things."

As the Barclays' lawyers from the New York firm Skadden Arps Slate, Meagher & Flom kept reminding them, buying Inc. was a dicey proposition. Hollinger's board might treat the Barclays as hostile bidders and try to thwart them, either by selling the Telegraph Group out from under them or by instituting a poison pill takeover defence to keep them at bay. David Barclay at various times suggested approaching the Hollinger board to appear friendly, but Black counselled the brothers to wait until their deal was sealed. "I think the shareholders have to be protected from these directors," Black explained. "I think they are a menace to the shareholders' interests."

Another thing that Aidan presumed was that Black would be negotiating with other parties right up until a deal was done, and this was astute of him. During November and December, while maintaining constant contact with the Barclays, Black discreetly juggled a number of potential suitors. Associated Newspapers, the owner of Britain's *Daily Mail*, was interested in buying half of Inc. if it were taken private, in a transaction that would include pre-emptive rights to buy the Telegraph papers down the road. In early December, CanWest CEO Leonard Asper – to whom Black had sold Hollinger's Canadian newspapers in 2000 – told Black that CanWest was interested in buying half or all of Inc., with the proviso that the company needed forty-five days to perform due diligence. CanWest had lined up an American partner for what it considered a very attractive opportunity. "A lot of people looked at this Inc. concept," said Asper. "Effectively, for US$400 million, you could get control of these assets instead of paying US$2 billion."

Axel Springer and the buyout firm Apax both floated similar ideas past Black, and the billionaire George Soros telephoned Black at home to express interest but never made a serious follow-up. At his New York apartment in mid-December, Black entertained executives from the buyout firm Cerberus, including Dan Quayle, the former U.S. vice-president. Aside from the Barclays, the most serious potential buyers were likely Nelson Peltz at Triarc, whom Black met regularly in New York, and the buyout firm Hicks Muse, whose chairman, Tom Hicks, he had brought into the office and introduced to Gordon Paris. Some of the bidders fell away early, but those that remained in the game at the end of the year included Hicks Muse, Associated, CanWest, and Triarc. However, none of their best offers could match the one made by the determined and deep-pocketed Barclays.

Initially, the twins proposed to buy out Ravelston's controlling shares in Inc., pending completion of due diligence by November 24 or 25. But during the due-diligence process, a couple of sticking points arose. One was whether the board of Hollinger International could sell the Telegraph Group without shareholder (that is, Inc.'s) approval. Another obstacle was Richard Desmond, the outrageous and unpredictable owner of Express Newspapers, the Telegraph Group's joint-venture partner in the West Ferry printing plant. Desmond, with whom Black had feuded in the past, was saying that any sale of the Telegraph papers would trigger his right to buy back the 50 per cent of the plant that he didn't own. "We hope any purchaser of *The Daily Telegraph* has their printing arrangements in place," Desmond crowed in the *Times*. (Desmond himself was bidding for the Telegraph Group, and this was his way of deterring rivals.)

Black suggested that David Barclay speak with Dan Colson to clarify Desmond's rights regarding West Ferry, and Barclay wrote back, "I suspect that Desmond is a bantam in more ways than one – the problem is he cannot keep his mouth shut."

A third issue was price, and Barclay and Black went back and forth with various numbers – for instance, Barclay was willing to pay only US$20 million for a premium for the super-voting shares and US$2 million to cover a redundancy payment for Black, whereas Black had asked for US$48 million and US$10 million.

On November 27, Conrad and Barbara spent Thanksgiving with Henry and Nancy Kissinger at their home in Connecticut. Black scrawled a handwritten note to Barclay – "I have been in the country battling with a turkey (eating it)" – in which he offered to split the difference on the numbers if Barclay was satisfied on his end with the legal questions. As the negotiations continued in private, a stream of negative stories about Black and Hollinger continued to pour out in the news media. But as he and Barclay edged closer to terms on a deal, Black was upbeat. In a November 29 note to Barclay, Black thanked him for his encouragement and wrote: "This is a rough country but the law will prevail and I will be vindicated." The following day he added: "I'm looking forward to suing the FT and The Sunday Times. It's time to turn this tide of vilification."

Black never followed up the threat of these lawsuits. On December 4, the deal showed signs of going off the rails when one of Black's own lawyers told a Barclay representative, Rigel Mowatt, that the November 15 restructuring agreement Black had signed with the Hollinger board precluded him from selling his shares in Inc. Mowatt brought David Barclay up to speed on the agreement's key points, including that Black had agreed not to do anything that would negatively affect a Hollinger transaction resulting from the Lazard review. If Inc. were forced to do something to solve its own liquidity problems,

Barclay wrote to Black, "I understand you would have to give Hollinger International reasonable notice. I am obviously very disappointed if this is the case. Have you any other ideas by which we can proceed? For example, can you sell us an option to conclude the deal that we have reached which could be taken up at the expiration of your agreement with the Hollinger International board?"

Black responded the next day that his lawyer at Sullivan and Cromwell had spoken to the Barclays' counsel at Skadden Arps and "they seem to have agreed that the prospects are more promising than your previous note indicated." Barclay wrote Black back by hand, thanking him and saying, "I appreciate that you may be under a lot of pressure and I want to take this opportunity to wish you every success and my best wishes."

Over the next few days, Barclay proposed buying half of Ravelston's stake in Inc. immediately and the remainder two or three months later, when all the legal questions were resolved in both the U.S. and the U.K. He also offered to pay US$32 million to Hollinger International to cover the unauthorized fees "if you think that would be a sensible thing to do." Barclay added that, given that Hollinger was a Delaware company, "I think it is important that we do not appear to be making a hostile bid for Hollinger International." Some of the alternatives that Barclay proposed might have avoided the death match that was looming, but Black rejected them all. He had been bluffing and stalling for so long now that he may have thought that, if he could drag things out a bit longer, he might be able to figure out a way to pull off a settlement with the special committee and hang onto his company.

Hollinger CEO Gordon Paris was hearing reports from a number of sources that Black was working on a deal of his own, including from Chris Browne, who sent him a letter on December 9 that said as much. Paris also heard that Dan Colson, who flew from London to Chicago to visit the *Sun-Times* in mid-December in his capacity as Hollinger's new COO, had given Tom Hicks of Hicks Muse a tour of the operation. Paris and Colson exchanged scathing e-mails on the subject, with Colson insisting that he had done nothing untoward.* Colson was in a particularly tough place. On the one hand, he seemed in the clear, because he was the most senior Ravelston executive who had not received any of the controversial non-compete payments – although he had complained about them to Black at the time they were paid. But he was torn between his decades-long friendship with Black ("I love the guy," he told the *Globe and Mail*) and his anger at him for taking his eye off the ball. Still, Colson didn't believe Black deserved the pillorying he was taking, and he had a growing disdain for Paris and Breeden, whose righteousness and motives he was suspicious of. "He didn't do anything to me," Colson said of Black to colleagues.

At another point, Black sent Paris an e-mail warning him that if he allowed Lazard Freres to send out books disclosing confidential Telegraph Group information to competitors, he would hold him "accountable" for his actions. That "could be construed as a threat of multi-faceted dimensions," Black later explained.

Black came to view Breeden as a holier-than-thou process wonk who seemed to think that the completion of his sacred special committee report was more important than the ongoing management of a large newspaper company. By the middle of December, Black was certain that his lawyers had unearthed enough evidence, in the form of audit committee minutes and material from Hollinger's auditors, KPMG, to show that the so-called unauthorized payments had in fact been authorized. "While I'm open-minded about this, I do not think any reasonable person in my position at this time would conclude that it's necessarily clear that I have a legal or moral duty to repay this money," he later explained.

Black was now convinced that Hollinger's board had breached the November 15 agreement in other ways, including restricting the flow of money to Ravelston. This, he felt, only exacerbated the financial problems at Inc. and thus gave him even more reason to pursue his secret deal with the Barclays. His logic was typically head-bending,

---

* At a December 17 board meeting Black said that he wanted it on the record that he "has been faithful to the Lazard process and has done nothing to disturb the Lazard process."

but Black was convinced that the special committee was in cahoots with the audit committee to spare themselves and Hollinger's other marquee-name directors liability and to hang Black and his associates out to dry. Now he added a new layer of complicity to complete his theory, arguing that Breeden and Paris, both of whom stood to make millions from their new roles at Hollinger, were manipulating the directors' mutiny in order to entrench themselves. Breeden's investigation, he said, was dragging on and running up millions in fees while Paris was being paid US$2 million a year as Hollinger's interim CEO. As far as Black was concerned, greed was the great culprit here – but not his. "Everyone can see Breeden is sucking the blood out of the company and he and Paris are just fattening their sinecures," Black later fumed to David Barclay.

To Paris, Breeden, and the independent Hollinger directors, this was classic Black sophism in overdrive. Their efforts in ridding the company of Black, Radler, and the other executives, and in cutting off the perks and flow of money to Ravelston, had added some US$700 million to the value of Hollinger through its rising stock price. "Black decided he no longer had to comply with the November 15 agreement with the company, as if he had a unilateral right to pick and choose what he would honour," Breeden said. "American corporate law in the early twenty-first century does not give controlling shareholders a right equivalent to medieval papal annulment."

Nevertheless, a new compromise was worked out between Black's lawyer John Warden and Richard Breeden on December 20. Hollinger now agreed to pay Ravelston a portion of the money it was owed from past management fees, and in return Black would agree to a standstill agreement under which he would make no deal for Inc. until January 4. "I have again emphasized, as you have, that I will not agree to anything that has a negative impact on the Lazard process," Black wrote to David Barclay that day. The tycoons agreed that they would aim to sign their deal on January 6 or 7, 2004.

On December 22, Black took an American Airlines flight from New York to Chicago to appear before the SEC, which had issued him a subpoena. During the interrogation, Black was uncharacteristically silent. He repeatedly invoked the Fifth Amendment, exercising his constitutional right to not make a statement that could incriminate him. (He maintained this was done because he was still conducting his investigation into the payments, and the SEC wouldn't grant him an extension.) That same day, Black had a reassuring phone call with Barclay in which he said they were on a "flight path" to completing a deal in January. Barclay replied, "As far as I'm concerned, it's a done deal."

Little else was going so smoothly for Black. The day after the SEC appearance, KPMG followed the lead of the Inc. audit committee and resigned as the Canadian company's auditor. Black said that the firm's action was "unseemly" because it was partly to blame for the poor paperwork that lay behind his troubles. Finding new independent directors to replace the departed audit committee of Inc. was proving to be a chore. To help shoulder the burden of stabilizing the company, Black enlisted his loyal friend, Ravelston partner, and original news-papering comrade Peter White to return to Inc. as co-chief operating officer, at a consulting fee of $75,000 a month.

On New Year's Eve, Black wrote to Barclay that he would like an option to keep 10 Toronto Street and the company's other Toronto real estate, worth maybe $15 million, once the deal was done. This sudden desire to hang onto his landmark office came amid reports that Black had shown his house in London's Cottesmore Gardens to prospective buyers and had formally listed his estate on South Ocean Boulevard in Palm Beach for sale. The asking price for the London house was reportedly in the £14 million range, while Palm Beach was on the market for US$36 million. The listing for the Florida house on www.realtor.com by Linda Gary Real Estate came complete with a helpful "estimated payment" calculator that showed that if a buyer put 20 per cent down, monthly payments on the mortgage would be US$168,153. This would not include maintenance, upkeep, help, or the annual taxes on the property of $351,225.

The listing of these properties added a new element to the swirl of speculation. Was it conceivable that Black, whose homes alone were estimated to be worth $100 million, was so cash-strapped that he couldn't come up with a mere US$850,000? Or was he simply setting the stage to bolster his position that Inc. was in such dire financial straits, he needed to sell to the Barclays to stay solvent? Sure enough, the December 31 deadline came and went, and no payment from Black arrived. Indeed, he had already suggested to David Radler that he needn't pay either, but both Radler and Peter Atkinson met the payment deadline. For Black, making the payment would have been a good stalling tactic; not paying only ensured that the enmity between himself and the Hollinger directors would grow.

As far as the non-compete payments were concerned, Black never directly pegged the blame on Radler, but he did tell Breeden that he felt that Peter Atkinson and particularly Mark Kipnis, the Hollinger legal counsel who worked closely with Radler in Chicago, bore responsibility for ensuring that all the documentation, approvals, and disclosures were in order.*

On Saturday, November 15, the day the special committee and Black worked out their agreement in New York, Radler had turned in his resignation from Chicago. That night he was at a birthday party for the *Sun-Times* columnist Michael Sneed when he took publisher John Cruickshank and editor-in-chief Michael Cooke outside and told them what had transpired. Radler explained glumly that he and his wife, Rona, were going to leave for Vancouver that night on the Hollinger jet before the company took back the keys. "But I'll be back," he said. 'I'm not sure how, but I'll be back."

There would be much derision of Radler's stewardship and business practices at the *Sun-Times* in the weeks that followed. (Few had forgotten that it was the only top ten newspaper in the United States that had decided it didn't have the budget to send its own reporter to Iraq to cover the war, or that the newspaper's marketing department had all but been eliminated, or that because of the penny-pinching

---

* When he was later deposed on the subject of US$5.5 million that was paid to himself, Radler, Boultbee, and Atkinson in February 2001, Black was asked if he "initiated" the payments, as Radler had claimed. "I am aware of the word 'initiated' in Mr. Radler's submission," said Black. "And what I did say was that he had conducted such a brilliant sale that this should be tangibly recognized. I didn't say how. And that is what he means by initiation." Black also said it was inaccurate to describe the payments as bonuses.

way that distribution of the paper was configured, the first 300,000 or so copies of the paper wouldn't have Cubs or White Sox scores from the night before.) Still, the executives who worked most closely with Radler felt he deserved credit for smartly buying up community newspapers in the Chicago area to fortify the *Sun-Times*'s position against the *Tribune*. They respected the fact that he never had pretensions about being anything beyond a businessman forever looking for a good deal. "Radler is not a monster," says Michael Cooke. "He's a very sharp money guy. It might be an exaggeration to say that he rescued the paper, but he made it safe – in the newsroom they'd throw rotten fruit at me for saying that."

The impact of Radler's departure from the *Jerusalem Post* was that it led soon after to the firing of combative publisher Tom Rose. By 2003 the paper was struggling financially because of the intifada's impact on advertising and a dispute over its contract to print Israel's Golden Pages; the *Post* no longer printed the directories despite investing in a customized US$5 million press and sued the directory company for US$8 million. For all Radler's boasts of money-making from the *Post* a decade earlier, it had accumulated losses of nearly US$30 million since Hollinger bought it in 1989. Still, he took great personal pride in his annual visits, which included meetings with Prime Minister Ariel Sharon and other government dignitaries. In 2001, when Radler was given an honorary doctorate from Haifa University, former prime minister Benjamin Netanyahu gave a speech praising him. "For him, the *Jerusalem Post* was something between a cause and a vanity," said another person who worked closely with Radler. "This was David's way of being a *macher* in the Jewish world."

Still, Radler never eased up the pressure to save money at the *Post*, including inviting its top executives and editors to Chicago in May 2003 for brainstorming sessions with his cadre of gruff Chicago executives. One of the attendees in particular recalled much discussion about one *Jerusalem Post* employee who had been at the paper for so long that terminating her would be a very expensive proposition under Israeli labour laws. "Can't you push her down the stairs?" one of Radler's deputies wondered. "Then we'd all go out for lunch," said the attendee. "It was a terribly depressing business culture."

Although he paid back the US$7 million, Radler had taken virtually the same position as Black in responding to the special committee – arguing in a letter from his lawyer Anton Valukas that the questionable payments appeared to have been authorized. Valukas's letter noted, for instance, that Radler recalled two meetings with James Thompson over the summer of 2000, in which the now disputed non-compete payments to officers were disclosed. And unlike Black, whose thousands of e-mails were being pored over by the special committee, Radler never used e-mail or put anything on paper.

Months before his forced resignation from Hollinger, Radler had wondered aloud whether he wanted to stick around the company or leave and focus on buying and selling small newspapers through Horizon, of which he became president in 2003 in addition to serving as Hollinger's president. He had become increasingly disillusioned after the Hollinger board began to object to his splitting his time with another company and in the summer of 2003 vetoed a US$100 million deal by Horizon to purchase newspapers from Alabama's Community Newspaper Holdings, the same company that had bought many of Hollinger's small-town titles in the past. "When things were still going well, David was amused by Conrad, by his love of titles," said one person who worked closely with him. "He found that kind of funny, and he also found it kind of sad that Conrad had spent so little time with his family. In the past couple of years, David had become more bitter about Conrad. They had been in trouble for so long now, that David's tone had become more acerbic." Speaking separately to two former colleagues soon afterwards, Radler was angry and dismissive of what was going on, saying, "They're going after the Jewish guy." In another conversation with a Hollinger executive, he said of Black: "He took the glory on the way up, he can take the crap on the way down."

Although Black was the primary target of Breeden's probe, Radler could not escape the fact that most of the transactions in question were done under his watch, including the sale of various groupings of newspapers, which had generated the controversial non-compete payments. It had also been Radler's task to propose the Ravelston management services fee each year to audit committee chairman

Thompson. According to the special committee's investigation, the management fee was set arbitrarily after a discussion among Radler, Boultbee, and Black. Radler then took the figure to Thompson who, along with the other audit committee members, apparently agreed to pay the fee without much questioning.

"Remember, the whole action we initiated was not against Conrad, it was against the board," explained Tweedy Browne's Christopher Browne. "And no one has focused on that. Ultimately, you have to say that if Conrad got all this money and it wasn't justified but the board approved it, what was the board doing?"

But Hollinger's blue-chip audit committee was not conceding any negligence on its part. "You don't serve on a board under the assumption that management is crooked," Thompson said later. Richard Burt explained the role of Hollinger's independent directors this way: "Like most directors, they rely on advisers. First of all, they rely on the truthfulness and honesty of senior management. Secondly, they rely on the thoroughness of the outside auditors to bring issues to their attention. Thirdly, they rely on the financial staff, and particularly the internal audit capability, to report to them when issues or questions arise. To that extent I don't think the Hollinger board performed any differently than most boards in the United States."

On this last point, at least, Black and his increasingly estranged board of directors would agree. "The independent directors should have plucked up their courage and said that all the payments they authorized to us were earned, appropriate, and disclosed, instead of imagining that they could sell the proposition that they had been deceived by David Radler," Black said later. "There was never a word of dissent, never anything they sought and did not receive, never any attempt to restrict their research of comparables and so forth, and never an occasion when the audit committee did not assure us that everything was fine and that they would have no difficulty justifying what they had approved."

On the point that the audit committee could have done more, at least, Hollinger's rebellious shareholders would agree with Black. The lawsuit brought by the Hollinger investor Cardinal Capital was unsealed by the court in early January 2004. According to the lawsuit, it presented "a saga of greed and deliberate indifference to fiduciary duties" that had allowed Black, Radler, and their associates to siphon US$300 million from the company. Cardinal's suit focused on what appeared to be a culture of rubber-stamping by directors, who approved whatever issue was brought before them by the executive committee, often retroactively and without much discussion and inquiry. And the executive committee consisted of Black, Radler, and Richard Perle, who was considered an insider because he was paid a reported US$5 million a year for his work on Hollinger Digital. Additionally, Black had Hollinger invest US$2.5 million in Trireme Associates, a venture capital firm Perle was involved in. Black and Kissinger both served on Trireme's strategic advisory board, and Black told Perle he would consider putting in up to US$25 million. "It's a great tragedy that it has come to this," Perle would say. "I think that as a public company it should have exercised more restraint than it did."

The pressure on the directors by Cardinal and, to a lesser degree, Tweedy Browne gave Black some encouragement because it bolstered his view that his board of directors – none of whom, unlike him, owned much stock in the company – were making a scapegoat of him. But as far as the special committee was concerned, there were two interlinked storylines. "I think we are drawing distinctions between those who profited and those who were stupid and inattentive," said special committee member Graham Savage. Moreover, having already moved against Black, Radler, and the others, the special committee wanted to keep the board onside while Lazard worked on selling the company.

Meanwhile, Cardinal and Tweedy were well aware that Hollinger had directors' and officers' insurance of some US$100 million. They harboured hopes that their legal actions against the board would result in a lucrative settlement from the directors (in addition to whatever might be recovered from Black and his associates). It would not be difficult to prove at least a lack of attention to detail among some of Hollinger's bold-face names. In a subsequent court deposition on February 12, 2004, Thompson, who in addition to being chairman of the audit committee was also the respected chairman of one of

Chicago's largest law firms and a member of the federal 9/11 commission, couldn't identify Wachovia Bank as Hollinger's chief lender, although Wachovia refinanced the company in late 2002.

"Did the company enter into a transaction with Wachovia?" Thompson was asked by the attorney Gregory Joseph.

"I don't recall that."

"Well, does the company currently have debt outstanding with Wachovia?"

"I don't know that as I sit here today."

"Is that a material matter on the financial statements?"

"I presume debt is a material matter, yes, but I just don't have any recollection, that's what I'm saying."

"You don't recall if today the company has any outstanding debt to Wachovia?"

"I don't recall Wachovia specifically."

"Does the company have outstanding debt of material size?"

"Yes."

"With whom?"

"I don't know as I sit here today."

"Understood," said Joseph. "I appreciate you are on multiple boards."

Black pegged Richard Breeden as a governance terrorist who had inveigled his way into his company to line his pockets, and Breeden was just as generous in his view of Black. He hypothesized that Black's efforts to sell Inc. were part of an intent to "get out of Dodge" and flee with the sale proceeds to some distant shore where he would be beyond the reach of any U.S. court judgments against him.

By early January 2004, Breeden, Paris, and the rest of the special committee were determined to prevent Black from seeing a penny from the sale of his company until the special committee had finished its work and all legal matters were resolved. Breeden said, "If those shares had been flipped to somebody else in a cash transaction and Mr. Black was now living in the Outer Hebrides with the money deposited in any of the banks around the world – Beirut or Gibraltar or who knows where – this could in essence mean that the special committee and company would spend the next twenty years trying to enforce a judgment."

In anticipation of the end of Hollinger's standstill with Black on January 4, Paris called a directors' meeting to discuss the adoption of a poison pill takeover defence to thwart any attempt by Black to sell Inc. A poison pill is a device under which a company is authorized to issue bushels of new stock to existing shareholders if an unwanted buyer has acquired a stake beyond a certain threshold; the new stock has the effect of diluting the company's existing shareholders to the point where no one is in control. Poison pills are quite common among American companies – some 2,500 businesses registered in Delaware have adopted them – but it was quite unheard of (and normally illogical) for a company to put one in place against its own controlling shareholder. Black learned about the pill in a group e-mail about it sent to him in his continuing though diminished role as a Hollinger director, and he went ballistic.

In phone calls to directors Henry Kissinger and Richard Perle – his closest remaining allies on the Hollinger board, neither of them strangers to combustible political situations – Black railed that he still controlled the company and that if the board tried to go forward with the poison pill he would exert his rights as controlling shareholder and fire them. "I saw it as an act aimed directly at trying to ensure the insolvency of Hollinger Inc. and therefore a mortal threat to me financially," said Black.

Perle was in France, but Kissinger offered to act as an intermediary to bring the sides together for more negotiation before either did anything rash. As a result, Black and Warden agreed to meet Paris and Breeden at the downtown offices of Sullivan & Cromwell on January 4 to see if any differences could be worked out without ending up in court. Black strode into the meeting determined to show that he was coming to the table not as a humble petitioner but as an equal who was also capable of inflicting legal pain.

To demonstrate this, Black kicked off the meeting by levelling a truculent glare at the two men across the table. He then launched into a tirade about how grievously damaged and defamed he had been, how he'd been accused of things that were base and untrue, and he listed all the different ways in which Breeden and Paris had violated their November agreement. Thus, he declared, he was certainly no longer obliged to pay back the US$7 million. Moreover, he continued, even if the laws of the United States did not restrain the defamatory behaviour that he had been subjected to, the laws of Canada and the laws of the United Kingdom did. "I have my rights, and I know where Ray Seitz has property in England and I know where Graham Savage lives in Toronto, and I'm going to launch a defamation action against them and their advisers, and I will take all their property and I will hold them accountable," Black vowed.

It struck Breeden as "an extraordinary beginning of a discussion that was supposed to be an attempt to see if we could resolve differences." Asked later if Black's threats had achieved their desired effect, Breeden would say only, "If you're going to try to intimidate somebody, I'm the wrong guy to try it with. And so is Gordon."

Nonetheless, both sides agreed to extend the standstill period until January 18 in exchange for Hollinger delaying until that date the deadline for Black to make his first US$850,000 payment. They agreed to continue to meet in the meantime in hope of working out a global settlement. Black wrote to David Barclay on January 4, saying, "We have just secured a deferral of the proposed [directors'] meeting, having frightened them with our threats of litigation and alteration of the composition of the board. We can finish our negotiations and tailor them to different contingencies. The standstill is extended two weeks. We will be ready for anything at the end of that time and we are having substantive negotiations with them in the meantime."

Barclay was not heartened by the news. He thanked Black for keeping him informed and asked, "Have you thought about an option which you can call on us to complete, when you have overcome the local difficulties? We could pay you say $20 million on account – if that would help."

It was indeed an uneasy peace between Black and his company. Hollinger issued a press release on January 5 in which Breeden testily replied to a comment from Black's spokesman in that day's *New York Times* that Lord Black had "yet to complete his own inquiry into the facts underlying whether the payment was in fact authorized." In the Hollinger release, Breeden said, "In the view of the Special Committee, there is not any doubt whatsoever that the payments in connection with these supposed 'non-compete' agreements relating to sales of U.S. community newspapers were not authorized by Hollinger International's Board, and this issue is not the subject of further review, inquiry or negotiation."

Black, not surprisingly, thought otherwise. A week before the extended standstill was due to expire, Barclay faxed Black a handwritten note saying that he had read in the press that Black's first payment of US$850,000 would be due at week's end and that there were rumblings that Black might not have the money to pay and was about to resign as Hollinger's chairman. "Please don't hesitate to call on me if you need any support," Barclay wrote. He went on to add: "You know as I do sometimes the best defence is to attack. I am sure you have thought about it, particularly with the board at Hollinger International."

Black replied in a handwritten note:

Dear David,
Many thanks for your kind note. The reason I didn't pay the $800,000 [sic] was because counsel have satisfied me that with new discoveries in the documentation, it is not due and cannot be collected. Everything is in suspense for our negotiations, which resume on Tuesday.

I will fax you after that encounter, but to the best of my judgment, we are on a glide-path to completion and if there is an attempt at legal obstruction, it will fail.

Black, Warden, Paris, and Breeden met as planned on January 13. On the agenda was a proposal, put forward by Black, that Hollinger and Inc. would merge – eliminating Inc.'s liquidity problems and ending Black's control over the company in the process. At the meeting, Black laid some cards on the table, saying that he had several groups interested in buying all of Inc. and another interested in a minority stake. He was willing to continue the standstill agreement while Hollinger considered his idea, he said, but only on the condition that he be reinstated as Hollinger's CEO. Paris responded that he was amenable to the idea of a merger, but only on the condition that any payment resulting to Ravelston from the combination would be set aside pending settlement or judgments from any legal claims relating to the special committee investigation. Black wouldn't agree to this, and they adjourned the meeting for two days.

On January 15, the two sides met by telephone, and again the result was inconclusive. Now Paris said it would take two months for him to make the necessary preparations for a merger between the two companies, and Black told him that was too long. Black also threw out the idea that he could offer Hollinger a right of refusal on any investment in or buyout of Inc. Once more, they agreed to continue the meeting the next day, again by telephone. Privately, the special committee viewed Black's new offers warily. As far as they were concerned, Black had signed an agreement in November and he was legally bound by it – the only real question was whether he was going to work with the board to get through the Lazard sale process. What's more, although they hadn't gone public yet, the committee had uncovered what it considered evidence of corruption and looting of Hollinger that went far beyond the US$32 million in dispute.

Black was not waiting for Paris and Breeden to come around to his way of thinking either. On January 14, David Barclay wrote to him, saying, "In my opinion now the press are onto us. The sooner we sign, the better." Black replied the following morning that they should make sure to present the Hollinger board with a "fait accompli, in advance of any attempt at a pill, which I doubt they have the votes for anyway. We are resuming discussions with the special committee chairman and counsel this afternoon. I will call you when those conversations are over. We are of course negotiating in good faith with them, but expect to complete with you." He added, regarding the wording of the Barclays' proposed letter to the Hollinger board, "I would prefer the references to me were less pejorative. Instead of references to 'negative media attention,' we could substitute 'media controversy.'"

Black may have thought that the stage was set for a smooth sale of his company to the Barclays and, with US$300 million in the bank, that he would regroup and face the legal challenges against him from a position of financial might. On the morning of Friday, January 16, he received his latest fax from David Barclay, who had heard that word was out on a possible Inc. deal and that Lazard Freres had been instructed to act as quickly as possible to dispose of Hollinger's assets.

Then, all hell broke loose. Black's lawyer John Warden was supposed to resume the negotiations with Breeden that afternoon but was told that Breeden had to cancel because he was in talks with the SEC. Warden was scheduled to fly to Florida to visit his parents that afternoon and asked Breeden to call him if anything was going on with the securities regulator that would require him to cancel his trip. Breeden never called, and it wasn't until Warden got to Florida that he heard the news: the SEC had obtained a federal court order against Hollinger to ensure that the special committee's continuing investigation would not be impeded if Black tried to sell control of the company or change the board.

Despite the extraordinary timeliness of the regulator's action, Paris said he hadn't seen it coming. He first learned of it on the night of January 15 and was informed that either he'd have to sign a consent decree approving the legal action by the regulator, or by the close of business on the following day the SEC would pursue alternatives that could include a fraud action or even a forced receivership of the company. After discussing the SEC's demands with members of Hollinger's special and audit committees, Paris signed the decree on behalf of the company. "There have been growing indications that some of the very same Hollinger International corporate insiders and related entities who improperly received corporate assets are attempting to thwart or obstruct the efforts of the special committee," said the lawsuit filed in the U.S. District Court for the Northern District of Illinois.

Based on the committee's previous findings and other information, the SEC charged the company with filing false 10-Q (quarterly) and 10-K (annual) reports from 1999 to 2001. In an unusual move, the court order called for the appointment of Breeden as "special monitor" of the company – an omnipotent role similar to the one he played at Worldcom – if any actions were taken by the board or the company's stockholders (in other words, Black) to interfere with the conclusion of the special committee process. If Breeden had played a direct role in the sudden turn of events, he wasn't saying. "That does seem fortuitous, doesn't it?" said Graham Savage. "If Richard had anything to do with it, it was brilliant."

Black wrote to Barclay, saying, "The action of the SEC today, with the connivance of some of Hollinger's management and the special committee, has been thoroughly examined by counsel for both of us and does not seem to me, to any of us, to affect what we are planning. An executive committee meeting has been called for 7 tomorrow (Saturday) evening, with a very unspecific agenda. In the circumstances, and given who we are dealing with, I suggest we aim at a 6 p.m. closing."

On the heels of the SEC action, the special committee decided it had had enough back and forth with Black and decided it was time to pre-empt anything he might try. The committee filed suit against him on behalf of Hollinger on January 16 in the U.S. District Court in the Southern District of New York.* Black, Radler, Ravelston, and Hollinger Inc. were named in the claim, which demanded the return of some US$300 million alleged to have been "diverted and usurped" via "systematic breaches of fiduciary duties." On top of the initial US$32 million in non-compete payments, the company was now seeking the return of the Ravelston management fees, as well as the CanWest non-competes, many of which were cited in the earlier Cardinal lawsuit. "The lawsuit is an attempt by the special committee now to divert attention from the fallacy of their earlier claims," Warden responded in a press release. It was notable that not only was Black no longer making grand public pronouncements himself, but he had also hired an external PR firm, New York's Robinson, Lerer and Montgomery, to handle his crisis communications.

When Black took part in the executive committee conference call that evening, a series of resolutions were proposed by Seitz, who had

---

* The venue for the lawsuit was later moved to the Northern District of Illinois.

become committee chairman after the November restructuring agreement. The meeting was attended by Black, Savage, Thompson, and
Burt. At the top of the agenda was the approval of the SEC order, and
then, to Black's shock, his removal as chairman of the board of
Hollinger as well as the removal of Ravelston executives from any
subsidiary boards (such as the Telegraph Group or the Jerusalem Post
company) within the firm.

The tetchy phone meeting concluded before eight p.m. on the
Saturday evening, and throughout it Black mentioned nothing of his
imminent deal with the Barclays. At 8:28 that night, a letter from
Black informing Hollinger of Ravelston's intention "tomorrow to
enter into an agreement with Press Holdings International Ltd., an
English company," popped out of the fax machine in Hollinger's
empty midtown office, addressed to Gordon Paris.

Paris found out about the Barclay deal to buy out Ravelston's
shares in Inc. – valued at US$466 million, including the assumption of
US$140 million of Inc.'s debts – the next morning, along with the rest
of the world. He and the other Hollinger board members also
received a fuller letter from Black, running more than three pages,
explaining his actions and his side of the story. Black reiterated his view
on the US$32 million that "the entire sequence of events based on the
premise that these were 'unauthorized payments' has been invalid" and
"this board was misled." He claimed that the November 15 restructuring proposal was invalid, and even if it weren't, that the special
committee had breached most of its provisions. Finally, he praised the
Barclays and their offer as one that "will not only provide substantial
value to all Hollinger Inc. shareholders, but also will allow the media
properties of Hollinger International to move forward unhindered by
recent controversy and uncertainty."

Black went on to list some of the new evidence he had of
approval for the payments, including handwritten notes of a conversation Thompson had had with lawyers from Shearman & Sterling
who were performing due diligence on Hollinger financial dealings,
in which Thompson allegedly said approvals were obtained and disclosed. "I want to be absolutely clear," Black concluded. "I fully

support a thorough, fair and complete airing of the facts relating to all of the questions that have been raised."

That day, Black wrote to David Barclay: "My lawsuits will begin tomorrow. The most important early test will be our challenge of the outrage with the SEC in Chicago. Counsel say our prospects are good. In any case, we will prevail eventually, and indications are the opposition is very flustered and befuddled about what to do. They have called a directors meeting for Tuesday morning and I will do some canvassing beforehand and keep you abreast of events."

Barclay wrote back the next day: "This is a done deal, there is no going back, and we are in for the long term. I hope you issued proceedings today – it is a conspiracy to defraud you out of your right to sell and get maximum value for your shares. It is vindictive and malicious."

The full Hollinger board met on January 20 to ratify the changes made by the executive committee. In addition to approving the filing of the lawsuit and Black's firing as chairman – an episode that included the dramatic *"Et tu, Brute"* exchange between Black and Henry Kissinger* – the meeting created a new corporate review committee, which would theoretically consider the Barclay deal on behalf of minority shareholders. The full board then adopted a resolution expanding the powers of the special committee to include, among other things, more power to launch legal actions and to co-operate with the agencies investigating the company, which had come to include the FBI as well as the SEC. Black and Amiel voted against everything, but it was clear that he was no longer in command.

Toward the end of the meeting, Kissinger also called for Breeden, on behalf of the special committee, to respond to Black's three-page letter to the board. Breeden said he didn't intend to present a highly detailed or complete recitation of facts discovered by the special

---

* Black later said, "In fairness to Henry, he does not profess to be particularly commercially knowledgeable and he . . . gave a statement of his great friendship in regard to me, which I was grateful to hear. And that was a very agreeable note to interrupt our long relationship, which will no doubt resume at some point."

committee in response to Black's letter, but he went on at length nonetheless. He noted that there was "no new evidence here" – rather, Black was providing new arguments and rationalizations regarding the meaning of documents that had already been reviewed by the special committee. Most of the documents purportedly showing that the US$32 million had been approved were already covered in Black's letter from November 10, 2003, he added.

Each of these payments, Breeden reiterated, had never been "explicitly reviewed" by the board or by the audit committee – "there were no minutes, no resolution, no evidence of any corporate action justifying the payments," half of which had been paid to executives and half to Inc. Breeden also pointed out that the US$15.6 million in payments to Black, Radler, and the other individuals were not disclosed in any of the men's January 2001 directors' and officers' compensation questionnaire, a standard part of preparing annual securities filings.

The former SEC chairman (who knew a thing or two about such filings) went on to say that Hollinger's 10-K annual information form filed in 2002 did refer to the US$15.6 million in payments made to the individuals but never disclosed the other US$15.6 million paid to Inc. Moreover, he said the disclosure was inaccurate because it referred to the payments as having being required by third parties as a closing condition of newspaper sales. He did make clear, however, that the special committee had not reached a judgment on whether Black actually knew of these inaccuracies. Breeden summed up by saying, "Disclosure cannot make something that did not happen something real."

Black asked if he could respond, and Paris agreed. On the "no new evidence" point, Black said, "It might not be new to you but it is new to me," and he said Breeden's claim that the evidence was "overwhelmingly clear" was not accurate. He maintained that O'Melveny & Myers, the counsel to the special committee, had withheld documents from him. He also repeated his contention that the special committee and the audit committee were operating jointly – which effectively meant that a cabal of Hollinger's independent directors were protecting themselves from shareholder litigation by blaming Black.

Railing against the "endless campaign to defame" him, he charged that members of Hollinger's management and staff of the special committee were releasing damaging information to the public and "endlessly harping about backdated documents et cetera." Despite this, Black said, the special committee had never offered "one single shred of evidence that I knew" about the lack of authorization for the non-compete payments. "Obviously I could have done things better," he admitted, but why wasn't anyone taking the audit committee to task for the fact that it too had signed off on an inaccurate 10-K?

Black finished by noting that he did not know whether he would ultimately be found to have committed an honest error, negligence, or some kind of malice, but he knew that all of the actions the board was taking were "mendacious" and being taken to destroy his reputation, financial position, and occupation, and to legally harass him. He would not stand for it.

Chapter Thirty-Two

THE LAST GREAT WAR

At various times the Barclays had talked about launching a bid for Hollinger International as well as Hollinger Inc., and Black now suggested that they do so sooner rather than later. On January 22, Black spoke to Sir Frederick Barclay, who had begun handling some of the talks with Black because his brother had fallen ill. In his "daily night-letter" to the brothers, Black wrote that he expected to halt the Lazard Freres auction of Hollinger assets, "but we don't know what they will try next. These are treacherous people.

"If you are considering bidding for all the stock, I urge you to do so. You could sell the other assets for enough to take out the minority: we could save you on the capital gains taxes payable, and you could get the Telegraph at a bargain price, and private. Not that you need us but we would be happy to come back in for $100–$150 million. This would end this drama."

David Barclay wrote back the following day that he and his brother were now considering an offer to all shareholders the following week. "We will be able to keep to our agreement," he wrote. "Thank you for your offer to come in with us, but we have the financial capability on our own."

Black replied that if the Barclays did make a bid for all of Hollinger, "it will be a great deal and a glorious victory over truly wicked people." In a separate note, he wrote to David, "I forgot to mention, you may want to call Bruce Wasserstein and tell him he would do a whole lot better waiting for your next deal than trying to sabotage anything."

The Barclays may have wanted to stay out of the feud between Black and his own company, but now they were in it with both feet. Aidan Barclay observed in a memo to his father that "the board's priority is to deprive Lord Black of the sale of his assets, not because it is in the interests of Hollinger International, but it appears to me out of some malicious response. However, in preventing Lord Black of disposing of his shares to us, they deprive us of lost opportunities."

Having moved into full military mode, Black sent the Barclays a copy of "the enemy's pathetic press release," in which Hollinger said its corporate review committee had met to consider the implications of the Barclay offer and to begin putting in motion a poison pill shareholder rights plan that would block the deal – just as the Barclays had feared. But Black was ready for this. Shortly after their meeting adjourned, the directors received notice that Inc. had executed a written consent changing Hollinger's bylaws. The SEC judgment barred him from interfering with the special committee probe, but the bylaw changes were aimed instead at the corporate review committee. The new bylaws would require, among other things, that a poison pill or sale of any significant company asset would require unanimous approval of all directors – including Black – at a meeting at which every director was present. In effect, Black was finally flexing his muscles as controlling shareholder to quash the poison pill and take over the Lazard sale process. Black's daily letter to the Barclays suggested the writer was even more fervid than usual.

"We caught them with their pants down, preparing more skull-duggery," he wrote. "They may have abandoned the Lazard fire sale nonsense. The New York press is finally on their backs. Counsel think we can already stop a poison pill with what we did today. They were going to do another Saturday night special. If we need to do more, we will. Obviously, the SEC won't bail them out this time."

Black was feeling so optimistic he again offered to buy some assets from the Barclays once they had acquired all of Hollinger. But after a phone call between Frederick Barclay and Bruce Wasserstein in which

Frederick said his family might be willing to consider a bid for US$18 a share and Wasserstein tried to bid them up, the Barclays decided the price was too rich and backed away for the time being, even after Lazard tried to pair them with Blackstone, a New York buyout firm.

Meanwhile, in addition to suing to try to reverse the SEC action, Black followed up on his earlier threat by launching a $646 million defamation suit against Breeden and the members of the special and audit committees: Seitz, Savage, Paris, Thompson, and Burt. This lawsuit, prepared by his long-time friend the prominent Canadian lawyer Eddie Greenspan, was as overwrought as anything Black had ever said or written. Breeden and the other insurgents, Black's defamation suit said, intended to enrich themselves at the expense of Hollinger International and Black; to destroy Hollinger Inc.; to divert attention from their own conduct while they were on the board; to make an example of Black to improve their own financial opportunities; and to bankrupt him. "The defendants were fully aware of their wrongdoing," the suit charged, and knew for months that their allegations that the non-compete payments were not authorized by Hollinger's board "were simply vicious vaporings and a vile tissue of lies."

As a result of their campaign against him, media reports of the committee's actions (several of which were attached as exhibits) had brought Black, the lawsuit claimed, "into hatred, ridicule, and contempt . . . Black would be pilloried and mocked mercilessly in the media throughout the world . . . socially, Black would be spurned and shunned by persons who had personally accepted his hospitality in London, New York and Palm Beach . . . Black would be compared falsely in the international media with white-collar criminals and with individuals who were charged with white collar crimes . . . Black would be transformed from a successful, well-respected businessman, the owner of an international chain of newspapers, into a social leper and a man whose reputation would be destroyed . . . he would become a symbol of corporate greed and misfeasance . . . their conduct would ignite a firestorm of international media vilification and defamation throughout the world against Black . . . they would create an atmosphere and a climate where the Black [sic] could be and would be mocked and reviled with impunity and without any restraint by the media throughout the world." And so on.

Long before Black's reputation could be defended in a Toronto court, the outcome of his months-long effort to sell Inc. finally came to a head in the court that is the modern-day corporate version of the Colosseum. On January 25, Hollinger International adopted the poison pill to stop the Barclay deal. It then sued in Delaware Chancery Court to block the bylaw changes by Inc. and to uphold the validity of the pill. Black quickly countersued. There were now a half-dozen legal actions underway involving Black and Hollinger, but this one was pivotal to the outcome of all of the others, as it would settle who was truly in control of Hollinger: Black or the board.

Under Delaware law, court cases are expedited when pressing matters – like a takeover bid – demand swift resolution. It's the legal equivalent of speed chess. Both sides put together scads of evidence and voluminous pretrial briefs for the judge to consider; then a limited number of trial days for witnesses are held. Black would have his day in court on the final day of a three-day hearing set to begin on February 18, although he was privately hoping that his show of force would lead to the global settlement that Warden was still pushing for. On January 28, he wrote to the Barclays: "We are now organizing the pre-trial and trial in Delaware, and much looking forward to it. There was almost violence between some of our lawyers over who would have the pleasure of questioning Breeden, Paris, and Thompson. They have been so sleazy and dishonest throughout the process, we will give them a real sleigh-ride. I only have to tell the truth and I have a reasonable grasp of the facts. I am looking forward to finally getting my story out. If they go to trial, they are making a serious mistake."

The case landed in the docket of Vice-Chancellor Leo E. Strine Jr. One of five jurists on the Chancery Court, Strine, at forty, was its youngest. Known for his oddball humour and casual approach as well as his lengthy written rulings, Strine had established himself as a staunch proponent of shareholder rights since being appointed to the court in 1998. When he wasn't presiding over multi-billion-dollar disputes, Strine still adjudicated smaller non-business matters, including one involving neighbours unhappy about a barking dog. ("Prinz eventually ran out of chances and had to move out of the neighborhood," he ruled.)

Black flew to Wilmington, Delaware, and set up camp in the Hotel du Pont, where he remained for the first two days of the trial. His wife was not among his entourage, which included Peter White and a battalion of legal advisers from three of the top law firms in America. Depositions had taken place in a flurry, with Black giving his own on the previous Friday over eight hours at the New York offices of Hollinger's law firm Paul, Weiss, Rifkind, Wharton & Garrison. Lawyers from both sides fanned out around the world to depose everyone from Thompson (Chicago) to Aidan Barclay (London) to Kissinger (then in Lyford Cay, Bahamas). Black was deposed by Hollinger's lead counsel in the case, Martin Flumenbaum. Bronx-born and educated at Harvard Law School, the squat, wide-faced, bespectacled litigator had honed his pit-bull approach as a U.S. attorney in the Southern District of New York.

The Chancery Court is housed in an unremarkable modern concrete and steel municipal building in downtown Wilmington; its business is business, which does not lend itself to the kinds of soaring wooden auditoriums full of rows of spectators that you see in John Grisham movies. Strine had ruled in some high-profile cases involving such companies as Healthsouth and Oracle, and he seemed bemused by the flotilla of international journalists who descended on his courtroom for a company of Hollinger's relatively small size; his room could accommodate only twenty or so spectators, so the court installed a closed-circuit feed to the courtroom next door to house the large overflow.

In Delaware Chancery Court, there are no opening or closing arguments; instead there are extensive written briefs full of cross-references to evidence, depositions, and case law, which are submitted to the judge both before and after the trial. Trial time is devoted to witness testimony and cross-examination. The briefs in the Hollinger vs. Hollinger (International vs. Inc.) imbroglio described the dispute from the starkly different angles that had defined relations between Black and his estranged directors for months. Hollinger International's case contended that Black had breached both his fiduciary duties and his contractual obligations under the November restructuring agreement by secretly dealing with the Barclays, and thus the poison pill was needed to stop the sale of Inc. and to let the Lazard process continue for the benefit of all Hollinger stockholders. Black's brief framed the argument around his and Inc.'s rights as Hollinger's indisputable controlling shareholder and Hollinger's repeated breaches of the same November agreement, which contributed to Inc.'s financial woes and to the need for the Barclay deal to solve its "liquidity" issues.

There are few grand hotels and fine dining options in Wilmington, a city of 70,000, so it was not surprising that the main players in the court drama found themselves congregated the night before Black's day in court in the main dining room at the Hotel du Pont. Black sat with his back against a wood-panelled wall, dining with three of his lawyers. In a nearby corner were Breeden, Paris, and several associates. Diagonally across the room from the Breeden table, Herbert Denton, the shareholder activist and adviser to Hollinger shareholders, was eating with Charles M. Elson, a governance expert and professor at the University of Delaware.

Taking it all in from his own table was Jacques Steinberg, a reporter from the *New York Times* who was covering the trial and dining with Hollinger's publicists from Kekst & Co. As Steinberg recounted, a member of the Breeden party breezed by and said, "Stand by." Soon after, a lawyer working with Breeden, holding a sheaf of papers behind his back, waltzed over to Black and served him with a copy of the US$200 million lawsuit the special committee had filed a month earlier. One of Black's lawyers briefly examined the papers and then made a show of dropping them dismissively on the floor beside the table.

The next morning, Black dressed in a navy suit, a light-blue shirt, and a tie of diagonal silver, red, and blue stripes that, set against his nearly white hair and pale skin, made him look as distinguished and lordly as could be. Although the case was scheduled to begin at 9:30 a.m., reporters had been lining up since seven because of the limited seating in Strine's eleventh-floor courtroom, and Black was enveloped by camera crews as he strolled into the court in a topcoat. "I'm here to be interviewed by the judiciary today, not the media," Black said quietly, keeping his narrow gaze focused ahead. This was no longer a flame-out he could get used to.

Because the doors to Strine's court had not yet been opened, Black came off the elevator with his retinue and drifted down the corridor past the line of fifty-odd waiting reporters. Normally, Lord Black would look over such a crowd, sizing up friend and foe, but this morning he kept his eyes focused ahead, a dour look frozen on his face. As he neared the entrance to the court, he silently walked by Seitz and Paris. "Morning, Conrad," Seitz said. Still looking straight ahead, Black replied, "Raymond."

Heading into the third and final day of the trial, it was impossible to predict the outcome of the case. Certainly the Hollinger witnesses who came before Black had got their licks in. Of all his opponents, Ray Seitz was the most credible because of his reputation, the fact that his friend Black had personally asked him the previous summer to join the special committee, and the fact that he would much rather have been sitting on his porch in South Carolina with his wife.

Black could argue to the court that the game of Paris, as CEO, and Breeden, as outside counsel, was self-enrichment, but the US$5,000 per week that Seitz received just for sitting on the special committee was not much of a jackpot. "Conrad does have this habit, when he gets in trouble, of reaching for whatever tools of intimidation he can find," Seitz said later. "And that serves to then alienate whoever is the subject of it. Right through the November negotiations, I had absolutely no interest at all in hanging Conrad out to dry or breaking Conrad's back. None at all. These things were wrong and they needed to be righted – simple as that. I would have been very supportive of any amicable resolution. Suddenly, a few weeks later it's a libel suit in Ontario; I'm getting served by gumshoes at home and told my personal property is in jeopardy. Conrad reaches too early for the nuclear option. And when Conrad reaches for the nuclear action, you react."

On the witness stand, Seitz was asked what he thought of the letter Black sent to the board the day the Barclay deal had been announced, repudiating the November agreement. "I had a feeling that this was a bit like the invasion of Czechoslovakia, and that I was in the unhappy role of Neville Chamberlain," Seitz replied, "because we had a perfectly good-faith agreement in November, and I had expected that would be adhered to."

Breeden had the press scribbling madly when he recounted Black's attempts to bully the Hollinger board. "Mr. Black begins many conversations by threatening everybody – or at least many of the conversations I've been involved with," Breeden testified. "I've heard him on many occasions . . . casually beginning the meeting, or somewhere during the meeting, suggesting that he was going to sue every independent member of the board if they didn't go along with what he wanted." During cross-examination, Inc.'s lawyer Gregory Joseph asked Breeden if he was aware of any other case where there had been so much legal process and regulatory attention, yet no convictions or indictments had been brought against the people involved. "No indictments, *yet*," Breeden replied. This prompted an angry reaction from Joseph, who demanded to know whether he was suggesting in front of dozens of reporters that indictments were coming. "That hasn't happened yet, but I have no way of knowing if it will or will not happen in the future," Breeden replied.

Meanwhile, Strine, with his boyish face, balding pate, and round glasses, leaned back in his swivel chair, delivering occasional zingers, some of them playfully at the expense of the officious court reporter, Ms. Flinn. "I have a standing rule on approaching," he told one lawyer who asked if he could come to the bench to give the judge a document. "You can approach until you become threatening, in which case Ms. Flinn is trained and authorized to use deadly force." At another point the video feed to the other courtroom full of reporters blinked out. "We are trying to get back on live in the other room, but our IT staff had Tivo'd Janet Jackson's half-time perform-ance" – a reference to the previous month's Super Bowl. "In lieu of the trial, we have shown that. It was, of course, shockingly inconsis-tent with the preceding numbers in the show, which were all, as you recall, Disney characters."

In their pretrial brief, Black's lawyers had argued that he had been duped and coerced into signing the November restructuring agreement. This resulted in Gordon Paris testifying about the dinner Black and Breeden had had at Le Cirque after their initial meeting. Strine found this particularly amusing. "It seems to me that one might well, at the end of a multi-course dinner – if there was wine at each course – be susceptible to coercion or any number of really fun things."

The final day was devoted to Black and Inc., but before Black took the stand, Inc.'s counsel called Peter White as a witness to testify to the failing financial condition of Inc., showing that Hollinger's deal with the Barclays was necessary to ward off pending financial disaster. To say it did not go well would be generous to White, whom one Hollinger director sitting in the wings described as giving a performance "like a third-rate sitcom actor." On the stand, White said that the company had US$4 million in cash, was spending US$1.3 million to US$1.5 million per month, and had a US$7.4 million interest payment due on March 1. White went on to explain that Inc. relied on funding from Ravelston under their "support agreement," and that nearly all of the shares in Hollinger that were owned by Inc. were pledged as collateral for Inc.'s bonds, and therefore the company could not simply sell some of its shares in the U.S. subsidiary to raise money. When Hollinger stopped paying Ravelston the management fee, the spigot to Inc. had been turned off too.

But under cross-examination from Flumenbaum, White described Ravelston as having roughly $500 million in assets and little debt. Although the vast majority of those assets were its Inc. stock, Flumenbaum ran though a range of steps Inc. could take to make its looming interest payment, including simply selling shares that secured loans to Black and Radler that were worth some US$7 million. Strine didn't ask questions himself very often, but when he did they tended to be pointed. "Is it your testimony that you have to sell the whole company to make a US$7.4 million interest payment?" Strine asked. White replied that in addition to the interest payment, Inc. had a series of preferred shares coming up for redemption at a cost of as much as US$100 million, and then another interest payment in September, so the troubles extended far beyond making the next payment. Flumenbaum pressed him on whether Inc. was obliged to pay the US$100 million right away (it wasn't) and succeeded in blowing holes in White's testimony. "I'm not an accountant. All I know is we don't have the money, we're broke," insisted White. "If that means yes we are insolvent, then I guess we're insolvent."

During a break, an intrepid *Toronto Star* reporter followed Black into the men's room with hopes of getting a comment but was stopped by the sight of Black being handed a writ by another process server, this one for a class action from the Louisiana Teachers' Pension Fund.

Black eased his frame onto the witness stand in mid-morning. His lawyers had counselled him to tone down his bombast before Strine, and he came across as more subdued than usual.* In private, Black may have convinced himself and the Barclays that he would wipe the floor with Hollinger's independent directors in court, but his demeanour now was that of a man in a jam. What he perhaps had not anticipated was the degree to which his character, rather than his corporate behaviour, would be on trial.

At one point early in his testimony, Black turned to Strine and asked plaintively, "Could I add one sentence, sir?"

"Sure."

"In consequence of the controversy that's arisen over these payments, I have been horribly defamed. In fact, I've been characterized and stigmatized as an embezzler," Black said. "I am trying, apart from the direct legal proceedings, to retrieve my reputation as an honest man."

Black cast Breeden as the villain, saying that he thought both sides were working toward some kind of settlement only to be hit over the January 16–18 weekend with the double whammy of the SEC action and the lawsuit against him. He only finalized the deal with the

---

* Black's sense of humour was still intact. At one point, as he ran through the chronology of events, Black testified about how James Thompson had "terminated" the company aircraft in November, "which I thought was an ambiguous use of terms." "So you have no reason to believe it was actually destroyed as an operable airplane?" Strine deadpanned. "I feared the worst," replied Black, "but no."

Barclays, Black testified, after his proposal that Hollinger buy Inc., "in which I invested great hope and original thinking, if I may say so, was clearly rejected. If I may expatiate one phrase, Chancellor," Black went on, his deep baritone slightly quaking, "I found it very disappointing to read testimony in deposition by directors comparing my offer to the antics of the Nazi government of Germany prior to the occupation of Bohemia in 1938."*

Black's testimony foundered once Flumenbaum swung like a dervish into his cross-examination. Flumenbaum attacked Black over his testimony that he did "not necessarily believe" that Hollinger International's financial disclosures under his watch had inaccurately reflected the US$32 million in payments. "Each filing is a federal offence if it's false – do you understand that?" Flumenbaum asked. "Of course," Black replied, adding that all the directors signed off on the statements.

When grilled on the non-competes, Black contended that he had an "open mind" about whether the money should be paid back but that he still wasn't convinced he had done anything wrong because he and his lawyers had not been able to review many key documents that the special committee had. When Flumenbaum jabbed away on the specifics behind the payments and the cheques he received, Black several times replied, "I'm not sure." In response to one question he said he wasn't sure whether he had received a certain cheque for $2.6 million because it was sent to his office in Toronto in February and he was not normally in Toronto at that time of year. "Isn't it a fact that you signed a non-compete with a subsidiary of Hollinger International?" Flumenbaum asked. "At one point I did, yes," Black replied. Here Black was basically admitting that he had agreed not to compete with himself, but he stuck to his view that this was the result of bad paperwork rather than intent to deceive anyone.

Black adopted the unusual stance that he didn't know how millions of dollars had found their way into his bank account without

---

* Seitz had quite deliberately made the Neville Chamberlain comment in court two days earlier, and his fellow former ambassador Richard Burt had also said it in his deposition.

approval, but he would spend the rest of his days trying to hunt down the perpetrators. In one tense exchange, Flumenbaum zeroed in on the US$15.6 million payment made in February 2001 that was backdated to December 2000 along with a non-compete agreement. Did Black know he had signed a backdated document? Without saying yes or no, Black replied windily that he knew that the money was paid to himself, Radler, and others and was related to the sale of American community newspapers but "the details beneath that" were "altogether secondary to the fact" that the sales had "generated a capital gain for the company of over US$90 million."

"You feel entitled to that money, don't you?"

"My understanding is that it was authorized," Black replied. "If you can shed any light, *Mister Flooomenbaum* [by now, Black had begun stretching out every syllable of his questioner's name in a condescending tone], on who would have backdated these cheques and for what reason, we would all be very grateful to you."

"Well, might it be possible that someone wanted those cheques to be a lot closer to the transactions that you were going to claim they were non-competes for, when there was no documentation for that? Is that a possibility?"

"No, I don't think so."

"No?"

"That implies something underhanded that I think is beneath the behaviour of any individual who would have the executive authority to do such a thing."

As the afternoon wore on, Black's eyes closed and he waved his big fingers around as he strained to find the right words to answer some of the questions. Visibly annoyed, Flumenbaum waved back at him. At moments, Black's voice became a hush. "Mr. Black, could you move the microphone close to you?" asked Strine. "It's late in the day and I understand people tend to drop their voice when they really want to take a nap, like I probably could do at this point."

The case concluded in a dramatic flourish, with Flumenbaum asking if it was correct that Black had said that critics of his policies were "a bunch of self-righteous hypocrites and ingrates."

"No, only certain of them," replied Black.

"Only certain of them?"

"Stock has risen 140 per cent since then, *Missster Flooomenbaum*."

"Does that give you the right to steal other people's money?"

"Objection!" One of Black's lawyers jumped up.

"Overruled," Strine called from the bench.

"The answer," Black said evenly, "is no."

"I have no further questions, your Honour."

As the lawyers gathered their papers, Black walked over to Flumenbaum, smiled for the first time all day, and said a few words to him, looking like a deposed heavyweight who wanted to let the kid who had just belted him into retirement know that he had thrown a lucky punch. Black put on his topcoat, walked out stonily past the TV cameras and reporters, got into a waiting Mercedes sedan, and was whisked away.

Judge Strine told the lawyers he would await final briefs from both sides over the weekend and take a week to write his ruling, releasing it by 5:00 p.m. the following Friday, February 27. Despite going to a conference in New Orleans in the middle of that week, Strine composed and delivered a devastatingly eloquent 130-page document a full day ahead of schedule. The judgment began: "The most interesting corporate law cases involve the colour gray, with contending parties dueling over close questions of law in circumstances where it is possible for each of the contestants to claim she was acting in good faith. Regrettably, this case is not one of that variety.

"Rather, in this case, defendant Conrad M. Black, the ultimate controlling stockholder of Hollinger International, a Delaware public company, has repeatedly behaved in a manner inconsistent with the duty of loyalty he owed to the company."

It only got bleaker for Black from here. Argument by argument, Strine cut through Black's assertions like a Japanese chef going through a pile of vegetables. He found Black's arguments in court were "unpersuasive" and "strain credulity"; his efforts to sell Inc. to the Barclay brothers behind Hollinger's back were "cunning and calculated"; his claim that he had been duped into signing the November agreement under false pretenses unconvincing, coercion at Le Cirque notwithstanding. "Black – an assertive and experienced businessman advised by his managerial subordinates, and his distinguished attorneys – did not lack the free will to sign a contract," wrote Strine. "His arguments to the contrary are frivolous."

Admitting that it was "no small thing to strike down bylaw amendments adopted by a controlling stockholder" (not to mention one from a foreign country), Strine blocked the proposed Inc. bylaw changes, allowed the poison pill to go ahead, and killed the Barclay deal on the spot.

He also ordered that Black repay the US$7 million he owed with interest and laid waste to the reputation Black said he wanted to retrieve. "Having had a three-day evidentiary hearing, I am in a good position to make certain credibility determinations and have done so. Generally, I found the key [Hollinger] International witnesses entirely credible," he wrote of Paris, Seitz, and Breeden. "As to Black himself, it became impossible for me to credit his word. On more debatable points, I found Black evasive and unreliable. His explanations of key events and of his own motivations do not have the ring of truth. I find it regrettable to say so but it is the inescapable, and highly relevant, conclusion I reach."

At trial, Black's side had tried to show that the minutes from a December 4, 2000, board meeting showed that Hollinger's executive committee had signed "consents" approving the payments in dispute stemming from the 1999 sale of community newspapers and the board had ratified them. "I like to think I am a close reader," said Strine, but he called the documents presented for board approval "a pile of legalese. They hardly put one on notice of what is contemplated, and surely do not purport to approve the specific terms of any non-competes" to be paid to Black, Inc., or the others. By his reading of the December 4, 2000, minutes, "the International board appears to have been told they were ratifying asset sales. There is no indication that there was any discussion of non-competes by the board or that the word even came up at the board." Moreover, that meeting predated the payments made to Black and his confreres in February 2001 that had been backdated to December 2000. "If anything, the December 2000 board minutes are suggestive of what, in the old days, might have been called constructive fraud," wrote Strine. "At worst, the [Hollinger] board was purposely duped and there was fraud on the board. At best, they were entirely uninformed."

Strine had equally harsh words for Black's fax to David Barclay suggesting the "outrageous strategy whereby" he tell Wasserstein to wait for the next deal and not try to sabotage an Inc. sale. "The same day he wanted the Barclays to convince Lazard to pull a Benedict Arnold," noted Strine, Black issued through Inc. his order to alter Hollinger International's bylaws.*

Black was in New York when he received word of Strine's ruling. The next day, the phone rang, and he picked it up. It was a reporter from the *Sunday Times* looking for a comment. "I understand the endless fascination with my downfall," Black told him. "Do what you want, I don't really care. I want to get to the relaunch of my life and will have nothing more to say to the press. I assume the sadistic fascination with my life will eventually come to an end." Then he hung up.

Although she had not been at his side in court, Barbara Amiel did have something to say. The week after Strine's ruling, Martha Stewart was convicted of obstructing justice in a peculiar case that revolved around her sale of some shares in the drug company Imclone in late 2001 that had netted her a mere US$51,000 profit. As a result, the billion-dollar company she had built faced potential ruin, her own personal fortune was greatly diminished, and she faced time behind bars for lying to investigators over a crime she was never charged with (insider trading). Amiel wrote in her *Daily Telegraph* column that Stewart "fell victim to the tall poppy syndrome sweeping the business world of the United States. America is a splendid country determined to better itself – sometimes by overkill. Corporate scandals have created an atmosphere where all public companies are potential wearers of the scarlet letter. Any hint of wrongdoing gets the elders out, solemn and judgmental." Without any mention of her personal

---

* Benedict Arnold was an interesting choice of metaphor, given that he was a turncoat in the United States but a hero in the United Kingdom.

knowledge of such matters, she concluded grimly: "Revolution has been sweeping the boardrooms of corporate America and the Terror is well under way."*

Black was encouraged by his lawyers, who told him he had mostly had the raw luck of coming before Strine. He announced through Inc. that he "respectfully disagreed" with Strine's ruling, and then filed an appeal, even while pledging (again) to support the Lazard sale process for Hollinger and its assets, which was now underway in earnest. Even though he had been fired, sued, and labelled a cheat and a liar by one of the most revered courts in America, Black remained adamant he'd done nothing wrong and continued to angle for a way to come out on top. "Hitler in his bunker was moving around paper armies and talking about making a comeback," noted one-time Argus director Hal Jackman.

Meanwhile, the two Hollingers showed no signs of impending reconciliation. Inc. reclaimed the Web domain Hollinger.com (prompting Hollinger to switch to HollingerIntl.com), and more lawsuits were filed by Black over income and the proceeds from stock options he claimed Hollinger owed him. (The company "impounded" for safe-keeping the US$1.6 million cheque he had sent to Chicago to exercise his options. Later, it claimed a large chunk of his options had "expired" as a result of his removal as chairman of the Telegraph Group.) Hollinger even moved some employees who were on its payroll and not Ravelston's out of 10 Toronto Street to 20 Toronto Street. The Blacks changed their e-mail addresses.

When Black asked Hollinger to pay the New York Public Library at least half of the US$100,000 he had pledged for co-chairing the Literary Lions benefit the previous year, the company refused. At the Metropolitan Opera, the bronze plaque bearing the names "Lord and Lady Black" was taken down and replaced with one engraved with just "Hollinger International, Inc."

---

* On the rare occasions when the Blacks had attended Hollinger board meetings in person since November, Amiel would deliver piercing stares at Gordon Paris and Graham Savage. "If looks could kill," said Savage, "I'd be a dead man."

Black continued to go out among the great and the good. For instance, on March 20, Black attended the sixty-fifth-birthday party for Brian Mulroney in Palm Beach, but not before calling Mulroney first to tell him Barbara couldn't make it and asking if it was okay if he came solo. Mulroney sat him next to the mayor of Palm Beach. Three weeks later, he went to Donald Trump's Palm Beach house, Mar-a-Lago, where what Trump called "an intimate Easter dinner of approximately 590 people" was served. "I think a lot of his friends have abandoned him," said Trump. "If he gets through everything and if it all works out, he'll be able to do something with respect to those so-called friends."

Friends who were still in touch noticed that in the few weeks after Strine's decision, Barbara and Conrad seemed to be spending more time apart than at any point in their twelve years of marriage. "Barbara could not face that crowd" at the Mulroneys, one said. "Conrad is oblivious." "Emotionally it is very difficult for her," Amiel's friend Krystyne Griffin said. "Everyone has dumped them." Barbara was spending more time in London and even made the scene at a couple of parties there in the Blacks' refurbished Rolls-Royce, yet her husband made no effort to rejoin her. "I said when I left London in mid-October that I would not return until the problems, which in one form or another, had been relentless since the start of the price war in 1993, had been resolved," Black said later. "They are not yet resolved. When they are, I will return there."

In the midst of the brouhaha the *Telegraph* had narrowly averted a strike and labour relations were only inflamed by the Hollinger revelations. Martin Newland, the *Daily Telegraph* editor, had tried to make the point to staff that whatever else he had done, Black had rescued the two papers from near-bankruptcy and served them well over the years. But by now many jaded employees viewed the Blacks as the spivs who siphoned away their pay raises.

The salon set in London looked on the Blacks' predicament with wry amusement and a bit of shock but acknowledged that, with the exception of Lord Weidenfeld, none of the Blacks' U.K. circle had been dragged into the mire of Hollinger's legal problems. At gatherings where Lady Thatcher or Lord Carrington might be found, talk of the Blacks led to a prevailing "folie à deux" theory in which the grand couple had fuelled each other's vices and become just too grand. While few doubted that Black had behaved greedily or high-handedly, no one could say whether he had done anything illegal; still, few were rallying to his defence. Among those who did was Dominic Lawson, the *Sunday Telegraph* editor. "What I have found truly disgusting," he said, "is the way in which in recent weeks many of those who enjoyed the Blacks' extraordinary hospitality have been cackling with glee and scorn at the revelations of corporate excess which have brought about their downfall. They are the very same people who drank the shareholders' champagne and swallowed the shareholders' caviar at the Blacks' Kensington home. Still, Conrad has a profoundly realistic appreciation of human nature. I don't think he will be surprised."

If the Canadian press was filled with *schadenfreude* about the Blacks' plight, the British media was almost gleeful in its coverage of the fall of Lord and Lady Black. In Hollinger's own *Spectator*, editor Boris Johnson published the cover story "The Legend of Connie and Babs," a devastating account of how the Blacks' social-climbing aspirations in the U.S. had done them in. "A few weeks ago executives were endeavouring to bring home to Conrad Black the full horror of his personal and corporate predicament, when a sight met their eyes," the piece by Peter Oborne began. "His wife Barbara, clad only in a leotard and shades, had swept into the room. For a moment nobody spoke. 'Oh Conrad', Barbara Black proclaimed: 'Let's just get out of here. They hate us.'"

Amiel wrote to the magazine and complained that she didn't own a leotard. Griffin had said the scandal left the couple distraught and Barbara physically frail, but she remained dedicated to her husband and convinced that he'd be vindicated. "Obviously he's done some very unwise things," Griffin commented. "It's very difficult for her because she loves him."

"I think there's a lot of rewriting of history and perversion of history to suggest he's nothing but a self-indulgent, self-important, pompous ass," Black's friend and lawyer Edward Greenspan said.* "I don't buy any of that. I don't see any of that. I think there's an incredible amount of depth with this guy."

If Canadians love to see the high and mighty fall and Fleet Street loves a scandal, New York society hates nothing so much as a poseur. One of the most damning assessments came from the *New York Observer*, the chattering-classes weekly that Black had tried and failed to buy. "Whereas the initial picture was of a narcissistic windbag with few qualms about doing business in an unscrupulous manner, the public portrait of Lord Black is progressing from 'sleazy' to potential crook," the *Observer* wrote in an unsigned editorial. "Indeed, it seems as if Lord Black woke up every morning thinking of some new way to rip off Hollinger shareholders."

While all this suggested that the Blacks had become social pariahs – indeed, Black himself had said as much in his defamation suit against Breeden and the Hollinger directors – this was not necessarily Black's read on the situation. "I don't feel as social as I once did, but I don't miss it and do not detect any lack of support from those whom I have considered friends," he said later. "There have been a few disappointments, but even more pleasant surprises. Like the theories that I was a crook, a broken man, a bankrupt, and that my wife was ditching me, the theory that I am an outcast is another product of the orgy of myth-making that has occurred."

For her part, Amiel, who resigned her post as Hollinger's vice-president of editorial after the Delaware decision, had prided herself on remaining a working journalist throughout her marriage. To her dismay, the *Telegraph* suspended her column in May after she was named as a defendant in the next bombshell to come from Breeden and the special committee – an amended complaint of the lawsuit filed in January in the U.S. District Court in the Northern District of Illinois. Now Hollinger was suing Black and his associates for US$380.6 million, plus US$103.9 million in interest, in a lawsuit bursting with

---

* Greenspan was a first-year Osgoode Hall Law School student with Black and liked to point out that the only two students who flunked out were Black and "the guy who invented Mr. Submarine." Greenspan had also known Amiel since high school.

damning new accusations. What's more, this time, the suit was modified to sue Black and others under the RICO law, which was originally designed for use against organized crime and drug kingpins and under which violators are subject to triple damages. RICO helped defeat some New York Mafia families in the 1980s, and then prosecutors used it against the junk bond king Michael Milken. Since then, RICO, a criminal statute, has often been used in civil actions.* Black's lawyer Warden called the racketeering charges "tabloid journalism masquerading as law."

The eye-catching RICO charge meant that Hollinger was now seeking a whopping total of US$1.25 billion from Black, Radler, Ravelston, Inc., and others – far more than their net worth. In addition to naming Jack Boultbee (but not Peter Atkinson, who settled with Hollinger and was set to become a key witness in the action against Black and the others), the suit now named Dan Colson and Amiel, and Horizon and Bradford, the two small private newspaper companies Radler and Black had helped create.

The charges in the revised Hollinger International complaint filed on May 7, none of which had been proven in court by the fall of 2004, portrayed Hollinger under Black, Radler, and their colleagues as an organization that they used for several years to bilk as much money as they could from public shareholders. The allegations fit broadly into several categories: non-compete fees like those received from the CanWest deal and other newspaper sales and totalling US$88 million; the Ravelston management fee, which totalled US$217 million from 1997 to 2003; abuse of fiduciary duties by using corporate assets like the jets, whose operation cost as much as US$6.5 million a year, for personal purposes;** and self-dealing on

---

* RICO stands for "Racketeer Influenced and Corrupt Organizations." It had also been included among the charges that Hanna Mining levelled against Black and Norcen in 1982.

** The Ravelston management services fee was alleged to have kept increasing, even after the sale of most of the company's North American papers, and until 2000 the cost of operating the jets had been covered under the services fee; since then the company had paid for it separately.

unfair terms to the company through Horizon and Bradford. The details amassed in the 175-page complaint were breathtaking in their scope and complexity. "If Hollinger was a cow, it would have sore udders indeed," said Herbert Denton, the adviser to Cardinal Capital Management and Tweedy Browne.

According to the suit, between 1997 and 2003 Black and the other defendants paid themselves nearly 72 per cent of the company's net income, totalling US$390 million. By contrast, during the same time the top five officers of the New York Times Co. and the Washington Post Co. (both of which are controlled through super-voting shares as Hollinger was) received 4.4 per cent of net income and 1.8 per cent of net income respectively. Where the management fee and his own take-home pay was concerned, Black was unrepentant. "My compensation level was modest for the value that has been, as recent stock price activity indicates, created," he said in the summer of 2004. "Most of the famous management fee went to sustain a large equity position. This has been much criticized, but much misunderstood; it was like stock options, except that we were borrowing to bet on the future upward movement of the stock."

The alleged depletion of Hollinger was accomplished, the lawsuit changed, through an astonishing array of techniques "in a manner evidencing complete disregard for the rights of all Hollinger shareholders." The biggest alleged misdeed was the payment of the Ravelston management fees to the "Black Group" that had been approved by Thompson and the audit committee. But the lawsuit also zeroed in on smaller items like the Blacks' use of the Hollinger Gulfstream to jet to Bora Bora; the fact that Black, Radler, and other Hollinger executives who were on the board paid themselves fees for attending directors' meetings that were customarily reserved for independent directors; US$900,000 and other "sham" broker fees "in amounts yet to be determined" that were sent without explanation to Moffat Management, a company owned by Black, Radler, and others in Barbados; the corporate purchase of the FDR papers for US$9 million at the time Black was writing his book; the Hollinger Digital bonus program; US$90,000 spent to refurbish the 1958 Rolls-Royce Silver Wraith owned by Ravelston and used by the Blacks in London;

and a tip (of an unrevealed amount) from Amiel to the doorman at the fancy clothier Bergdorf Goodman that she put through on her expense account.* The special committee estimated that US$1.4 million was paid toward the Blacks' personal staff in New York and London, including salaries for "chefs, senior butlers, butlers, under butlers, chauffeurs, housemen, footmen and security personnel." In addition to being paid for her columns at regular *Telegraph* rates, Amiel had also been paid some US$1.4 million over several years, plus millions in stock options, for "an executive position to which she devoted no meaningful time or effort."

The lawsuit's descriptions of the structure and intricacy of the way non-compete and other payments were extracted from the sales of Hollinger's community newspapers were eye-popping. To take just one of many examples, when the first group of Hollinger newspapers was sold to Horizon in March 1999 for US$43.7 million, US$5 million was allocated to a non-compete. But several months later, according to the suit, Radler had another US$1.2 million sent up to Inc. from Hollinger, a payment allegedly never approved by the company's independent directors.

In another accusation, the lawsuit claimed that Black and Radler arranged for Hollinger to sell two tiny papers in Washington State, the *Skagit Valley Argus* and the *Journal of the San Juan Islands*, to Horizon for US$1 "plus or minus a working capital adjustment," which meant that Hollinger actually paid Horizon US$150,000 to take the papers off its hands. Black and Radler "provided a slanted negative portrayal of the properties to the audit committee and board and hid the properties' true earning potential," the suit said. It claimed that the board wasn't told that a buyer was willing to pay US$750,000 just for the *Journal*, and in any case Horizon then flipped both papers eighteen months later for US$700,000. Radler disputed the allegations,

---

* Paul Healy told Richard Breeden he thought the attention-grabbing tip might be "gratuitous" next to some of the bigger allegations in the suit, to which Breeden replied, "Good pun!" Greenspan claimed the tip was for US$20 and the expense was filed not by Amiel, who knew nothing about it, but by the Blacks' driver, Gus, who tipped the doorman for allowing him to park on the curb.

noting, among other things, that "these papers were losing money at the time of their sale by Hollinger. By purchasing these papers, Horizon spared Hollinger further losses on their operations and the cost of shutting them down."

The founding of Horizon, as portrayed in the suit, was dubious from the outset – rather than a passive investment to back some former Hollinger executives, Radler and Black were in command. The suit claimed that when Horizon was created in 1998, Black and Radler each contributed US$1.5 million for a 24 per cent stake in the company and told the Hollinger board that they would be minority investors. In April 1999, Todd Vogt, a Hollinger executive in Chicago who had worked closely with Radler until recently, was installed as Horizon's president and CEO. The company operated out of the offices of the old American Publishing division in Marion, Illinois, renting from Hollinger. Vogt, who already owned about 6 per cent of Horizon, was allegedly designated as the registered holder of a further 25 per cent stake in Horizon that was "secretly" held by Radler through a separate company. Vogt could vote those shares only "as directed by" F.D. Radler Ltd. Yet in a 2002 wrongful dismissal lawsuit in the Supreme Court of British Columbia, Radler had testified that in 1999 he and Black owned 24 per cent each of Horizon and Vogt owned around 35 per cent. (Radler denied, after the Hollinger suit was filed, that he had misrepresented his ownership in Horizon.)

Regardless of who was in control, by 2003 Radler had become Horizon's president and as far as the special committee was concerned, it had bilked Hollinger in a series of deals.

Another transaction that was astonishing in its sheer contrivance involved the sale of four small Hollinger newspapers to Bradford, the other private company set up in 2000 by Radler, Black, and a former executive who worked for Radler. The sale price was US$37.6 million, but that allegedly reflected a falsely adjusted earnings figure for the company to achieve a lower price. Moreover, the lawsuit said, other buyers were willing to pay as much as $7.5 million more for the papers, although Hollinger's board wasn't told this. It went deeper still, with accusations that Black and Radler "caused" Hollinger to loan Bradford

US$6 million of the purchase price over ten years, interest-free – and couched it as a non-compete payment. This loan was apparently structured in such a way that only a fraction had been paid back.

One thing that was clear from the amended complaint was that it appeared to target Radler more closely – possibly to encourage him to settle with the company and aid it in its ultimate objective of battling Black. Unlike Black, Radler made no obvious effort to retrieve his reputation and gave the impression of someone who merely wanted to get the whole nightmare over with, spend time with his family, and go back to buying and selling newspapers. Similarly, the inclusion of Dan Colson in the lawsuit on some of its less sensational charges – receiving bonuses under the Hollinger Digital plan and receiving a US$1.3 million bonus because he wasn't among the recipients of the non-compete payments – was perceived at least partially as a legal tactic to keep him from coming to Black's defence. (Colson had resigned from Hollinger and the Telegraph Group in March after sparring incessantly with Paris.)

Through his spokesman, Radler said the amended complaint was "without merit." In order to "set the record straight on certain facts," Radler pointed out that the Ravelston management fee was fully disclosed and approved by the Hollinger audit committee and board, and that in 2001 KPMG had done an independent analysis of the fees and found them to be "not only appropriate but conservative." The CanWest fees were negotiated by Black but similarly approved by both the audit committee and the board. Where the Horizon transactions were concerned, Radler reiterated that the papers purchased by Horizon were ones that Hollinger had previously tried and failed to sell – and, as Black had, he pointed out that the sales of all Hollinger's community newspapers resulted in capital gains to the company of more than US$600 million. "The special committee has done everyone a service by finally making its allegations in court where they can and will be vigorously defended."

Like Black, Radler contended that he had done nothing wrong – he was a successful entrepreneur who had been run out of his own company and now faced a wall of lawsuits and possible civil or criminal charges from the SEC and the FBI. Whatever the two men had once thought the future held for them, it was clear that it was not supposed to be this.

It was an unusually warm spring day in a place from long ago, a place that he would never forget and that would never forget him. On the afternoon of Friday, May 28, 2004, Conrad Black was back in the auditorium at Upper Canada College, the school where, nearly forty-five years earlier, he had been caught trying to sell stolen exams to other students and had been expelled. Dressed in a light grey suit and silver tie, he arrived alone, without Barbara, to attend the graduation of James Black, his youngest son. Jonathan and Alana and their mother, Joanna, were also there, and Conrad sat with them for the ceremony. As part of the day's program, UCC was awarding an annual fellowship to a prominent Torontonian who had contributed to society. The recipient turned out to be Hal Jackman, the tall, distinguished financier who had backed Black's Argus takeover a quarter century earlier. Even though Jackman considered Black a friend, like many in the old Toronto establishment he hadn't actually spent time with Black in years. Nonetheless Jackman, more than anyone else from the old days that Black had seemed so determined to catapult beyond, had led the "I told you so" brigade, assailing Black in interviews for having "a death wish." As far as Jackman was concerned, Black was entertaining and brilliant but should have stuck to making speeches and writing books. Stepping down from the podium after accepting the fellowship, Jackman walked past the crowd, noticed Black, smiled, and said hello. Black nodded and said hello back. Jackman moved on.

As if on cue, Doug Blakey, the school's retiring principal, launched into his graduation address to the newest old boys of the elite private school. The subject was corporate greed and doing the right thing. He cited Enron and Worldcom and warned the boys of how easy it would be, as they became young men and joined the business world, to fall into the trap of doing things that were self-serving in a corporate sense and a personal sense. How easy it is, he noted, to gratify yourself and step across the ethical line and put a little extra money in your pocket.

How hard it is not to. "He kept citing these corporate greed examples," recalled another parent whose son was graduating. "I'm sure Conrad was squirming in his chair." Afterwards, the graduates and their parents congregated for drinks outside, standing around in family clusters on the student commons, which was adorned with blue and white balloons. Two years earlier, at an event like this, Lord Black of Crossharbour would have been swarmed by parents and students alike hoping for a word with him. Now people eyed him but kept their distance. Black looked unbothered and posed proudly for a photograph with his sons. Someone asked him if he wanted to have his picture taken with Hal Jackman. "Hardly," he said.

Epilogue

THE FALL OF 2004

On June 22, 2004, Hollinger International announced that it had struck a deal to sell the Telegraph Group, including the *Daily Telegraph*, the *Sunday Telegraph*, and the *Spectator* magazine, to the Barclay brothers' Press Holdings International for US$1.2 billion. For the time being, Hollinger would hold onto the *Chicago Sun-Times*, the *Jerusalem Post*, and remaining smaller newspapers, because complicated tax issues and the overhang of litigation at the company had prevented the investment banker Bruce Wasserstein and his Lazard Freres colleagues from producing a buyer for the whole business.

It might have been the end of the story, with Black's prized *Telegraph* wrested from his once-mighty clutch. But Black never stopped plotting a comeback. He saw the announcement of this new Barclay deal as an opening for a last-ditch plan to try to keep at least part of the Telegraph Group, get back in the saddle at Hollinger, and exact vengeance on the directors who had fired him. (At least, he could get back into a position where he could threaten such action and induce Hollinger to settle its massive racketeering lawsuit against him.) "The biggest mistake we can make now is to underestimate Conrad," said Raymond Seitz, the Hollinger director and special committee member. "I don't think he's sitting at home watching reruns. I think he will be very confident that he will land on his feet until his ankles are cut out from under him."

Indeed, under the auspices of Toronto-based Hollinger Inc., where he remained chairman and CEO, Black returned to the Delaware Chancery Court after Hollinger International's Barclay deal was announced to argue that under the state's laws, the sale of "substantially all" of a company's assets must be approved by shareholders – and Inc. still controlled 68 per cent of the American company's votes and 18 per cent of its equity.* It was highly ironic that Black was trying to block a deal to sell the *Telegraph* newspapers to the same buyer that this court had barred him from selling to. But while Black's thwarted Inc. deal with the Barclays would have put some US$300 million into his pocket, it was unclear that the Barclays' purchase of the Telegraph Group from Hollinger would lead to a penny making its way up the pyramid of Black's companies and into his personal coffers.

Vice-Chancellor Leo Strine Jr. had all but invited Black to return and argue the case – although between the lines of Strine's comments to Black and Hollinger was the message that they ought to try to settle their differences, which had led to a full-employment program for lawyers. The various manifestations of the dispute had cost Hollinger US$24 million over the past year, including US$7 million spent on the operations of the special committee alone in the second quarter of 2004.

Given the deep pools of bitterness between Black on the one hand and Breeden and the insurgent board on the other, there was no settlement forthcoming. And despite the legal pummelling he had taken, Black was encouraged that Strine's previous rulings – which prevented him from changing Hollinger's bylaws or firing its board – were extended only until the end of October 2004. He compared Hollinger's attempts to sell the *Telegraph* or its other assets to "chasing a dancing football."

---

* In May, Black reduced Inc.'s stake in Hollinger through a complex financing that staved off Inc.'s financial troubles but prompted yet another legal action, this one from a Canadian shareholder, Catalyst Fund General Partner I, which demanded in Ontario Superior Court that Inc.'s conduct be investigated.

Indeed, soon after the Delaware court blocked his deal with the Barclays, Black was again furiously trying to entice potential partners, such as Nelson Peltz's Triarc and the buyout group Cerberus, to join him in a bid to buy out Hollinger International, especially since what he called the "faltering" strategic process was not going to yield a bid for all the company's shares. Black figured that with a financial partner he could buy out Hollinger's public shareholders, sell half the Telegraph Group to the Barclays or Associated Newspapers to help fund the buyout, and be left with a promising private company based on half the *Telegraph* and all of the *Sun-Times* and its related Chicago-area papers. "This could be a rare opportunity," Black wrote to Peltz, "involving absolutely premier assets and clearly proven, fanatically motivated (after recent abrasions) management."

Black's rivals' retort to all his manoeuvring was that he was fooling himself and lacked the wherewithal, given his diminished reputation and the severity of the legal actions and investigations he was facing, to get a deal done.

In filing his new lawsuit in Delaware to earn the right to block the sale, Black took steps to improve his standing with the court. He finally paid back the US$30 million in non-compete fees and interest that Strine had ordered (although Black included the proviso that he was appealing the ruling and hoped to get the money back someday). He also granted to the two directors who now constituted Inc.'s audit committee sole authority over all litigation matters, as well as the sole power to decide whether to vote in favour of the Telegraph Group sale, should Inc. prevail in Delaware. The directors, Gordon Walker, a lawyer and long-time friend of Hollinger co-president Peter White, and retired general Richard Rohmer, "Canada's most decorated citizen," had joined the board in January to replace the four who had resigned in November. They were told by White on June 23 – the day after the Telegraph Group sale was announced – that their directors' fees were being doubled to $100,000 apiece, four times the fees paid to other, "non-independent" Inc. directors. Hollinger's lawyers took delight in pointing this out to the Delaware court, as well as noting the fact that Walker and Rohmer did not appear to have challenged Black on a single issue since coming aboard.

Determined to avoid a repeat of February's "Strine disaster" (as he called it), Black heeded the advice of his lawyer Edward Greenspan when he was deposed once more by Hollinger's counsel Martin Flumenbaum in advance of the second Delaware hearing. Greenspan warned Black to be more plain-spoken and told him that for every five-syllable word he used in the deposition he would have to pay $50; the fine would be $40 for four syllables and $30 for three syllables. When they broke at eleven a.m., Greenspan congratulated Black: "So far you owe me only 80 bucks."

A one-day hearing took place on Friday, July 23, although this time there were no witnesses, just briefs and oral arguments before the court. Hollinger's lawyers pointed out that Black's correspondence had included a missive in which he railed that he was "fighting truly evil people" including "Breeden and his fascists . . . who are a menace to capitalism as any sane and civilized person would define it." This prompted Strine to look around the courtroom and muse: "Mr. Black and Mr. Breeden aren't here. I understand they're taking family vacations together."

Armed with depositions from Black and others, Inc.'s lawyers argued before Strine that the *Telegraph* was Hollinger's "crown jewel" and that its chief remaining asset, the *Chicago Sun-Times*, was a "second-place" title that was "racked by circulation issues." Without the *Telegraph*, Hollinger would be reduced to a "back-bench" outfit.

As it happened, the circulation issues were a new wrinkle in the Hollinger debacle and were brought to light only in the days before the Telegraph Group sale was finalized. John Cruickshank, publisher of the *Sun-Times*, unearthed them after the paper increased its cover price in April from 35¢ to 50¢. He noticed that the expected monetary boost was not in line with the number of papers being sold. Eventually, it was determined that the paper had been overstating its Monday-to-Friday circulation of 486,936 by as much as 23 per cent to advertisers. Two *Sun-Times* executives who had run the circulation department resigned, and the company was hit by lawsuits from merchants who had been buying space in the paper on the basis of the inflated values. Although David Radler was publisher of the paper during 2002 and 2003, when the sales inflation was said to have taken place, he denied any knowledge of it. The misrepresentation seemed to follow a pattern of similar circulation scandals at newspapers around the United States.*

At the hearing, Strine dwelt with some amusement on the relative merits of the *Telegraph* versus the *Sun-Times* and how to quantify the notion that the *Telegraph*'s prestige lent greater value to its company. Hollinger's Paul Healy had memorably testified at his deposition that as proprietor of the *Telegraph*, "you can have dinner with the Queen." "Is there anyone who came out of London any finer than Belushi?" Strine deadpanned at one point, presumably referring to the late *Saturday Night Live* comedian John. "That's a real test."

"Don't know the answer to that, your Honor," Inc.'s lawyer Gilchrist Sparks replied.

When Strine got down to the more serious task of rendering his decision, Black came up empty once again. Six days after the hearing, Strine ruled that the Telegraph Group represented "approximately half" of Hollinger's assets, which is not the same as "substantially all," and took a pointed swipe at Black by noting that Inc.'s exclusion from the Telegraph Group sale process was "self-inflicted." Inc. immediately filed an appeal with the Delaware Supreme Court, which stayed up late that same evening to reject it with unusual dispatch, clearing the way for the sale of the Telegraph Group to the Barclays to close as planned at 10:00 a.m. London time on Friday, July 30.

For his part, Black moved on quickly from the sale of the Telegraph Group and focused on the fact that Strine's rulings were in effect only

---

* The scandal unleashed another torrent of criticism against Radler's regime. "The news that our former top bosses were apparently pirates came as a shock; knowing that the paper was solidly profitable, I assumed they were merely skinflints," noted the famed *Sun-Times* movie reviewer Roger Ebert. "Radler shut down the building's escalators to save money on electricity and maintenance. Who would have thought such a pennypincher might possibly be pinching millions for his own pockets?" Radler told Michael Miner of the *Chicago Reader* that he was working on a response to Ebert's outburst, but several weeks later it had not appeared. "When it comes to profits, no one blames me for that. I quadrupled profits," Radler complained.

until the end of October, and that the strategic process managed by Lazard was complete. "Hollinger Inc. does not have to sell Hollinger International," he said in August, "and will repossess its control position, unless someone makes us a brilliant offer." When Richard Breeden heard from one of Hollinger's executives that Black and Radler believed they were coming back to assume control over the company, he said ominously, "Maybe. But they'd have to come back to this jurisdiction." Breeden and the special committee followed up the tough talk by issuing their final report in late August, a 500-page indictment that called Hollinger under Black and Radler a "corporate kleptocracy" and leaving it to "appropriate governmental and judicial authorities" to determine what actions should be brought against the company's former rulers. Through Ravelston, Black issued a retort that "The Special Committee's report is recycling the same exaggerated claims laced with outright lies that have been peddled in leaks to the media and over-reaching lawsuits since Richard Breeden first began his campaign against the founders of Hollinger International."

Black turned sixty years old on August 25, and found that Barbara had filled the dining room at Park Lane Circle with red, white, and blue balloons for a quiet celebratory dinner with Black's children, their close friend George Jonas (Barbara's ex-husband), former *National Post* editor Ken Whyte, his old friend Brian Stewart, and their spouses. Since the beginning of the summer Conrad and Barbara had once again become inseparable, but people who saw them commented on how thin she was. Asked two days before his birthday about the impact of the previous ten months on him and Barbara, Black said, "If you mean on the quality of our relations, they are stronger than ever. If you mean on us as individuals, the events have been trying and such ordeals are the stuff of many clichés. It will fortify us, as individuals and as a couple, but it is a strain. It is a transition, not the sort of transition any sane person would seek, and reaching the end of it will not redeem the unpleasantness of it. But we will be fine at the end of it and are philosophical."

Black claimed not to bear a grudge against most of the directors and Hollinger executives who forced his removal from the company. "I must hold myself primarily responsible. I had a view of how the company should be run and of the limits to which a controlled company that had been built by the majority shareholder should collegialize its management. I had the full support of the directors. I underestimated the force of the corporate governance movement. I believe my skepticism toward that movement and its exponents in our company was well founded, but I must secondly blame the legal personnel of the company for leaving the vulnerability of incomplete documentation that they did. Without that, we would have come through the special committee process unscathed."

Amiel told friends that she was going to write a book on the events of the past decade in her life, through which, no doubt, some scores would be settled. Conrad had been considering writing his next book on Richard Nixon, another "great man much reviled" whom he had grown to admire. The new life the Blacks began to envision for themselves would revolve mainly around Toronto and New York. Over the summer, each penned an op-ed piece for the *Wall Street Journal*, Conrad's on the eve of the Canadian election and Barbara's during the Democratic National Convention.

A press lord no more, Lord Black put his Cottesmore Gardens home in London up for sale, and he was considering putting Palm Beach back on the market. According to Greenspan, it had been withdrawn only after Breeden had publicly floated the idea of Black fleeing the country with the money from his earlier Barclay deal, and Black wanted to quash anything that might seem to support that accusation. "My house in London was never for sale until the *Telegraph* was sold," Black said. "A few people looked at it on the basis that if they wanted to make an irrefusable offer, they could, but no offers were solicited. Obviously, we have no need of such a house in London now. Palm Beach was for sale for one month, after these events, but before we were able to refinance Hollinger Inc. I thought I might need to put up a good deal of the money to keep Hollinger Inc. afloat, after the audit and special committees reneged on the restructuring proposal understandings and set out to bankrupt Hollinger Inc. . . . With the sale in London, I do not anticipate any more residential changes."

Between meetings at 10 Toronto Street and phone calls with his lawyers, Black found himself acclimatizing to a life reconfigured around Park Lane Circle, where each of his children was spending at least part of the summer. Jonathan, twenty-six, who had worked as a model and in the music industry, had moved back to Toronto from Los Angeles with ambitions to get into the restaurant business. Alana, twenty-one, was entering her last year of study at Concordia University in Montreal, and James, eighteen, would be entering his freshman year at the same school.

The recurring question of how Black would end up financially once all was said and done raised the concern of his first wife, Joanna, over the status of their children's finances. A trust fund, created when Conrad and Joanna divorced in 1992, had been set up so that a stake in one of his private companies would be set aside and distributed among the Black children once they were well into adulthood. In the meantime, the kids' expenses would be covered either by the trust's earnings or by Black himself.

Conrad and Joanna were both designated trustees, but Joanna felt that she had received poor legal advice. She considered herself yet another person who was outsmarted by Black in a legal agreement. Although she believed Black "lived up to the letter" of the agreement, she was unable to determine from the statements she was receiving what value, if any, remained in the private company in which the trust held a share certificate, and whether the trust was segregated from his other finances. "I've been trying to figure out if there's any value to that certificate beyond the 10 cents' worth of paper from Grand & Toy," she said. "We're supposed to be trustees on behalf of our children, and I'm told by my lawyers that it is my fiduciary duty to get this information." While Joanna was considering legal arbitration to try to extract more information, Conrad told her: "Once I've got everything sorted out, we'll address this. Don't worry, the kids are going to get everything anyway in the end."

"Everything of what?" she wondered.

Where would Black end up? As always with Black, there were many shades to the story. His hero William Randolph Hearst lost control of his newspaper company for several painful years before regaining it later in life, although Hearst remained a kind of figurehead and did not face the possibility of jail. Still, there were echoes in Black in 2004 of the portrait in *Citizen Hearst*, the book that inspired him as a young man to dream of presses and ink. "No one could dispute his title as the champion loser of his time," W.A. Swanberg wrote of Hearst. "The inspiring thing about him was his ability to see himself trounced in one fight and to come back swinging in the next." Maybe this was how Black saw himself, although his inability to give up the fight could seem less than inspiring – more as if he was digging himself an ever-deeper hole.

To a degree, Black's legacy would be shaped by events that were yet to come. Still, a few conclusions could already be drawn. He made a mark on Canada with his originality and style, his relentless urge to stir things up, and his rare candour among business people. At the height of his powers, Black seemed like a human steamroller, trampling rules, foes, and conventions that blocked his path. He adamantly refused to be told what to do, even growing indignant at the sight of an outstretched seatbelt. On the subject of Conrad Black, most people's views were as strong as his own. Those who admired him did so precisely because he was someone who did exactly what he wanted in life. Those who did not found him infuriating and surprisingly thin-skinned.

At the same time, Black's failings defined him; for someone who talked the talk of a swashbuckling capitalist with such bravado, he never quite lived up to his promise by the measure of capitalism's ultimate scorecard: the stock market. Similarly, his need to surround himself with the great and the good didn't make him one of them. The rapidity with which that crowd distanced itself from him when scandal struck underlined the point. One former Inc. director said: "Conrad wasn't as good as everybody said he was in the heyday. I don't think he's as bad as everyone's making him out to be now."

Where his record as a press owner was concerned, Black was either a great newspaper mogul or a wasted talent – or both. Martin Newland, once the deputy editor of the *National Post*, fondly recalled how Black was practically run out of Canada by Jean Chrétien because of the *Post*'s coverage of the prime minister's business dealings. "Did I hear one word of recrimination from him? Not one,"

Newland, who later became editor of the *Daily Telegraph*, said of Black. "That is the measure of a great newspaper proprietor. With Conrad's passing, the whole world of thinking about exciting ways to make newspapers comes to an end. What we do will be worse off for the loss of Conrad."

Looking back, the argument could be made that Black's pinnacle was his takeover and turnaround of the *Telegraph* from the mid-1980s until the early 1990s. "You had this golden period when Conrad had all of his abilities but less of his arrogance," said a long-time associate. "For a long time he got it fundamentally right about the *Telegraph*. He bought it brilliantly, and he understood what to do with it and how to restore its reputation and its commercial success. He tried hard and cared about the journalism and was very interested in the politics of the time."

Then came the breakup of his first marriage, his remarriage, the price war in London with Rupert Murdoch, and the endless succession of deals and battles to build the world's fastest-growing press empire – including the exhilarating but disappointing run of Black's *National Post* – and the fateful decision to move Hollinger's base of power to the United States. Somewhere in the wake of the *Post* adventure, the peerage flap, and his brother's death, Black's colossal personal ambitions disastrously intersected with the darkening mood in corporate America.

There were, naturally, no shortage of theories on what got Black booted from his perch; one proposed a confluence of greed, hubris, and self-delusion, perhaps exacerbated by his relationship with an equally unrestrained wife, all of which rendered him incapable of seeing that the way he was running his affairs left him wide open to attack. "In most human areas Conrad is so spectacular and makes such a powerful mark on you," said another former director of one of his companies. "But in this one area – business – he is a total, absolute, utter disappointment. When I was on the board, he ran the business like a medieval fiefdom. He was arrogant and totally unaware of reality and of everyone else's concept of a public company."

There was also the distinct possibility that Black remained exactly who he always was, and his style had simply caught up with him.

"Here's a man who lived on the edge all the time, and when you do that it eventually goes wrong," said Victor Rice, who worked for Black more than two decades ago when he was the president of Massey-Ferguson. "He's very brave and very articulate and thinks he can intellectually dominate anybody – and he can't."

It is also worth remembering that, unlike many people, Black had no concept of "conflict avoidance," so the threat of having to tussle would not cause him to back away from a fight. Certainly there were many points over the past two or three years at which Black might have played his cards differently and achieved a less painful result – from making more of an effort to placate shareholders like Tweedy Browne to letting the Hollinger strategic process he had initiated run its course without trying to finagle his own deal with the Barclays.

There are, of course, unanswered questions. For instance, why would Black and Radler bother to mislead a lackadaisical board of directors that seemed willing to approve anything that was put in front of them? If Black is to be believed, the answer is that his downfall was the result of bad paperwork, governance zealots, and a cowardly board. "He believes that if people tell the truth, he will prevail," says Greenspan.

If his accusers are right, Black's sense of entitlement was so warped that he didn't feel the need to ask anyone's permission for what was coming to him, let alone a hand-picked board that seemed better suited to discussing Middle East policy than dividend policy. But, as Black discovered in Strine's court, his alleged breaches of his own fiduciary duties to the company and its shareholders couldn't be defended merely by saying that his directors or underlings said they were okay. "There is a point at which this went over the top – way over the top. It was a pattern of behaviour that was outrageous," said Hollinger interim chairman and chief executive Gordon Paris. "He conducted himself around this whole notion of being 'the proprietor.' And he perceived that this was his company. Period, end of story."

By the fall of 2004, it looked as though the barrage of lawsuits and countersuits, the investigations into Hollinger and Black by the SEC and FBI, and whatever charges might result from the investigations could take years to play out. As to where he would end up,

Black offered this scenario: "It will be clear that I am innocent of wrongdoing and that my financial condition is good. Some of the shortcomings of the corporate governance movement will be much more evident than they have been. The story is not the trajectory of · my career so much as the rush to judgment in November and December, and the credulous reception of the enormities of the special committee process. The underlying facts are the quality of the assets we built and the absence of intentional wrongdoing and illegality, and those who deserve to benefit from those facts, will."

Unless and until the truckload of accusations against Black were proven in court, he would continue battling and plotting his comeback until he had exhausted every possible angle. "This is a long-running drama," Black contended, "and it may have a surprise ending."

Or, looked at another way, the story of Conrad Black's rise and fall was over, but a new story had surely begun.

AUTHOR'S NOTE

This is a revised and updated version of a book that was first published in 1995 with the subtitle *Conrad Black and the World's
Fastest Growing Press Empire*. My editors tell me it's actually
quite rare that you get to revisit a book with a fresh eye almost a decade
on, so this *Shades of Black* is a remake, or, to use the latest Hollywood
buzz lingo, a "reimagining." This time around, my aim was to write less
of a business and media biography and just tell, as definitively as possible, Black's extraordinary, and ultimately sorry, story. As a result, in
addition to adding new material, I have cut and revised sections that
are no longer central to the overall narrative.

It's worth recalling the reasons why I was drawn to write a book
about Black back in 1992, when I started research. After his controversial career as a Canadian financier, in less than a decade Black had
put together the world's largest company singularly dedicated to publishing newspapers, with titles including London's *Daily Telegraph* and
the *Jerusalem Post*, those published by Australia's John Fairfax and
hundreds of small American dailies and weeklies; over the course of
my research he added Canada's Southam chain and the *Chicago Sun-
Times*. At the time there was even more doom-saying about the
future of newspapers than there is now, making Black's interest in
them a curiosity. Then there was Black himself, with his ambitious
intellectual and geopolitical pursuits, an arsenal of gigantic words and

military analogies at his command, and the propensity to tongue-lash – or sue – anyone who got in his path.

The first time Black agreed to meet me to discuss my book was at his 10 Toronto Street headquarters late on the humid Friday afternoon of June 18, 1993. His customary half-hour late, Black strode into the small library across the hall from his second-floor office. While I attempted to stop myself sinking into a soft yellow couch, he eased his imposing frame into an armchair like a statesman: upright, tie straight, suit buttoned up, hands on knees, as if an official portrait were about to be taken. His hands were fleshy and his head seemed disproportionately large. Although our conversation was "cordial" (a common word in Black's lexicon), his hooded eyes betrayed nothing but the confident gaze of a man used to having things his way.

At our meeting, Black told me he would not impede my access to anyone, and he didn't. He never asked to see, nor was he shown, prior to publication, any of what I had written. We spoke on fifteen or twenty occasions over the next two years, usually on the telephone but also in person in Toronto and London.

Ultimately I came to view Black as someone who, despite his denials, cared a lot about what people thought of him. In our last conversation before the book first came out in November 1995, he asked me repeatedly how he came off in it. "Say you're on a bus and you're sitting next to some guy from Texas and you tell him you've written a book on this guy Conrad Black," Black asked me. "And the guy says, 'What's this guy Black like?' What would you say?"

Months later, I was told by one close friend of his that Black was annoyed by the book, but I didn't hear from Black. (Nor did he sue me, to answer the first question people usually ask.) A year or so later I went to observe an all-day conference that Hollinger was holding for stock market analysts at the Plaza Hotel in my capacity at the time as a correspondent for a Canadian newspaper. At a cocktail reception I ended up joining a small group of adoring suits who were chatting with Black. At one point he turned to me and said, "I haven't spoken to you in a while, but I thought your book was fair." I thanked him, and that was that. A few months later on a sunny New York day I ran into Black as he was walking up Fifth Avenue. He was extremely friendly, telling me excitedly of his plans to launch a national newspaper in Canada. The next time I encountered Black was in the offices of *Business Week* magazine in spring of 1998, where I had just been hired as media editor but hadn't officially started.

Black had come in for a long-standing "meet and greet" with senior editors, and to my chagrin I was the suddenly the recipient of the famed Black bombast. As soon as I walked into the editor-in-chief's office, Black started dressing me down over something I had said to the *Columbia Journalism Review* for a recent profile on him. I had not a clue what he was talking about, but as he vented, it became clear that what he took great exception to was my being quoted as saying that people in Canada don't like his style because he "shoots his mouth off."

"I do not shoot my mouth off," he argued while my new co-workers looked on, perplexed. "Surely you were misquoted. If not, I can defend that." At the end of the meeting, Black shook my hand and said with a slight smirk, "Richard, don't shoot your mouth off." "Ditto," I replied.

I didn't see Black in person again for six years until his appearance in a Delaware court in February 2004, and the dramatic course Black's life took over that period is recounted in the new chapters of the book. Some readers might wonder whether Black played a role in my becoming the *Sunday Telegraph*'s New York columnist. He did not. In the spring of 2002, Robert Peston, whom I had come to know when he was at the *Financial Times*, was appointed business editor of the *Sunday Telegraph* and invited me to become a contributor. A few months later we were chatting and Peston mentioned that he had not heard from Black about me or any other subject. In January of 2004, when I began covering Black's troubles in his own newspaper, I heard from someone else at the *Telegraph* that Black was "surprised" to learn that I worked there as a weekly columnist (apparently he hadn't been reading the paper closely, or I wasn't having much of an impact). I sent Black a note asking if he would grant me an interview for his own pages – while he still owned them – but he politely replied that he was not going to co-operate with me or any other journalist for the time being and would write his own story at some point. However, as the deadline for this edition approached, I felt it was important that Black respond to several of the questions raised by my research, and he did.

Some of the 200 people who were interviewed for the original *Shades of Black* were reinterviewed for this edition, and more than 50 others have contributed fresh stories, perspectives, and documents as my pursuit of the story took me to London, Chicago, Toronto, and Jerusalem in these past few months. The result is the entirely new section "Titanic," in which much of the information in the later chapters is the subject of court filings and proceedings. Wherever I am able to identify my sources, I have done so in the "Notes and Sources" that follow. The earlier edition had a lengthy list of people on three continents whom I thanked for their time and indulgence, including Conrad Black and his closest friends and executives. This time around, in view of the ongoing legal battles, so many people shared at least some of their insights on condition that they not be identified that the best way to express my gratitude is generally, but genuinely, to them all.

I would also like to express personal appreciation to a few key people for their support and encouragement while I toiled away on this new edition: Cholene Espinoza, Roger Karshan and Ali Levine, Samantha and Robert McRaney, Eric Pfanner, Ann Shortell and Herb Solway, Michael J. Wolf; my esteemed colleagues at the *Sunday Telegraph*, city editor Robert Peston and editor-in-chief Dominic Lawson; chairman Ted Magder and the brilliant faculty of New York University's Department of Culture and Communication; the book's indefatigable contributing reporters, Gayle MacDonald and Laurie Ludwick, and my diligent assistant, Elizabeth Costa. Thank you of course to my wonderful colleagues at McClelland & Stewart, especially Doug Gibson, Doug Pepper, and Dinah Forbes, and to Bill Hamilton of the AM Heath agency in London.

Finally and firstly, thank you to Jacquelyn and Eugene Siklos and family, to Suzanne Siklos, and to Laine, with whom all is possible.

New York
August 2004

SOURCE NOTES

Abbreviations

ALIP   Conrad Black, *A Life in Progress* (Toronto: Key Porter Books, 1993).
CB   Conrad Black, interview with the author
DC   Daniel Colson, interview with the author
DEL   Delaware court testimony
DEP   Delaware court deposition
DR   David Radler, interview with the author
MB   Montegu Black, divorce testimony
PW   Peter White, interview with the author

Introduction: "ET TU, BRUTE"

x   "I realize the allegation is about": CB.

xiii   "It was an unpleasant meeting this morning": Correspondence
       between Conrad Black and the Barclays, filed in Delaware court.

xiii   "All his life, Hearst had a conviction": David Nasaw, *The Chief:*
       The Life of William Randolph Hearst (Gibson Square Books, 2003),
       foreword by Conrad Black (for paperback edition).

xiv   "There's a terrible amount": *Chicago Tribune*, September 18, 1994.

xiv   "The one thing I remember": Tom Wolfe, interview with author.

xiv   "This is a guy who at his annual meeting said": Richard Burt, DEP.

xv   "The only way one can possibly understand": Herbert Denton,
       interview with the author.

xv   "Pursuing a grand vision": Richard Breeden, interview with the
       author.

461

xv   "smear job": Correspondence between Conrad Black and the
      Barclays, filed in Delaware court.

xv   "There's a serious war going on here": Edward Greenspan, inter-
      view with the author.

PART ONE: MAN OF DESTINY

Chapter One: HIS FATHER'S SON

4   "As Coleridge once observed": George Black Jr., interview with
      Maurice Hecht, 1973, E.P. Taylor Archives.

4   "He has tried his hand at most sports": *Saturday Night*, March 26,
      1955.

5   "seven financially lean": George Black Jr., foreword to C.S. Riley's
      memoirs, published by his family.

5   growth of Winnipeg: J. Castell Hopkins, *The Canadian Annual
      Review of Public Affairs, 1912* (Toronto: Annual Review Publishing,
      1912) pp. 70–80.

6   "bore my callow unsophistication": Riley memoirs.

6   "After all": George Black, interview with Hecht.

6   "a hopeless bunch of ghouls": Ibid.

7   "So if anybody says": Ibid.

7   "Hold onto your hat": Ibid.

7   "I think you should come to Toronto": Ibid.

8   formation of Argus: *Financial Post*, November 24, 1945.

9   "there was beer and blood": Ibid.

9   "I've fired so many people": Ibid.

10   "too many policies and decisions": Richard Rohmer, *E.P. Taylor:
      The Biography of Edward Plunket Taylor* (Toronto: McClelland and
      Stewart, 1978), p. 205.

10   "I am opposed philosophically": section on Canadian Breweries
      from author interviews with CBL colleagues; George Black, inter-
      view with Hecht; newspaper clippings; company documents; and
      Rohmer, *E.P. Taylor.*

10   "I find the phone works just as well": *Globe and Mail*, October 7,
      1958.

11   "If you can't turn around": George Black, interview with Hecht.

11   E.P. Taylor on George Black Jr.'s abilities: E.P. Taylor, interview
      with Maurice Hecht, 1973, E.P. Taylor Archives.

11   "I did the best I could, Eddie": George Black, interview with Hecht.

12   "I have all the money I'll ever need": Ibid.

Chapter Two: AIMLESS YOUTH

13   "Certainly there was a good chance": George Hayhurst, interview with the author.

14   "Mostly we played with the slot machine": Ibid.

14   "His father was a bit distant": Ibid.

14   "I don't think it does any harm": George Black, interview with Hecht.

14   meeting Prince of Wales: *Winnipeg Tribune*, October 13, 1924.

15   "To Conrad this was torment": Brian Stewart, interview with the author.

15   [Footnote] "He had an extraordinary affection": Sarah Band, interview with the author.

15   "accumulated life savings of $60": Conrad Black, address to Harvard Business School Club of Toronto, September 16, 1992.

16   "[Campbell] had come to the house": Joanna Black MacDonald, interview with the author.

16   "I was very young": CB.

16   "That's the only time": Hal Jackman, interview with the author.

17   "[rushing] home early from school": Conrad Black, address to Harvard Business School Club of Toronto, September 16, 1992.

17   "It was an unbelievably great speech": Brian Stewart, interview with the author.

17   "His father had an outstanding memory": Ibid.

17   "Where do you think North Carolina comes": George Black, interview with Hecht.

18   "You always have to be careful": *Toronto Star*, June 17, 1978.

18   "I know he rarely, if ever, did any work": George Hayhurst, interview with the author.

18   "gauleiters": John Fraser, *Telling Tales* (Toronto: Collins, 1987), pp. 75–83.

18   "This place is a concentration camp": CB.

19   unattributed comments of UCC colleagues of Black: Author's interviews.

19   "All those who, by their docility: ALIP, pp. 11–12.

19   "a systematic campaign of harassment": ALIP, pp. 11–12.

20   "A lot of money for a fourteen-year-old": CB.

20   "I was not seeking attention": CB.

20   "Those who had been among the most eager": Fraser, *Telling Tales*.

21   "I am neither proud nor ashamed": ALIP, pp. 14–16.

21   "I concluded the courses": CB.

21   "Diefenbaker's government": Conrad Black, speech to Carleton University convocation, Ottawa, June 8, 1989.

21   "He's extraordinarily hard working": *Toronto Star*, December 15, 1979.

22   "Paul Martin was very, very ponderous": PW.

23   George Black's health: CB.

23   "Conrad was the apple of his father's eye": PW.

23   "discussing the world": Brian Stewart, interview with the author.

24   "He had just read the book *Citizen Hearst*": Ibid.

24   "Conrad clearly had a mystical love of America": Ibid.

25   "Conrad has always been impressed": Ibid.

25   "Social unrest had become severe": Conrad Black, address to Harvard Business School Club of Toronto, September 16, 1992.

26   "He was really wondering": Brian Stewart, interview with the author.

Chapter Three: "WHERE HAS THIS BUSINESS BEEN ALL OUR LIVES?"

27   history of *Eastern Townships Advertiser*: PW.

28   "bucolic redoubt": Conrad Black, *Duplessis* (Toronto: McClelland and Stewart, 1977), p. 172.

28   "He was a young kid": Maureen Johnston-Main, interview with the author.

29   "He was always very curious": PW.

29   "We used to regularly have long boozy dinners": DC.

30   purchase of *Sherbrooke Record*: DR; PW; Ivan Saunders, interview with the author.

31   inherited at least $200,000: CB. According to court documents, Black inherited money from his grandparents which was held in trust by his father until he reached the age of twenty-five, in 1969. In 1964, the value of the trust was $468,050. Black did not recall seeing any of that money, and noted it was mainly in illiquid private company stock and therefore of debatable value.

31   "Conrad was crapping in his pants": DR.

31   "Diversity of opinion": quoted in Maude Barlow and James Winter, *The Big Black Book* (Toronto: Stoddart, 1977), p. 1–2.

32   "great mentors for somebody": Crosbie Cotton, interview with the author.

32   "downward payroll adjustment": Irwin Ross, "The Boy Wonder of Canadian Business," *Fortune*, July 29, 1979.

33   "a certain playfulness": Lew Harris, interview with the author.

33   "I used to go get a dictionary": Crosbie Cotton, interview with the author.

33   *scutcheon:* Words from *Duplessis*, which Black was writing at the time.

35   "I announced myself to the Marine guard": Philip Marchand, "Rich, Young, Powerful and Heir to Bud McDougald's throne . . . Meet Conrad Black," *Toronto Life*, August 1977.

35   "the highlight of my sporadic career as a journalist": ALIP, p. 65.

35   "less coverage, more wires": Charles Bury, interview with the author.

36   "Of course, the personal lives of journalists": Conrad Black, speech to Canadian Association of Journalists, Ottawa, April 8, 1994.

36   "an avid devourer": Black, *Duplessis*, p. 660.

36   "a gentleman could allow himself": Ibid., pp. 664–65.

36   "decried as dictatorship and corruption": Ibid., p. 679.

36   "It would be unjust to omit all reference": Ibid., p. 218.

37   "I can remember vividly": DC.

37   "we would say, 'Remove your tie, Conrad'": Laurier LaPierre, interview with the author.

37   "gratuitously insulting": CB.

38   "I have no idea why he's so upset": Marchand, "Meet Conrad Black."

38   "We didn't suddenly sit down one day": *Toronto Star*, June 17, 1978.

39   "We used to tell the bank": DR.

39   Cranbrook airplane crash coverage: Peter Newman, *The Establishment Man* (Toronto: McClelland & Stewart, 1982), p. 54.

40   "Radler told us he wrote some editorials": Royal Commission on Newspapers, July 1, 1981, p. 94.

40   "The English community here": ALIP, pp. 136–37.

Chapter Four: COMING OF AGE

42   "no degrees, but several attempts": MB.

43   "the key to Argus's success": Marchand, "Meet Conrad Black."

44   "He was happy enough": CB.

44   "came the unnerving crack": ALIP, pp. 169–70.

45   "He was getting a bit incoherent": CB.

45   "I never heard him say that": CB.

45   "The physical symptoms": ALIP, p. 52.

46   Draper, Dobie phone instructions: Joanna Black MacDonald, interview with the author.

46   "Doesn't she *know* who I am?": Ibid.

47   "ample experience": ALIP, p. 108.

47   "as if he is encased in cement": Laurier LaPierre, interview with the author.

47   "The curious sense he projects": Marchand, "Meet Conrad Black."

Chapter Five: BOY WONDER

49   sliced his hand while carving a turkey: Douglas Creighton, interview with the author.

50   "a tired group of entries": *Financial Post*, May 29, 1989.

50   "Argus didn't do anything": Hal Jackman, interview with the author.

51   "bring him along exceedingly slowly": *The Canadian Establishment, Part I: 10 Toronto Street*, CBC, first broadcast in 1980.

51   "We were happy to co-operate": Ibid.

52   "We are running this company": Hal Jackman, interview with the author.

52   "McDougald was a real divide-and-conquer kind of guy": Ibid.

52   "You're rushing your fences": *The Canadian Establishment, Part I.*

52   "Well, I need hardly tell you": MB.

53   "Knowing something of the propensity": Conrad Black, James Gillies Alumni Lecture, Toronto, June 18, 1991.

53   "Bide your time": Rod McQueen, "The Young Lion: How Conrad Black Made Argus His Own," *Maclean's*, June 26, 1978.

54   "enthusiastic urging": Ibid.

55   "When the inevitable publicity ensued": Conrad Black, James Gillies Alumni Lecture, Toronto, June 18, 1991.

55   "I agree with everything": *Globe and Mail*, June 15, 1978.

55   "There is no doubt that these ladies were aware": Ibid.

56   "If Bud McDougald were here": Dixon Chant, interview with the author.

56   "On the day that Conrad heard about the ladies' ploy": *Canadian Lawyer*, September 1980.

57   "We're talking about business": Hal Jackman, interview with the author.

58   "I'm sorry I have to keep bringing this up": Brian Stewart, interview with the author.

58   "the new Mrs. Black": *Toronto Star*, June 18, 1991.

58   "When they phoned my mother-in-law": CB.

59   "I'm a man of the people": McQueen, "Young Lion."

59   "We had a very difficult time": Mariellen Black, divorce proceedings transcripts.

59   "I really don't understand": Ibid.

59   "it's a Monopoly game": MB.

60   "was startled that this amount of money": MB.

Chapter Six: FINANCIAL ENGINEERING

62   "seriously disquieted": Conrad Black, James Gillies Alumni Lecture, Toronto, June 18, 1991.

62   "asset upgrade": Ibid.

62   "my brother and I had known Argus": Ibid.

62   "I was slightly miffed": CB.

63   "We had to . . . eliminate those companies": MB.

63   "It was a revealing encounter": *Wall Street Journal*, November 8, 1994.

64   "a wild bowdlerization": Ibid.

64   "There is mounting evidence": *Globe and Mail*, December 30, 1978.

65   "I am amazed by the number": Gillian MacKay, "Massey Faces the Grim Reaper," *Maclean's*, September 22, 1980.

65   [Footnote] "I am a historian by vocation": Ibid.

65   "I thought to myself": CB.

66   "Herb Gray's remark to us": Dixon Chant, interview with the author.

66   "I was not prepared to tolerate": Conrad Black, *Financial Times of Canada*, October 6, 1980.

66   "The truth of the matter": Victor Rice, interview with the author.

66   "as surprising and controversial": Peter Cook, *Massey at the Brink* (Toronto: Collins, 1981), p. 258.

67   "For a self-appointed spokesman": Ibid., p. 259.

67   "the sort of irresponsible, self-serving action": *Toronto Star*, October 9, 1980.

67   "I worked at Massey-Ferguson": *Toronto Star*, October 11, 1980.

68   "For the record": *Toronto Sun*, October 14, 1980.

68   "I was being a success": Victor Rice, interview with the author.

69   "The major item": MB.

70   "You've got to take these opportunities": CB.

70   "I understand you're negotiating": David Hayes, *Power and Influence: The* Globe and Mail *and the News Revolution* (Toronto: Key Porter Books, 1992), p. 160.

70   "Well, I'm not against this": CB.
70   "We will have to do something": Richard J. Doyle, *Hurly-Burly: A Time at the* Globe (Toronto: Macmillan, 1990), p. 421.
71   "He's just getting rich": *Financial Post*, March 23, 1985.
72   organization charts: Jack Boultbee, interview with the author.

Chapter Seven: THE HANNA BRAWL
The reconstruction of the events surrounding Norcen's investment in Hanna Mining is based on court transcripts and examinations for discovery in the ensuing court case. The author is particularly grateful to Ian Austen, who covered the story for *Maclean's*, for sharing his files. Black's deposition took place on April 10, 1982, in Palm Beach. The trial began five days later in Cleveland.

76   "In the companies that we had in Argus Corporation": MB.
77   "Palm Beach isn't everyone's cup of tea": Newman, *Establishment Man*, p. 202.
77   "a fierce litigious and regulatory firefight": Conrad Black, James Gillies Alumni Lecture, Toronto, June 18, 1991.
86   "Our thought was that we had a real good shot": CB.
86   "He had some cardinal in tow": Dominic Rushe, "Black Narcissi," *Sunday Times Magazine*, March 28, 2004.
86   "It was the adventures of King Pyrrhus": Ibid.
87   "He elected to find fault elsewhere": William Kilbourne, interview with the author.
89   "strained and unpersuasive": Decision of Judge Manos, June 11, 1982, p. 39.
89   consent decree with SEC: *Globe and Mail*, July 2, 1982.
90   "I never had any fears": Newman, *Establishment Man*, p. 257.
90   "Conrad was astounded": PW.
92   Conrad Black's visit to McMurtry: Linda McQuaig and Ian Austen, "The Law and Conrad Black," *Maclean's*, February 21, 1983; plus tapes of McQuaig and Austen's interviews with Black and McMurtry.
93   "in such a way as to make it look": Conrad Black, interview with Linda McQuaig.
94   "I have always got along well with him": ALIP, p. 299.
94   "I can guarantee you": Brian Mulroney, interview with the author.

94 "I'm willing to take up the cudgels": *Globe and Mail*, December 25, 1982.

95 "a lot of police were going round": *Globe and Mail*, December 25, 1982.

95 "Isn't that *tragic*": Conrad Black, interview with Linda McQuaig and Ian Austen.

96 "Maybe we should all try it": McQuaig and Austen, "The Law."

96 "If you're the attorney general": Hal Jackman, interview with the author.

96 cockroach anecdote: John Fraser, "Basic Black," *Saturday Night*, July 1994. Fraser confirmed in an interview with the author that the man called "R" in the magazine was Roy McMurtry.

97 "He was as wounded": Peter Atkinson, interview with the author.

97 his wife would assure him: Joanna Black MacDonald, interview with the author.

97 "not unusual at all": Ian Austen and Linda McQuaig, "Power in High Places," *Maclean's*, April 25, 1983.

98 "We have been completely exonerated": Ibid.

98 "I suppose I overreacted a bit": CB.

Chapter Eight: A DARKER SHADE

99 "He's not keen on the spotlight": Sarah Band, interview with the author.

100 "Monte is an extraordinarily capable person": Ibid.

100 "already in steep decline": Conrad Black, "Black's Arts," *Report on Business*, July 1987.

101 "It was a dry rot": Dixon Chant, interview with the author.

101 "become a relatively soft competitor": *Toronto Star*, February 14, 1985.

102 "We had all kinds of people": *Toronto Star*, June 28, 1989.

102 "was run by an inbred, furtive": *Report on Business*, July 1987.

102 "In commerce, as in matters of mundane physiology": *Report on Business*, February 1986.

102 withdrawals of funds in 1986: *Financial Times of Canada*, April 28, 1986.

103 "Dominion's managers saw the pension funds": Judgment of Justices Reid, Montgomery and Ewaschuk, August 18, 1986, p. 10.

104 "In my opinion, the commission failed": Ibid., p. 32.

104 "I have a question for the premier": Legislative Assembly of Ontario, *Hansard*, January 27, 1986, p. 3477.

104 "a symbol of swinish, socialist demagoguery": *Toronto Sun*, January 30, 1986.

104 "I never said that anything": Ibid.

104 "We had $30 million in produce stolen": *Globe and Mail*, January 29, 1986.

105 "I recommended that a scythe": ALIP, p. 326.

105 "The overhaul really should have been done": *Financial Post*, March 23, 1987.

Chapter Nine: THE HOUSE THAT BLACK BOUGHT
This section benefited from Duff Hart-Davis's interview of Conrad Black for his book *The House the Berrys Built* (London: Hodder and Stoughton, 1990), an interview Hart-Davis generously shared with the author.

107 "I am just trying to do my job": *Report on Business*, April 1985.

107 "The end of the line was coming": MB.

107 "Quite clearly there wasn't enough work": MB.

108 "Conrad and I put in money each year": MB.

108 Arrowwood meeting: CB; Andrew Knight, interview with the author; Conrad Black, interview with Duff Hart-Davis.

109 "one more fiery little Armagnac": Andrew Knight, interview with the author.

109 "the *Daily Telegraph* looks somewhat unstable": Ibid.

111 "Send me the stuff": Ibid.

111 The reference to Thomas Riley's owning part of the *Telegraph* comes from *The Memoirs of Robert Thomas Riley*, published privately in 1947. No reference to Riley's involvement is found in the published histories of the newspaper, but under commercial structures of the day his interest may have been as small as one sixty-fourth. The best histories of the paper are Lord Burnham's *Peterborough Court: The Story of the* Daily Telegraph (London: Cassell & Co., 1955); Duff Hart-Davis's *The House the Berrys Built* (London: Hodder and Stoughton, 1990); and H.R. Fox Bourne's *English Newspapers: Chapters in the History of Journalism*, Vol. II (New York: Russell and Russell, 1966), first published in 1887. Other sources for the history of the *Telegraph* are *Sunday Times*, December 15, 1985, and *Financial Times*, December 14, 1985.

113 "It appeared very odd": Conrad Black, interview with Duff Hart-Davis.

114   newspaper circulations: Private placement document.

114   the most elderly readership profile in Fleet Street: David Goodhart,
       Eddy Shah and the Newspaper Revolution (London: Coronet Books,
       1986).

116   "Stay away from it": John Tory, interview with the author.

116   "I would have had to be fairly unobservant": CB.

116   "I've never heard of him": Lord Hartwell, interview with the
       author.

116   "They were making hay or something": Rupert Hambro, interview
       with the author.

117   "The trouble was I introduced myself": Ibid.

Chapter Ten: "GOOD MAN, CONRAD RITBLAT"

118   The section on the airport meeting is based on Duff Hart-Davis's
       interview with Conrad Black and on the author's interviews with
       Daniel Colson, Conrad Black, Andrew Knight, Sir Evelyn de
       Rothschild, Rupert Hambro, and Lord Hartwell.

120   "Lie down until the feeling passes": DC.

120   "Good man, Conrad Ritblat": *Sunday Times*, December 15, 1985.

121   "I'd gone all through that instant baptism": CB.

121   "I have generally been disappointed": *Spectator*, August 10, 1985.

122   *Economist* dinner: Andrew Knight and Frank Rogers, interviews
       with the author; Frank Rogers quoted in Hart-Davis, *Berrys*, p. 309.

124   "I was told I could wait": *Financial Times*, November 18, 1989.

124   "Many of us felt we should sue": Rupert Hambro, interview with
       the author.

125   "I didn't get the advice": *Oldie*, October 16, 1992.

125   "handed the Berry family's balls": Duff Hart-Davis, *Berrys*, p. 307.

125   "our kind of people": Lord Hartwell, interview with the author.

126   November 15 meeting with Lord Hartwell: DC.

127   "I told the then-governor afterwards": Lord Swaythling, interview
       with the author.

129   "No ordinary medic": John Fraser, *Report on Business*, May 1986.

129   "What exactly is it": DC.

130   "a screaming match": DC; Nicholas Berry, interview with the
       author.

132   "I do not know him very well": *Daily Telegraph*, December 14, 1985.

132   "Why are you doing this?": Lord Hartwell, interview with the
       author.

132   "The trouble is that we are a family": *Daily Telegraph*, December 14, 1985.

133   "The British as a matter of course": *Toronto Star*, December 24, 1985.

Chapter Eleven: DROWNING THE KITTENS

134   Park Lane Circle: The house was featured anonymously in *Architectural Digest*, April 1988. Although the article did not identify Black by name, it was not hard to recognize the "power to be reckoned with in Canada" who owned "a major London daily."

134   "As Thierry was finishing up here": Ibid.

135   "I'm not a great sportsman": Ibid.

135   Worsthorne lunch with Andrew Knight: Peregrine Worsthorne, interview with the author.

135   "Perhaps because of all the excitement": Peregrine Worsthorne, *Tricks of Memory* (London: Weidenfeld and Nicolson, 1993), pp. 245–46; and interview with the author.

136   "thinking very seriously": Max Hastings, interview with the author.

136   "Ah, yes . . . HMS *Warspite*": Ibid.

136   "except for the proprietor's almost obsessional preoccupation": Worsthorne, *Tricks*, pp. 245–46.

137   "I think he was probably anxious to show": Peregrine Worsthorne, interview with the author.

138   "They said when I had been in newspapers": *Financial Times*, February 22, 1992.

138   "the most important single thing": Andrew Knight, interview with the author.

138   "I am still editor-in-chief": Lord Hartwell, Lord Swaythling, Adrian Berry, and Daniel Colson, interviews with the author.

139   "I suppose if I'd had any guts": Lord Hartwell, interview with the author.

139   Shah's early triumph: Charles Wintour, *The Rise and Fall of Fleet Street* (London: Hutchinson, 1989), pp. 253–55.

140   showdown at Wapping: William Shawcross, *Murdoch* (New York: Simon & Schuster, 1993), pp. 270–75.

141   "It's a terrible bore": Adrian Berry, interview with the author.

141   "distant ogre in Canada": Andrew Knight, interview with the author.

141   "Conrad played that role brilliantly": Ibid.

142   "I'm afraid some of the senior managers": Dixon Chant, interview with the author.

142   "You can't trust these banks": CB.

144   "love at first sight": Charles Powell, interview with the author.

144   "It became evident during the lunch": Andrew Knight, interview with the author.

144   "The revolution you have wrought": Conrad Black, speech to the Canadian Club, London, July 1, 1987.

145   "Although the *Daily Telegraph*": Max Hastings, interview with the author.

145   "a bad call": Ibid.

146   "seriously fallacious analyses": CB.

146   "good at drowning the kittens": Max Hastings, interview with the author.

146   "Well, you've sacked lots of other people": Ibid.

146   "Given Conrad's devotion": Ibid.

146   "You have to defend your editor": CB.

147   "This consisted of a good, informative newspaper": Conrad Black, James Gillies Alumni Lecture, Toronto, June 18, 1991.

148   "He brought a sinister reputation": Charles Moore, interview with the author.

148   "In recent years": *Spectator*, October 12, 1991.

149   "From my observation of you": *Guardian*, December 7, 1992.

151   "A company's cash flow is like a dictator's army": *Quaynotes*, September 1989.

154   [Footnote] "We all sat in the Cabinet Room": CB.

154   "The *Telegraph* was not always a strong ally": Charles Powell, interview with the author.

154   "His [Napoleon's] talents as a military commander": CB.

155   [Footnote] "Now there was a man associated with a terrible war": CB.

155   "The proprietor of the *Daily Telegraph*": Francis Wheen, interview with the author.

PART TWO: THE WORLD'S FASTEST-GROWING PRESS EMPIRE

Chapter Twelve: "NEWSPAPERS WANTED"

159   "expanding funnel": Conrad Black, James Gillies Alumni Lecture, Toronto, June 18, 1991.

160   "Conrad is the master opportunist": PW.

160   "My associates always": Conrad Black, James Gillies Alumni Lecture, Toronto, June 18, 1991.

161 "Arthur, count the chairs": Jennifer Wells, "Paper Chaser," *Report on Business*, August 1994.

161 "probably closer to an American-style brokerage company": DR.

162 "the *Simpsons'* Montgomery Burns": Rushe, "Black Narcissi."

162 "Where are you guys going?": DR.

162 "What do you think motivates": DR.

162 "I remember one day": DR.

163 "I know what he thinks": DR.

163 "the Refrigerator": John Fraser, interview with the author.

165 "had nothing against Protestantism": Black, *Duplessis*, p. 679.

165 "Ah . . . but would I be invited?": Ron Graham, *God's Dominion* (Toronto: McClelland & Stewart, 1990), p. 134.

165 "Those who find trendy and undignified: *Spectator*, February 26, 1994.

166 "There was a hitch": Norman Webster, interview with the author.

167 "When I arrived at Toronto Street": Robert Fulford, *Best Seat in the House* (Toronto: Collins, 1988), pp. 245–53.

168 "an extremely uncommon millionaire": Ibid.

168 "He was talking about the role": John Fraser, interview with the author.

169 "What, that faggot?": James Fleming, *Circles of Power* (Toronto: Doubleday Canada, 1991), p. 311; John Fraser, interview with the author.

Chapter Thirteen: ISRAEL

170 "You're going to send the Italian guy": *Financial Post*, November 14, 1992.

170 David Radler's meeting with Arye Mekel, 1988: David Radler and Arye Mekel, interviews with the author.

171 "The aim of this paper": *Jerusalem Post*, sixtieth-anniversary supplement, May 6, 1992.

172 "a certain irony": DC.

173 "they thought it was a typo": Ari Rath, interview with the author.

173 "It wasn't that our bid was higher": *Jerusalem Post*, March 30, 1990.

173 "This part of the world": Ibid.

173 "I consider Bob to be the main author": Ibid.

174 "I think it was to shut him up": DC.

174 "They have a responsibility to be aware": *Jerusalem Post*, April 28, 1989.

174   "Let's not play games": *Jerusalem Post*, March 30, 1990.

175   "I knew it was over": *Independent*, January 4, 1991.

175   "I smell a rat": Ibid.

175   "Ari, if anything is happening": Ari Rath, interview with the author.

176   "Generally speaking . . . I knew we were standing": Yehuda Levy, interview with the author.

176   "This is not a left-right bullshit thing": DR.

177   "It's not just a job": David Horovitz, interview with the author.

177   "Has the *Post* been a headache?": DR.

177   "Radler, I think, relished the fact": David Horovitz, interview with the author.

178   "It was one of the few moments": Max Hastings, *Editor: A Memoir* (Pan, 2003), p. 251.

178   "You don't understand, Max": Ibid.

178   [Footnote] "Advertisers threatened to withdraw": Dominic Lawson, *Sunday Telegraph*, January 25, 2004.

Chapter Fourteen: MINDING THE KINGDOM

179   "one of the most important and successful presidents": *Daily Telegraph*, February 3, 1991.

179   "Black once said that he was prepared": Alexander Chancellor quoted in Nicholas Garland, *Not Many Dead: Journal of a Year in Fleet Street* (London: Hutchinson, 1991), pp. 109–10.

181   "As a Canadian, I wish I could sit here": *Canadian Business*, November 1991.

181   "Do you realize that anyone": *Financial Post*, May 9, 1988.

181   "He loves the atmosphere over there": Ibid.

181   "He charmed an enormous number of people": Rupert Hambro, interview with the author.

183   "He's very remote": Charles Moore, interview with the author.

183   "I actually think I ought to step aside": Andrew Knight, interview with the author.

183   "We have created a kingdom": *Financial Times*, November 18, 1989.

183   "That may be good for him": *Financial Times*, October 11, 1989.

183   "a rather picturesque illustration": Conrad Black, speech to Canadian Association of Journalists, Ottawa, April 8, 1994.

184   "I brought my hobnailed jackboot": Ibid.

184   claiming that Knight had only three days earlier: ALIP, pp. 407–8.

184   "If you lose one of your best managers": *Sunday Correspondent*, January 14, 1990.

184   "I advised you again and again": *Observer*, January 14, 1990.

185   "deluged with so many calls": Ibid.

185   "The Constant Smiler": *Sunday Telegraph*, January 7, 1990.

186   "Charles was very funny": Garland, *Not Many Dead*, p. 164.

186   "Unlike, let's say, Rupert": Max Hastings, interview with the author.

186   "I wouldn't say Conrad": Sir Evelyn de Rothschild, interview with the author.

187   "I couldn't and can't stand that man": Lord Hartwell, interview with the author.

187   "I don't think non-executive directors": Ibid.

187   "a sort of *Almanach de Gotha*": Alexander Ross, *Canadian Business*, November 1991.

188   "Conrad's role to some extent": DR.

188   [Footnote] "if he were younger": CB.

188   "They're almost too rich": William F. Buckley Jr., interview with the author.

189   "It was an experience": Peter Munk, interview with the author.

189   "Frankly . . . a lot of the use of these boards": CB.

189   "I liked him": Raymond Seitz, interview with the author.

189   "The newspaper industry in London": *Saturday Night*, December 1992.

190   "will always remain a model": Ibid.

191   Joanna Black's change of first name: Joanna Black MacDonald, interview with the author.

192   "Our cash flow": Conrad Black, James Gillies Alumni Lecture, Toronto, June 18, 1991.

Chapter Fifteen: SOUTH PACIFIC

193   Warwick Fairfax's meeting with Conrad Black: Participants' interviews with the author.

194   "It didn't seem to appeal to us": Ken Thomson, interview with the author.

194   "I would be a little bit leerier than Mr. Black": Arthur Sulzberger Sr., interview with the author.

194   "This Fairfax company is unbelievable": Andrew Knight, interview with the author.

194   "Andrew . . . I find it hard enough": Ibid.

195   "In the end we took the bait": DC.

195   Conrad Black met Kerry Packer at Sir James Goldsmith's home: ALIP, pp. 433–34.

196   Fairfax history: A fuller history of the company can be found in Gavin Souter's *Heralds and Angels* (Penguin Books Australia, 1992), in his earlier volume *Company of Heralds* (Carlton: Melbourne University Press, 1981), and in John Fitzgerald Fairfax's *The Story of John Fairfax* (Sydney: J. Fairfax and Sons, 1941), published to mark the company's centenary.

198   "when economic conditions open up such opportunities": Conrad Black, speech to 1991 Hollinger annual meeting.

198   "The government of Ontario": Ibid.

198   "As the Samaritanly philanthropist": *Sydney Morning Herald*, July 18, 1991.

198   "Conrad, did you really say that?": Colleen Ryan and Glen Burge, *Corporate Cannibals* (William Heinemann Australia, 1992), p. 202.

199   "I hope that my arrival": *Bulletin* (Sydney), July 23, 1991.

199   "If it had been necessary": CB.

200   "heavy baggage": *Sydney Morning Herald*, November 2, 1992.

200   Black whistling "Waltzing Matilda": Nicholas Coleridge, *Paper Tigers* (London: William Heinemann Ltd, 1993), p. 337.

200   Conrad Black interview with Jana Wendt: *A Current Affair*, Nine Network, October 22, 1991.

201   Kerry Packer interview with Jana Wendt: *A Current Affair*, Nine Network, October 23, 1991.

201   "Mr Murdoch has not enjoyed competing with me in London": *Sydney Morning Herald*, November 2, 1991.

201   [Footnote] "completely false": *Australian*, November 4, 1991.

202   "an interventionist, right-wing, pro-Thatcherite owner": *Age*, November 28, 1991.

203   "sleazy, venal, and despicable": *Sydney Morning Herald*, December 12, 1991; also Ryan and Burge, *Corporate Cannibals*, p. 432.

203   "Contrary to widespread rumours": Canadian Press, December 17, 1991.

204   "There do seem to be rather attractive women": *Financial Post*, April 17, 1993.

205   "Normally I take Malcolm": *Australian Business Monthly*, January 1993.

205   "When he is here": Malcolm Turnbull, interview with the author.

Chapter Sixteen: MEDIA MERGER

206 "I was attracted to the *real* Conrad Black": Joanna Black MacDonald, interview with the author.

207 "Joanna . . . you *must* come back": Ibid.

208 "For months after my wife left me": *Maclean's*, August 2, 1992.

208 "I didn't leave him for anybody": Joanna Black MacDonald, interview with the author.

208 "I can remember Conrad": Max Hastings, interview with the author.

208 "the summit of my most ardent": ALIP, p. 463.

209 "power is sexy": Barbara Amiel, "Why Women Marry Up," *Chatelaine*, May 1986.

209 "She was worried that Conrad": Miriam Gross, interview with the author.

209 "not going to make the same mistakes": Joanna MacDonald Black, interview with the author.

210 "She looks like Gina Lollobrigida: *Evening Standard*, May 10, 1988.

210 "Conrad and Barbara": Rosemary Sexton, *Glitter Girls* (Toronto: Macmillan Canada, 1992), p. 182.

210 "They're doing this to spice up their CVs": Ibid.

211 "Now, the knives are drawn": *Maclean's*, January 27, 1992.

211 "You couldn't think of two people": Peter Munk, interview with the author.

211 "an ideologically uplifting Christmas": Newman, *Establishment Man*, p. 268.

211 "I've suffered from insomnia all my life": Jean Sonmor, *The Little Paper That Grew* (Toronto: Toronto Sun Publishing, 1993), p. 216.

212 "a lacquered apparition": Barbara Amiel, *Confessions* (Toronto: Macmillan Canada, 1980), p. 74.

212 "I believe it to be morally wrong": Ibid., p. 144.

213 "I remember it very well": Peregrine Worsthorne, interview with the author.

213 "On the appointed day": Hastings, *Editor*, p. 235.

214 "I think it is quite in order": Ibid.

214 "The fashionable intellectual would": Miriam Gross, interview with the author.

214 "Everybody likes you": Joanna Black MacDonald, interview with the author.

214   "I so loathe the permissive promiscuous society": Judith Timson, "Barbara Amiel: Nothing Succeeds Like Excess," *Chatelaine*, June 1980.

215   1992 Hollinger Dinner: Tape of event.

215   "sleazy, tasteless and neurotic": Newman, *Establishment Man*, p. 191.

216   "a more resonant rationale": The column also ran in the *Toronto Sun*, August 9, 1992.

218   "It was a very chirpy evening": Edward Klein, "Black Mischief," *Vanity Fair*, November 1992, p. 283.

218   trying to find a fax machine: Conrad Black, interview with Patricia Best.

218   "They've become incredibly glamorous": Miriam Gross, interview with the author.

218   "Nowadays . . . he's absolutely full": Max Hastings, interview with the author.

219   "They're intellectually very well suited": Miriam Gross, interview with the author.

219   "It's an all-round paradise": *Evening Standard*, December 9, 1992.

220   "I was always skeptical": CB.

220   "You walk down the main staircase": Elizabeth Lambert, "A Classically English Attitude: Proportion and Scale Support Traditional Themes in a Graceful London Town House," *Architectural Digest*, March 2000, p. 198. (The Blacks' London home was featured anonymously, without any obvious clues to who the owners were).

221   "Is This London's Most Powerful Woman?": *Evening Standard*, October 21, 1992.

221   "made the subject of all sorts of common tittle-tattle": CBC Newsworld, November 14, 1993.

221   "I was aware that there was a myth": *Maclean's*, August 1, 1994.

222   "Many journalists and most of the more talented ones": Conrad Black, speech to Canadian Association of Journalists, Ottawa, April 8, 1994.

223   "hit the nail on the head": *Sunday Times*, October 17, 1993.

223   "Now that she is rich": *Evening Standard*, October 20, 1993.

223   "one of the differences": *Sunday Times*, November 7, 1993.

224   "Mind you, you were the one": Author present.

Chapter Seventeen: THE HUNT

225   "media businesses will prove considerably less marvellous": *Forbes*, August 1, 1991.

225   "It's murder out there": Ibid.

226   "I think Conrad is sometimes inclined": Max Hastings, interview with the author.

226   "Conrad felt that the law": Hastings, *Editor*, p. 243.

227   "The reaction from institutional investors": *Sunday Times*, July 5, 1992.

227   "Well, it would be lighter on the payroll": DR.

229   Martin Maleska's meeting with Black: Martin Maleska, interview with the author.

229   "I think Conrad": Rupert Murdoch, interview with the author.

229   "I have no interest": Edward Klein, "Black Mischief."

230   "He has given the store away": CB.

230   "We have much more of a focus": Mort Zuckerman, interview with the author.

233   "absolute liberty of content": Conrad Black, speech to Canadian Association of Journalists, Ottawa, April 8, 1994.

233   "very politely" rebuffed: CB; St. Clair Balfour, interview with the author.

233   [Footnote] "When people came to us": Ibid.

234   "There is a chance": David Galloway, interview with the author.

234   "David, I just want to reiterate": Ibid.

235   "as a multiple proprietor": *Ottawa Citizen*, March 4, 1993.

235   "pompous farrago of nonsense": Ibid.

235   "I'm actually slightly touched": CB.

235   "The problem with Conrad": Hal Jackman, interview with the author.

235   "Well, that's absolute crap": CB.

235   "I like to bring him": Ibid.

238   "There was an awful lot of shilly-shallying": CB.

Chapter Eighteen: MAN OF LETTERS

244   "They were so good": CB.

244   "I didn't see why": CB.

244   "set the record straight": CB.

245   "the work of a man": *Canadian Business*, November 1993.

245   "some sort of celebratory sash": ALIP, p. 281.

245   [Footnote] "To Allan": Allan Fotheringham, interview with the author.

246   "only took him by the shoulders": Author's correspondence with Jean A. Roy, agent of Maurice Richard, March 30, 1994.

247   "infuriated" Mulroney: PW.

247   "He cannot imagine why he gave Conrad": PW.

247   "At an appropriate time": Brian Mulroney, interview with the author.

247   "was really rather positive": CB.

247   "The fact is I like to mix it up": *Morningside*, CBC Radio, October 29, 1993.

248   "It's a profit centre for me": CB.

248   [Footnote] "Anyone who has witnessed": CB.

248   "Perry went on TV": CB.

249   "It doesn't matter who you are": Peter Atkinson, interview with the author.

250   "In the midst of this book": Conrad Black, speech to Canadian Friends of the Hebrew University of Jerusalem, Toronto, December 9, 1990.

251   "Any respect I had for him": Ron Graham, interview with the author.

Chapter Nineteen: A QUESTION OF BALANCE
The principal sources for this chapter include uncorrected proofs of *Hansard*, as reproduced in the *Report of the [Australian] Senate Select Committee on Certain Aspects of Foreign Ownership Decisions in Relation to the Print Media*, June 1994 (here referred to as "Senate Report").

253   Conrad Black's descriptions of Paul Keating and John Hewson: Conrad Black, *A Life in Progress* (Random House Australia, 1993), pp. 453–4.

254   "might be disposed to support": *Sydney Morning Herald*, November 26, 1993.

254   "The word 'balanced' was in quotes: Senate Report, pp. 646, 650.

255   "a bit mischievous": CB.

255   "Well, that's Conrad": *Sydney Morning Herald*, November 30, 1993.

255   "best Mo Dean outfit": CB.

256   part of an international conspiracy: Submission to senate inquiry by Citizens Electoral Councils of Australia, April 27, 1994.

256   "Black is a man": Senate Report, p. 137.

256   "allegations emanating from him": CB.

256   "He is an urbane character": Senate Report, p. 163.

256   "At the obvious risk": Senate Report, p. 523.

258   "despite being unimpressed with me": Senate Report, p. 656.

258   "he simply cannot be relied upon": Senate Report, p. 746.

258   "I did not hear anything more from him": Senate Report, p. 748.

259   "What possesses Bob Hawke": *Sydney Morning Herald*, April 23, 1994.

260   "were simply an exercise": Senate Report.

260   "I thought that was a scream": CB.

260   "Black's writings and interviews": Senate Report.

261   "I'd rather buy shares in a company": Conrad Black and Rupert Murdoch at Davos: Tape of interview by Joanne Gray, Bloomberg Business News.

261   "I'd rather have a shareholder like you": Ibid.

Chapter Twenty: PRICE WARRIORS

262   "He's sort of a funny guy": CB.

263   "He's a plunger by nature": CB.

263   "I'm a great admirer of his": Rupert Murdoch, interview with the author.

264   "The argument that newspaper price increases": *Daily Telegraph*, September 8, 1993.

265   "took the quality premium away from the price": *Financial Times*, January 6, 1995.

265   "The *Telegraph* usually cuts the figure": *Independent on Sunday*, June 26, 1994.

266   The *Times* is the natural competitor": Andrew Knight, interview with the author.

266   "his numerous spear carriers": CB.

266   "They'll hang in for a while": CB.

266   "The problem is the future": Meeting with investors at Toronto's National Club, June 10, 1994.

267   "Anyone who wants to get something": Ibid.

267   "Murdoch is a Darwinian": CB.

268   "the first time in recent memory": *Financial Times*, July 1, 1994.

268   "It was an orgy": CB.

268   "The credibility of the management": *Maclean's*, August 1, 1994.

268   "He has pissed off the establishment": Ibid.

268   "You can't make war and peace at the same time": *Financial Times*, June 25, 1994.

269   [Footnote] "We're basically buying dimes for nickels": *Financial Post*, February 23, 1995.

Chapter Twenty-One: CHICAGO

271   "If you ever decide": DR.

271   "That's a telephone call you will get": Leonard Shaykin, interview with the author.

271   "After you lose your enamour": Ibid.

271   "We were in this kind of nondescript boardroom": DR.

272   "Conrad was the logical buyer": Leonard Shaykin, interview with the author.

273   "Then there's the style thing": DR.

273   "The most interesting example of Radler": *Chicago Reader*, June 25, 2004.

274   "For such an architecturally well-endowed city": *Chicago Tribune*, September 18, 1994.

Chapter Twenty-Two: ALL OVER THE MAP

277   "too old to be called a 'whiz kid'": CB.

278   "No, not a bit": CB.

278   "You always have a military analogy": CB.

278   "So I got out General Fuller's life": CB.

279   "If you want to be rich, you've got to do it once": CB.

280   "By those criteria . . . I suppose I should aspire": *Political Memoirs*, produced by MCTV, first broadcast December 5, 1993.

280   "Most of what goes on": CB.

281   "I'm not interested in popularity": CB.

281   "That is a perfectly legitimate question": CB.

281   "He does seem to lead a lifestyle": Peter Munk, interview with the author.

281   "In an ideal world": CB.

PART THREE: TITANIC

Wherever possible, the author has tried to give the source of a direct quote. However, some of the quotes that appear in the text without attribution in Part Three have been provided on that basis, and therefore don't appear in these notes. I have tried to be selective of the use of unattributed quotes, using them only when the teller has a first-hand account or when a quote could be independently verified.

Chapter Twenty-Three: "THE GREATEST CORPORATE FRIEND CANADIAN PRINT JOURNALISTS HAVE"

285   "I'm always representing the *Daily Telegraph*": *Ottawa Citizen*, July 1, 1997.

285   "Mr. Black got his chance at pageantry": Ibid.

286   "We want the *Citizen*": *Ottawa Citizen*, March 3, 1997.

286   "Hollinger poured a lot of resources": Tim Jones, "That Old Black Magic," *Columbia Journalism Review*, March 1998.

286   "I don't go around trying to stir up foreign wars": Ibid.

286   "Conrad's version of this is different than mine": Chris Cobb, *Ego and Ink* (Toronto: McClelland & Stewart, 2004), p. 12.

287   "We don't doubt our ability": *Ottawa Citizen*, May 28, 1997.

287   "For years I've personally loathed the homogeneity": Barbara Amiel, "Let Me Declare My Conflict of Interest," *Maclean's*, October 19, 1998.

289   Gosevitz putting Black and Godfrey back in touch: Cobb, *Ego and Ink*, p. 32.

290   "They took all of the best people": John Cruickshank, interview with the author.

290   "I don't think Conrad ever saw": Martin Newland, interview with the author.

291   "My overarching impression of him": Ken Whyte, interview with the author.

291   "the greatest corporate friend": Jones, "Black Magic."

292   "Boris Yeltsin, a Russian politician": Montreal *Gazette*, November 1, 1998.

292   "tits and analysis": Jones, "Black Magic."

292   "Whether you love Conrad Black or hate him": Derek DeCloet, "Black and White and Dread All Over," *Canadian Business*, October 15, 1999, p. 40.

292   "shook up old bones": *American Mercury*, May 1927.

293   "I am married to": Amiel, "Let Me Declare."

294   "You just never know": Michael Cooke, interview with the author.

294   "The fact is that Canada": Cobb, *Ego and Ink*, p. 282.

Chapter Twenty-Four: FLYING HIGH

297   The accusations against Black, Radler, and other Ravelston executives are in the amended lawsuit filed by Hollinger International
against them on May 7, 2004, in the U.S. District Court for the
Northern District of Illinois.

297   "We have bought and sold hundreds": Ibid.

297   "It's always best to have two planes": Peter Oborne, "The Ballad of
Connie and Babs," *Spectator*, January 24, 2004, p. 13.

298   [Footnote] "I have never seen": *National Post*, February 9, 2004.

298   "Oh, you'll never guess": Joanna Black MacDonald, interview with
the author.

298   Purchase of Ocean Boulevard house: *Palm Beach Post*, August 6, 1997.

299   "He died looking at the house": *Ottawa Citizen*, January 8, 2004.

300   "Poised for a U.S. move": Anthony Holden, *Talk Magazine*,
November 2000, p. 63.

300   "The nadir of this activity": Hollinger International 1998 Annual
Report.

300   [Footnote] "I have just been obliged": Hastings, *Editor*, p. 256.

301   "attractive diversification opportunity": *Vancouver Sun*, July 24, 1998.

301   "There are some of us who would say to Mr. Black": Ibid.

302   "In my view he did not commit a crime": *National Post*, May 29,
1999.

303   "Intermittently, there is fear": CB.

303   "We fear that over the next few years": Hollinger 1993 Annual
Report.

303   "there's a lot of absolute bunkum": *Wall Street Journal*, August 1, 2000.

304   The sections on Hollinger's digital investments and Radler's quote
are based on court documents including the amended lawsuit,
internal Hollinger documents, and background interviews with
executives.

Chapter Twenty-Five: PEERLESS

The chief sources for Black's peerage controversy are the legal filings
from his lawsuit against Jean Chrétien; Calvin Trillin's *New Yorker* article
"Paper Baron: What Would Conrad Black Do to Become a British Lord?"
December 17, 2001; and Chapter 21 of Chris Cobb's book *Ego and Ink*.

306   "I do not really know anything": *Globe and Mail*, June 9, 1999.

307   What made Black's situation different: *Globe and Mail*, June 21, 1999.

307   "Do you know what that bastard has done?": Trillin, "Paper
      Baron," p. 62.

308   "I don't think the prime minister": Cobb, *Ego and Ink*, p. 254.

308   [Footnote] "I thought we hammered": Ibid.

309   "They know what our numbers are": Arthur Carter, interview
      with the author for *BusinessWeek* Online, July 16, 1999.

309   "the Great Commoner": *Guardian*, May 21, 2004.

310   Chrétien has no chance: *Calgary Herald*, March 4, 2000.

310   "For a man who has espoused the values": *Globe and Mail*,
      August 27, 2001.

310   "Do you think the public": Cobb, *Ego and Ink*, p. 294–95.

311   "It's profitable as ever": Canadian Press, March, 3, 2000.

312   "Even the devil": *Globe and Mail*, April 3, 2000.

312   "For any offence Mr. Black has caused me": *Globe and Mail*,
      April 13, 2000.

313   Tom Wolfe letter: *Globe and Mail*, May 25, 2000.

314   "I own a few shares": Ibid.

314   "big whale, spouting profits": Ibid.

315   Amiel ordered her hamburger: John Cruickshank, interview with
      the author.

315   "I thought Barbara Amiel": Mark Steyn, "The Last Press Baron,"
      Spectator, February 14, 2004.

Chapter Twenty-Six: GOODBYE, CANADA

317   "Do you remember that cartoon character": *New York Times*,
      August 3, 2000.

318   "myth that I aspired": CB.

319   "One intuits that he has a gravitational pull": *Talk*, November 2000.

320   "On occasion, I mused": Hollinger International 2000 Annual
      Report, p. 4.

320   "Conrad Black is licking his wounds": *Globe and Mail*, August 2,
      2000.

321   1,700-word raspberry: *National Post*, August 5, 2000.

321   [Footnote] Céline Dion comparison: *Globe and Mail*, August 2,
      2000.

323   "It was probably the saddest party I've ever been to": Joanna Black
      MacDonald, interview with the author; and interviews with other
      attendees.

Chapter Twenty-Seven: HELLO, CROSSHARBOUR

325   "Having opposed for thirty years": *National Post*, May 19, 2001.
326   "There was intense discussion": Leonard Asper, interview with the author.
327   "I wouldn't be so concerned": Ibid.
328   "They were both very upset": Ken Whyte, interview with the author.
331   "Unless you're going to take": *National Post*, November 10, 2001.
332   "Take that, Mr. Chrétien": Ibid.
332   "Obviously, when you're walking in": Ibid.

Chapter Twenty-Eight: THE A-LIST

335   "In her professional life": Krystyne Griffin, interview with L. Ludwick.
336   "The little panels of metal": "Being Bold," *Vogue*, August 2002, p. 310.
337   "I took her to lunch": David Wynne-Morgan, interview with L. Ludwick.
337   "She was always": Robert Gage, interview with G. Macdonald.
338   "You're all fired": Paul Healy, interview with the author.
338   "out of commission for three to four days": Anthony Holden, *Talk*, November 2000, p. 63.
339   "Barbara was like a lighthouse": Bret Stephens, interview with the author.
340   "I have an extravagance that knows no bounds": *Vogue*, August 2002, p. 204.
340   [Footnote] "I have been saying that": *National Post*, February 9, 2004.
341   "vaulted into circles": Barbara Amiel, "A Girl's Best Friend," *FQ*, Winter 2003, p. 38.
341   "Taki never spoke": Tim Bower, "Meet Conrad Black," *Gotham Magazine*, April 2002, p.110.
341   "It's an odd thing": Hal Jackman, interview with the author; and Rushe, "Black Narcissi."
342   "The opulence of my lifestyle": CB.
343   "London's biggest bore unhung": Oborne, "Ballad," p. 12.
343   "He just happens to be": *Globe and Mail*, November 22, 2003.
344   "It's very embarrassing": Eleanor Mills, interview with the author.
344   "a potentially difficult situation": *National Post*, February 9, 2004.
345   "Recently, the ambassador of a major E.U. country": *Daily Telegraph*, December 17, 2001.

346 "They're definitely on the A-list": *Globe and Mail*, November 22, 2003.

346 "I used to say to the kids for years": Joanna Black MacDonald, interview with the author.

Chapter Twenty-Nine: INVESTOR RELATIONS

349 "His legal problems": transcript of May 23, 2002, Hollinger International AGM.

350 "I'm friends with all my shareholders": Paul Healy, interview with the author.

351 "not guys in the Social Register": Christopher Browne, interview with the author.

357 "We have said for some time": Hollinger International lawsuit against Black and others.

358 "There has not been an occasion": Ibid.

358 Support payments needed to meet Hollinger Inc. payments: Louis Zachary, DEL.

358 "I think we should concentrate": Hollinger International amended lawsuit against Black et al., May 7, 2004, U.S. District Court for the Northern District of Illinois.

359 "appeared to be quite a flush company": Conrad Black, DEP.

359 "US$8 million was not something": *Financial Times*, August 18, 2003.

359 "had some really wonderful, belly-laughing good times": Paul Healy, interview with the author.

361 "Healy did his job quite well": CB

362 "Kozlowski with class": Christopher Browne, interview with the author.

Chapter Thirty: HEART OF BLACKNESS

364 "Conrad does what Conrad wants to do": Gene Fox, interview with the author.

364 "We tend to seek out situations": Herbert Denton, interview with the author.

365 "We had a very prestigious board": Christopher Browne, interview with the author.

365 "The question was, Would Lord Black": Herbert Denton, interview with the author.

366 "I will certainly go to great lengths": Richard Burt, DEP.

366 [Footnote] "He really succeeded here, hasn't he?": Ibid.

366   2003 annual meeting: Transcript of Hollinger International 2003 AGM; and Devin Leonard, "Black and Blue," *Fortune*, October 13, 2003, p.166.

368   "Like all fads, corporate governance has its zealots": Transcripts of Hollinger International 2003 AGM.

368   "He mentioned that they might amount": Henry Kissinger, DEP.

370   "I don't believe in mixing": Paul Healy, interview with the author.

370   "Like any astute politician": Raymond Seitz, interview with the author.

370   "Would you please do it": Ibid.

371   "I went into this": Graham Savage, interview with the author.

371   "I don't think MCI would have survived": *Wall Street Journal*, April 20, 2004.

372   "Suddenly the flavour changed": Raymond Seitz, interview with the author.

373   "moved from the peculiar to the bizarre": Raymond Seitz, DEL.

374   "After Marie-Josée resigned": Henry Kissinger, DEP.

375   "I'll surrender control to the undertaker": *National Post*, October 16, 2003.

375   "Dear Conrad": Correspondence between Conrad Black and the Barclays, filed in Delaware Chancery Court.

377   "I just wish to reiterate": Ibid.

378   "He said that he had been asked": Richard Burt, DEP.

379   "I think my letter": Conrad Black, DEP.

380   "volunteered that I had been": CB.

381   "I was not convinced": CB.

383   "Dear David": Correspondence between Conrad Black and the Barclays, filed in Delaware Chancery Court.

Chapter Thirty-One: UNRAVELLING

385   "He couldn't lie straight in bed": London *Times*, November 8, 2003.

385   "monumental and masterful biography": London *Times*, November 29, 2003.

385   "It's hard to avoid a sense of crossover": *New York Times*, December 21, 2003.

386   "Mr. Black, anything to say to your shareholders?": Transcript and video, courtesy of the CBC.

389   "When was the last time you flew commercial?": John Cassidy, "Baron/Biographer," *The New Yorker*, December 8, 2003.

389   [Footnote] "Roosevelt punished his enemies": Conrad Black, *Franklin Delano Roosevelt: Champion of Freedom* (New York: Vintage, 2003).

391   "We should all find it distressing": Peter White, speech sponsored by the Faculty of Arts of McGill University, Toronto, February 12, 2004.

391   [Footnote] integrity questions about the audit committee members: Conrad Black, DEP.

391   "Mr. President, . . . you famously concluded a speech": Christopher Grimes and John Lloyd, "The End of the Line," *FT Magazine*, January 24, 2004, p. 22.

392   "was sparsely attended": Ed Koch, interview with the author.

392   "What can we do?": Chris Browne, interview with the author. The quote also appeared in *Vanity Fair*, April 2004.

394   "a once in a lifetime opportunity": Aidan Barclay, DEP.

394   "he says that about a lot of things": Ibid.

395   "the more aggressive half": Louis Zachary, DEP.

395   "Some of this stuff": Aidan Barclay, DEL.

395   "I think the shareholders have to be protected": Conrad Black, DEP.

396   "A lot of people": Leonard Asper, interview with the author.

397   "We hope any purchaser of *The Daily Telegraph*": London *Times*, November 18, 2003.

399   "I love the guy": *Globe and Mail*, November 22, 2003.

399   "could be construed as a threat": Conrad Black, DEL.

399   "While I'm open-minded about this": Ibid.

400   "Black decided he no longer had to comply": Richard Breeden, interview with the author.

402   [Footnote] "I am aware of the word 'initiated'": Conrad Black, DEP.

404   "He took the glory on the way up": David Radler as quoted by Paul Healy, interview with the author.

405   "Remember, the whole action": Christopher Browne, interview with the author.

405   "You don't serve on a board": *Chicago Tribune*, January 11, 2004.

405   "Like most directors": Richard Burt, DEP.

406   "a saga of greed and deliberate indifference": Cardinal Capital lawsuit against the Hollinger International directors.

406   "It's a great tragedy": Bloomberg News, January 8, 2004.

407   "Did the company enter": James Thompson, DEP.

407   "get out of Dodge": Richard Breeden, DEL.

407   "If those shares had been flipped": Ibid.

408   "I saw it as an act": Conrad Black, DEP.

409   "an extraordinary beginning of a discussion": Richard Breeden, DEL.

409   "If you're going to try": Richard Breeden, interview with the author.

410   "Please don't hesitate to call on me": Correspondence between Conrad Black and the Barclays, filed in Delaware Chancery Court.

410   "Many thanks for your kind note": Ibid.

413   "The action of the SEC today": Ibid.

415   "My lawsuits will begin tomorrow": Ibid.

415   [Footnote] "In fairness to Henry": Conrad Black, DEL.

Chapter Thirty-Two: THE LAST GREAT WAR

418   "daily night-letter": Correspondence between Conrad Black and the Barclays, filed in Delaware Chancery Court.

418   "it will be a great deal": Conrad Black, DEL.

418   "I forgot to mention": Conrad Black, DEL.

419   "We caught them with their pants down": Correspondence between Conrad Black and the Barclays, filed in Delaware Chancery Court.

421   "We are now organizing the pre-trial": Ibid.

422   "Prinz eventually ran out of chances": *Wall Street Journal*, June 26, 2001.

423   The incident in the dining room at the Hotel du Pont was the basis for Jacques Steinberg, "For Lord Black and His Foes, a Suit Is Served Before Dessert," *New York Times*, February 20, 2004.

425   "I had a feeling": Raymond Seitz, DEL.

432   "I understand the endless fascination": *Sunday Times*, February 29, 2004.

432   "fell victim to the tall poppy syndrome": *Daily Telegraph*, March 8, 2004.

433   [Footnote] "If looks could kill": Graham Savage, interview with the author.

433   "Hitler in his bunker": *Sunday Times*, February 29, 2004.

434   "If he gets through everything": Donald Trump, interview with the author.

434   "Emotionally it is very difficult": Krystyne Griffin, interview with L. Ludwick.

434   "I said when I left London": CB.

435 "What I have found": Dominic Lawson, *Sunday Telegraph*, January 25, 2004.

435 "A few weeks ago executives were endeavouring": Oborne, "Ballad."

435 "Obviously he's done some very unwise things": Krystyne Griffin, interview with L. Ludwick.

436 "I don't buy any of that": Edward Greenspan, interview with the author.

436 "Whereas the initial picture was of a narcissistic windbag": *New York Observer*, February 9, 2004.

436 "I don't feel as social": CB.

438 "If Hollinger was a cow, it would have sore udders": Herbert Denton, interview with the author.

440 "these papers were losing": press release from David Radler, May 9, 2004.

Epilogue: THE FALL OF 2004

444 "The biggest mistake": Raymond Seitz, interview with the author.

445 "chasing a dancing football": London *Times*, May 20, 2004.

447 "Strine disaster": Conrad Black, DEL.

447 Greenspan warned Black: Edward Greenspan, interview with the author.

447 "fighting truly evil people": DEL.

447 circulation issues at *Sun-Times*: *Chicago Tribune*, June 17, 2004.

448 [Footnote] "The news that our former top bosses": *Chicago Reader*, June 25, 2004.

449 "Hollinger Inc. does not have to sell": CB.

449: "If you mean": CB.

450 "My house in London": CB.

451 "I've been trying to figure out": Joanna Black MacDonald, interview with the author.

452 "No one could dispute": W.A. Swanberg, *Citizen Hearst* (New York: Scribner's, 1961), p. 525.

452 "Did I hear one word": Martin Newland, interview with the author.

454 "Here's a man": Victor Rice, interview with the author.

454 "He believes that if people": Edward Greenspan, interview with the author.

454 "There is a point": Gordon Paris, interview with the author.

455 "It will be clear": CB.

455 "This is a long-running drama": CB.

INDEX

493